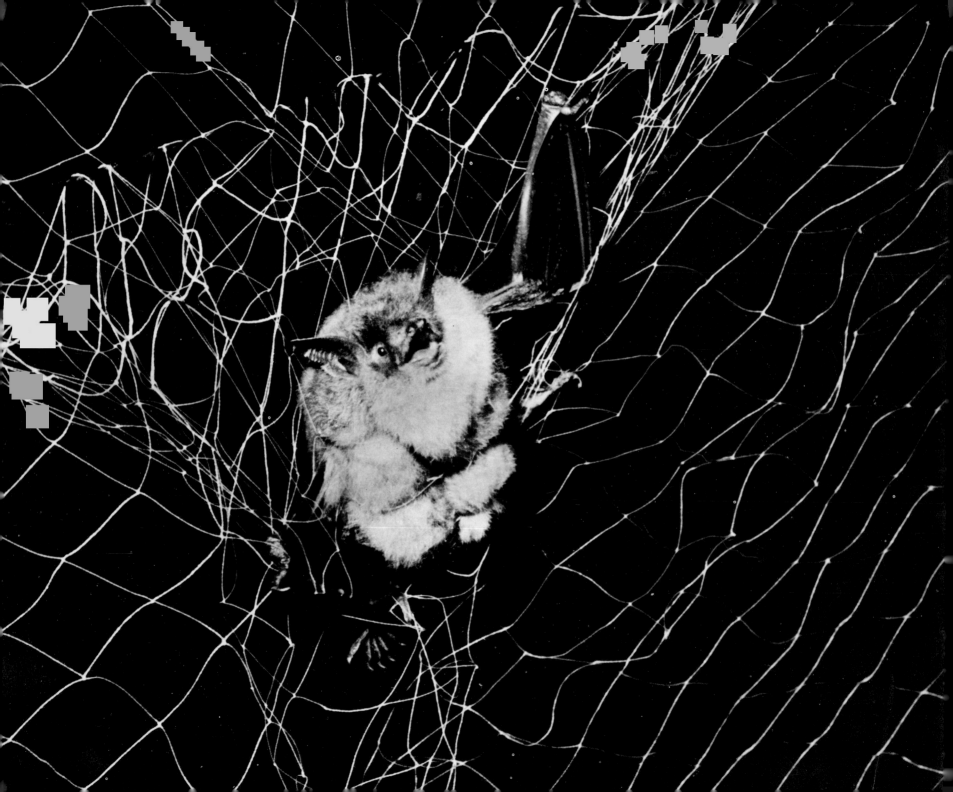

Bats of America

Roger W. Barbour &

Wayne H. Davis

The University Press of Kentucky

TO

Bernice & Shirley

Standard Book Number 8131-1186-2
Library of Congress
Catalog Card Number 73-80086

Copyright © 1969 by
The University Press of Kentucky

A statewide cooperative scholarly publishing agency
serving Berea College, Centre College of Kentucky,
Eastern Kentucky University, Kentucky State
College, Morehead State University, Murray State
University, University of Kentucky, University of
Louisville, and Western Kentucky University.
Editorial and Sales Offices:
Lexington, Kentucky 40506

Contents

The Molossidae

Preface

We have long recognized the need for a single reference that presents information enabling one to identify bats from the United States and summarizes the available information on their life history.

Many people are interested in bats. Research scientists, public health workers, and naturalists need to be able to identify them. At present, this is a skill acquired mainly by experience with bats in the field and museum. With a few exceptions, however, adult bats found in the United States are rather easily identified when the necessary information is available. We have designed this volume to provide this information and, hopefully, to encourage the further study of these interesting animals.

The scope of this book was determined by necessarily arbitrary decisions. We have intended to present an account of the known life history of each species native to the United States. The literature on bats is enormous and includes numerous specialized papers in areas such as physiology and anatomy, which are of marginal interest for the present work. In these areas we have tried to include anything likely to apply to the species in question and to exclude that which would apply to bats or mammals in general. For instance, we would include data on the size of a red blood cell of a species only if this factor appears important for the survival of that species in its particular habitat.

We have treated only those species currently found in the United States. Fossil forms have been ignored as have fossil and sub-fossil records of present-day species. For example, we do not list the vampires from Florida and Texas. We have not included the little fruit-eating bat, *Enchisthenes hartii*, a specimen of which has recently been taken in Tucson, Arizona. This specimen was probably an accidental which could have been imported by man or may have wandered beyond its normal range. It is one of many tropical species known from our neighboring Mexican states. They all have tickets in the accidental sweepstakes and any may appear in the United States at any time.

No attempt was made to survey the literature on parasites. We have mentioned, however, the parasites treated in the accounts we have read. As we are not competent in this area, information on parasites was taken at face value directly from the original sources.

This book is not a taxonomic treatment. For the distribution of the subspecies refer to Hall and Kelson (1959), or to later works where available. For nomenclature we have accepted the opinions of the last reviser, when suggested changes seem based upon adequate evidence. The first listed common name for each species is from Hall's (1965) list of suggested common names for North American mammals. Exceptions are for *Leptonycteris* and *Choeronycteris* for which we have listed first the more descriptive names of "long-tongued bat" and "hog-nosed bat," respectively. Hall listed these names as "long-nosed bat" and "long-tongued bat," respectively. We think his choice is unfortunate since *Choeronycteris* has a longer nose than *Leptonycteris*. Both genera have long tongues. We like the commonly used name of hog-nosed bat for *Choeronycteris*, as the resemblance of its snout to that of a hog is striking. The name *Choeronycteris* means "nocturnal pig."

In the species accounts we have deviated from the standard practice of presenting mammalian measurements of total length, length of the tail, length of the hind foot, and length of the ear. We have presented measurements of the length of the forearm and, when available, wingspread. These are used because they are helpful in identifying a bat, and can be made easily and accurately by an inexperienced person.

Our distribution maps are modified from Hall and Kelson (1959), with the addition of more recent records. Any method of drawing boundaries on a range map is arbitrary. We have been conservative and have avoided including any large area from which no specimens are known. In cases where marginal records in the literature seemed likely to have been based upon questionable identification, we have examined the pertinent specimens. This has resulted in shrinkage of several ranges.

We originally intended to include chapters on various aspects of bat biology such as migration and hibernation. William Wimsatt, however, is compiling a book on the biology of bats which will include such information. His work will probably appear about the same time as the present volume.

Our experiences in bat studies span a total of about 50 years. RWB has studied bats and other animals in his work with various aspects of the natural history of vertebrates, primarily in the eastern United States, since his college days. His experience as a wildlife photographer covers about 30 years. WHD has worked almost exclusively with bats during his professional career. He has studied bats in most of the states and provinces of the United States, Mexico, and Canada. During the summer of 1966 we went together to the Southwest to obtain experience with some species which we had not previously encountered in the field and to obtain photographs needed to complete our series. All photographs not otherwise credited are by RWB.

To compile this book we have collected about 1,000 published papers and books and read the pertinent sections of each. In addition to these sources, we have drawn upon our own unpublished observations accumulated during the years of our studies of native bats. We have been collecting papers and references on the bats of the United States for several years. We have regularly examined *Biological Abstracts*, scanned lists of current literature and citations, and have been in contact with most of the people who are currently doing research with bats.

All publications that contain information we have used are listed in the Bibliography. We have intended to list all papers containing life history information on native bats published prior to December 31, 1967. We have omitted most systematic treatments published prior to Hall and Kelson (1959). No doubt we have overlooked important papers containing information which should be in this book. We have probably also missed bits of useful information in papers we have read. Such oversights, though unfortunate, are perhaps inevitable.

We are indebted to the Research Fund Committee of the University of Kentucky for several grants that made this volume possible. We acknowledge the help of numerous people who have contributed in various ways. We are especially thankful to Robert J. Baker for providing us with numerous specimens of live bats and for helping us in the field in Arizona, Mexico, and New Mexico. Others whose help we gratefully acknowledge include George M. Baer, E. Lendell Cockrum, Mr. and Mrs. Dale M. Davis, Russell Davis, David A. Easterla, Carl H. Ernst, W. Gene Frum, Bryan P. Glass, Marion D. Hassell, Bruce Hayward, Gordon C. Hubbell, Richard K. LaVal, Brian McNab, Robert T. Orr, Erwin W. Pearson, Roger Potts, Clyde Senger, David H. Snyder, S. Edwin Sulkin, Stanley K. Taylor, and Frederic A. Webster. Elizabeth Rogers Pugh is due especial thanks for patiently typing various revisions of the manuscript and protecting us from unnecessary interruption during critical periods.

We would also like to express our appreciation to certain individuals who have indirectly contributed to this volume. RWB would like to name three: Dr. Wilfred A. Welter, who first recognized, appreciated, and encouraged his youthful interest in wildlife and photography, pointed him into graduate school, and served as friend and advisor until his untimely death in 1939; Drs. L. Y. Lancaster and Gordon Wilson, whose counsel, encouragement, and friendship over the past 35 years have been invaluable. WHD is especially indebted to his parents, Hannibal A. and Tyreeca E. Davis, mathematicians and plant taxonomists, whose encouragement of his early interests in natural history went far beyond that normally to be expected of sympathetic parents. He is also thankful to W. Gene Frum who channeled an interest in small mammals into the specialty of bats at a time when few people had become interested in these animals.

Introduction

Bats are the only flying mammals. This unique characteristic, coupled with their nocturnal habits, has no doubt been largely responsible for their prominent position in folklore and superstition. Throughout history they have been objects of much interest and speculation.

Of the 16 living families of bats three occur in the United States. The Phyllostomatidae, or leaf-nosed bats, constitute a tropical American family, five species of which range northward into the southwestern states. The Vespertilionidae, of worldwide distribution, range farther into the temperate regions than any other family and include most of the hibernating species. They occur in all 50 states. Molossidae, the free-tailed bats, are widely distributed throughout the warmer regions of both hemispheres and range across the southern United States.

Structure: The most notable features of a bat are those adaptations which enable it to fly. The fore limbs are built upon the same general pattern as those of other mammals—an upper arm, forearm, wrist, and hand with thumb and four fingers—but in a bat the bones of the hand and fingers are greatly elongated and serve to spread and manipulate the wing. The flying surface, which consists of the wings and the interfemoral membrane, is made up of double layers of skin forming a continuous membrane that encloses the fore limbs, the hind limbs, and the tail.

The hind limbs of a bat also exhibit peculiar modifications. They are attached at the hip in a reverse manner from other mammals; when bent the knee points backward, and the bottom of the foot faces forward. This adaptation doubtless facilitates the bat's alighting upside down and hanging by its toes. One of the ankle bones, the calcaneous, bears a long spur, the calcar, which projects toward the tail and helps to support the interfemoral membrane between the hind limbs and the tail.

A bat's ear contains a well developed tragus, a thin, erect, fleshy projection rising from the inner base of the ear. It has not been shown to function in hearing, and despite much speculation and research its significance remains unknown.

Aside from these features, the anatomy of a bat is similar to that of most mammals. The major external anatomical features are illustrated in figure 1.

Distribution: Bats are common in the United States and can be found easily in most regions. On warm evenings they can be seen in flight almost anywhere from the largest eastern cities to the deserts of the Southwest, and from the sea coast into the high mountains. However, they are most abundant in the southwestern United States. Bats are basically tropical animals, and many species that are essentially Central American in distribution range into this region.

Habitat: Wide though their distribution may be, bats show certain common preferences in their choice of foraging areas. They are most often found feeding over a pond or stream, along a forest edge, beside a cliff or ravine, or among buildings. Many species seem attracted by water, not only in arid regions but also in areas of abundant rainfall.

In the daytime bats seek shelter in a wide variety of places. Many species live in buildings, some in caves and mines, and a few roost among the foliage of trees. Window shutters, loose bark, rock crevices, and various other nooks and crannies also often shelter bats. Most day roosts are dark and secluded, but many shelters which are too exposed for use by day are used at night by bats resting between foraging flights.

During the winter most species retreat beneath the ground to hibernate in caves, mines, and other comparable shelters. These hibernacula are characterized by high humidity and by temperatures that are usually above freezing. Some species hibernate in buildings and a few apparently pass the winter in hollow trees.

Activity: Most bats spend the day hanging quietly in a secluded retreat. The body temperature usually approaches that of the environment, and metabolism is at a low level. When bats are hanging in groups some individuals are usually active, especially on warm days. If the environmental temperature reaches the normal body temperature of active bats (about 100° F.; 38° C.), the entire group may become noisy and active.

At the approach of evening the roosting bats become restless and begin squeaking and crawling about. If their shelter is large enough, they begin flying inside an hour or so before emerging, often approaching the exit to sample the waning light.

Upon leaving the roost most bats fly to a pond or other body of water to drink. They drink while in flight, skimming low over the water and scooping it up with the lower jaw. A feeding period of up to about an hour follows, and when the stomach is filled, the bat retires to a roost where it rests most of the night. A second feeding period often occurs just before daylight. By daybreak, or shortly after, the bats are back in their daytime retreat. This general behavior pattern is modified when the bats have tiny young.

Food and Feeding: Although in different parts of the world bats feed on such diverse items as blood, fish, mice, lizards, and fruit, all our species are basically insectivorous except for

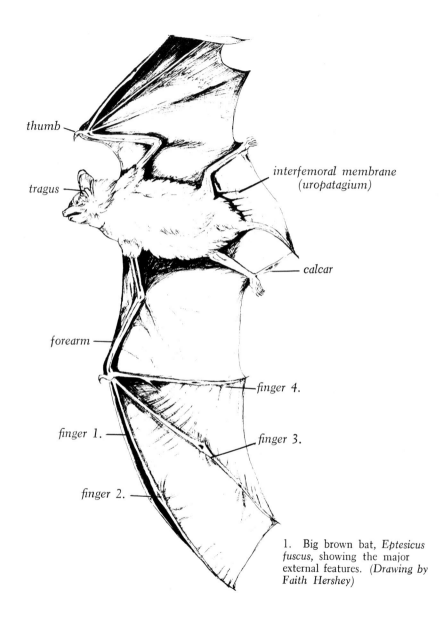

1. Big brown bat, *Eptesicus fuscus,* showing the major external features. (*Drawing by Faith Hershey*)

9

three that feed on nectar. When foraging, bats utter a continuous series of supersonic cries and locate flying insects by the echoes. Once detected the insect is caught in a wingtip, quickly transferred to a cup formed by the interfemoral membrane, and then eaten. Sometimes bats catch insects too large to be handled in flight and must alight to devour them. At least one species commonly forages on the ground where it feeds upon beetles and crickets.

Reproduction: In the United States bats mate in fall and winter. The female of most species retains the sperm in the uterus until spring when ovulation and fertilization occur. The annual litter is usually produced in May or June. However, parturition ranges at least from April through July, varying with the species and the climate. Most bats produce a single young, but several species have twins, and two kinds often give birth to litters of three or four.

Most species congregate in nursery colonies ranging in size from a dozen or so to several million bats. The pregnant females assemble in buildings, caves, mines, or other dark retreats. No nest is built. The mother hangs head upward as the young is born, and the baby is received in a pocket formed by the interfemoral membrane. In some species which have a poorly developed interfemoral membrane the female hangs head downward when giving birth. At birth bats are large and well developed. As soon as they are born they crawl to the mother's breast and attach to a nipple. In most species the very young remain attached throughout the day, and if disturbed at such times, the mother takes flight with the young usually clinging tightly to her by mouth, thumbs, and feet.

When the mother emerges in the evening to feed, the young are left behind, where they usually form clusters. Mothers return at intervals throughout the night to nurse the small young; as the young mature they return less frequently. Most bats apparently can recognize their young and pick them out from the clusters to nurse; but in at least one species, *Tadarida brasiliensis,* the mothers seemingly nurse the first young that reaches them when they return to the roost.

Young bats grow rapidly and most are able to fly within three weeks. As they become increasingly adept at flying and obtaining their own food, they become less dependent upon the mother. As the young are weaned the maternity colonies begin to disperse.

Migration: Most species of bats leave the nursery colony and migrate to suitable winter quarters. The Brazilian free-tailed bat of the Southwest migrates up to nearly a thousand miles to reach its winter quarters in Mexico. Several other species are suspected of migrating long distances, but definitive data on their movements are not yet available.

Bats which hibernate in caves do not necessarily migrate on a north-south axis, but travel in whatever direction necessary to reach suitable caves. Such movements commonly involve 200 miles or more; unfortunately, the migratory habits of bats which live even farther from suitable underground retreats remain unknown.

A few bats frequent the same cave in both summer and winter, but other species that form nursery colonies in caves may migrate a hundred miles or more to winter in other caves. The few bats known to winter in buildings usually choose structures other than the one used in summer; the winter quarters may be close by or many miles away.

Fall migration starts early. In most species the nursery colonies begin dispersal in July, and during August most bats are on the move. The pattern of the late summer movement is not yet understood, but bats are frequently found outside their usual range at this season.

Hibernation: Most of the bats of the United States are capable of hibernating during cold weather. In the northernmost latitudes the hibernation season lasts more than eight months with torpid bats frequently being found in the caves from September through May. In the southernmost states, on the other hand, hibernation may be sporadic with bats arousing to feed during warm spells in winter.

Before hibernating, bats deposit layers of fat amounting to about a third of their weight. In some species which migrate considerable distances to winter quarters, some of the stored fat is used in travel, and they must fatten again after arrival. Young bats store less fat than adults and are thus less likely to survive the winter. Perhaps they have difficulty acquiring the skill to catch sufficient insects, since they commonly remain active and feed later into the fall than the adults.

Most bats choose hibernation sites where the temperature usually remains a few degrees above freezing. When hibernating, a bat's temperature approaches that of the environment, with the optimum temperature about 41° F. (5° C.). If the environmental temperature rises, the rate of fat utilization increases. If the temperature drops the bat responds by raising its metabolism and thus also uses more stored fat. The end result is the same—a shortening of the time the bat can survive in hibernation.

A hibernating bat is helpless and barely able to move. If pulled from a cave wall, such a bat responds by slowly extending the wings, opening the mouth and emitting a long drawn-out squeak. If given opportunity at this time it will bite a person, hanging on with such tenacity that it is difficult to remove. After disturbance a hibernating bat arouses quickly. Heart rate increases, and the rate of breathing accelerates. Within 15–30 minutes after being disturbed, the bat is ready to fly.

Longevity: Although most small mammals do not usually survive more than a year in the wild, bats frequently live 10 years or more. There are several records of 20-year-old bats, and one little brown bat is known to have lived at least 24 years.

Probably the facts that these bats hibernate and, being able to regulate their metabolic rate at will, spend little of their time at full activity, are factors contributing to their long life.

Economic Importance: Bats are of little economic importance. Most feed entirely upon insects, and thus are beneficial. The guano of bats is sometimes marketed as nitrogen-rich fertilizer. In some southwestern caves inhabited by millions of bats, the guano is deposited at a rate sufficient to produce a significant annual income for the landowner.

Sometimes a colony occupies a house or other buildings in such numbers as to be a genuine nuisance. They may be noisy and dirty and can create an odor which permeates the entire household. Such bats are best dealt with by carefully sealing all entrance holes after the bats have left for the winter.

Like other mammals, bats sometimes carry rabies. This disease remains widespread and common in the United States despite persistent control efforts by public health agencies. With the growth of inoculation programs, rabies has become less common in domestic animals and man, but seems relatively stable in wildlife. Although reported most frequently in skunks, foxes, and racoons, it is also rather common in bats. They seem to be the only animals that can contract rabies and survive. There are apparently healthy bats which react positively to rabies tests. Fortunately, bats do not readily transmit the disease to other species.

The Need for Conservation: Bat populations have been decreasing at an alarming rate in the United States during the past 20 years. The causes are unknown but many possible factors may be responsible. Disturbance by man has affected many cave populations, since many bats are rather sensitive to intrusion and will leave a favored site after repeated molestation. The increase in popularity of cave exploring has made many caves less suitable for bats. In some caves bat banders have noted decreased populations apparently as a result of their own banding activity.

Insecticide poisoning is probably a factor contributing to the decrease of the bat population. Bats are highly sensitive to some insecticides. Large quantities of the chlorinated hydrocarbon pesticides are slowly stored with the fat in late summer and fall and may cause the death of many bats as they use this fat during hibernation. Observers have recently noted a scarcity of bats in the irrigated valleys of Arizona and in the tobacco raising region of Connecticut and suspect that this may be due to the heavy use of sprays in these regions.

Diseases may have caused the decrease of some bat populations. There are several recent reports of massive deaths in bat colonies in the Southwest and Mexico which are thought to have resulted from disease or perhaps pesticides. Extensive destruction of bats by man in rabies control projects has been reported in several states.

The collection of bats by irresponsible people for various scientific research projects has decimated several bat colonies during recent years. With their low rate of reproduction our bats cannot withstand heavy cropping and still maintain their population.

If bats are to remain a conspicuous part of our fauna, we must initiate conservation measures. Although we do not yet know enough about bat biology to formulate an adequate conservation plan, certain needs are obvious. Some caves harboring important colonies should be protected from undue human disturbance. The trend away from the use of the dangerous residual pesticides must be continued. People who work with bats should try to minimize the disturbance, and those who use bats in research should take them, whenever feasible, from buildings where they constitute a nuisance.

Finally, more people should become aware of the many aspects of a bat's life; such awareness should make people more interested in the protection of these fascinating animals. The creation of such an attitude toward our dwindling wildlife resources is a major purpose of this volume.

The Identification of Bats

So far as feasible, the accompanying key to the adult bats of the United States has been designed to enable one to identify a bat in the flesh. Juveniles are more difficult to identify. They can easily be recognized by the cartilagenous areas in the finger joints (fig. 2); the larger the area, the younger the bat. Juveniles old enough to fly can often be identified, but baby bats cannot.

The external features referred to in this key and in the species accounts are illustrated in figure 1.

In using the key, it is important to consider each of the two alternatives; one would fit the animal in hand and lead to another pair of alternatives or the name of the animal.

In a few cases it is necessary to examine the skull. Salient features are illustrated in figure 3. The skull should be removed and soaked overnight in water. It should then be brought to a boil and allowed to simmer for about five minutes. The flesh then can be removed with a knife or forceps.

In attempting to identify a bat, especially a dried specimen, difficulties in choosing an alternative may occasionally be encountered. In such cases one should follow each alternative, and examine the photographs and species accounts for final determination.

Within a population of animals any measurement will show individual variation. Since such variation approximates a normal distribution, the larger the sample examined the greater the extremes of measurements expected. In most cases a specimen will fall somewhat near the middle of the range. Occasionally, however, a bat will be encountered whose measurements fall outside the range given in this book.

For this and other reasons, no key is infallible. After taking an animal through the key, it should be compared with the photographs and species account for verification.

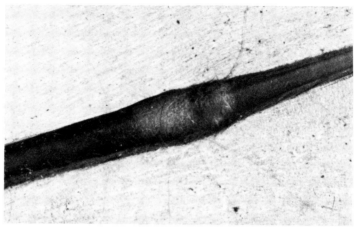

2. Finger joint of a juvenile *Eptesicus fuscus*. The light region is cartilage; the adult joint is knobby and lacks cartilage.

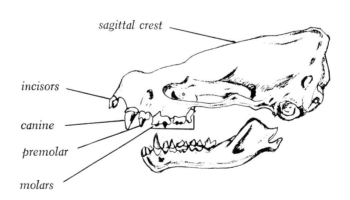

3. Skull of *Eptesicus fuscus* showing major features. (*Drawing by Faith Hershey*)

la.

la,2a

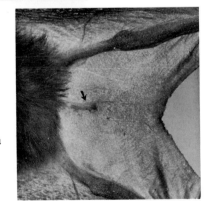
4a

A KEY TO ADULT BATS OF THE UNITED STATES

1. a. With prominent facial adornments in the form of chin or nose flaps (Family PHYLLOSTOMATIDAE)—2

   b. Without prominent facial adornments in the form of projecting skin flaps—6

2. a. Face pug-like, with a series of grooves and flaps on the chin, no prominent flap on end of snout—*Mormoops megalophylla*

   b. Face not pug-like, without conspicuous chin folds, with an erect, leaf-like flap on end of snout—3

3. a. Ears large, over 25 mm. in length; tail prominent, over 30 mm. long—*Macrotus waterhousii*

   b. Ears less than 25 mm. long; tail absent or vestigial—4

4. a. Tail present, minute; forearm less than 48 mm.—*Choeronycteris mexicana*

   b. Tail absent; forearm more than 48 mm.—5

14

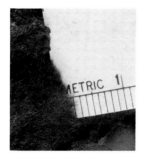

5a

5b

8a

8b

5. a. Total length of longest finger, including metacarpal, less than 105 mm.; forearm usually less than 55 mm.; fur short, usually less than 5 mm. on back—*Leptonycteris sanborni*

b. Total length of longest finger, including metacarpal, more than 105 mm.; forearm usually more than 55 mm.; fur on back usually more than 5 mm. long; occurs in U.S. only in Big Bend region of Texas—*Leptonycteris nivalis*

6. a. About half the tail projecting beyond the interfemoral membrane (Family MOLOSSIDAE)—7

b. Tail inclosed in interfemoral membrane, with no more than a few millimeters at most projecting free (Family VESPERTILIONIDAE)—12

7. a. Forearm less than 55 mm.—8

b. Forearm more than 55 mm.—9

8. a. Ears occasionally meeting, but not joined basally at midline; dorsal hairs whitish on basal quarter or less—*Tadarida brasiliensis*

b. Ears clearly joined basally at the midline; basal half of dorsal hairs whitish—*Tadarida femorosacca*

9a

11a

11b

14a

9. a. With a few guard hairs on rump projecting 7–10 mm. beyond fur—*Eumops underwoodi*

    b. Without guard hairs on rump projecting appreciably beyond fur—10

10. a. Forearm more than 70 mm.—*Eumops perotis*

    b. Forearm less than 70 mm.—11

11. a. Ears projecting beyond snout, almost parallel to body, and nearly obscuring eyes—*Tadarida macrotis*

    b. Ears not projecting beyond snout, but upward at an angle, and not obscuring eyes—*Eumops glaucinus*

12. a. Ears enormous, over 28 mm. from notch to tip—13

    b. Ears less than 26 mm. from notch to tip—17

13. a. Fur black, with 3 large white blotches on back—*Euderma maculatum*

    b. Color various, but not black; no white blotches on back—14

14. a. With a pair of leaf-like structures projecting over the forehead from the base of the joined ears—*Plecotus phyllotis*

    b. No leaf-like projections over forehead; ears not joined at base—15

15b

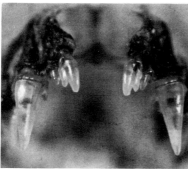

16a

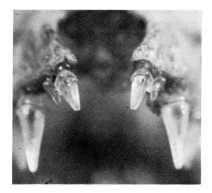

16b

15. a. Without a conspicuous lump on each side of snout; fur light at base; dorsal color pale yellowish—*Antrozous pallidus*

b. With a conspicuous lump on each side of snout; fur dark at base; dorsal color light brown to gray—16

16. a. Belly fur white, first upper incisor bifid—*Plecotus rafinesquii*

b. Belly fur tan to brown; first upper incisor unicuspid—*Plecotus townsendii*

17. a. At least the anterior half of the dorsal surface of the interfemoral membrane well furred—18

b. Dorsal surface of interfemoral membrane naked, scant-haired, or at most lightly furred on the anterior third—24

18. a. Color of fur black, but many of the hairs distinctly silver-tipped—*Lasionycteris noctivagans*

b. Color various, but never uniformly black; fur may or may not be silver-tipped—19

19. a. Posterior half of dorsal surface of interfemoral membrane essentially bare—20

b. Posterior half of dorsal surface of interfemoral membrane nearly as well furred as the anterior half—21

17

21a

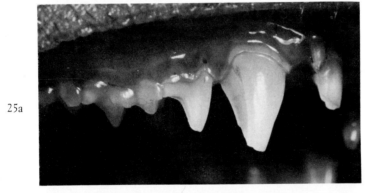

25a

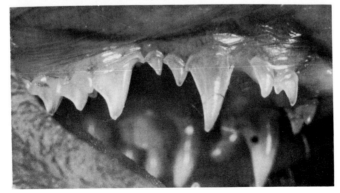

25b

20. a. Total length over 120 mm. (occurs from Texas to Virginia)—*Lasiurus intermedius*

    b. Total length less than 120 mm. (occurs from California to New Mexico; see species account)—*Lasiurus ega*

21. a. Ears conspicuously black-edged, and with patches of yellowish hair scattered inside them—*Lasiurus cinerus*

    b. Ears not conspicuously black-edged, bare, or at most scant-haired inside—22

22. a. Color red-orange—*Lasiurus borealis*

    b. Color rich mahogany brown or yellowish brown, not red-orange—23

23. a. Color rich mahogany-brown; not yellowish except about face—*Lasiurus seminolus*

    b. Color pale yellowish brown—*Lasiurus borealis*

24. a. Black, with conspicuously silver-tipped fur—*Lasionycteris noctivagans*

    b. Not black; fur not silver-tipped—25

25. a. From a side view, the first visible tooth behind the upper canine approximately half as high as the canine and in contact with it at the base—26

    b. From a side view, the first visible tooth behind the upper canine less than ⅓ as high as the canine, or if half as high, then separated from the canine by a noticeable gap—28

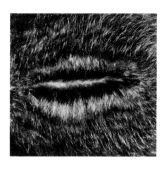

28a

29a

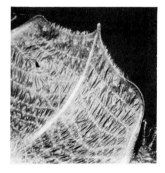

30a

31a

31b

26. a. Forearm more than 40 mm.—*Eptesicus fuscus*

 b. Forearm less than 40 mm.—27

27. a. Wingspread more than 240 mm.; interfemoral membrane naked; color brown—*Nycticeius humeralis*

 b. Wingspread less than 230 mm.; interfemoral membrane sparsely furred on anterior third of dorsal surface; color yellow to sooty gray—*Pipistrellus hesperus*

28. a. Hairs on back dark at base and tip, but lighter in the middle—*Pipistrellus subflavus*

 b. Hairs on back dark at base and lighter at tip, or uniformly colored; no light band in the middle—29

29. a. Tragus less than 5 mm. long, blunt, and curved—*Pipistrellus hesperus*

 b. Tragus more than 6 mm. long, pointed, and straight—30

30. a. With a conspicuous fringe of hairs projecting backward from the posterior edge of the interfemoral membrane—*Myotis thysanodes*

 b. Without a conspicuous fringe of hairs projecting backward from the interfemoral membrane—31

31. a. Hairs on back uniformly colored from base to tip; wing attached to foot at the ankle—*Myotis grisescens*

 b. Hairs on back darker at base than at tip; wing attached to foot at base of the toe—32

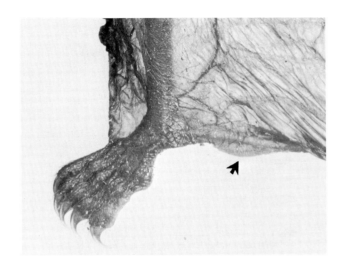

35a

37a

32. a. Ear when gently laid forward extending more than 2 mm. beyond tip of nose; i.e., ear more than 16 mm.—33

b. Ear when gently laid forward extending less than 2 mm. beyond tip of nose; i.e., ear less than 16 mm.—35

33. a. Ears black—*Myotis evotis*

b. Ears dark, but not black—34

34. a. Ear when gently laid forward extending about 4 mm. beyond tip of nose; i.e., ear 17–19 mm.—*Myotis keenii*

b. Ear when gently laid forward extending about 8 mm. beyond nose; i.e., ear 20–22 mm. (occurs in Southwest only)—*Myotis auriculus*

35. a. Calcar with a keel—36

b. Calcar not keeled—40

36. a. Foot over 8.5 mm.; forearm usually more than 35 mm.—37

b. Foot under 8.5 mm.; forearm usually less than 35 mm.—39

37. a. Under surface of wing furred to a line from elbow to knee; anterior 25 percent of dorsal surface of interfemoral membrane furred (occurring west of the Great Plains)—*Myotis volans*

39a

39b

40a

40b

b. Under surface of wing not furred to a line from elbow to knee; anterior dorsal surface of interfemoral membrane naked, or at most with a narrow fringe of hairs about the base—38

38. a. Foot more than 10 mm.; Texas and westward—*Myotis velifer*

b. Foot less than 10 mm.; Ozarks and eastward—*Myotis sodalis*

39. a. Frontal area of skull rising abruptly from the rostrum; dorsal fur dull, not glossy; third metacarpal usually over 30.5 mm.—*Myotis californicus*

b. Skull flattened, frontal area rising gently from rostrum; dorsal fur glossy; third metacarpal usually less than 30.5 mm.—*Myotis leibii*

40. a. With a few scattered long hairs on foot extending to the tip of the claws or beyond—41

b. No long hairs on foot extending to tip of claws—46

41. a. Occurring east of a line from Corpus Christi, Texas, through Oklahoma City, Oklahoma, to Grand Forks, North Dakota—42

b. Occurring west of a line from Corpus Christi, Texas, through Oklahoma City, Oklahoma, to Grand Forks, North Dakota—43

42a   42b

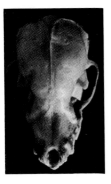

43a

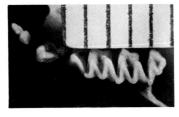

45a   45b

42. a. Frontal area of skull rising abruptly from rostrum; sagittal crest usually present; braincase viewed from side almost spherical; dorsal fur dull, not glossy—*Myotis austroriparius*

b. Frontal area of skull rising gently from rostrum; sagittal crest lacking; braincase viewed from side flattened, not spherical; dorsal fur usually with a conspicuous sheen—*Myotis lucifugus*

43. a. Forearm usually more than 40 mm.; skull with a prominent sagittal crest—*Myotis velifer*

b. Forearm usually less than 40 mm.; sagittal crest absent, or at most low and inconspicuous—44

44. a. Greatest length of skull usually not more than 14 mm.; fur usually dull, not glossy (see species account)—*Myotis yumanensis*

b. Greatest length of skull more than 14 mm.; fur usually glossy (see *M. lucifugus* account)—45

45. a. Length of row of upper molariform teeth less than 4 mm.—*Myotis lucifugus*

b. Length of row of upper molariform teeth more than 4 mm.—*Myotis occultus*

46. a. Foot 10 mm. or more; forearm usually more than 40 mm.; skull with a distinct sagittal crest; Texas and westward—*Myotis velifer*

b. Foot under 10 mm.; forearm usually less than 40 mm.; sagittal crest lacking; Ozarks and eastward—*Myotis sodalis*

The Phyllostomatidae

MORMOOPS MEGALOPHYLLA Peters

Leaf-chinned bat; leaf-chin bat; Peter's leaf-chinned bat; lappet-chinned bat; old man bat; moustache bat

Recognition: Forearm, 51–59 mm.; wingspread, about 370 mm. A rather large pug-faced bat with conspicuous folds of skin stretching from ear to ear across the chin. The short tail projects from the upper side of the interfemoral membrane. Color, reddish to brown.

Confusing Species: Although there are bats in tropical America similar to M. *megalophylla*, there is no reason to confuse this bat with any other species in the United States. The folds of skin across the chin are unique among our bats.

Range: From South America north through Central America and Mexico into the United States, where it is known only from Arizona and Texas. Two specimens were taken near Patagonia, Arizona, in 1954; there are no additional records. In Texas there are records from six caves in four counties on the Edwards Plateau where colonies as large as an estimated 4,000 individuals have been reported. There are also scattered records from the Big Bend region, Comstock, and Edinburg. The winter and summer ranges coincide.

Habitat: This bat occupies a diversity of habitats, ranging from desert scrub to tropical forests. A colonial species, it may be found in caves, mines, tunnels, and rarely buildings. It is

4. Head of *Mormoops megalophylla* showing prominent chin lappets. The mouth is open but the teeth are partially obscured by the numerous long labial hairs.

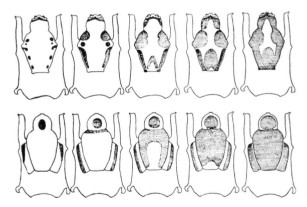

5. Molting sequence in *Mormoops megalophylla*. Upper row, dorsal surface. Lower row, ventral surface. New pelage appears in stippled areas. Molt progression is indicated from left to right. (*Courtesy of Denny G. Constantine, from the* Journal of Mammalogy)

occasionally taken in nets set over water holes. In some regions, it is one of the more abundant bats.

Behavior: Little is known of the behavior of *M. megalophylla*. Apparently it emerges late in the evening and forages for insects. However, Alvarez (1963) was able to shoot one as it flew at a height of six feet in Tamaulipas. The flight is strong and swift. It gives no indication of being able to detect a mist net, colliding with it at full speed.

Unlike most colonial bats *M. megalophylla* apparently does not form clusters. Members of the colony roost singly spread out about six inches apart over the ceiling of a cave. Where they shared a shelter in Texas with *Myotis velifer* and *Tadarida brasiliensis* each species occupied a different chamber of the cave (Raun and Baker, 1958).

When asleep during the day this species rests with the back arched and the head tucked ventrally almost to the chest. Hall and Dalquest (1963) noted that two individuals they found hanging on a cave wall in Veracruz were alert and twisted and turned to watch the light; however, they made no attempt to fly as they were plucked from the wall.

Although a permanent resident in the United States (specimens have been taken in Texas caves in all months except April, June, July, and September), several observers have commented on the nomadic behavior of this species in the United States and Mexico. Its presence at a given locality is highly unpredictable; caves known to be frequented by this species may or may not be occupied on any given date, with no apparent relation to time or season. Constantine (1958e) found 3,000–4,000 in Frio Cave, Texas, in August, November, and December. They were not present in April and July. Four individuals were found hanging from the rough ceiling of a junior high school in Edinburg in January and February.

In a cave in Nuevo Leon, Villa (1967) found a colony of

over 500,000 individuals in November. By December the number was reduced to 50,000 and in January only Brazilian free-tailed bats occupied the cave. In Coahuila he noticed that colonies formed in caves in October and November but disappeared by spring.

Apparently this species does not hibernate, but there is almost no information on the subject. In Frio Cave, Jameson (1959) found 1,500 individuals on January 22, 1956, in a room which has a winter temperature of 80° F. (27° C.). In November, Villa (1967) found half a million *Mormoops* in a cave where the relative humidity was 86 percent and the temperature 70° F. (21° C.). Outside temperature was 59° F. (15° C.).

Reproduction: The only data on reproduction are from the Mexican populations. Although nursery colonies probably occur in the caves of the Edwards Plateau in Texas apparently none have yet been found in the United States. One of two females netted in Arizona on June 10, 1954, contained an embryo. In the border states of Nuevo Leon, Coahuila, and Sonora, Villa (1967) found eight females containing one embryo each in March, April, and May. One taken March 24 in Coahuila had an 18 mm. embryo; one on May 12 in Sonora carried a 23 mm. embryo. There is obviously a rather wide range of birth dates.

Parasites: Jameson (1959) examined 14 specimens from Frio Cave in Texas, and found two species of mites and one each of nematodes and trematodes.

Pelage and Molt: Constantine (1958d) described color variation and molt within a Texas population. Molt occurred in August. The old, faded, lighter coat was replaced by darker fresh fur in the sequence shown in fig. 5.

Distribution of *Mormoops megalophylla* in the United States

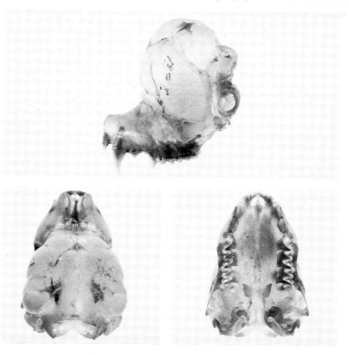

Skull of *Mormoops megalophylla*, x3

25

Remarks: Davis and Carter (1962a) described a reddish subspecies, *Mormoops megalophylla rufescens* from northwestern Mexico, ranging into Arizona. However, Villa (1967) considered it to be a synonym of *Mormoops megalophylla megalophylla* Peters. He said there was no significant size differences between the two, and that the reddish color could be found in any population and was not a geographic variation. Since *Mormoops megalophylla senicula* Rehn from Texas had previously been submerged by Villa and Jiminez (1961), there are now no recognized races of *M. megalophylla*.

In the caves occupied by large numbers of *T. brasiliensis* ammonia concentrations frequently reach levels high enough to cause bleaching of the fur. Some of the color variation in *M. megalophylla* may be due to such bleaching (Constantine 1958e).

There are places in Mexico where *M. megalophylla* is so abundant that it produces large deposits of guano. This material, rich in usable nitrogen from the chitinous exoskeletons of the insects upon which the bats feed, is used by the local people as fertilizer.

Villa (1956b) described a spectacular mortality among these bats in the Mexican border state of Nuevo Leon. He found hundreds of thousands dead in a cave and several thousand dead in a mine several miles away. No live bats were seen. The cause of the deaths is unknown.

While we were in Arizona studying bats, Dr. E. Lendell Cockrum told us our best chance to obtain a live *Mormoops* was to go to Sonora, Mexico, where a colony was known to inhabit Cueva del Tigre, about 200 miles south of Tucson. Fortunately Robert J. Baker, who knew the area, could go with us as a guide. The cave itself is at the end of a little desert footpath off the end of an unimproved road. It is beyond doubt the most isolated area in which we have collected; we would never have found it without a guide.

An estimated half-million *T. brasiliensis* made the air so rank with ammonia that about five minutes was all a man could stay in the cave; we made several quick sallies looking for our bat. In addition to the omnipresent *Tadarida*, we found several thousand *Leptonycteris sanborni*, and smaller groups of *Natalus stramineus*, *Pteronotus davyi*, and *Macrotus waterhousii*. We were disappointed to find no *Mormoops*, but not surprised, because of its unpredictable movements.

Baker was sure we could find the animal in an abandoned mine near Alamos, about 300 miles farther down the highway. *Mormoops* had been taken there on several occasions, either in the mine by day or in nets set in the entrance at night.

No *Mormoops* were in the mine when we arrived at midday. Before netting that night, we took Baker's advice and used an old parachute to seal the thousands of *Glossophaga* and *Natalus* in the mine; we did not care to pick them, one by one, from the back side of our nets. We stretched two 30-foot nets in a V over the water in the mouth of the mine. The apex was some 15 feet back in the mine, and the arms projected about the same distance out from the entrance.

Shortly after dusk we began catching a wide variety of interesting bats. After about an hour and a half, a *Mormoops* entered the mine at high speed, struck the bottom of a net, and fell into the water. We pounced upon him just as he was rising from the surface and forced him into the net where he became entangled.

Apparently *Mormoops* is a most fragile bat, said to be difficult to keep alive for even a short period. Since we were afraid our animal might succumb before we could get it to a place where we could photograph it, we hoped to catch another one or two. However, after half an hour went by and we saw no more *Mormoops* we folded our nets, retrieved our parachute, and left. We spent the hours after midnight in a stuffy Mexican motel photographing our prize.

MACROTUS WATERHOUSII Gray

Leaf-nosed bat; California leaf-nosed bat

Recognition: Forearm, 47–55 mm.; wingspread, about 340 mm. A rather large bat with big ears. A triangular flap of skin projects upwards from the end of the nose. Color, grayish; bases of the dorsal hairs are nearly white.

Variation: Seven subspecies have been recognized. Only *Macrotus waterhousii californicus* Baird occurs in the United States.

Confusing Species: The other big-eared bats, such as *Antrozous pallidus* and *Plecotus townsendii* could be confused with this species. However the combination of large ears and a triangular nose leaf of *M. waterhousii* is distinctive. No other big-eared bat has a nose leaf; no other leaf-nosed bat has big ears.

Range: The Caribbean islands, Guatemala, and Mexico, northward to the United States, where it occurs across southern California and the southern half of Arizona, with an extension into extreme northwestern Arizona and southern Nevada. *Macrotus* is a permanent resident in the United States.

Habitat: This species is a resident of lowland desert scrub of the Southwest. Abandoned mine tunnels are its favored daytime retreats. In the Riverside Mountains of southern California, Vaughan (1959) found that it inhabited deserted mine tunnels on the steep sides of the rocky canyons, in groups of from several to 100 or more, usually within 30–80 feet of the entrance. In short tunnels the bats sometimes took refuge within 20 feet of the entrance in fairly bright light. Small

6. *Macrotus waterhousii.*

27

groups were also found in natural rock shelters in the walls of the canyon. The mines used by the bats suggested that *Macrotus* prefers a shelter with considerable ceiling surface and flying space. The mines were generally about 5–7 feet high and equally wide.

The shelters these bats use in the daytime must provide protection from the heat and drying effects of the desert climate. In August Vaughan found that the temperature where a group was resting 45 feet inside a mine tunnel was 84° F. (29° C.), whereas the temperature outside was 110° F. (43° C.) in the shade.

Like most other bats, *Macrotus* uses resting places during its nocturnal forays. Such night roosts may be open buildings, cellars, porches, bridges, rock shelters, and mines. Any sort of shelter offering overhead protection and adequate flight approach may serve as a night roost. *Macrotus* will not crawl through a crevice into a building as do many kinds of bats.

Behavior: M. *waterhousii* begins to emerge about one hour

Distribution of *Macrotus waterhousii* in the United States

after sunset, considerably later than most other species. Emergence is spread over about three hours with small groups of bats often leaving together. When netting at the entrance to a day roost, Vaughan (1959) found that frequency of capture was greatest from about one hour 15 minutes to two hours after sunset, but many bats were still being taken 15 minutes later. After foraging for about an hour each bat retired to a night roost.

A second foraging period begins sometime after midnight but is not so clearly defined as the earlier one. The greatest activity in the morning begins about 2½ hours before sunrise and lasts about 2 hours. At the day roosts there is an especially large influx of bats with full stomachs about 45 minutes before sunrise. Vaughan estimated the total foraging time per bat as about 1¾ hours per night, with perhaps part of this time spent at night roosts consuming the larger prey species.

When at rest M. *waterhousii* hangs pendant by gripping the ceiling of its roost with one or both feet. Their long legs, large feet, and long nails seem adapted to hanging from a horizontal surface which they seem to choose more frequently than most other species. Much of the time at rest is spent hanging from a single foot with the other leg relaxed and dangling to the side. The free foot is often used for scratching and grooming the fur, the bat swinging gently like a pendulum.

Like our other leaf-nosed bats, *Macrotus* has rather large eyes and apparently can see well. When encountered by man in its daytime retreat it becomes alert immediately. It holds its large ears erect and, often hanging by one foot, twists and turns to get a better view of approaching danger. Facing the intruder, it is ready for instant flight.

Because of its apparent good vision and alertness, it is difficult to approach. When captured and handled, it utters no audible sounds and is reluctant to bite.

Although this species is usually found in groups, it does

not form tight clusters as do many other kinds of bats. The individuals hang in such a way that their bodies do not touch one another. A bat becomes restless and moves when it comes into contact with a neighbor.

M. *waterhousii* is unusual in that it is apparently unable to crawl. Whereas most of our bats readily scramble about using the wrists as front feet, Vaughan (1959) thought that this species was unable to perform quadrupedal locomotion; he was never successful in forcing the animals to crawl. These bats, however, can perform a most peculiar bipedal walk while hanging from a ceiling. A bat releases its hold with one foot and swings the body dorsally. After the free foot gains a new hold, the other foot releases, and the body again swings to begin a new stride. The bat progresses across the ceiling in a series of steps. It moves in the direction of its dorsal surface, keeping the head lifted, apparently looking about. A bat can travel a foot or two in a few seconds in this manner.

Flight: This leaf-nosed bat usually launches into flight by dropping from the roosting site. After falling a foot or less the bat pulls upward in a shallow arc into level flight. A second type of launching is exhibited by bats moving a short distance along the ceiling. The wings are stroked rapidly while the bat retains its grip with the feet. This brings the body horizontal and the bat moves off with the wings often beating against the roof of the mine (Vaughan, 1959).

In flight this is one of the most alert and agile of all our bats. An individual is difficult to capture even when cornered in a small dead end mine tunnel. We once spent half a hour catching one in a small attic of a building in Arizona. We divided the attic with a hanging mist net and chased the two bats present with wide-mouthed dip nets. Most kinds of bats can be easily chased into a mist net under such circumstances, but these persistently maneuvered over, under, or around the net. We finally caught one in a hand net.

This bat flies rapidly upon occasion, but the foraging flight is slow, buoyant, and quieter than that of most bats. In level flight the wings make a soft fluttering sound that is less sharp and carrying than that of other bats. Thus, Vaughan (1959) was able to identify *Macrotus* as they flew in and out of caves at night.

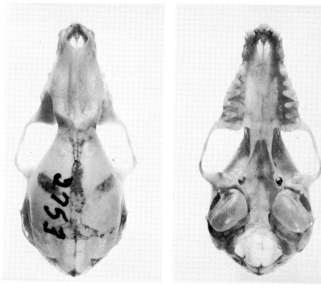

Skull of *Macrotus waterhousii*, x3

Like other leaf-nosed bats *Macrotus* can hover in flight. The body is vertical, the ears are erect, and the head points forward. The legs are apart, with the uropatagium fully spread, and the wings make rapid, shallow beats (Vaughan, 1959).

By analyzing high-speed photographs Vaughan was able to describe the remarkable intricate alighting maneuver of *Macrotus*. The bat makes a level approach to the roosting spot. When about six to eight inches below the ceiling the bat sweeps the wings in a deep downstroke that is directed nearly straight forward, and the hind limbs and uropatagium are lowered. This causes the bat to swoop sharply upward toward the ceiling. The wings are then pulled back in an upstroke while the bat loops more than 180° with its back facing downward and the long legs reaching for the ceiling. At the peak of the upstroke the head is downward and the bat is almost upside down as the feet grasp the ceiling. The wings then make a last downstroke that steadies the body and cushions the impact of landing.

Food and Feeding: These bats appear to be entirely insectivorous. Food items include grasshoppers, cicadas, noctuid moths, caterpillars, and beetles of the families Scarabaeidae and Carabidae. Remains of sphinx moths, butterflies, and dragonflies have been found beneath the night roosts.

Many food species are insects that are flightless, seldom fly, or fly in the daytime. Probably these are picked from the ground or vegetation by the hovering bats. The capture of a *Macrotus* in a mouse trap set on the desert floor (Grinnell, 1918), and the finding of willow leaves beneath a night roost (Huey, 1925) constitute circumstantial evidence for such a feeding behavior. Being unable to crawl, they cannot alight on the ground and forage as the desert pallid bat does, but must detect their prey while in flight.

Vaughan (1959) described the feeding behavior of **M.** *waterhousii* in southern California. The bats regularly foraged within three feet of the ground over a dry wash and the nearby desert. They often dropped nearer to the ground and occasionally hovered there for a few seconds. They also foraged close to the vegetation and probably picked food items off the bushes.

Many of the food items were fairly large and were carried to a night roost to be consumed. The night roost is often the daytime roost, or may be any other nearby shelter. Vaughan (1959) believes that *Macrotus* has a small foraging range. Some colonies seemed to feed within a few hundred yards of the daytime roost; others were observed up to about a mile away.

Reproduction: Testes and epididymides enlarge during July and August while the males live in small bachelor groups in various mine tunnels other than the ones used as nurseries. They join the females in September. Insemination, ovulation, and fertilization occur during September, October, and November. Most females are fertilized during October and all are pregnant by the end of November. Young females born the previous spring (3–4 months old) participate in the breeding, but insemination usually occurs later in October than it does in older females. Young males do not breed their first year.

Embryological development is delayed during the winter months, but accelerates by March. Because of this retarded development, the gestation period is about eight months (Bradshaw, 1962).

Like many other species, *Macrotus* forms maternity colonies where the females congregate to give birth and rear their young. In Arizona, they give birth in May or June. In Durango, Mexico, Jones (1963) found females carrying young on June 13, but in Baja California where *Macrotus* is one of the most common bats, females were still pregnant on July 7 and 8 (Jones *et al.*, 1965).

Only the right ovary is functional, and implantation occurs in the right uterine horn. Although there is one record of a female carrying two embryos (Cockrum, 1955), normally each female gives birth to a single young. The young are nursed for about a month before they join the evening feeding flights.

Remarks: The distribution of this species in Arizona is peculiar. It seems to be absent from the vicinity of the Chiricahua Mountains but is common in the area of Tucson. Abandoned mine tunnels and desert scrub vegetation are readily available in both places, and the bat fauna is similar with respect to most other species. Apparently there is some critical ecological difference important to *Macrotus* which is not yet recognized.

Near Carbo, Sonora, we saw a colony of *M. waterhousii* in a cave occupied by half a million or so Brazilian free-tailed bats. Ammonia was present in such concentration as to make the cave decidedly uncomfortable for us. Mitchell (1963) studied the effects of ammonia on *Macrotus* and found that they could tolerate concentrations that would be lethal to man.

These leaf-nosed bats do not hibernate. Although they spend the winter in the mines about Tucson, they are less active during this period. Apparently they maintain a somewhat lowered body temperature during these months, but a sustained body temperature below 79° F. (26° C.) is lethal (Bradshaw, 1962).

Nelson (1966) described the deciduous dentition of *M. waterhousii*; this is one of the few species for which such information is available.

CHOERONYCTERIS MEXICANA [Tschudi]

Hog-nosed bat; long-tongued bat; Mexican long-tongued bat

Recognition: Forearm, 43–45 mm.; wingspread, 330–360 mm. A rather large bat with a long slender nose. A triangular erect flap of skin arises at the tip of the snout. The minute tail, easily overlooked, extends less than halfway to the edge of the interfemoral membrane (fig. 7). Color, sooty gray to brownish.

Variation: Two subspecies have been named; only *Choeronycteris mexicana mexicana* (Tschudi) occurs in the United States.

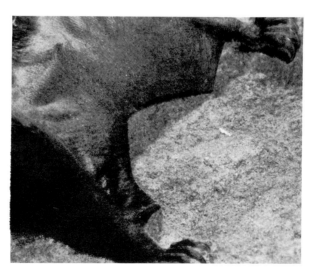

7. Interfemoral membrane of *Choeronycteris mexicana* showing the minute tail.

8. *Choeronycteris mexicana* giving birth. Left, young emerging. Center, the newborn young still wet and partially enclosed by the embryonic membranes. Right, within an hour after birth the youngster is dry and attached to the mother's breast.

9. *Choeronycteris mexicana* showing prominent nose leaf and large eye.

10. Newborn young of *Choeronycteris mexicana*.

Confusing Species: Leptonycteris sanborni and *Leptonycteris nivalis* are similar, but neither has a tail.

Range: From Venezuela northward through Central America and Mexico to the United States, where it is known only from southeastern Arizona, extreme southwestern New Mexico, and San Diego, California. Winter range unknown.

Habitat: In southeastern Arizona and adjacent New Mexico the desert is broken by isolated mountain ranges which rise abruptly several thousand feet above the desert floor. The deep canyons cut into these mountains carry streams that contain enough moisture to support dense vegetation, including large trees. These canyons support a surprising diversity of bat species and are the only places in the United States where the hog-nosed bat is resident.

The favored day roosts are caves and mines, where the bats hang an inch or two apart, but they are occasionally found in a variety of other shelters, including buildings. In Mexico, a group of these bats was once found hanging from the exposed roots of a tree on the bank of a deep ravine (Davis and Russell, 1954). Hoffmeister and Goodpaster (1954) found them in nearly every mine tunnel and cave investigated in the Huachuca Mountains. They usually shared their quarters with big-eared bats, *Plecotus townsendii*.

Behavior: Choeronycteris mexicana usually are found in the dimly lighted zone near the entrance of their roost. Like other leaf-nosed bats, they are extremely wary. Hanging from a single foot, they can rotate nearly 360° to watch an intruder, their large eyes glowing ruby red in the beam of a light. When disturbed, they will readily leave the shelter and fly out into the sunlight, seeming reluctant to retreat deeper into their shelter. In flight, the wings make a swishing sound similar to that produced by *Leptonycteris*.

33

Distribution of *Choeronycteris mexicana* in the United States

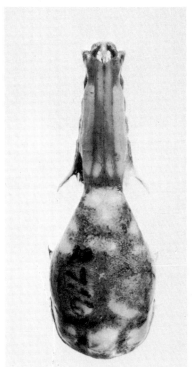

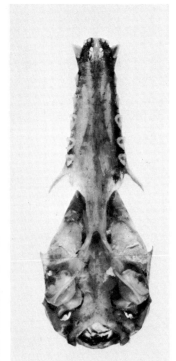

Skull of *Choeronycteris mexicana*, x3

34

Although Olson (1947) and Huey (1954b) reported that *Choeronycteris* they captured in San Diego bit viciously and repeatedly, we found those we handled in Arizona to be quite gentle. None attempted to bite.

Food and Feeding: *C. mexicana* probably feeds on nectar. Individuals have been captured whose heads and faces were covered with pollen. We found that in captivity they readily lap up sweetened water.

Reproduction: In Arizona and New Mexico young apparently are born in June and early July. Litter size is one. We have netted females near term in the Chiricahua Mountains on June 9 and June 29. Mumford *et al.* (1964) found newborn young in New Mexico on June 9 and Mumford and Zimmerman (1962) captured pregnant females there on June 19. In Sonora, Burt (1938) captured a mother with young on April 14 and took other young in April, May, July, and August.

We watched a *C. mexicana* give birth near Portal, Arizona, on June 10, 1966. Parturition took about 15 minutes as the bat hung head down from a vertical rock surface (fig. 9). The young are born in a remarkably advanced state of development and are surprisingly well furred (fig. 10). An embryo weighing 4.5 g. was taken from a female which weighed 19.9 g. Thus the female carried a fetus which was nearly 30 percent of her post partum weight.

The mother bat can carry a rather large baby in flight. Mumford and Zimmerman (1962) flushed one which flew with an attached young which weighed 8.2 g. They noted that the burden of young did not seem to impair flight.

Perhaps the mother carries her baby while she is feeding. Mumford *et al.* (1964) netted a female over a stream 200 yards from her day roost. She was carrying a 5.9 g. baby. However, she may have been moving her youngster from one roost to another.

Remarks: *C. mexicana* is known from southern California as a result of an invasion in September 1946 when the animals appeared at many scattered localities in the city of San Diego. From September to December Laurence Huey collected thirty-nine from such places as hallways, patios, and garages. Most were roosting singly but one group of about 40–50 lived in the cave-like understructure of a house for about a month. We know of no records of this bat in California before or since this invasion, except for a single individual captured in San Diego in October, 1963.

Stains and Baker (1954) described the replacement of the deciduous teeth in this species. The order of elimination is: in the upper jaw, second premolar, first premolar, incisors, canine; in the lower jaw, first premolar, third premolar, second premolar, canine, incisors. In the lower jaw the minute deciduous incisors are still present when the third lower molar erupts and sometimes persist in adults. They are not replaced by permanent teeth.

In the Chiricahua Mountains we found *C. mexicana* to be rather common during June 1966. We netted several over the South Fork of Cave Creek among the oaks at 5,200 feet elevation. In Rucker Canyon we found them among the yellow pines at 6,080 feet.

11. Juvenile *Leptonycteris nivalis* in Big Bend National Park, Texas.

LEPTONYCTERIS NIVALIS [Saussure]

Mexican long-tongued bat; long-nosed bat

Recognition: Forearm, 55–60 mm.; wingspread, about 410 mm. A rather large bat with a long nose supporting a triangular erect flap of skin at its tip. There is no tail. Color, sooty brown.

Confusing Species: It is most like *Leptonycteris sanborni*, from which it differs in being larger, with a longer forearm, and with the total length of the third finger including the metacarpal greater than 105 mm. It also has longer, more brownish fur. *Choeronycteris mexicana* is similar, but has a short tail.

Range: In summer, known only at higher elevations in Big Bend National Park, Texas, and a few localities in the neighboring Mexican states of Coahuila and Nuevo Leon. In winter, known only in Mexico, south at least to Morelos and Jalisco.

Habitat: This is a colonial, cave-dwelling species. Its favored habitat is the high pine-oak country from snow line down to about 5,000 feet. The only known colony in the United States occupies a cave on Emory Peak in the Chisos Mountains at an elevation of 7,500 feet.

Behavior: Available evidence suggests that this species emerges late in the evening and moves down to lower elevations to feed. Koestner (1941) found a colony of 10,000 in a mine in Nuevo Leon at an elevation of 11,500 feet, but did not find them flying at night at this elevation. In Big Bend

National Park we found them foraging well after dark among the agave and desert scrub in the dry rocky canyons and on the lower hillsides. David Easterla has netted *L. nivalis* at three localities in the Park, one of which was along the Rio Grande.

This species is a strong flier, flying more directly than most, with the wings making a characteristic swishing sound. It is highly maneuverable, able to fly straight up while keeping the body horizontal.

Food and Feeding: This bat feeds on the nectar and pollen of flowers. When we put one of our captives on the flowering stalk of an agave, it quickly thrust the long snout into each of several blossoms and apparently lapped the nectar from them.

Reproduction: In Texas one or two young per female are born in April, May, or June (Davis, 1960). In July adults of both sexes and half-grown young were found intermingled in the cave on Emory Peak.

We netted a juvenile over a pond in the valley below Emory Peak on July 5, 1966. It was virtually full grown and had been born probably in late May or early June.

Remarks: Essentially nothing is known of the life history of this species. This lack is due in part to the fact that not until 1962 was it recognized that two species of *Leptonycteris* occur in the United States and Mexico. *L. nivalis* apparently is a rare species throughout its range. Certainly it is one of the rarest bats in the United States. On July 4, 1967, David Easterla examined what is apparently the entire population of *L. nivalis* in the United States. There were an estimated 13,650 adults and young in the cave, arranged in four clusters the largest of which was 4 x 10 feet.

In July 1944, Davis (1960) noted that *L. nivalis* shared the

Skull of *Leptonycteris nivalis,* x3

cave with a large colony of big-eared bats, *Plecotus townsendii.*
The two species were in clusters about 20 feet apart. When
David Easterla visited the cave in 1967, he found only one
P. townsendii.

On July 5, 1966, we visited Big Bend National Park in quest
of this species. The cave inhabited by the bats is far up the
mountain via horse trail and not easily located. Since we
arrived so late in the afternoon that we could not make the
round trip before dark, we decided to try to net *L. nivalis*
that night. We asked the park naturalist and the superin-
tendent the location of the nearest waterhole to the cave.
After some thought, they directed us to the sewage settling
ponds below the campground. Water is scarce in west Texas.
Although the sewage ponds were too large to stretch a net
across, we put a 60-foot net over part of one end and waited
for dusk. Bats soon appeared in great abundance. We saw
dozens of western pipistrelles and netted 25 *Tadarida
brasiliensis* and 22 *Antrozous pallidus.* By 10:00 p.m. we had
also taken two *L. nivalis,* an adult and a young of the year.

One can recognize a cave inhabited by a large colony of
these bats by the musky smell. The odor is somewhat similar
to that of the Brazilian free-tailed bat, *T. brasiliensis.*

Distribution of *Leptonycteris nivalis* in the United States

LEPTONYCTERIS SANBORNI Hoffmeister

Sanborn's long-tongued bat; long-nosed bat

Recognition: Forearm, 51–56 mm.; wingspread, about 380 mm. A rather large bat with a long nose supporting a triangular erect flap of skin at its tip. There is no tail. Color, gray to reddish brown dorsally; brownish ventrally.

Confusing Species: It is most like *Leptonycteris nivalis*, from which it differs in being about 10 percent smaller, usually more reddish with a smaller forearm, with the total length of the third finger including the metacarpal being less than 105 mm., and having shorter, denser fur. *Choeronycteris mexicana* is similar, but has a short tail.

Range: Lowland deserts of Mexico, from Oaxaca and Veracruz to Baja California, and northward into the United States where it is known from several localities in south central and southeastern Arizona and adjacent New Mexico. Seasonal distribution is unknown, but apparently it is absent from the United States in winter.

Habitat: This bat is a resident of the desert scrub country. It is colonial, occupying mines and caves at the base of the mountains where the alluvial fan supports agave, yucca, saguaro, and organ pipe cactus.

Behavior: At rest *L. sanborni* hangs by its large claws from a rough surface with the head projecting downward. When slightly disturbed, it raises its head and peers at an intruder. Like other leaf-nosed bats, it has rather large eyes and likely can see well. When the beam of a light strikes them the eyes glow a ruby red. It hangs with its feet so close together that it can turn nearly 360° to watch a moving person. It is shy and takes flight quickly when disturbed.

When launching, it gives several strong wing beats, bringing the body into a horizontal position before releasing its grip. It is an agile flier and difficult to capture, even when cornered in a mine passage. It is able to fly nearly straight up while maintaining a horizontal body position.

The flight is rapid and direct, showing none of the erratic movements characteristic of the insectivorous bats. When the bats are aroused in a cave or mine, the strong wing beats

12. *Leptonycteris sanborni.*

produce a distinctive roaring sound, which can be recognized from even a single individual in flight.

Like *Choeronycteris* and *Macrotus*, *Leptonycteris* is a remarkably gentle bat. When handled it seldom attempts to bite. There is no bickering and fighting within the colony as there is in insectivorous species.

Food and Feeding: Leptonycteris emerges late in the evening, about an hour after sundown, and immediately moves out to feed. Food consists of nectar, pollen, and insects. The long tongue, covered with hair-like papillae on the upper and anterior surfaces, is well adapted for feeding at flowers. Apparently fruits are utilized after the flowering season is past. In captivity it will eat various kinds of fruit. Winter feeding habits are unknown (Cockrum and Hayward, 1968).

Cockrum and Hayward (1968) placed *L. sanborni* in an outdoor enclosure and described the feeding behavior. Bats landed on the flowering stalks of *Agave schotti* and worked over the flowers, inserting their long snouts into each blossom. At other times they appeared to hover in front of the flower, like a hummingbird, sometimes grasping the blossoms with their feet. Close analysis showed, however, that they did not really hover, but that the feeding was done during a braking wingbeat. The bats did not back off from the flower but turned at the last instant. If they did not obtain all the nectar in one pass, they returned to that flower again and again until the supply was exhausted.

After feeding for several hours the bats have such distended stomachs that they appear to be in late pregnancy. The volumes contained in the stomach range up to 4.5 cc. and the stomach walls are so thin as to be transparent (Cockrum and Hayward, 1968). When the stomach is filled, they retire to a night roost where they hang up and rest. Such a night roost has been described by Hoffmeister (1954) who found bats

40

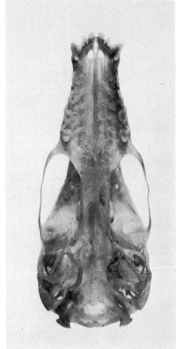

Skull of *Leptonycteris sanborni*, x3

using a barn at the mouth of Miller Canyon at the base of the Huachuca Mountains in Arizona in August. This group of about 100 bats consisted of adult females and their nearly grown young. Although no bats were there in the daytime, their use of the barn was betrayed by yellow spatterings of fecal material.

Reproduction: In Arizona females in late pregnancy form maternity colonies, numbering into the thousands of individuals, in early May. The single young is born from a few days to three weeks later. They are normally flying by late June. During the latter part of July the maternity colonies break up and scatter. The adult males congregate in small bachelor groups in various mines and tunnels while the young are being raised.

Cockrum and Ordway (1959) examined 10 females from a mine near Paradise, Arizona, on August 14, 1955, and found 5 of them pregnant. The largest embryo had a crown-rump length of 10 mm. Three of the ten bats had lactated earlier in the year; none of these was pregnant. Cockrum and Hayward (1968) suggested that these pregnant bats would migrate to Mexico and give birth there in the fall.

Migration: During September, *L. sanborni* apparently leaves the United States to winter in Mexico, returning in early May.

Remarks: Some of the lower incisors are frequently missing. These teeth may be vestigial. Hoffmeister (1954) pointed out that their loss may be advantageous as the tongue must rub over these incisors as it is protruded in feeding. Davis and Russell (1954) described a specimen which lacked all lower incisors and had no trace of alveoli.

L. sanborni does not hibernate. Although body temperatures may drop to 91° F. (33° C.) in the laboratory, prolonged exposures to cold are lethal (Cockrum and Hayward, 1968).

On June 21, 1966 we visited Cueva del Tigre, some 15 miles from Carbo, Sonora, where several thousand female *L. sanborni* had their young. Robert Baker pointed out to us that the bright red color which stained the rocks indicated the presence of *Leptonycteris*. The stain is produced by spattering of the thin fecal material. Dalquest (1953) said that this stain was from the fruit of the organ pipe cactus, which was abundant in the flats below Cueva del Tigre.

Distribution of *Leptonycteris sanborni* in the United States

41

The Vespertilionidae

MYOTIS LUCIFUGUS [LeConte]
Little brown myotis; little brown bat

Recognition: Forearm, 34–41 mm.; wingspread, 222–269 mm. A medium-sized *Myotis* usually with sleek glossy fur. There are long hairs on the toes extending beyond the tips of the claws. The ears are rather small (14–16 mm.); the foot is rather large, nearly always measuring 10 mm. The skull lacks a sagittal crest and is usually 14–15 mm. long. Rarely there is a slight keel on the calcar. Color, pale tan through reddish brown to dark brown.

Variation: Three subspecies are recognized in the United States. *Myotis lucifugus lucifugus* (LeConte) occurs in the eastern United States and northward across central Alaska; *Myotis lucifugus carissima* Thomas is a slightly paler form occurring in the Rocky Mountains. *Myotis lucifugus alascensis* Miller is a dark race on the Pacific Coast west of the Cascades from California to Alaska.

Confusing Species: In the east this species is most frequently confused with *Myotis sodalis* from which it can be distinguished by the presence of long hairs on the toes extending beyond the claws (fig. 14), and the absence of a keel on the calcar. Also commonly confused with *Myotis keenii*, which has longer ears (17–19 mm). *M. keenii* also has a longer, more narrow and pointed tragus, which easily separates these two species. *Myotis austroriparius* has dull, wooly fur, and a higher, more

13. Little brown bat, *Myotis lucifugus*. The nose is darker than that of the very similar *M. sodalis* (see fig. 43).

globose braincase. The baculum is also distinctive (fig. 26). *Myotis leibii* is smaller and has a much smaller foot (8 mm.). *Myotis grisescens* is larger, has monochromatic fur and has the wing membrane attached at the ankle.

In the west *M. lucifugus* most closely resembles *Myotis yumanensis*. The latter has dull fur and is usually smaller. The skulls of most *M. yumanensis* are 14 mm. or less in greatest length and the forearm is usually less than 36 mm. In most places these two species are distinct, but in parts of the Northwest from California to Washington they are very similar. A few specimens from these areas appear to be intermediate, and we suspect that occasional hybridization occurs.

Myotis volans is similar in appearance, but it is easily distinguished by its strongly keeled calcar and by the underwing which is furred to the elbow and tibia (fig. 51).

Myotis occultus is usually more reddish and usually lacks one of the small upper premolars while *M. lucifugus* usually has them both on each side. The molars of *M. occultus* are much larger; the length of the maxillary toothrow is usually greater than 5.5 mm. *M. occultus* has a sagittal crest on the skull. Findley and Jones (1967) consider *M. lucifugus* and *M. occultus* to be only subspecifically distinct.

Myotis velifer is usually larger, has a distinct sagittal crest on the skull, and never has glossy fur. *M. leibii* and *Myotis californicus* are smaller and have noticeably smaller feet (8 mm. or less). *Myotis evotis*, *M. keenii*, and *Myotis auriculus* have longer (17–24 mm.) ears.

Range: This is a northern species of wide distribution and may be the most abundant bat in the United States. It ranges from the coast of Labrador across the Northwest Territories and central Yukon to Alaska. In the United States it is known from much of Alaska and all the northern states, ranging southward in the mountains to Georgia and southern Cali-

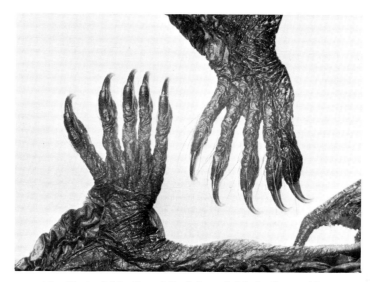

14. Foot of *Myotis sodalis*, left, and *M. lucifugus*. Note the hairs extending beyond the toes of the latter.

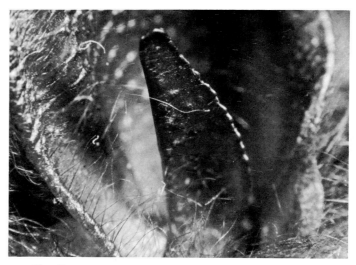

15. Ear of *Myotis lucifugus* showing tragus. The tragus of *M. keenii* is longer and more pointed (see fig. 34).

43

fornia. It is scarce and local in the southern part of its range. Stragglers have been taken in the coastal Carolinas, Alabama, Mississippi, Texas, and New Mexico.

A population of bats that seems to be this species occurs in the high country of southern Mexico in the Distrito Federal and the states of Mexico and Tlaxcala. These animals are larger than *M. lucifugus* from the United States and they probably represent an undescribed race.

The winter and summer ranges in the east are identical. In the west, the winter range is unknown. Specimens have been found hibernating in Jewell Cave in the Black Hills of South Dakota (Jones and Genoways, 1967b).

Habitat: In summer *M. lucifugus* inhabits buildings, usually choosing a hot attic, where nursery colonies of hundreds and even thousands form. Less frequently colonies form beneath tar paper, siding, shingles, or other similar sheltered spots. In the west colonies have been found beneath bridges and in caves. Single males have been found in attics, behind shutters, under bark, in rock crevices, behind siding, and under shingles. Groups of males occasionally occur in caves (Krutzsch, 1961).

Colonies are usually close to a lake or stream; the bats seem to prefer to forage over water. If water is not close by, they forage among trees, in rather open areas such as a tree-lined village street.

In winter they are found in caves and mines throughout the eastern part of their range. Apparently they never hibernate in buildings in the east (Davis and Hitchcock, 1965).

Behavior: In a summer colony the bats remain alert on warm days. In any large group a few are usually active, crawling about over the others, biting and bickering. A colony can be heard as far away as 100 feet. Toward evening the bats become more active until a constant squeaking can be heard as they gather about the exits. They begin to emerge at late dusk. At colonies where there is water nearby, most of the bats head at once for the water where they begin feeding a few feet above the surface as they continue to disperse. One of us (WHD) once counted 1,000 in 15 minutes as they moved up Otter Creek in Vermont after leaving their day roosts in houses in the village of Middlebury. At the other end of the village even greater numbers could be seen moving in the other direction.

Where a body of water is not nearby, the bats begin feeding among trees and over lawns, pastures, or streets near the roost. Here they forage at heights of about 10–20 feet.

In foraging, a bat often repeats its flight pattern. Hough (1957) watched one follow a set hunting pattern around a house and tree. Each evening it repeatedly followed the same narrow path. Davis and Hitchcock (1965) and Humphrey (1966) noticed that some individuals flew in a steady circular path that repeatedly brought them back to the roost entrance.

At dawn when bats return to the roost most individuals make numerous passes at the entrance before entering. As they approach the entrance they frequently defecate. The moist droppings strike and adhere to the wall beneath the opening. This results in a spattered appearance clearly visible on the side of a light-colored house. Often a bat will alight momentarily several times before finally entering the roost.

Food and Feeding: Food apparently consists of a variety of insects. Although no study of the diet has been made, Griffin (1958) found one that had caught a tiny gnat and others that had captured an 8 mm. ichneumon wasp and assorted beetles. Poole (1932) saw them catch a crane fly and noctuid moths.

Insects are found by echo-location and normally taken on the wing. They are usually captured with a wing tip, im-

16. Multiple exposure of a little brown bat, *Myotis lucifugus*, in flight. It had been trained to capture mealworms tossed into the air. The bat apparently mistook a pine needle for the mealworm, which can be seen at the top of the picture. Note the open mouth as the bat utters its ultrasonic echolocation cries. *(Courtesy of Frederic A. Webster)*

17. Multiple exposure of a *Myotis lucifugus* capturing a moth under difficult conditions. *(Courtesy of Frederic A. Webster)*

mediately transferred into a scoop formed by the down and forwardly curled tail and interfemoral membrane, and then grasped with the teeth. Smaller insects are eaten in flight. Larger ones, too difficult to handle in flight, are held in the mouth, and the bat alights to eat them. This bat is very efficient at capturing insects in flight. In the laboratory, with a plentiful supply of flying *Drosophila*, Donald Griffin found that a bat could capture them at the rate of one a second. In the field, he (1958) estimated feeding efficiency at about one capture per seven seconds and darting sallies after insects at about twice this rate. Feeding attempts are not always successful.

Some noctuid moths have developed an amazing ability to avoid capture. They can hear the echo-locating sounds. When a hunting bat approaches, the moth begins a zig-zag flight, making its capture difficult.

Reproduction: M. lucifugus breeds in the fall. Occasionally, a mated pair may be encountered during winter. In any large hibernating colony, some are active; it is not unusual to find an active pair mating. Wimsatt (1945) observed a hibernating pair in coitus. The sperm is stored in the uterus of the female, where the cells remain viable throughout the winter. Fertilization occurs when the bats emerge from hibernation in the spring (Wimsatt, 1944a). The gestation period is 50–60 days (Wimsatt, 1945).

M. lucifugus establish maternity colonies in the attics of old buildings and in similar warm, dark retreats. In Vermont these colonies start to form during the latter part of April. On Cape Cod they begin during mid-May (Griffin, 1940) and in southern Illinois by the first of April (Cagle and Cockrum, 1943).

Most summer colonies range in size from a few individuals to about a thousand. Cockrum (1956a) reported a colony of more than 30,000. Colonies of 300–800 are rather common and consist primarily of females and their young. In New England, until the young are weaned, few adult males occur in the maternity colonies; they appear in numbers in late summer. In Illinois Cagle and Cockrum (1943) found that males made up 38 percent of the colony in June. In Kentucky, where summer colonies of *M. lucifugus* are uncommon, adult males comprise 20–30 percent of the colonies (Davis *et al.*, 1965). Here they are found among the clusters of females and young, whereas in the north the few adult males are normally separated from the clusters.

Parturition dates vary with latitude and also show considerable variation within a colony. In Vermont birth dates range from June 7 to July 10; in Wyoming the young are born in July (Findley, 1954a); in southern Illinois, from May 17 to July 12; and in Kentucky, from May 21 to June 21. Older bats give birth earlier than yearlings. About half the yearlings are nonparous (Davis and Hitchcock, 1965).

A single young is produced each year. Although the ovum is shed as frequently from one ovary as the other, the embryo almost invariably develops in the right uterine horn, which is larger than the left. The uterus can thus easily accommodate only a single ovum, but exceptions are known. Gates (1936) found two minute embryos in February, and Wimsatt (1945) found two females each with two well developed embryos. We captured a female in Kentucky which had just given birth to twins.

Wimsatt (1960a) described birth in *M. lucifugus*. As time for parturition approached, the bats became restless and showed obvious signs of nervousness and irritability. This behavior usually lasted only a few minutes. As parturition begins the female hangs head upward, the reverse of the normal resting position, and the tail and interfemoral membrane are cupped ventrally forming a basket which receives the emerging fetus.

The baby emerges breech first. If the amnion is not already ruptured, the mother tears it apart with her teeth at the first opportunity. Thereupon the baby actively participates in its own delivery by groping movements of the legs, followed by grasping and pulling. The feet clutch whatever they encounter. After gaining footing, the baby flexes the legs vigorously and helps its body emerge from the birth canal. Birth is completed in 15–30 minutes.

When the young is born the placental and umbilical circulation is still intact. If the cord is broken the fetus bleeds to death in a few minutes. After a normal delivery, free circulation through the umbilical vessels continues for 3–10 minutes after which there is a rapid blanching of the cord as circulation ceases. The cord then quickly dessicates and breaks, and the placenta falls.

Care of the Young: The single young clings tightly to a nipple during its early days of life. When the mother is at rest during the day, she keeps the baby beneath a wing. If disturbed she takes flight and carries the baby attached to a nipple. It has not yet been established whether or not the mother carries the newborn during her feeding flights. Probably she leaves it at the roost. In an extensive study of two European species of *Myotis*, Nyholm (1965) found only two instances of females carrying the young at night. When the baby is about half grown, it begins to release the nipple during the day and hang beside the mother.

Growth and Development: The newborn weigh 1.5–1.9 g., about one-fourth the weight of the post partum mother. Their state of maturity at birth is a reflection of the long gestation period. The initial behavior of the newborn is to seek out and obtain secure attachment to a nipple. They are born blind, but the eyes open on the second day.

The young grow rapidly and are first capable of flight at about three weeks of age. They usually learn to fly within their home shelter and venture outside at the age of about one month at which time they have attained adult weight. After learning to fly and to find their way about outdoors, they are faced with the substantial problem of learning to catch insects on the wing. They must learn to detect flying insects by echo-location, distinguish them from such things as twigs, leaves, and wires in their environment, and capture them in flight. It has been suggested by Davis and Hitchcock (1965) that it takes some time to acquire these skills. They found that the full grown young bats did not store as much fat as the older ones, and they were active in the fall after the fat-laden adults had entered hibernation.

Population: Davis and Hitchcock (1965) found that the local distribution and abundance of this species was spotty in New England. Abundance was apparently related to water and availability of hibernation sites. For a favored section encompassing a major part of the region they estimated the summer population as 26 bats per square mile.

M. lucifugus has a remarkable life span. The oldest on record is 24 years (Griffin and Hitchcock, 1965), and there are several records of 20-year-old bats. Since these bats produce but one young per year a long life span is an effective way to maintain the population.

Hitchcock (1965) found that the males live longer than females. An analysis of the population dynamics of this species has not been conducted.

Migration: In the latter part of July, after the young are weaned, the maternity colonies begin to disperse and gradually decrease in size until only a few individuals are left after the middle of September. After leaving the maternity colonies many of the bats travel to certain caves where they congregate by the thousands during August. The bats fly into and out of the caves at night, sometimes accompanied by several other species, and then depart for their summer range, sometimes more than 100 miles away. An entirely new group of individuals convenes at the cave the following night. The significance of these late summer conventions is not yet understood. The same individuals return later in the fall to hibernate in the swarming caves or others nearby.

The distances traveled in migration seem to depend upon the availability of adequate wintering sites. On Cape Cod there are no adequate hibernation sites, and *M. lucifugus* residing there travel 150 miles or more to winter in a cave in Vermont. Humphrey and Cope (1964) have described the migration of bats from a summer colony in central Indiana to winter quarters about 200 miles away in a Kentucky cave. They made numerous recaptures of banded bats at caves between the two areas. Many of those in northern Indiana, which is also devoid of caves and mines, travel to the Mammoth Cave region of Kentucky, a distance of 290 miles for some individuals. On the other hand, most of the several thousand *M. lucifugus* which hibernate in Carter Caves State Park in northeastern Kentucky migrate less than 100 miles to spend the summer in southwestern Ohio (fig. 18). The wintering grounds of this species in northern Ohio remain unknown despite rather intensive study by Smith (1954) and others.

Spring migration begins in Vermont about the first week in April. The females leave earlier than the males, and most females are gone by the second week in May. The males begin leaving in numbers about the end of the first week in May, and few bats remain in the cave by the end of the first week in June.

Upon leaving the cave the bats move to their summer homes. The major exodus is to the southeast in a rather narrow

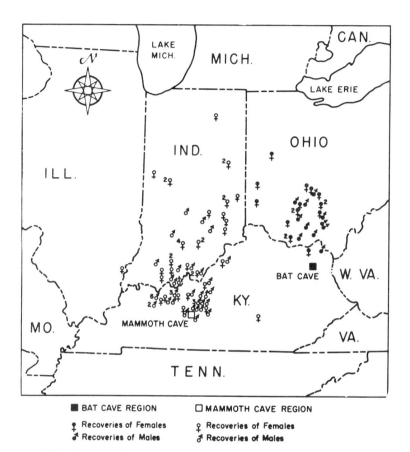

18. Summer distribution of the little brown bats, *Myotis lucifugus*, which winter in two of Kentucky's cave regions, based upon recoveries of banded individuals. Numbers indicate multiple recoveries from the same locality.

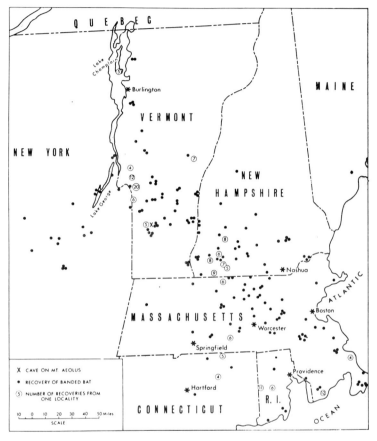

19. Dispersal of *Myotis lucifugus* from a cave in Vermont. From the *Journal of Mammalogy*.

band leading to Cape Cod (fig. 19). Some move northward into the Champlain Valley and a few scatter in other directions (Davis and Hitchcock, 1965).

The bats can travel rapidly in migration. One banded at a Vermont cave in April was recaptured in a house 80 miles away after three nights. One which we banded at a cave in Kentucky in August traveled even more rapidly; it was captured in a house 50 miles to the north after one night.

Little is known of the migratory habits of *M. lucifugus* in western North America where it is one of the most abundant bats. Bailey (1926) reported that it occupies a large cave called Devil's Kitchen in Yellowstone Park in great numbers during summer, but apparently leaves during the cold season. He also found a large breeding colony under a bridge over the Bitterroot River in Montana where the bats returned each spring. Twente (1960) reported that the species is common in summer nursery colonies in Utah, but he was unable to find any among the over 500 mines and caves and 100 buildings he investigated in that state in winter.

Homing: Several workers have studied the homing ability of *M. lucifugus.* Hitchcock and Reynolds (1942) showed that half of them returned to the home roost after being displaced over 70 miles. Schramm (1957) recovered 2 out of 34 bats back at the home roost 17 and 22 days after they had been released 270 miles away. Cope *et al.* (1961c) calculated the speed of homing as about four miles per hour. Mueller (1965) found that in homing from a distance of 58 miles the greatest speed of the fastest bat averaged about 19 miles per hour. In measuring flight speeds of individuals released in a building corridor he obtained readings ranging from 5.9 miles per hour to 11.7 miles per hour. However, he noticed that under natural conditions where the bats were leaving their diurnal roosts and moving off to their feeding grounds they traveled at rates ranging from 12.5 miles per hour to 21.7 miles per hour.

It has not been established that these bats can return home over unfamiliar territory. Even the greatest distance of successful homing experiments is within the known migratory range of some individuals. Davis and Hitchcock (1965) studied the fate of individuals which were not successful in homing; some were apparently lost and wandered off, while others established new summer and winter homes in the vicinity of release.

Hibernation: During September *M. lucifugus* in the eastern part of its range moves into caves and mines to hibernate. Bats from a summer colony may scatter to several such sites (Humphrey and Cope, 1964); conversely the bats using a particular site may come from many different summer colonies. The hibernating colonies range in size from a few individuals to many thousands. A cave in Vermont harbors a winter population of about 300,000 bats, part of which represents the total population from 8,600 square miles of New England.

When large numbers of these bats hibernate in one cave they form clusters in favorable spots (fig. 20). Throughout much of the east the winter clusters are distinctive and easily recognized. They are not so tightly packed as those formed by *M. sodalis*, which frequently uses the same caves. *M. lucifugus* sometimes form a linear arrangement along a cave wall (fig. 21).

In Canada and other northern regions, *M. lucifugus* sometimes form tightly packed clusters, which are not easily distinguished from those of *M. sodalis*. In a mine in the Adirondacks of New York many thousands form such clusters, which include a few individuals of the latter species.

M. lucifugus picks a spot to hibernate where the temperature normally remains several degrees above freezing and the humidity is high (85–100 percent), often so high that droplets

20. Cluster of little brown bats, *Myotis lucifugus*, hibernating in a recess in the ceiling of a Kentucky cave. Several are banded.

21. Little brown bats, *Myotis lucifugus*, hibernating in a Kentucky cave.

51

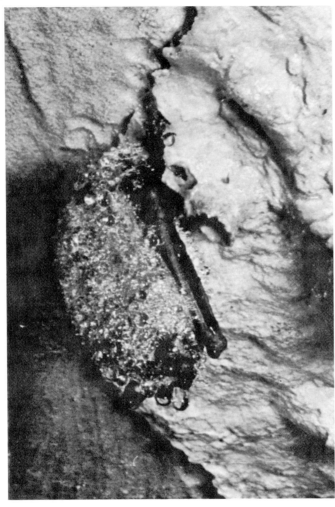

22. Droplets of water have condensed upon the fur of this little brown bat, *Myotis lucifugus*, hibernating in a cave.

of water condense on the fur of the torpid bat (fig. 22). The bats arouse at intervals of about two weeks and, if conditions have changed, may move to a more favorable spot. During an extreme cold spell, with the wind blowing into the cave, the more exposed bats may regulate their body temperature by increasing metabolism enough to maintain themselves a few degrees above air temperature (Davis and Reite, 1967). Prolonged exposure to subfreezing temperatures is fatal, and many individuals, especially young of the year, die during exceptionally cold weather (Davis and Hitchcock, 1965).

Temperature Relations: This bat exhibits probably the greatest range of body temperature known in vertebrates. Davis and Reite (1967) cooled an individual to 20° F. (–6.5° C.) with no apparent harmful effects to the animal. A maternity colony has been found living next to the ceiling in an attic where the temperature was 131° F. (55° C.) (Davis *et al.*, 1965), and Robert Stones has informed us of finding a body temperature of 129° F. (54° C.) in this species.

Maternity colonies are usually situated where the temperatures reach high levels; this likely contributes to the rapid growth of the young. Since *M. lucifugus* is a northern species, such rapid growth is probably necessary so that the young can get on the wing and fatten before the hibernating season. The high temperatures of the nursery colonies is probably a factor contributing to the lower survival rate of the females of this and some other species of bats.

In August females are heavier than males, apparently as a result of greater fat storage (Davis and Hitchcock, 1965). For hibernation the males tend to select the colder regions of the caves (Davis and Hitchcock, 1964). Since the metabolism of a bat is lower at lower temperatures (Hock, 1951), males probably require less fat to survive the winter. Thus males, by avoiding the high temperatures in maternity colonies and by choosing cooler spots in winter, would have a lower annual metabolism than the females. These are likely factors contributing to the higher survival rate of male *M. lucifugus* reported by Hitchcock (1965).

Menaker (1962) found that in summer little brown bats put into hibernation and maintained at 37° F. (3° C.) could not arouse when stimulated, whereas those taken in winter could. The summer bats could not generate enough heat to become active. He concluded that the bats cannot use the caves and mines in New England as roosts in the summer, for once they let their body temperature drop to that of the cave they would be trapped.

Captivity: Little brown bats do poorly under ordinary laboratory conditions. Even those which eat well usually die within a week or two. Stones and Wiebers (1965b), realizing that this species naturally dwells in attics where temperatures are high, decided to try raising them in warm quarters. The bats do nicely in their laboratory at 92° F. (33° C.), feeding on live meal worms.

Parasites: The species harbors a few fleas and numerous mites during summer. Mites can be found on the wing membranes of most individuals. The most conspicuous parasite is the large bat bug, *Cimex* sp. These bugs are occasionally seen on the forearm of a bat but are much more frequently encountered in the summer roost. In a roost inhabited by a large colony of bats the bugs can be seen by the thousands. All sizes are present. They sometimes are so abundant as to nearly cover the rafters where the bats hang.

Cimex is responsible for the common rumor that bats carry bedbugs. Such an idea is understandable, for these bugs are closely related and similar in appearance. Although most bugs stay near the bats, some occasionally move down out of the attic where they come to the attention of man. This seems to happen more frequently when the bats have been shut out of a building, or have left the site for the winter.

This bat may harbor trematodes, cestodes (Ubelaker, 1966), and chiggers (Jones and Genoways, 1967b).

Predation and Accidents: Several animals are known to prey upon *M. lucifugus.* Judging from reports of recoveries of banded bats, house cats must take them frequently. At a colony in a house in New York the resident told how his cat perched on the roof in the evening and struck at the bats as they emerged, catching some. We have also heard it recounted how a cat would crouch in high grass and spring at low flying bats.

Mink enter caves and feed upon bats (Goodpaster and Hoffmeister, 1950). Racoons, which commonly enter caves, surely feed upon this species at times. Voles have been reported as preying on the bats in a cave (Martin, 1961a), and Hitchcock (1965) suspected a wood mouse, *Peromyscus leucopus,* of preying on bats hibernating in Ontario.

Borell and Ellis (1934) watched trout eat bats which were shot over a lake in Nevada. One which we banded in Kentucky was recovered from the stomach of a bass, and one which Harold Hitchcock and Wayne Davis released while banding in Vermont was captured by a broad-winged hawk.

Kinsey (1961) watched a leopard frog, *Rana pipiens,* consume a *Myotis* which it had captured. Rat snakes, *Elaphe obsoleta,* probably also take them. Barr and Norton (1965) watched one capture a *Myotis sodalis* in the ceiling of a cave in Kentucky.

Accidents also take their toll. DeBlase *et al.* (1965) described the destructive effects of a flood in a Kentucky cave. Hundreds of drowned bats were found. There are several reports of these bats becoming entangled in the dried burs on a burdock,

Arctium minus, and perishing there. Hitchcock (1965) found one which had become impaled on a barbed wire fence. He also (1963) reported the accidental death of about 350 *M. lucifugus* which had become entrapped in a china jar in the attic of a building.

Remarks: As with several other species of bats in which the females form nursery colonies, the whereabouts of most of the males while the young are being raised is not known. Probably most lead a solitary life during this period and roost in a great variety of sheltered sites. Single males are frequently encountered behind window shutters. They appear to be transient, as such spaces are seldom occupied for more than a night or two.

Krutzsch (1961) reported colonies of several hundred males in Hellhole Cave, West Virginia, in July and August, and smaller numbers in June. We think it is likely that Hellhole is a center for summer swarming bats and these colonies represent bats that find themselves in the cave at daybreak. A similar situation is found at Dixon Cave, Kentucky (Davis, 1964b).

An evolutionary trend toward the loss of the tiny upper premolars is evident in this species. Frum (1946) noted the frequency of missing premolars in eastern populations. Findley and Jones (1967) found premolars occasionally missing in the Colorado population, and we have noticed the same in specimens from California.

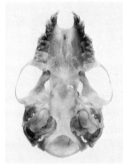

Skull of *Myotis lucifugus*, x3

Distribution of *Myotis lucifugus* in the United States

MYOTIS YUMANENSIS [H. Allen]

Yuma myotis

Recognition: Forearm, 32–38 mm.; wingspread, about 235 mm. A rather small *Myotis* with fairly large feet (10 mm.) and short ears (14–15 mm.). Calcar not keeled. Skull short, usually less than 14 mm., with no sagittal crest. Color, light tan to dark brown; underparts, whitish to buffy.

Variation: Five subspecies are recognized in the United States:
1) *Myotis yumanensis yumanensis* (H. Allen), a pale, buff colored bat of the southwestern deserts.
2) *Myotis yumanensis phasma* Miller and Allen, a larger animal found in Utah and Colorado.
3) *Myotis yumanensis sociabilis* Grinnell, a tan to olive bat that ranges from central California into Canada, generally east of the Cascade Range.
4) *Myotis yumanensis oxalis* Dalquest, a dull, ash-gray to brown race of the San Joaquin Valley in California.
5) *Myotis yumanensis saturatus* Miller, a dark reddish to dark brown race of the northwestern coastal region west of the Cascade Range.

Confusing Species: *Myotis lucifugus* is very similar, but has longer, glossier fur, and is larger. Its skull is similar but distinctive, usually more than 14 mm. in length, flattened, and somewhat broader. *Myotis leibii, Myotis californicus* and *Myotis volans* have keeled calcars. *Myotis velifer* is larger. *Myotis occultus* usually has only one small premolar behind each upper canine; if two are present, one is crowded out of alignment. Some specimens from various localities in Cali-

23. *Myotis yumanensis* echolocating just prior to launching into flight.

55

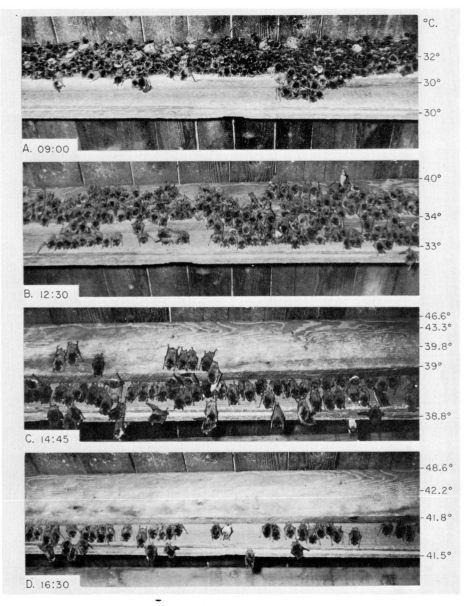

°C.

- 32°
- 30°
- 30°

A. 09:00

- 40°
- 34°
- 33°

B. 12:30

- 46.6°
- 43.3°
- 39.8°
- 39°
- 38.8°

C. 14:45

- 48.6°
- 42.2°
- 41.8°
- 41.5°

D. 16:30

24. Movements of *Myotis yumanensis* in response to heat in their natural roost. Time of day is shown on the left and temperatures on the right. (*Courtesy of Paul Licht and Philip Leitner, from the* Journal of Mammalogy)

fornia and Washington are apparently hybrids between *M. lucifugus* and *M. yumanensis*.

Range: Western North America from British Columbia south in Mexico to Hidalgo and Michoacan. In the United States, westerly from Texas, Oklahoma, Colorado, and Montana, with a hiatus in northern Utah and most of Nevada. Winter range unknown. There are a few winter records from coastal California.

The similarity between *M. yumanensis* and *M. lucifugus* has led to many mistaken identifications in the literature and consequent difficulty in plotting the ranges of the two species.

Habitat: M. *yumanensis* seems to be more closely associated with water than any other North American species of bat. From the cottonwood lined streams of the desert southwest to the redwood canyons of the Pacific coast, nearly all habitats of this bat show a common feature—some open water nearby. Although locally abundant, the species seems to be absent in many apparently suitable feeding areas. Perhaps adequate day roosts are a limiting factor. Large nursery colonies are most frequently located in buildings, under bridges, and in caves and mines.

The night roosts of the *M. yumanensis* often show little or no evidence of use. Careful search of abandoned cabins, attics, porches, and similar sites will usually reveal droppings. Many times, however, no droppings are found on the floors of buildings in which bats can be captured at night (Dalquest, 1947a).

Behavior: M. *yumanensis* emerges early in the evening and feeds over ponds and streams, just a few inches above the surface of the water. Like other insectivorous bats it is an efficient feeder. Individuals with full stomachs have been taken at resting places 15 minutes after dusk.

Dalquest (1947a) observed a colony of about 5,000 that inhabited a church belfry at Wadsworth, Nevada. Shortly after sunset the bats became active and started squeaking. It was nearly dark before they began to emerge, first in twos and threes and then in larger groups until a steady stream poured forth. They flew swiftly to the Truckee River, 100 feet away, skimming the tops of the low willows and cottonwoods, rarely over 30 feet above the ground. After feeding for several minutes they began to drink. Two hours after dark no bats were seen along the river, although some were feeding about street lights of the town, and others were seen and heard over the open desert.

M. yumanensis sometimes forms nurseries in buildings where temperatures rise to 122° F. (50° C.) in the afternoon. Licht and Leitner (1967a) studied the behavior of such a colony. They found that as the temperature rose, the bats moved to cooler spots. In the morning they formed tight clusters in the warmest place at the top of a beam just beneath the roof. As temperatures there increased to about 104° F. (40° C.), the bats began to move down the beam. Finally, if the temperature rose above 104° F. (40° C.) on all sections of the beam, the bats began to fly to seek cooler spots elsewhere in the barn (fig. 24).

Dalquest (1947a) found that nursery colonies would not tolerate disturbance. In all colonies from which he collected specimens, he found numbers much reduced, or the sites deserted, on subsequent visits.

Reproduction: M. yumanensis gives birth to a single young. Parturition dates vary from late May to July. Data presented by Dalquest (1947a) suggest that in California the young are born from late May to mid-June. In Arizona the time of birth is about the middle of June. When we visited a nursery colony beneath a bridge in Graham County on June 17, 1966, many

25. Adult female *Myotis yumanensis* with her baby tucked beneath her left wing. The baby's feet are evident, one clinging to the rock and the other to the mother's foot.

Skull of *Myotis yumanensis*, x3

Distribution of *Myotis yumanensis* in the United States

bats had small young and the rest appeared to be in late pregnancy. Commissaris (1959) reported that 30 bats examined in New Mexico on June 15 were all pregnant. In a nursery colony of several thousand in a Nevada cave, Hall (1946) found all adults examined on July 11 pregnant or with newborn young.

As is so commonly the case with *Myotis*, the sexes segregate when the young are being raised. Males are usually absent from the large maternity colonies and live as solitary individuals scattered in buildings and other suitable retreats. Often they are accompanied by a few adult males of other species (Dalquest, 1947a).

Migration: M. *yumanensis* abandon the nursery colony sites in fall, but their destination and winter habits are unknown. There are a few winter records from California. Dalquest (1947a) observed transients at the ventilators of a building in Berkeley, California. He saw one female on February 20, 1945, and captured an occasional individual during March, April, and May. Albert Beck and Philip Leitner have been studying M. *yumanensis* extensively in California during recent years, but have been unable to locate them in winter. The bats arrive at the nursery colonies in April and leave by the end of September.

Parasites: M. *yumanensis* seems surprisingly free of ecto-parasites. Dalquest (1947a) found the bat bug and many fleas, but no ticks, mites, lice, or flies.

Remarks: M. *yumanensis* is closely related to M. *lucifugus* and apparently the two species have been derived from the same stock in the rather recent geologic past. In some places in California the two species apparently are not reproductively isolated and introgressive hybridization occurs (Harris and

Findley, 1962). Albert Beck, who has studied the species extensively in California, says that he is unable to identify specimens from certain localities in that state. In most instances, however, the two are separable, even where they occur together. For example, Hall (1946) shot seven *M. yumanensis* and nine *M. lucifugus* in August as they flew through an opening in the trees at the north end of Lake Tahoe, Nevada, and found no evidence of intergradation.

One of us (WHD) observed *M. yumanensis* in the bottom of Grand Canyon during the summer of 1954. The bats appeared at dusk over Bright Angel Creek where it joins the Colorado River. They all flew downstream just above the surface of the water. None was ever seen at the edge of the stream where *M. californicus* and *Pipistrellus hesperus* were foraging. The yuma myotis flew so close to the surface of the stream that a most effective way of collecting them was to knock them into the water with a stick. A stick about six feet long was cut, all leaves removed, but several branches left on the end. Swinging the stick in an arc, sweeping the surface of the water from one bank to the other knocked the bats into the stream. In each of three evenings more than a dozen bats were captured; all were *M. yumanensis*.

MYOTIS AUSTRORIPARIUS [Rhoads]
Southeastern myotis; southeastern bat; Mississippi myotis

Recognition: Forearm, 36–41 mm.; wingspread, 238–270 mm. A medium sized *Myotis* with a globose braincase and a slight sagittal crest. The calcar is not keeled. The fur has a wooly appearance, and there is little contrast between the base and the tip; there are long hairs on the toes, extending well beyond the tips of the claws. Color, russet to gray above, tan to whitish beneath.

Variation: Three subspecies are recognized. *Myotis austroriparius austroriparius* (Rhoads) occupies most of the coastal Southeast. *Myotis austroriparius mumfordi* Rice is a gray race with white underparts found in the lower Ohio River Valley. A reddish race, *Myotis austroriparius gatesi* Lowery, occurs in the lower Mississippi Valley. A gray phase is frequently encountered in Louisiana and Arkansas.

Confusing Species: Myotis grisescens is easily separated by its peculiar wing attachment. *Myotis sodalis* lacks the long hairs on the toes and has a slight keel on the calcar. *Myotis keenii* has longer ears (17–19 mm. versus 15 mm.). *Myotis leibii* is smaller, has a keeled calcar, and a smaller foot (8 versus 10 mm.). It is most similar to *Myotis lucifugus*, but with wooly rather than smooth, glossy fur. The shape of the skull is distinctive, as is the baculum (fig. 26).

Range: Southeastern United States, from coastal North Carolina west to Louisiana. It occurs sparingly in extreme

59

26. Bacula (penis bones) from *Myotis austroriparius* (A and B) and *M. lucifugus* (C and D). *(Drawing courtesy of Charles L. Rippy)*

northeast Texas and southeastern Oklahoma. An apparently isolated population occurs in southern Illinois and Indiana south into Kentucky. Summer and winter range identical.

Habitat: In the cavernous regions of Florida, caves are the favored day roosts, although buildings and other shelters are sometimes used. Maternity colonies numbering in the many thousands are known in caves. Throughout the rest of the Deep South *M. austroriparius* resides in buildings and hollow trees. In the Ohio River Valley it roosts almost exclusively in caves. During their extensive work in Indiana, Russell Mumford and James Cope have found only one *M. austroriparius* roosting outside a cave; it was among hundreds of *M. lucifugus* in an attic.

In winter all but a few leave the great maternity caves of central Florida and take up residence in small groups at various outdoor sites. At this time they are usually found over water in places which are protected from climatic extremes, but which are more exposed to cool temperatures than are the caves—in crevices between bridge timbers, in storm sewers, road culverts, the vertical drain pipes of concrete bridges, in boat houses, in various other buildings, and in hollow trees (Rice, 1957).

In February 1955, E. V. Komarek showed one of us (WHD) a hibernating colony of these bats in a fertilizer plant at Thomasville, Georgia. The building is a large shelter, open on all sides. About 300 bats were present, all tightly packed into a long narrow crevice between two of the rafters supporting the roof. When dislodged with a long pole, the torpid bats fell to the floor where they were gathered and banded.

Behavior: This species is usually associated with water. It emerges late in the evening and flies to a nearby pond or stream to feed. In feeding, it flies very low, just above the surface of the water; in this behavior it is similar to *Myotis yumanensis* of the western United States.

Russell Mumford has studied the winter behavior of *M. austroriparius* in Indiana caves. The bats formed clusters on the walls and ceiling ranging in number from 8 to 45 bats. They were also frequently found in crevices in the ceiling where there was room for only one bat. In this respect the behavior is like that of *M. keenii*. Up to six individuals have been found in longer crevices, and a few *M. lucifugus* sometimes occupied the same crack. Even in mid-winter the clusters were often composed of active individuals which flew when disturbed.

Reproduction: Reproductive data on this species are available only for the Florida populations studied by Sherman (1930) and Rice (1957). The time of mating is unknown. Rice (1957) believes that the population in peninsular Florida breeds in the spring and that yearling males are reproductively active, but he presented little supporting evidence. Apparently yearling females produce young.

The maternity colonies in the caves of central Florida begin to form about the second week in March; all bats arrive by early April. They gather in large dense clusters containing

60

about 150 bats per square foot. Colonies range in size from 2,000 to 90,000, and they are found only in caves which have standing water. A few males are present in the nursery colonies, but most are in other caves or shelters, singly or in small groups. After the young mature, many adult males join the colony.

Parturition begins at the end of April and reaches a peak about the second week of May. Ninety percent of the pregnant females produce twins; the remainder give birth to a single young. This species is unique among the *Myotis* of the United States in that all others normally produce a single young.

The nursery colonies disperse mainly during October, and the bats leave for their winter quarters. Males tend to depart earlier than females.

Care of the Young: The young often hang in clusters separated from the adults during the day (Sherman, 1930). They are left behind when the mothers go out to feed in the evening. Within about five or six weeks after birth the young take flight (Rice, 1957).

Migration and Homing: In Florida the bats occupy different quarters in summer and winter, but the patterns of movement among sites are unknown. Rice (1957 listed a few recoveries of banded bats showing movements of up to 27 miles.

In limited homing experiments Rice found that some of the bats he removed from a nursery colony in May returned from distances of 18 and 45 miles. He had no returns from 108 and 178 miles.

Population Dynamics: The population dynamics of **M. austroriparius** in Florida seem substantially different from other bats in the United States. Rice (1957) found only 42 percent

27. *Myotis austroriparius* from Gainesville, Florida.

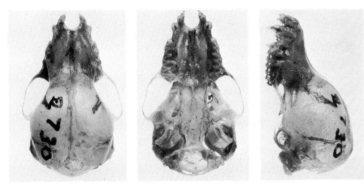

Skull of *Myotis austroriparius*, x3

Distribution of *Myotis austroriparius*

males among the winter population. Since the sex ratio at birth is 1:1, he suspected a higher death rate among the males. This would be contrary to what has been found for more northern species in which the males live longer (Hitchcock, 1965; Davis, 1966). The production of two young per litter is also peculiar to this *Myotis*. Perhaps these population parameters represent adaptations to life in milder climates. Here bats are active a greater portion of the year and thus subject to higher mortality rates than the more northern bats which hibernate for up to eight months.

In parts of Florida this species is extremely abundant. Rice (1957) estimated the population for a large area of central Florida as 77 per square mile during May. This contrasts sharply to the estimate of 26 per square mile for *M. lucifugus* in some of its most favorable habitat in New England (Davis and Hitchcock, 1965).

Predation: Rice (1957) believes predation is the most important mortality factor for *M. austroriparius* in Florida. Rat snakes (*Elaphe obsoleta*) and corn snakes (*Elaphe guttata*) were frequently found in the bat caves and were thought to be the most important predators. They are excellent climbers and readily feed upon bats. Various carnivorous mammals and owls take some. Hawks are apparently not a factor, since *M. austroriparius* emerges late in the evening. Cockroaches (*Periplaneta americana* and *Periplaneta australasiae*) are abundant in the bat caves and eat very young bats which have fallen to the floor.

Parasites: Several species of ectoparasites are found on *M. austroriparius* in Florida. Mites are abundant on the wing membranes. Nycteribiid flies, *Basilia boardmani*, are common in the fur. Streblid flies, *Trichobius major*, are the most conspicuous parasites; most of the bats harbor several (Rice, 1957).

Remarks: Apparently most of the caves in central Florida are too warm (69° to 73° F.; 21°-23° C.) to be suitable as hibernation sites for this species. If the bats remained active during the winter, they would suffer in cold spells when flying insects were scarce. Probably the few active individuals occasionally found in the maternity caves in winter are transients.

At Gainesville they are residents about the sewage disposal ponds of the University of Florida where they are so abundant as to be easily captured with an insect net. They may be found any evening when it is warm enough for insects to fly. Apparently the bats reside in the large concrete drain tiles which connect the ponds.

The population of *M. austroriparius* in the lower Ohio River Valley is apparently isolated from the remainder of the species. It is known only from a few caves in Indiana, Illinois, and Kentucky, where its numbers have been steadily declining. Apparently, this race is nearing extinction.

One of us (WHD) observed a colony of this race in a cave beside the Ohio River in Hardin County, Illinois, on November 29, 1953. The bats were in a tightly packed cluster on the ceiling within easy reach. When gathered for banding they were found to be torpid. There were 120 bats in the cluster, 55 percent of which were males.

MYOTIS GRISESCENS [Howell]
Gray myotis; gray bat; Howell's bat; cave bat

Recognition: Forearm, 40–46 mm.; wingspread, 275–300 mm. A large, big-footed (12 mm.) *Myotis.* The wing membrane is attached to the foot at the ankle (fig. 28). Calcar not keeled. A distinct sagittal crest on the skull. Color, uniformly gray from base to tip of hair; occasionally russet.

Confusing Species: Most likely to be confused with *Myotis lucifugus, Myotis sodalis, Myotis austroriparius* and *Myotis keenii.* From all of these, it may be recognized by the uniformly colored fur; all others have the base and tip of the fur in contrasting shades. Also, the attachment of the wing membrane is unique.

28. Feet of *Myotis* showing attachment of the membranes. Left, *Myotis grisescens,* showing attachment at the ankle. Right, attachment at the base of the toe, as seen in other species of *Myotis.*

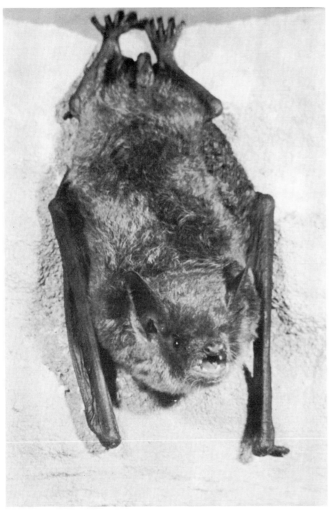

29. *Myotis grisescens* at Mammoth Cave National Park, Kentucky.

Range: Concentrated in the cave region of Missouri, Kentucky, Tennessee, and Alabama. Occasional colonies and stragglers occur in adjacent states. Summer and winter range identical.

Habitat: *Myotis grisescens* is almost unknown outside of caves. Most banding recoveries represent individuals that have encountered mishap in transit from one cave to another. No mine has yet been found harboring the species. Wilson Baker has found a few transients in a tunnel on the campus of the University of Georgia. A small maternity colony occupies a storm sewer in Pittsburg, Kansas (Hays and Bingman, 1964).

Thomas C. Barr, Jr., who has probably seen more summer colonies of *M. grisescens* than anyone else, has generalized for us the requirements of this species. He finds the maternity colonies nearly always in rather large caves containing substantial streams. With few exceptions, the colonies are accessible only by boat or by wading deep water.

The species winters in caves; apparently almost the entire population hibernates in five or six major caves.

Reproduction: The males become reproductively active in autumn. Sperm is found in the testes and tubules in October and November and persists until May. Copulation occurs in late fall. Some females have sperm in the uteri as early as October; specimens taken November 11 and December 3 contained many active spermatozoa (Guthrie, 1933b).

In summer *M. grisescens* forms maternity colonies of from a few hundred to a quarter of a million individuals in many large caves in the central part of the eastern United States. Here the bats and their young form great masses clustered on the ceiling. The bats are intolerant of disturbance and take flight in mass when a light is turned on the cluster. Repeated disturbance causes them to move to remote regions of the cave or to abandon it.

Guthrie (1933b) found that in Missouri pregnant and lactating females could be found together in summer. Females in their second summer were nonparous and were rarely in the maternity colonies; more frequently they were with the males in another area of the cave.

Sometime during June a female produces a single young. She rarely carries it, normally leaving it in the cave when going out to feed.

Migration: In autumn the colonies disband and leave the caves where the young were raised. Only rarely are a few found in winter in these caves. Until the work of Richard Myers in Missouri in the late 1950s the winter home of *M. grisescens* was unknown. He discovered three caves where they collect from widely scattered areas to hibernate. More recently John Hall discovered such a cave in Kentucky and Merlin Tuttle one in eastern Tennessee. Probably another great wintering cave exists somewhere in that state. Sealander (1956) found small groups of *M. grisescens* wintering in Arkansas.

Evidence suggests that these bats travel in flocks between summer and winter caves. Tuttle followed their movements from several scattered summer colonies to the wintering cave near Rogersville in northeastern Tennessee. Bats came from as far as 130 miles. He observed bats at a cave near Concord, Tennessee, which seems to serve as a rest stop for transients. This cave often contained 500 to 2,000 *M. grisescens* during the day in spring and fall. Sometimes bats were absent during these seasons. Once during the spring of 1961 he visited this cave and found no bats. Returning that night at 11:00 p.m., he was surprised to find several thousand gray bats. Next day all were gone. Smith and Parmallee (1954) found a cluster of hundreds in an Illinois cave on October 1. None was seen there on June 25, and none could be found in December.

Hall and Wilson (1966) found that bats from summer colonies scattered over about 10,500 square miles of Kentucky, southern Illinois, and Tennessee migrated to a cave in Edmonson County, Kentucky, to hibernate.

Hibernation: Hall (1962) described the clusters of 100,000 gray bats which used to hibernate in Coach Cave, Kentucky. They formed great mats several tiers thick on the ceiling. The forearms of the bats, instead of being held parallel to the body as in other species, stuck out at sharp angles making the cluster appear interwoven.

The gray bats chose areas slightly warmer (45°–50° F.; 7°–10° C.) than those chosen by *M. sodalis.* However there was some area of overlap between the species and in these areas the *M. grisescens* would sometimes hang directly on the clusters of *M. sodalis.*

30. Part of the nursery colony of *Myotis grisescens* at Sauta Cave, Alabama. This is the largest known colony of the species, estimated at about 200,000 individuals. (*Courtesy of Lyle G. Conrad*)

Parasites: Ubelaker (1966) found three species of mites, one species of flea, and one species of streblid fly in a summer colony in Kansas. Among internal parasites he found four species of trematodes, two kinds of nematodes, and one cestode.

Remarks: The large winter colonies of *M. grisescens* are in deep caves accessible only by use of the elaborate gear needed for vertical cave work. These colonies were long unknown because they were so inaccessible; however, in the last few years human disturbance has threatened the very existence of the species. Cave exploring has become extremely popular in recent years and vertical pits are an intriguing challenge. One of the wintering caves in Missouri has become very popular with spelunkers. Another is commercialized and stocked as a fallout shelter; the owner wants to get rid of the bats. The cave in which *M. grisescens* of Kentucky and Illinois hibernate has recently been commercialized apparently resulting in the loss of this population. Hall and Wilson (1966) located several maternity colonies in this area in the late 1950s, but the bats were not present in the summers of 1963 and 1964.

Summer colonies of this species are also receiving ever increasing harassment. The largest known colony (200,000–300,000) inhabits Sauta Cave in Alabama. This cave has been converted into a fallout shelter and is being commercialized. The bats were present as late as 1967 but their fate is uncertain. Old Nickajack Cave, the type locality and one of the best known colonies of *M. grisescens*, is being destroyed. The Tennessee Valley Authority has built a dam which will flood the cave.

Thus it seems that *M. grisescens* is destined to continue a rapid decline in numbers and probably faces extinction. It should be on the list of rare and vanishing species. No cave regularly inhabited by this species is protected. Mammoth

Cave National Park, which currently protects about 100,000 *M. sodalis* in winter, serves as a shelter for only a few transient *M. grisescens*.

Skull of *Myotis grisescens*, x3

Distribution of *Myotis grisescens*

MYOTIS VELIFER [J. A. Allen]

Cave myotis; cave bat; Mexican brown bat

Recognition: Forearm, 37–47 mm.; wingspread, 280–315 mm. A large *Myotis* with robust teeth and a well developed sagittal crest on the skull. Calcar not keeled. Foot, 10–12 mm., usually 11 mm. Color, light brown to nearly black.

Variation: The population in the United States consists of two distinct subspecies which differ strikingly in appearance. *Myotis velifer incautus* (J. A. Allen), found in Kansas, Oklahoma, Texas, and eastern New Mexico, is a light brown animal. It is the largest of our *Myotis*, the forearm measuring 43–47 mm. The western form, *Myotis velifer brevis* Vaughan, common across southern Arizona, is gray to nearly black and is smaller (forearm 37–43 mm.). The two races intergrade across New Mexico and in western Texas. Specimens from Arizona and New Mexico referred to *Myotis velifer velifer* (J. A. Allen) by Miller and Allen (1928), before *M. v. brevis* was described, probably should be reassigned to *M. v. brevis*.

Confusing Species: The geographic variation exhibited by this species renders it confusing. In the eastern portion of the range (Kansas, Oklahoma, central Texas) other species of *Myotis* are scarce, and all are smaller, with forearms less than 43 mm. In the western portion many species of *Myotis* occur. *Myotis auriculus*, *Myotis evotis*, and *Myotis thysanodes* have longer ears (over 16 mm.). *Myotis yumanensis*, *Myotis californicus*, and *Myotis leibii* in this region are all smaller (forearm less than 37 mm.); *Myotis volans* has a distinct keel on the calcar and lacks a sagittal crest; *Myotis occultus* is usually

31. *Myotis velifer* from an Oklahoma cave.

russet brown and has but one small premolar behind each upper canine. If two are present, one is crowded out of alignment.

Range: Southwestern United States at lower elevations from Kansas to southern Nevada and southeastern California, southward through Mexico to Honduras.

This is an abundant bat in the cave country of central Texas and in the band of gypsum caves from south central Kansas to the Texas panhandle. It is found in more of the caves than any other species of bat and is a year-round resident. Bats of the western subspecies are locally abundant in summer, but their winter distribution is unknown.

Habitat: Myotis velifer is a highly colonial species, inhabiting the Sonoran and Transition life zones of the arid Southwest. In summer they congregate in caves, mines, and apparently less often in buildings. In winter they hibernate in caves, at least in the eastern part of their range and in the highlands of Mexico.

They are tolerant of high temperatures and low humidities. Constantine (1958e) found a group of 75 in the attic of a house in Gila County, Arizona. In July the temperature at the roost was 99° F. (37° C.) and the relative humidity was 23 percent.

Behavior: The flight of this species is stronger, more direct, and less fluttery than most other members of the genus *Myotis*. The bats begin emerging from the daytime roost well before dark, fill their stomachs within about a half an hour of foraging time, and retire to some shelter such as a building, cave, or mine for a night resting period. There is no clearly defined second foraging period in early morning as there is with some other species of bats (Vaughan, 1959).

Twente (1955a) described the pattern of emergence of a nursery colony of 15,000 to 20,000 adults in a cavern in Kansas. All members of the clusters were alert and ready to fly at any time of day. As evening approached the bats began squeaking loudly. Fifteen minutes before the first ones emerged bats began to fly into the light zone, turn around, and fly back into the cavern. As the light decreased the bats flew farther and farther toward the outside until the small opening of the cave became filled with milling *Myotis*, still five minutes before emergence. Two minutes before emergence bats were flying outside the entrance and returning quickly to the cave. Once the emergence flight began very few bats turned around to go back into the cavern and within 30 minutes the cave was deserted.

This behavior clearly suggests a light sampling pattern which informs the bats of the proper time to emerge. Emergence generally begins 10–15 minutes after sunset; it is about 10 minutes earlier on overcast evenings.

After emergence most bats traveled directly to a stream while feeding at a height of 15–20 feet. Their cruising speed was 13–15 miles per hour. Other bats flew up and down the canyons feeding at tree top level. By 11:00 p.m. many bats had returned to the cavern and at 2:00 a.m. all seemed to be back. A morning flight occurred after this, but the bats remained near the cavern to feed at that time.

Vaughan (1959) found that *M. velifer* foraged over the desert, floodplains, and water, usually at a height of 6–15 feet. When feeding among sparse desert shrubs they preferred to fly close to the vegetation, often within a few inches of the foliage. Frequently individuals flew back and forth over definite foraging beats about 50–70 yards long. They may also be seen foraging beneath street lights in desert villages.

Bailey watched *M. velifer* emerge from limestone hills in the dry country near Carlsbad, New Mexico. The bats flew in a straight line across several miles of desert to an artificial pool (Miller and Allen, 1928).

Twente (1955a) found that after feeding the bats selected the warmest locations in the caves where they remained active. When adverse conditions, such as heavy rain, prevented feeding, the clusters retreated to the coldest parts of the caverns and became torpid, as if trying to conserve energy.

Reproduction: Nursery colonies may form either in the caves where the bats hibernate (Glass and Ward, 1959), or in other nearby caves. In the panhandle of Texas, nursery colonies were found in the least accessible caves (Tinkle and Patterson, 1965), in the warmest parts of the warmer caves, and were used by bats from several hibernation caves.

In Kansas and Oklahoma a single young is born during the last week of June and the first two weeks of July. Presentation is breech as in many species of bats. The newborn crawls unaided to a nipple and begins to nurse while the umbilical cord and placenta are still attached.

Care of the Young: During early July the females carry their young in flight when disturbed, but leave them in a cluster when they go out to feed. Twente (1955a) thought the females recognized their own young. When a colony moved 5,000 babies from one room to another in a cave, 5 youngsters were left. These died within a few days; probably their mothers had not returned from foraging. When a colony has been disturbed and the females are moving their young, they alight on a cluster of young and nuzzle many of the babies until they apparently find their own. Each female then crawls over the baby and with her nose pushes the youngster about until it attaches itself to her with its teeth and claws. The female then flies with the baby to another part of the cavern.

Development of the clustering behavior is apparently gradual. The very young are spaced about the ceiling where the mothers have left them in the evening, although they are well able to crawl about. As they grow older they begin to form clusters, and by the time they have juvenile pelage they form the same tight clusters as the adults. In Oklahoma some young can fly by July 17 (Glass and Ward, 1959).

Population Dynamics: Twente (1955b) separated a population of *M. velifer* into six age groups based upon tooth wear. On the basis of the distribution of the sexes within these groups he decided that there was no differential mortality of the sexes. He then constructed a theoretical population structure based upon the assumption that survival rate is .667 per year and is independent of age as well as sex. Such an assumption is probably invalid. Davis (1966) found that survival rate varied sharply with age in pipistrelles and Tinkle and Patterson (1965) found mortality higher in males among *M. velifer*.

Migration: The populations in Kansas and Texas seem to be permanent residents. Many banded individuals have been found in the same region both summer and winter. Banding recoveries reported (Cockrum, 1952a) give little indication of significant migrations. On the other hand, Stager (1939) made observations in several mines in southeastern California at all seasons, and found *M. velifer* present only from May through August. In Arizona the great colonies found in many mines disperse in late summer. Where they go is unknown. Villa (1967) found that *M. velifer* which he banded in Mexico moved up the mountains to hibernate in caves at higher elevations.

In Kansas, the hibernating clusters break up in late March and early April. They disperse to warmer caves in the vicinity where they congregate in large clusters in crevices. These transient groups appear irregularly throughout April and May

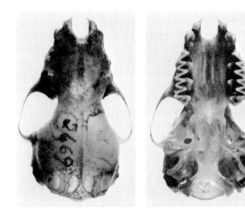

Skull of *Myotis velifer*, x3

Distribution of *Myotis velifer* in the United States

70

before the nursery colonies are established. At this season, they are likely to be found seeking temporary shelter in varied retreats where they are not ordinarily found. Buchanan (1958) found several hiding in cliff swallow nests in Texas.

Both Twente (1955b) and Tinkle and Patterson (1965) found that the bats readily moved among several nearby caves during winter. A few individuals moved between caves 90 miles apart in mid-winter. Intracave movement was studied by painting the ears of the hibernating bats in a cluster; one color for bats on the edge of the cluster, and a different color for those in the center. Observations were made weekly. Within three weeks the bats from the marked cluster had scattered, with no apparent tendency to remain together or for individuals to occupy a similar position in another cluster.

Hibernation: As fall approaches these bats deposit fat stores preparatory to hibernation. In Kansas fall weights average over 15 g.; females are heavier than males. One fourth of this weight is lost during hibernation (Twente, 1955a), the greatest loss being early in the hibernation period.

Twente (1955a) studied the factors which determined where the clusters form within the cave. Since it is important to a hibernating bat not to use stored fat too rapidly, the choice of a spot with the proper temperature and stability is necessary. Metabolism falls with temperature (Hock, 1951) but rises again at air temperatures below 41° F. (5° C.), as the bat regulates his body temperature to prevent freezing (Reite and Davis, 1966). Thus the optimal temperature range for most hibernating bats is about 41° F. (5° C.). Twente believed that the bats arrived at the most favorable spots within a cave by trial and error. He found that *M. velifer* were scattered when hibernating in the fall, and that those which were in the less favorable spots awakened sooner than those in the more favorable locations. He suggested that the length of inactivity is inversely proportional to metabolic rate and the bats awaken when the urinary bladder is filled. Since M. *velifer* is social, those which awaken more frequently would tend to gather with those which are in the most favorable spots, thus giving rise to the great clusters as the winter progresses. Although Twente's hypotheses seem reasonable, he gathered no evidence to support them.

The tight clusters of hibernating bats, which number about 158 per square foot, are sometimes in the open on the walls and ceiling of the cave and at other times packed into crevices. Tinkle and Patterson (1965) found that this behavior was dependent upon temperature changes. When temperatures were stable in a favorable range, the bats clustered in the open. When air temperatures in the caves fluctuated beyond the optimal range, the bats retreated into crevices where the microenvironment was more stable.

Like most bats M. *velifer* needs rather high humidity at the hibernation site. Tinkle and Patterson found that the large hibernating clusters were frequently over water where the relative humidity was close to 100 percent. Twente (1955a) found torpid bats scattered over a range of humidities from 20 to 100 percent in October, but by February none was found at localities below 55 percent.

In the caves where large numbers of M. *velifer* hibernate, the individuals which are active at any time gather in loudly squeaking clusters in select spots in the warmest part of the cave. Bats which are handled and released appear in these clusters prior to selecting a spot to reenter hibernation. The same behavior has been found in *Myotis sodalis*, another species which winters in huge clusters (Hall, 1962).

Captivity: Unlike most *Myotis* this species apparently takes well to captivity, and eats various foods. Stager (1939) fed them beef heart which they consumed without hesitation.

The meat was placed on a flat piece of wood in the center of the cage floor, and here the bats crowded around and fed until the last bit of heart disappeared. In captivity M. *velifer* seemed more quarrelsome than most species. When Stager confined them with several other species of bats they attacked and devoured *Macrotus waterhousii*.

Associated Species: M. *velifer* is often a close associate of the freetail bat, *Tadarida brasiliensis*; they frequently cluster together. Twente (1955a) found that male M. *velifer* lived with *Tadarida* throughout the summer. Buchanan (1958) found males of the two species living together in cliff swallow nests in Texas in March.

M. *yumanensis* is another common associate of M. *velifer*. On June 17, 1966, we saw several hundred of each species occupying a cave-like chamber at the end of a bridge in Graham County, Arizona. It was a nursery colony for M. *yumanensis*, most of which carried young or were in late pregnancy, but there were no young M. *velifer*. Several caught and examined were males. Cockrum and Musgrove (1964b) found the two species in a nursery colony in southern Nevada. On June 29 they were found together in one cluster, along with their young, which were estimated to be a week to 10 days old.

Predation and Disease: Twente (1955b) believed population size in M. *velifer* is controlled primarily by predators. He recorded predation in Kansas by hawks, owls, racoons, and corn snakes (*Elaphe guttata*), but considered the latter to be one of the most important predators. Cockrum (1952a) noted a wood rat, *Neotoma micropus*, carrying a M. *velifer* in a Kansas cave.

Apparently disease is sometimes an important mortality factor. Raun (1960) found thousands dead in a cave in Texas.

Many were hanging on the walls in mummified condition. Cockrum (1952a) also reported many dead *M. velifer* hanging from the ceiling of a cave in Kansas.

Parasites: Stager (1939) examined over 100 *M. velifer* for ectoparasites in California. He found only the flea *Myodopsylla*, but this insect was abundant on all specimens examined. He said that in roosts harboring large numbers of *M. velifer* the walls were alive with fleas.

Jameson (1959) examined 27 *M. velifer* from north Texas, and found a variety of internal and external parasites. Worms included trematodes, cestodes, and nematodes. Insects found were *Trichobius major, Myodopsylla collinsi* and nycteribiids. Mites recovered included *Ornithodores, Spinturnix,* and *Ichoronyssus longisetosus.* Ubelaker (1966) found additional species of mites and a trematode parasitizing *M. velifer,* and George and Strandtmann (1960) reported two species of fowl mites on this bat.

Molt: Molt occurs once a year. In central Texas adults molt during July and August, the males molting several days earlier than the females. Molting is completed in about a month. The new pelage is somewhat darker than the old, which has faded or may have been bleached by the ammonia present when there are large summer bat colonies (Constantine, 1957; 1958e). The molt pattern is shown in figure 32.

Remarks: The sex ratio among known hibernating populations is nearly 1:1. Twente found slightly more males than females in Kansas; Tinkle and Patterson found more females than males in Texas. Ward (1891) collected 193 *M. velifer* from torpid clusters in a cave high in the mountains of Veracruz, Mexico; 78 percent were males. Twente noted a difference in behavior between the sexes. The larger clusters deepest in

72

the cave contained more females and the smaller scattered clusters contained a preponderance of males.

This species was reported from Utah by Miller and Allen (1928) on the basis of two young specimens from Thistle Valley in the United States National Museum. We have examined these specimens. They were very young when collected, probably less than three weeks, and flightless. The skulls are fragmentary. The feet are large (10 mm.), the calcars not keeled, the ears small, and the fur pale (perhaps faded with age in alcohol). Although we cannot identify these bats with certainty, we believe that they are either *M. yumanensis* or *M. lucifugus,* not *M. velifer.*

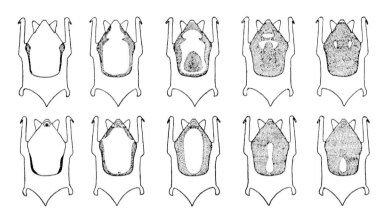

32. Molt pattern of *Myotis velifer incautus.* Upper row, dorsal view. Lower row, ventral view. New hairs appear in the stippled areas. Molt progression is indicated from left to right. Dorsal molt is almost completed before ventral begins. (*Courtesy of Denny G. Constantine, from the* Journal of Mammalogy)

MYOTIS OCCULTUS Hollister

Arizona myotis

Recognition: Forearm, 36–41 mm.; wingspread, 245–275 mm. A medium-sized brightly colored *Myotis* of the southwest. Skull with a distinct sagittal crest; teeth massive for a *Myotis.* Calcar usually not keeled. Most individuals have only one small premolar behind each upper canine; when two are present, one is crowded out of the toothrow. Color, tawny ocher.

33. *Myotis occultus* from the mountains of New Mexico.

Confusing Species: Similar to *Myotis lucifugus* which lacks a sagittal crest and has smaller cheek teeth. The maxillary toothrow is generally greater than 5.5 mm. in *Myotis occultus*, less than 5.5 mm. in *M. lucifugus.* The usual absence of one or more of the small upper premolars is rather distinctive, but this condition is occasionally seen in *M. lucifugus*, *Myotis thysanodes*, and *Myotis volans.* Findley and Jones (1967) consider *M. occultus* only subspecifically distinct from *M. lucifugus.*

Within the range of *M. occultus*, *Myotis velifer* is usually much darker, the sagittal crest is more prominent, and the two small upper premolars on each side are usually not crowded out of alignment. *Myotis californicus* and *Myotis leibii* are smaller. *M. thysanodes*, *Myotis evotis*, and *Myotis auriculus* have larger ears. *M. volans* has a distinctly keeled calcar and has the under side of the wing furred to the elbow and knee.

Range: Extreme southeastern California through Arizona, New Mexico, and south central Colorado south into Chihuahua.

73

Skull of *Myotis occultus*, x3

Distribution of *Myotis occultus*

One specimen has been taken in extreme western Texas. Winter range unknown.

Habitat: Although this species is found in the low desert along permanent water courses, it is most commonly encountered in the pine forests at 6,000–9,000 feet elevation.

Day roosts have been found beneath bridges and in attics of buildings. *M. occultus* may commonly share their day roosts with *Myotis yumanensis*, *M. velifer*, and *Tadarida brasiliensis*. Stager (1943a) found a maternity colony of about 800 living in small crevices between horizontal timbers of a highway bridge at Blythe, California. The bats were present at least from April 20 to August 13, but none were found in February. Hayward (1963) found a nursery colony clustered in crevices around a chimney in the attic of an abandoned house in Middle Verde, Arizona, at an elevation of 3,400 feet. The house was beside a stream lined with cottonwoods, willows, and sycamores. A colony occurs in a garage in Bosque del Apache National Wildlife Refuge, New Mexico.

Stager (1943a) took one adult male from a mine in Riverside County, California, in August. We know of no other records of this species from mines or caves. It is not among the many that commonly can be netted at these sites at night.

At lower elevations the bats have been observed foraging in an orchard and beneath large cottonwood trees (G. M. Allen, 1921). In the high country they forage over ponds and in clearings among the pines.

Reproduction: Apparently a single young is produced. Mumford (1957) collected a female carrying an 11 mm. embryo on May 27. The little data available suggest that the young are born mostly in June. Hayward (1963) found that none of 41 adults had given birth on June 4, but most had given birth by June 29. The young at that date ranged from nearly naked individuals weighing 1.8 g. to those nearly ready to fly and weighing 6.6 g.

Parasites: Stager (1943a) examined 63 specimens from California for parasites. He found only two species of fleas.

Remarks: M. occultus seems to be most common in the high country of New Mexico and Arizona where it is a resident of fir, spruce, and ponderosa pine forests. When netting over two ponds and lakes in New Mexico during the summer of 1966 we found this to be the most common of the four species of *Myotis* taken. About two dozen were captured in four nights. This species was particularly gentle when being removed from the net and handled. This is unusual for a *Myotis*, most of which bite when handled.

Findley and Jones (1967) studied many specimens of *M. occultus* from New Mexico and *M. lucifugus* from northern Colorado and found that the two were clearly separable. However, two specimens from southern Colorado and one of two from northern New Mexico appeared to be somewhat intermediate. On the basis of these specimens they tentatively concluded *M. occultus* is only a subspecies of *M. lucifugus*.

We think that other possible explanations should have been considered. The three specimens may be hybrids between the two species. More likely they may be individuals which by sampling chance happen to lie near one end of the variability spectrum. Data presented by Findley and Jones show that they clearly fall within the range of variability of *M. occultus*, whereas they are not within the range of variability indicated for *M. lucifugus*. We have not seen these specimens, but based upon these data we consider them to be *M. occultus*.

Findley and Jones may well be correct. However, we believe it is undesirable to change the present nomenclature until more evidence is available to support the change. The resolution of the status of *M. occultus* must await the study of adequate material from southern Colorado.

Miller and Allen (1928) recorded the measurement of the forearm of the type of *M. occultus* as 33 mm. Since this is exceptionally small for this species, one of us recently examined this specimen for verification. Both forearms had been shattered and obviously shortened in collecting and preparing the specimen.

MYOTIS KEENII [Merriam]

Keen's myotis; Keen's bat; Acadian bat

Recognition: Forearm, 32–39 mm. (usually 35–39); wingspread, 228–258 mm. A medium-sized *Myotis* with long ears (17–19 mm.) and a narrow pointed tragus. Calcar not keeled. Color, brown; fur, not glossy.

Variation: Two subspecies are recognized. *Myotis keenii keenii* (Merriam) occurs in the Northwest. *Myotis keenii septentrionalis* (Trouessart) is a paler race widespread in eastern North America.

Confusing Species: This species is most similar to *Myotis auriculus* which is larger, has longer ears (20–22 mm.), and does not occur within the range of *Myotis keenii*. *Myotis evotis* also has longer ears (22–25 mm.). *Myotis lucifugus* has shorter ears (14–16 mm.). *Myotis thysanodes* has a fringe of hair along the posterior border of the interfemoral membrane.

Range: Myotis keenii keenii ranges from Alaska south along the coast and coastal islands of British Columbia to the area of Puget Sound in Washington. Another population, *Myotis keenii septentrionalis* is widely distributed across eastern North America. It ranges from Manitoba across southern Canada to Newfoundland, south to northern Florida, and west to Wyoming. It has been reported from west central Saskatchewan. Winter range of *M. k. keenii* is unknown. Winter and summer ranges of *M. k. septentrionalis* are apparently identical.

Habitat: In British Columbia *M. k. keenii* is an inhabitant of the dense timber. Apparently it is a solitary species, roosting

34. Ear of *Myotis keenii* showing the long pointed tragus. For comparison with *M. lucifugus* see fig. 15.

in tree cavities and cliff crevices. It forages high along the forest edge and over ponds and clearings (Cowan and Guiguet, 1965). This is the only information we have about this race and we have no personal experience with it in the field. The rest of our treatment of the species deals with the eastern race.

Myotis keenii is a northern species. It is most commonly encountered in the mines and caves of eastern Canada and in the United States from Nebraska to Vermont. Here in winter these bats are found hibernating with *M. lucifugus*, *Eptesicus fuscus*, and *Pipistrellus subflavus*. They are never abundant; concentrations of 100 or more in one mine are unusual. These bats usually hang singly. Although they frequently hang in the open, they seem to prefer tight crevices and holes. Sometimes only the nose and ears are visible, and they are easily overlooked. When seen in such crevices, they can be recognized by their long ears.

Myotis keenii shows a preference for cooler hibernation sites than *M. lucifugus*. In this respect it is similar to *E. fuscus* and *Myotis leibii* but these latter two are more tolerant of low humidity. The sites favored by *M. keenii* are near the entrance, but in areas where the humidity is so high that water droplets sometimes cover the fur.

In summer they roost by day in a variety of shelters. Individuals have been found beneath the bark of trees. Russell Mumford often finds them behind window shutters in Indiana, and there are several records from buildings. One was found in August beneath tar paper on a beehive in West Virginia. Except for small maternity colonies, these bats are generally found singly.

In summer *M. keenii* commonly uses caves as night roosts. Robert Goslin searched Ray's Cave in Indiana on June 16, 1932, and found no bats; at 10:30 that night he found eight male *M. keenii*. In June 1957 John Hall and Wayne Davis had a similar experience in a cave in western Kentucky. No bats were found in the cave during the day but after dark numerous bats were seen flying in and out of the cave. One *Pipistrellus subflavus* and one *E. fuscus* were captured in the cave where they had hung up to rest; at the entrance five *M. keenii* and three *M. lucifugus* were shot. All were males. Jones (1964) found *M. keenii* a common resident in quarry tunnels in eastern Nebraska.

Poole (1932) found *M. keenii* to be common at night in certain Pennsylvania caves during August. He stretched a net across a passage and captured 65 in one night as the bats were entering the cave.

Reproduction: Breeding data are scarce; essentially nothing is known of reproduction in this species. Apparently small nursery colonies are formed. A nursery colony estimated at 30 animals was found beneath the bark of a dead elm tree in Indiana on July 8 (Mumford and Cope, 1964).

A small maternity colony was discovered in July by Harold Hitchcock and Wayne Davis in a barn near Fitzwilliam, New Hampshire. A cluster of two adult females and three young was found hanging from the roof in the full light from a window at one end of the barn. Eight additional specimens were encountered in other places in the barn. The barn was also occupied by about 300 *M. lucifugus*, but these were hidden in dark crevices. The *M. keenii* were asleep when approached, whereas the other bats were awake and noisy.

Brandon (1961) found *M. keenii* living beneath the wooden shingles of a shelter on the shore of Roosevelt Lake in Shawnee State Forest, Scioto County, Ohio, on June 12. Bats were heard squeaking in the roof at night, and several flew about the shelter. Occasionally a bat entered the space between the roof and the shingles where a female nursing her young could be seen. During the night two young bats which fell

35. *Myotis keenii* feeding on a beetle.

36. *Myotis keenii* from Indiana.

78

from the ceiling were captured and put in a shoe. Next morning the shoe also contained an adult female which was nursing one of the young. Apparently she had attempted to retrieve her fallen baby.

Migration and Homing: Although *M. keenii* is rather scarce in the Appalachian Mountains, Merlin Tuttle has found them in eastern Tennessee under circumstances which suggest migration through that area. On February 5, 1961, he found only 3 in Little Mammoth Cave, but on March 11 he found about 75. Thirty were in a single cluster and the rest were scattered throughout the cave; all were alert and many flew when a light was turned on them.

M. keenii are taken in various numbers during the August swarming season at mines and caves. James Beer once captured several hundred with a hand net at the entrance of an iron mine at Hurley, Wisconsin, in late August and early September; most were young of the year. Harold Hitchcock and Wayne Davis regularly captured *M. keenii* when netting at Aeolus Cave, Vermont, during August, but never in large numbers. The most taken in any one night was 43.

James Cope and his colleagues capture a dozen or so *M. keenii* annually in their late summer netting at Wyandotte Cave, Indiana. However, only an occasional straggler is netted in the Mammoth Cave region in Kentucky.

The bats of Bat Cave, in Carter Caves State Park in eastern Kentucky, have been about as intensively studied as in any cave in the United States. We have never taken this species there. However, at a cave a few miles away, in a similar wooded area, we netted six of these bats in two hours one evening in August.

Poole (1932) banded and released *M. keenii* which he captured in a cave in Pennsylvania in August. Two were recaptured at the cave after being released 18 miles away.

Remarks: Although not especially rare *M. keenii* appears to be locally and irregularly distributed. It is a common bat in Indiana and Illinois, but scarce in Kentucky and West Virginia. Intensive investigations on the bats hibernating in the numerous caves of West Virginia over several years revealed *M. keenii* to be scarce and irregular. However, at one cave in Pocahontas County the species occurred regularly in winter in numbers up to a dozen or so.

The wide geographical separation of the two races of *M. keenii* has long been puzzling to taxonomists. Until recently specimens of the nominate race have been very scarce in collections. We are currently studying specimens from the west coast. Their relationship to *M. evotis* and *M. thysanodes* in that region and to *Myotis k. septentrionalis* in the east is not clear at this time. We suspect that the latter might not be a subspecies of *M. keenii* in which case it would take the name *Myotis septentrionalis* (Trouessart).

Jones and Genoways (1967b) collected chiggers, *Leptotrobidium myotis*, from the ears of a specimen shot in South Dakota. Among four specimens they netted in late July in that state, two were molting, one had completed molt, and one had not yet begun.

Skull of *Myotis keenii*, x3

Distribution of *Myotis keenii* in the United States

79

MYOTIS AURICULUS Baker and Stains

Mexican long-eared myotis

Recognition: Forearm, 37–41 mm.; wingspread, about 270 mm. A rather large *Myotis* with long ears (20–22 mm.) and a narrow pointed tragus. Calcar without a keel. Ears brown. Color, brownish; fur, not glossy.

Variation: Two subspecies are recognized, but only *Myotis auriculus apache* Hoffmeister and Krutzsch occurs in the United States.

Confusing Species: *Myotis keenii* is smaller, has shorter ears (17–19 mm.), and does not occur within the range of *M. auriculus*. *Myotis evotis* has longer ears (22–25 mm.), which are nearly black. *Myotis thysanodes* has a conspicuous fringe of hair along the posterior edge of the interfemoral membrane.

Range: Mexico, at intermediate elevations from Veracruz, Distrito Federal, and Jalisco, northward into New Mexico and Arizona. In the United States, it is known from a restricted area in southwestern New Mexico and southeastern Arizona. Winter range unknown.

Habitat: This is a bat of arid woodlands and desert scrub. It ranges most commonly from the mesquite and chaparral through the oak forests into the piñon-juniper habitats. It seems to reach its greatest abundance in areas of extensive rocky cliffs where some water is available.

So far as we can determine, this species has never been found during the day. At night they are known to roost in

37. *Myotis auriculus* from southeastern Arizona.

buildings and caves. Hoffmeister (1956) found them at night hanging singly, never more than two or three at a time, from the center rafter of a building at 8,700 feet in the Graham Mountains of Arizona. We netted four males and six females as they entered a mine at night in the Chiricahua Mountains. The mine was at an elevation of 5,700 feet on a dry, brushy slope, and contained the only water supply in the vicinity. Near Alamos, in southern Sonora, we netted two as they were entering a mine which contained a pool of water. The surrounding hilly countryside was covered with dense shrubby vegetation and at the time was extremely dry.

Reproduction: In the United States a single young is produced in June. A female taken over Cave Creek in Arizona on June 8 contained an 18 mm. embryo and was apparently near term. The latest date we captured a pregnant female there was June 18. Farther south the young apparently are born later. On June 22 we netted two females at the entrance to a mine near Alamos in southern Sonora. Each contained an embryo, one 17 mm. and the other 12 mm.

Remarks: During the summer of 1966 we became familiar with this bat in the Chiricahua Mountains. It was one of the more common bats found among the oaks along Cave Creek at elevations of 5,000–6,000 feet. They were readily taken in mist nets stretched across the stream. All but one of the specimens taken were females.

This species has a short but painful nomenclatorial history. It was recognized as an apparently undescribed bat almost simultaneously by Hoffmeister and Krutzsch who had discovered it in Arizona and by Baker and Stains who had captured specimens in Coahuila and Tamaulipas. Both groups published descriptions of the new bat in 1955, considering it to be a subspecies of *M. evotis*. The paper by Baker and Stains was printed

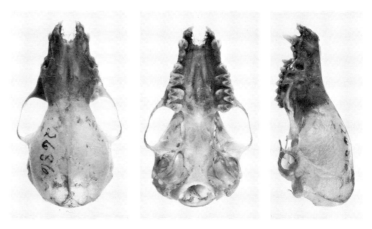

Skull of *Myotis auriculus*, x3

Distribution of *Myotis auriculus* in the United States

81

18 days the earlier. Findley (1960) found that this bat occurred with *M. evotis* in New Mexico and concluded that the two could not be conspecific. He noted the striking resemblance of this bat to *M. keenii* and decided that it should be classified as a subspecies of that form. Most recently Jones and Genoways studied the bat in question and concluded that it is a distinct species which now takes the name *M. auriculus* Baker and Stains. Their results are now in press. They found that the one described from Arizona is somewhat different in color and thus should take the name *M. auriculus apache* Hoffmeister and Krutzsch.

Recently one of us examined the type of *Myotis micronyx*, which was described in 1909 by Nelson and Goldman from a specimen taken at Comondu, Baja California. This name has resided in synonymy since Miller and Allen (1928) decided that it was not distinguishable from *M. evotis*. However, since they also decided that specimens of the present species from Veracruz, Jalisco, Chihuahua and Arizona were identical to *M. evotis*, we thought it best to clarify the matter. The specimen is a *M. evotis*.

38. *Myotis evotis* from the mountains of New Mexico.

MYOTIS EVOTIS [H. Allen]

Long-eared myotis

Recognition: Forearm, 36–41 mm.; wingspread, about 275 mm. This bat has the longest ears (22–25 mm.) of any American *Myotis*. The ears and other membranes are heavily pigmented, usually black. Fur, long and glossy. Color, brown, buffy below.

Variation: Two subspecies are recognized. *Myotis evotis evotis* (H. Allen) occupies most of the range. *Myotis evotis pacificus* Dalquest has been described as a darker race from the Northwest. The status of this form, as well as that of *Myotis keenii* and *Myotis thysanodes* in western Washington, is confused at this time.

Confusing Species: M. *thysanodes* can be readily recognized by the conspicuous fringe of hair along the posterior margin of the interfemoral membrane. M. *keenii* and *Myotis auriculus* have smaller, lighter colored ears.

Range: The western mountains, from British Columbia, Alberta and Saskatchewan, south into the highlands of New Mexico, Arizona, and southern California. On the west coast it ranges down to the sea. A specimen is known from Baja California. Winter range unknown.

Habitat: The favored habitat is the coniferous forests of the high mountains of the West. In the Pacific states it ranges down into the coastal forests.

Although never abundant, it is regularly distributed and a bat net stretched over a pond in a ponderosa pine or spruce forest will usually take a few specimens. Individuals are frequently encountered in sheds and cabins. Probably they also take shelter beneath the bark of trees.

Davis (1939) reported this species residing in a cave. He captured two specimens from among dozens thought to be this species as they emerged from the cave at dusk in July.

Although these bats seldom reside in caves, they frequently use them at night and one of the most effective ways to capture this species is to net a cave. Albright (1959) found this to be the most abundant species in Oregon Caves during August. Using a butterfly net he captured 185 males and 28 females.

Reproduction: Apparently small maternity colonies are formed. In British Columbia groups of 12 to 30 individuals have been encountered in buildings (Cowan and Guiguet, 1965). Miller and Allen (1928) reported a group of adults and young found in a deserted ranch house in Colorado.

A single young is produced, but little else is known of the reproduction of this species. Pregnant females have been captured on June 14 and 24 in Nevada (Hall, 1946), and 2 of 12 females taken in British Columbia on July 7 were pregnant (Cowan and Guiguet, 1965). In South Dakota Jones and Genoways (1967b) took two specimens which carried embryos measuring 14 and 15 mm. on June 17 and 19, respectively. A juvenile male taken on August 6 was nearly full grown. An adult male taken in August had enlarged testes which measured 7.5 mm.

Remarks: Myotis evotis emerges late in the evening and forages among the trees and over woodland ponds with *Myotis volans*, *Myotis lucifugus*, *Eptesicus fuscus*, *Lasionycteris noctivagans*, and *Lasiurus cinereus*.

We have captured this pretty little bat at several localities in the mountains of New Mexico and Colorado at elevations of 6,500–8,500 feet, taking them in nets stretched over ponds in the coniferous forests. Only a few were taken each night at each locality.

The single specimen of this species known from Mexico was taken at Comondu, Baja California, on November 8, 1905. It was described by Nelson and Goldman (1909) as a new species, *Myotis micronyx*. One of us (WHD) examined this specimen. It is a small *M. evotis*.

Comondu, at 700 feet elevation, is in the desert scrub, far from any habitat where one would expect to find this species. Possibly the species is a migrant or winter resident in the area.

Molt apparently occurs in July and August. In South Dakota Jones and Genoways (1967b) found three females and two males in new pelage in early August, whereas two other males had nearly completed molting.

Although *M. evotis* is widespread and not uncommon, very little is known of its habits.

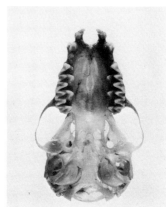

Skull of *Myotis evotis*, x3

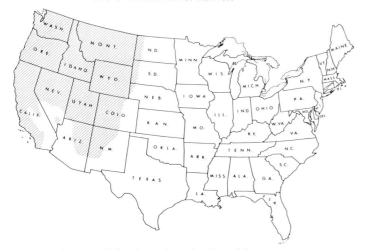

Distribution of *Myotis evotis* in the United States

84

MYOTIS THYSANODES Miller

Fringed myotis; fringed bat

Recognition: Forearm, 39–46 mm.; wingspread, 265–300 mm. A rather large *Myotis* with long ears (16–20 mm.). This is our only *Myotis* with a conspicuous fringe of hair along the posterior border of the interfemoral membrane (fig. 39). Upperparts, usually reddish brown, but varying to dark brown; underparts, usually pale.

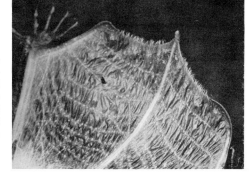

39. Tail and interfemoral membrane of a fringed bat, *Myotis thysanodes*, showing the conspicuous fringe of hairs.

Variation: Two subspecies are currently recognized in the United States. *Myotis thysanodes thysanodes* Miller is a brown to russet race with pale underparts and a well-developed fringe. It occupies the major part of the range. *Myotis thysanodes pahasapensis* Jones and Genoways has larger ears, a shorter forearm, and a smaller, narrower skull; it is known only in the Black Hills of South Dakota and Wyoming. A small, dark, undescribed race with a reduced fringe occurs in southwestern Washington.

Range: Western North America from British Columbia south to Veracruz and Chiapas. In the United States, it is common in the lower and intermediate elevations throughout much of the Southwest; irregular, local and usually scarce northward. Winter range unknown.

Habitat: This species is a resident of the forests of oak, piñon, and juniper and the desert scrub of the Southwest. It usually occurs at elevations of 4,000–7,000 feet, but ranges down to the sea on the west coast. However, we once took a specimen in a spruce-fir forest at 9,350 feet in New Mexico.

Favored roosting sites, both day and night, are caves, mines, rock crevices, and buildings. Many shelters uninhabited by day are used as night roosts. Droppings on the floor often give a clue to the use of a site as a night roost.

Reproduction: *Myotis thysanodes* is a highly colonial species. Nursery colonies of several hundred are not uncommon. Bailey (1931) found a mass of these bats a yard in diameter on the ceiling of a cave in southwestern New Mexico on August 9, 1908. He collected 87; all were adult females and young. A small nursery colony inhabits Carlsbad Caverns where they sometimes roost in a cluster with a few *Myotis velifer*. A nearby cave contains a much larger colony estimated at about 300 bats (Baker, 1962). A nursery colony of 30 to 40 individuals

40. Fringed bat, *Myotis thysanodes*, from southeastern Arizona.

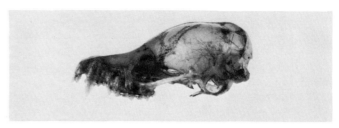

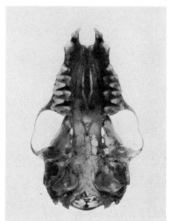

Skull of *Myotis thysanodes*, x3

41. Example of the small dark race of *Myotis thysanodes* from southwestern Washington.

Distribution of *Myotis thysanodes* in the United States

was found in the attic of a house in British Columbia (Maslin, 1938). Colonies are also known from buildings in Utah and California.

Adult males are usually absent from the nursery colonies. Hoffmeister and Goodpaster (1954) found a cluster of adult males in a mine in the Huachuca Mountains of Arizona in August.

Except for the fact that a single young is produced annually, practically nothing is known about reproduction in this species. Two females taken near Colorado Springs on June 18 each had one embryo; one was 6 mm., the other 10 mm. Two females collected in Chihuahua on June 28 each contained a large fetus nearly ready for birth. Young in various stages of development were found in an attic colony in southern California on July 3. Cockrum and Ordway (1959) reported that all those examined from a nursery colony of about 200 bats in a cave in the Chiricahua Mountains on July 19 were lactating females with young attached, and that on July 26 all the young of this colony were able to fly. Bailey (1931) found nearly full grown young in southwestern New Mexico on August 9.

Remarks: We found *M. thysanodes* one of the more common species among the oaks in the Chiricahua Mountains at elevations of 5,000–6,000 feet where we captured them in mist nets set over water.

A good way to catch this species is to net at night at a cave, mine, or the open entrance to a building. In the West an abandoned building with gaping doors and windows or a barn with the hayloft door open is a good place to capture bats. One of us (WHD) netted such a barn just north of Colorado Springs in June 1954. Although no bats could be found in the barn by day, they entered regularly at night. Of the several species captured, *M. thysanodes* and *Myotis volans* were most common.

In June 1966, we netted bats at a mine in the Chiricahua Mountains of Arizona. The mine goes all the way through the mountain and carries a stream which emerges into the desert scrub, apparently the only available water in the vicinity. We found no bats there in the daytime, but evidence indicated that the mine was heavily used by nocturnal transients. We arranged two mist nets to block the entrance, forming a V leading into the cave. Bat traffic into the mine was rather heavy; within two hours we had captured six species and over 70 individuals. Eleven of these were male *M. thysanodes*.

At Oregon Caves, Albright (1959) captured 26 male and 3 female *M. thysanodes* with an insect net at night during August. No bats were found in the cave during the day. Easterla (1966) caught adults of both sexes and fully grown young by stretching a mist net across the entrance to a cave in Utah during August. Thorough inspection of the cave in the daytime had revealed no bats. Likely all were transients or used the cave only as a night roost.

As with many other western species of bats nothing is known of the winter habits of *M. thysanodes*. The maternity clusters apparently break up in the fall but their movements are unknown. Few *M. thysanodes* have been banded and we know of no recoveries. This is a species that would well repay careful study. It is probably much more common than the records indicate.

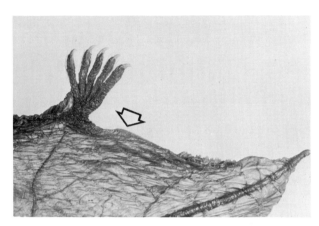

42. Keeled calcar of *Myotis sodalis*.

43. *Myotis sodalis*. Compare the pale nose with *M. lucifugus*, fig. 13.

MYOTIS SODALIS Miller and Allen

Indiana myotis; Indiana bat; social bat

Recognition: Forearm, 35–41 mm.; wingspread, 240–267 mm. A medium sized *Myotis* of the eastern United States. Foot rather small (9 mm.). The calcar has a slight keel (fig. 42). Color, dark gray, usually nearly black, sometimes brownish. Fur dull, not glossy.

Confusing Species: Myotis lucifugus has long hairs on the toes (fig. 14), no keel on the calcar, a slightly larger foot (10 mm.), and usually a glossy sheen to the fur. *Myotis grisescens* has fur the same color from tip to base and a large foot with an unusual membrane attachment (fig. 28). *Myotis austroriparius* has long hairs on the toes and a slightly larger foot (10 mm.). *Myotis keenii* has longer ears (17–19 versus 15 mm.). *Myotis leibii* is smaller. *Pipistrellus subflavus* is smaller, with a light-colored forearm and usually paler, tricolored fur.

Range: Eastern United States, from Oklahoma, Iowa, and Wisconsin east to Vermont, and south to northwestern Florida. In summer, apparently absent south of Tennessee; in winter, apparently absent from Michigan, Ohio, and northern Indiana where suitable caves and mines are unknown.

Habitat: Myotis sodalis is known primarily from the caves in which it hibernates. In winter it congregates by the thousands in tightly-packed clusters in the relatively few caves and mines which it finds suitable to its needs. Two caves in Kentucky and a cave and a mine in Missouri each harbor about 100,000 in winter, accounting for about 90 percent of the known population of the species; the rest occur in groups of from a dozen to a few thousand in several dozen caves and mines.

Summer records are rather scarce; no breeding colonies are known. A few males inhabit caves in Kentucky and neighboring states. Occasional individuals have been encountered under a bridge, beneath the bark of a tree, and in buildings. We have reason to believe that they do not commonly inhabit buildings. The recovery rate of banded individuals is very low, compared to the recovery rate for the attic dwelling *M. lucifugus*. If *M. sodalis* regularly lived in buildings, surely more would be encountered.

Although no breeding colonies are known, likely the nursery retreats are in rather cool places. *M. sodalis* is much less tolerant of high temperatures than is *M. lucifugus* which resides in extremely hot attics in summer. Body temperatures of 93–95° F. (34–35° C.) are frequently fatal to *M. sodalis*, whereas *M. lucifugus* can tolerate body temperatures at least 18° F. (10° C.) higher (Henshaw and Folk, 1966). Our guess is that most *M. sodalis* spend the summer singly or in small groups in hollow trees or beneath loose bark.

Reproduction: *M. sodalis* breeds in the caves in fall. At Bat Cave in Kentucky most breeding occurs during about 10 days in early October. At night the bats scatter in pairs over the ceiling of the cave where they can be seen copulating by the hundreds. The breeding occurs mostly in a large room near the upper entrance to the cave. During the day the bats cluster at several localities within the cave and the sexes are almost completely segregated. The males form clusters in the breeding room and the females at the other end of the cave, about 3,000 feet away.

M. sodalis seems to have a more definite mating season than *M. lucifugus*, which commonly breeds throughout the winter. Only occasional *M. sodalis* breed in winter. Hall (1962) noted limited mating activity in late April as the bats were leaving hibernation.

The scant data available suggest that *M. sodalis* produces a single young in the latter part of June. Nothing is known of parturition or development. The only record of a pregnant *M. sodalis* is of one shot as she flew along the edge of a small woodlot on June 18 in northern Indiana. She was carrying a single large embryo (Mumford and Calvert, 1960).

Several immature *M. sodalis* have been taken from beneath a concrete bridge in Indiana. The youngest seen there was captured on July 24. It is questionable whether or not it could fly. Three larger young were captured there on July 27, five years later (Mumford and Cope, 1958).

Migration: The colony of about 100,000 *M. sodalis* hibernating in Bat Cave, Carter Caves State Park, Kentucky, begins to disperse in late March. The females begin leaving first to go to their summering grounds to the northwest. The greatest exodus occurs in late April when nearly half the population leaves within a week. By the end of the first week of May the cave is vacant. A few males usually remain in the vicinity, and can be netted at the cave entrance at night. Most males, however, migrate to the northwest.

In Mammoth Cave National Park where about 100,000 *M. sodalis* also hibernate, several hundred males spend the summer. Hall (1962) found that these formed an active band which wandered about from cave to cave in the area throughout the summer. Such groups also occur in the caves in Missouri.

Although recovery rates for banded bats of this species are low, enough have been banded in Kentucky to determine an approximate migration pattern. After leaving the caves in spring the females and nearly all of the males move northward and occupy Indiana, the western half of Ohio, and southern Michigan (fig. 44).

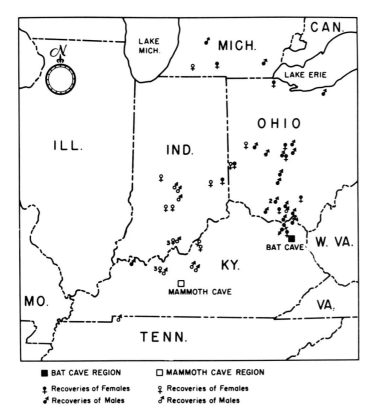

BAT CAVE REGION · ☐ MAMMOTH CAVE REGION

♀ Recoveries of Females · ♀ Recoveries of Females

♂ Recoveries of Males · ♂ Recoveries of Males

44. Summer distribution of *Myotis sodalis* which winter in two of Kentucky's cave regions, based upon recoveries of banded individuals. Numbers indicate multiple recoveries from the same locality.

Migrants next appear in numbers during August when nocturnal swarming occurs at the caves. Bats appear at some caves by the hundreds; a net tended all night at the mouth of such a cave may yield nearly a thousand. At this time the population of a cave has almost a complete turnover each day, and only rarely is an individual recaptured at the same cave. It is not known where the bats go after leaving the caves. However, one which was netted at Dixon Cave, Kentucky, the night of September 2 was captured in a barn over 300 miles away in Michigan on September 10. Many of the bats appearing in August can later be found hibernating in various caves in the area.

The wintering population begins to build up in mid-September, and by late November the great mass of bats has settled for the winter. A few straggle in through December.

Homing: That *M. sodalis* has remarkable navigational abilities has been established by several workers. Hassell and Harvey (1965) took groups of 500 from Bat Cave, Kentucky, and released them simultaneously at distances of 200 miles north, south and west of the cave. Two-thirds of the bats from the northern locality were recaptured at the cave, nearly as many as among controls banded and released there. However, that release locality was within the normal summer range, and the bats might be expected to be familiar with the area. Much more remarkable was the recovery of nearly a third of those released south of the cave in North Carolina across the Smoky Mountains, outside the normal range of this population. The recapture of these bats at the cave strongly suggests that they were able to orient and navigate over many miles of rugged, unfamiliar territory. From the western release point only 16 percent of the bats were recaptured at the cave. Possibly the bats can orient better on a north-south axis when in unfamiliar territory.

Hassell (1963) released groups of bats at 12-mile intervals west of the cave at distances up to 144 miles. Some bats returned from all sites, but percentages decreased with distance from 68 percent at 12 miles to 4 percent at 144 miles. We have recently found that the return percentage from the north is essentially unrelated to distance, at least up to 200 miles.

The high rate of return over the rugged and apparently totally unfamiliar territory to the south of the cave poses some interesting questions. How do the bats know which direction they need to go and how do they maintain a course? That they know where they are going is evident from the time lapse; many returned within the first week. That they are accurate in navigation is suggested by the recovery of one bat released in North Carolina and recovered 54 days later near Virgie, Kentucky, on November 28. This locality is roughly half way between the release point and the cave and precisely on a line between the two.

We have investigated the vision of the bats as a possible clue to their navigational abilities. Laboratory tests showed that they can see and that they use their eyes in flight (Davis and Barbour, 1965). Further, we were unable to demonstrate homing of blinded bats from 125 and 200 miles north of the cave (Barbour *et al.*, 1966). More recent experiments, however, have shown that blinded bats can return to the cave from distances of 5, 15, 25, and 40 miles to the north. Return percentages were not as high as controls, and it took the blinded bats longer to return.

Hibernation: M. *sodalis* enters the hibernation caves in the fall. Hassell (1967) found that when they first entered Bat Cave in Kentucky they roosted in the warmest parts of the cave. Many bats became active and left the cave nightly to feed during September and October.

Hall (1962) found that they put on most of their fat after they had arrived at the caves. Weight was minimal about the first of September and the deposition of fat preparatory to hibernation occurred during that month (fig. 45). This contrasts to M. *lucifugus* which becomes very fat by the second week in August. Perhaps M. *sodalis* uses its stored fat during its migration from summer to winter home and must deposit more for the hibernation period.

Hassell (1967) found that the bats moved down a temperature gradient in the cave as the autumn progressed with ever more bats congregating at the wintering site in the colder part of the cave. The clusters form at the same spots on the cave walls and ceilings year after year; such spots can be recognized by brown stains.

The sites favored for hibernation are places in the caves where the temperature averages 37°–43° F. (3°–6° C.) in midwinter (Hall, 1962; Henshaw and Folk, 1966). Temperatures in this range probably require minimum expenditure of energy (Davis and Reite, 1967). In Bat Cave, Kentucky, the temperature where the clusters form ranges from 29°–48° F. (–1.6°–9.2° C.) during December, January, and February, with an average

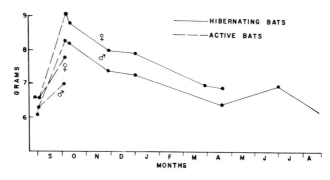

45. Weight changes of *Myotis sodalis* throughout the year. Each dot represents the average weight of 50 or more bats taken in a cave in Edmonson County, Kentucky. From Hall (1962).

46. Typical hibernating cluster of *Myotis sodalis*.

47. Clusters of *Myotis sodalis* hibernating in Bat Cave, Kentucky. Bands are evident on several bats.

of about 42° F. (5.6° C.). When the temperature drops below freezing this bat, like several others, responds by increasing its metabolism sufficiently to maintain its temperature a few degrees above that of the environment (Henshaw and Folk, 1966; Davis and Reite, 1967).

M. sodalis chooses a hibernation site where the humidity is rather high. However, saturation seldom occurs; droplets of moisture do not form on the fur, as they sometimes do on other species. In Bat Cave during the winter months relative humidity at the cluster sites ranges from 66 to 95 percent, with an average of 87 percent (Hassell, 1967).

The hibernating cluster is a characteristic of this species (fig. 46). It appears more tightly packed than any other. Each individual bat grasps the cave ceiling with its feet; they do not hang on one another. The forearms are held close and parallel to the body, not angled outward as in *M. grisescens* (Hall, 1962). All that is visible in a blanket of hibernating *M. sodalis* on a cave ceiling are noses, ears, and wrists (fig. 48).

In a cave occupied by great numbers of *M. sodalis*, a few are always active even in the coldest part of winter. Individuals awaken from hibernation approximately every 8–10 days (Hardin, 1967). At any time during the winter one can find dozens of active bats in Bat Cave. These bats form squeaking clusters at four sites in the cave where temperatures are higher (54°–57° F., 12°–14° C.). Hall (1962) described a similar behavior pattern for caves in western Kentucky. A bat which awakens and moves to the active cluster may return to any of the hibernation clusters, not necessarily the one whence he came.

Hall (1962) placed plastic sheets beneath the clusters of active *M. sodalis* in Kentucky caves and measured the deposition of guano. He found that even during the period of January to March the guano deposited was rich in insect remains. Apparently the bats had been feeding during winter.

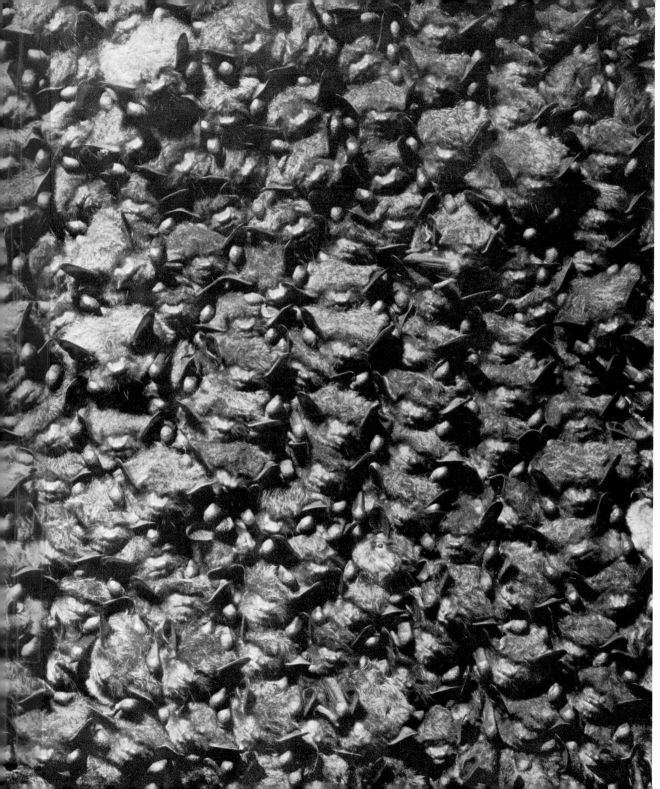

48. Tightly packed hibernating cluster of *Myotis sodalis*. One bat is awake.

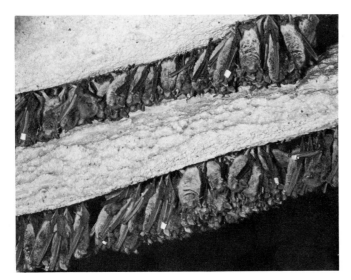

49. *Myotis sodalis* hibernating in a cave.

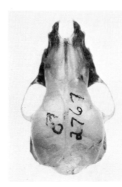

Skull of *Myotis sodalis*, x3

Distribution of *Myotis sodalis*

50. *Myotis sodalis* with an abnormal color pattern. White spots are frequently seen, but they are rarely this extensive.

Where several hibernating populations are close together, bats move from one cave to another. If a hibernating group is disturbed even in mid-winter, some individuals may move to neighboring caves.

As the bats arouse and leave the cave with the coming of spring, they reverse the behavior pattern exhibited in the fall. They move through the cave in a period of several days resting in progressively warmer areas. After reaching the warmest areas, they leave the cave for their summer home (Hassell, 1967).

The two great populations in Kentucky which hibernate 180 miles apart are almost totally separate. Hall (1962) reported one bat that moved from one cave to the other. Movements between other distant populations are also rare. Hall (1962) found a bat from a hibernating population in northern Illinois, in Coach Cave, Kentucky, 320 miles away. In Bat Cave we recovered two bats banded by James Cope as autumn transients at Wyandotte Cave in Indiana. One male banded by Merlin Tuttle in mid-winter in a cave in Campbell County, Tennessee, spent subsequent winters in Bat Cave, 145 miles to the northeast. The Tennessee cave had been converted to an air raid shelter. This disturbance may have caused the move.

Remarks: M. *sodalis* has shown a drastic decrease in numbers in recent years. Thirty years ago there were several caves and mines in New England, New York, and Pennsylvania which harbored colonies numbering in the hundreds. Now, only occasional individuals can be found throughout most of this area. During the 1950s it has also nearly disappeared in West Virginia, Indiana, and Illinois, and several populations in Missouri have been severely depleted. Causes of such losses are unknown, but are most likely due to man's interference. Unless adequate protection is afforded the hibernation caves, the species will probably-disappear within a few years. Fortunately, one major colony is in Mammoth Cave National Park where the bats are protected. The great colony in Bat Cave in Carter Caves State Park, Kentucky, is not yet adequately protected.

One frequently see a conspicuous white patch of fur on M. *sodalis.* Such blotches may be on the dorsal surface or the belly. They vary in size from a small spot to an area involving a third or more of the fur (fig. 50). The frequency of such markings varies from about 1 in 300 in some populations to one in several thousand in others.

Ubelaker (1966) listed a mite and two species of trematodes taken from M. *sodalis.*

DeBlase and Cope (1967) once found a M. *sodalis* impaled on a barb of a barbed wire fence. Although such accidents are common among bats of the genus *Lasiurus,* they have not been reported before for other groups.

Information on the summer habits of the Indiana Bat is slowly accumulating. Perhaps 20 or so have been shot at dusk by collectors at scattered localities in Indiana as the bats fed over fields and clearings. Young have been taken beneath a bridge in Turkey Run State Park, Indiana, and several have been found among little brown bats in buildings. We found a single juvenile male among over 600 M. *lucifugus* in a building in Logan County, Kentucky, on August 1, 1963. Any careful observation of this species in summer will be a real contribution.

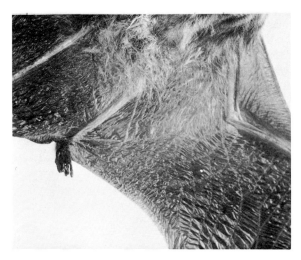

51. Underside of *Myotis. volans* showing furred wing and keeled calcar.

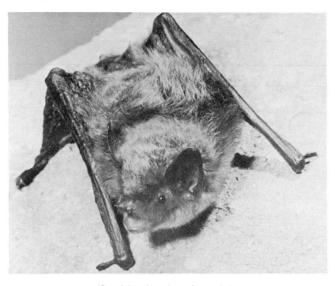

52. *Myotis volans* from Arizona.

MYOTIS VOLANS [H. Allen]

Long-legged myotis; long-legged bat; hairy-winged myotis

Recognition: Forearm, 35–41 mm.; wingspread, 250-270 mm. The only large western *Myotis* with a well developed keel on the calcar. The short rostrum and globose braincase are distinctive. The underwing is lightly furred outward to a line from the elbow to the knee (fig. 51). Color, usually dark, but variable, ranging from russet red to nearly black.

Variation: Two subspecies occur in the United States. *Myotis volans interior* Miller occupies the major part of the range; the darker *Myotis volans longicrus* (True) is found in the Pacific Northwest.

Confusing Species: Myotis californicus and *Myotis leibii* are smaller, with wingspread less than 250 mm. All other similar *Myotis* in the west, such as *M. lucifugus, M. yumanensis,* and *M. occultus* lack a well developed keel on the calcar. The big brown bat, *Eptesicus fuscus,* also has a strong keel, but is much larger. *Myotis volans* is the only brown bat with the belly fur extending onto the wing to a line joining elbow and knee.

Range: Western North America, from Alaska to Veracruz; east to the Dakotas and Nebraska. This is the common *Myotis* of the western United States and over large areas is probably the most abundant species. Although most at home in the forested Transition and Canadian life zones, the species is common among the oaks and junipers down to about 4,000 feet. Along the coast it ranges down to sea level. It seems to be absent from the lowland deserts of the Southwest. Winter range

96

unknown; there is a March record from a cave in Washington. Apparently a few hibernate in Jewel Cave, South Dakota (Jones and Genoways, 1967b).

Habitat: Maternity colonies form in buildings, rock crevices, and trees during summer. Caves and mines are not used by day, although *M. volans* is easily taken in such places by netting at night. Probably trees are the most commonly used sites for nursery colonies. Baker and Phillips (1965) collected 33 of these bats from a colony beneath a piece of bark in Mexico in July. The bark was loose at the bottom and the bats crowded in between the bark and the trunk of the tree.

Davis (1960) found *M. volans* living in crevices in the face of a cliff in western Texas. Quay (1948) found a colony of about 180 in a crack in the ground in the badlands of northwestern Nebraska. A stream had formed ledges and overhanging banks by lateral erosion. The collapse of these banks had formed cracks parallel to the edge of the stream; one of them harbored the bat colony. When the bats were disturbed they flew out in all directions and dropped into other crevices in the surrounding badlands. All of the several dozen that were caught and examined were females.

Habits: This species emerges in the evening while it is still light enough for them to be readily seen. They commonly forage 10–15 feet high over water and in openings in the woods. As the evening progresses they tend to drop closer to the ground. According to Dalquest (1948) *M. volans* flies more slowly and less erratically than *M. lucifugus* and *M. yumanensis* and can be recognized in flight when feeding with these species.

Reproduction: *M. volans* forms large nursery colonies, often numbering in the hundreds. In the southwestern states they

Distribution of *Myotis volans* in the United States

53. Head of *Myotis volans*. The ear is more rounded than in other species of *Myotis*.

97

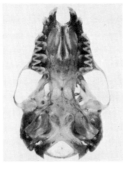

Skull of *Myotis volans*, x3

give birth to the single young earlier in the season than most other bats. Of 100 females taken from a building in southern California on June 2 and 4, nearly all were pregnant and the embryos were nearly ready for birth (Dalquest and Ramage, 1946). In the Chiricahua Mountains of Arizona, Cockrum and Ordway (1959) found several females carrying 13 and 14 mm. embryos on May 31 and June 2. Netting over a pond in the same area at 5,800 feet elevation, we captured 45 lactating females on June 18. None was pregnant at that time. On July 2 we took a flying young, and five more the following night. Hall (1964) shot 63 female *M. volans* at various localities in Nevada and found pregnant ones from June 10 to July 14. All of the 14 pregnant females examined had a single embryo each. In Colorado Findley (1954a) found three pregnant *M. volans* on July 31 and August 1. The embryos were remarkably large, ranging in crown-rump measurements from 24 to 34 mm. In northern Wyoming he found females carrying fetuses of 12–17 mm. on July 11 and 13. Jones and Genoways (1967b) reported embryos 20 and 22 mm. on June 29-30 in South Dakota. Clyde Senger found a juvenile hibernating in a cave in southwestern Washington on March 23, 1967. Obvious cartilaginous gaps at the epiphyses suggest that it was little more than a month old when it entered hibernation.

Thus, there is extreme variation in the time of parturition in this species. The variation is probably as greatly influenced by altitudinal distribution as by latitude.

Migration: Apparently the adults and young leave the maternity colonies in the fall, but nothing is known of their subsequent movements. Few have been banded, and we know of no recoveries.

Parasites: Dalquest and Ramage (1948) found a heavy infestation of parasites in a colony of about 500 *M. volans* in a California building—crab lice, bat bugs, mites, wingless flies, and fleas. Chiggers and bat flies have also been reported (Jones and Genoways, 1967b).

Remarks: One of us (WHD) found this species common in a spruce forest at 9,000 feet near Aspen, Colorado, in the summer of 1952. It was the most common bat on the south rim of the Grand Canyon in 1954. A colony inhabited the Park Headquarters Building; numerous individuals were seen emerging from the corners of the building in the evening. Mist nets over earthen tanks among the pines in this area took dozens of *M. volans*, almost to the exclusion of other species.

During June 1966 we found this species to be abundant in the Chiricahuas of Arizona and in the mountains of New Mexico. We banded and released 131. Of the 19 species of bats captured, only *Lasiurus cinereus* was caught in greater abundance.

Jones and Genoways (1967b) found that males taken in South Dakota in mid-June and the middle of July had begun to molt.

Although this species does not use caves by day it frequently enters such shelters at night. We took 44 adults of this species (24 males and 20 females) in two hours by netting the Hilltop Mine in the Chiricahua Mountains one night in June.

MYOTIS CALIFORNICUS [Audubon and Bachman]
California myotis

Recognition: Forearm, 29–36 mm.; wingspread about 230 mm. A small bat with a tiny foot and a keeled calcar. Color, extremely variable, from light tan to nearly black.

Variation: Three subspecies are recognized in the United States. *Myotis californicus californicus* (Audubon and Bachman) occupies a major part of the western United States. A paler form, *Myotis californicus stephensi* Dalquest, is found in the lowland deserts of the Southwest. *Myotis californicus caurinus* Miller is a dark race in the Pacific Northwest.

Some populations exhibit wide variation in color, and the ranges of the three subspecies are poorly understood. A careful investigation of geographic variation in this species is needed.

Confusing Species: Only three other western species of bats approach the small size of *Myotis californicus*. Of these, the western pipistrelle is usually recognizable by its smaller size. *Myotis* has two tiny premolars behind each upper canine; *Pipistrellus* has but one. *Myotis leibii* is remarkably similar to *M. californicus* (fig. 55). The skulls of the two are distinct in that the former is flattened, while the latter rises abruptly. In the flesh some individuals are difficult to distinguish unless one is thoroughly familiar with both species. The fur of *M. californicus* is generally dull and not glossy as in *M. leibii*. *Myotis yumanensis* is similar but has a larger foot (10 mm. versus 8 mm.) and lacks a keel on the calcar.

Range: Western North America from Alaska to Chiapas. In

54. *Myotis californicus* from southeastern Arizona.

the United States it ranges throughout the desert Southwest and in the lowlands and river valleys to Montana, Utah, and Colorado. Winters in California, Nevada, Utah, and Arizona; limits of winter range unknown.

Habitat: M. *californicus* is a bat of the western lowlands, ranging from the sea coast through the desert regions of the Sonoran life zones into the oak and juniper of the Transition life zone up to an elevation of about 6,000 feet. It seems most at home in the rock-walled canyons where open water is readily available and where it can feed among trees such as sycamore, cottonwood, willow and oak. These bats are also common, however, in the desert scrub where a few can be netted over a stockpond or even a dry arroyo among the cat's-claw and mesquite.

Perhaps more than any other species, this bat uses manmade structures as night roosts, and one of the easiest ways to collect specimens is to take advantage of this fact. In the desert where buildings are scarce almost any shack may serve as a night roost. Careful search will reveal their tiny droppings beneath the chosen spots. One can then return at night and find the bats resting after their feeding flights. Krutzsch (1954) found them using night roosts most extensively between 9:00 p.m. and midnight. He found that they would use almost any open shelter such as garages, barns, houses, outbuildings, porches, bridges, and corridors. Most such structures were wooden but several were adobe or cement. Darkness, shelter from the wind, and proximity to their foraging area seem to be the factors governing selection of a night roost. Mines and caves are also frequently used as night roosts and this is one of many species easily taken by netting the entrance to such a retreat at night.

The summer daytime roosts of M. *californicus* include a large variety of crevice-like places. They have been found in houses, barns, stables, under bridges, behind sign boards, in

55. Two of our most similar species of *Myotis.* Upper, M. *leibii.* Lower, M. *californicus.*

mine tunnels, in rock crevices, in hollow trees, and beneath loose bark. Krutzsch found a nursery colony of 25 adults behind a sign on a stable. Dalquest (1953) found one among the dead leaves of a tree yucca in Mexico. Warner and Beer (1957) found a group of 13 males in crevices in an overhang at the base of a cliff in a tropical forest in Puebla during the late fall. In winter a few hibernate in mines in the United States.

Behavior: This species has a slow erratic flight pattern and usually feeds within about 5 to 10 feet of the ground. During the summer of 1954 one of us (WHD) observed M. *californicus* foraging at the bottom of the Grand Canyon. At night they fed over the trail through the trees beside Bright Angel Creek at Phantom Ranch. They were not seen until it was too dark to shoot bats, but because of their slow, fluttery flight we succeeded in collecting a dozen or so by knocking them down with switches.

Except for occasional small maternity colonies, summer bats appear to be transients and move about without regard to any habitually used hiding place. Krutzsch (1954) suggested that they apparently roost in the most readily available site when their evening foraging is over. He found a bat in a fold of a temporary canvas shelter less than 24 hours after it was erected, another in a space between rafters of a building where no bats had been present before, and another in a previously unoccupied space between the beams of a bridge. An old rag hanging inside an unused building served as a hiding place for two adults with young; previous searches had disclosed none. Bats taken from such sites were marked and released, but subsequent searches of the roosts produced no marked individuals.

Reproduction: The little available evidence indicates that the males in southern California become reproductively active in the fall. Krutzsch (1954) found males with enlarged testes in

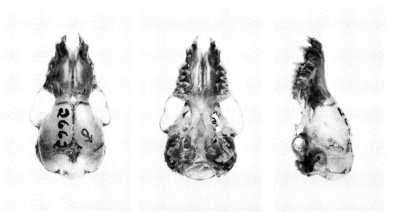

Skull of *Myotis californicus*, x3

Distribution of *Myotis californicus* in the United States

101

September and October. The single young is born between late May and mid-June. By July 20 some young are able to fly.

Hibernation: This is one of the few species of western bats for which there are many winter records in the United States. They are known to hibernate in small numbers in mines in Nevada, Utah, and Arizona; in spite of their scarcity in such situations, they are exceeded in numbers only by *Plecotus townsendii*. In southern California Krutzsch (1954) found occasional individuals active on warm days throughout the winter. O'Farrell *et al.* (1967) found this species active in Nevada during winter, regularly capturing specimens throughout the fall and winter. Nearly half the bats were taken when the temperature was below 43° F. (6° C.).

Parasites: Krutzsch (1954) found this species to be relatively free of ectoparasites. Only the mites *Ichoronyssus* and *Spinturnix* were found. Fleas, ticks, bat bugs, and flies which are so common on other western species were not found. Ubelaker (1966) listed two species of trematodes found in this bat.

Remarks: We found this species one of the more common bats in the lower canyons of the Chiricahua Mountains of Arizona in June of 1966, especially near Portal where they foraged over Cave Creek. Two distinct color phases were present.

56. *Myotis leibii* from West Virginia.

MYOTIS LEIBII [Audubon and Bachman]

Small-footed myotis; least brown bat

Recognition: Forearm, 30–36 mm.; wingspread, 212–248 mm. A small bat with a tiny foot (8 mm.), flattened skull, keeled calcar, black ears, and a black facial mask; the wings and interfemoral membrane are dark brown, almost black. Color, usually brown, but varying from pale yellow or light tan to dark brown.

Variation: Three subspecies are recognized. *Myotis leibii leibii* (Audubon and Bachman) is a glossy brown race found in the eastern United States. A much paler, light tan form, *Myotis leibii ciliolabrum* (Merriam) ranges through the western Great Plains. *Myotis leibii melanorhinus* (Merriam) is variable in color, but usually brown; it occurs generally west of the continental divide. A pale yellow population occurs in the Big Bend region of Texas; apparently it is an undescribed subspecies.

Confusing Species: *Pipistrellus hesperus* is usually smaller and paler. *Pipistrellus subflavus* and *Myotis yumanensis* lack a keel on the calcar and have larger feet. It is most similar to *Myotis californicus* (fig. 55) from which it can be distinguished with confidence only by the shape of the skull. The skull of *Myotis leibii* is flattened; that of *M. californicus* rises more abruptly. Occasional individuals are difficult to separate. All other species of *Myotis* found in the United States are usually larger and always have larger feet.

Range: This animal is most common and widespread in the western half of the United States, ranging from Saskatchewan, Alberta, and British Columbia in Canada south to Chihuahua in Mexico. In the east, it ranges from New England southward in the mountains to Georgia. In the central United States, incidental records, sometimes in substantial numbers, exist for several localities. It may be expected in almost any area in the United States except the Deep South and perhaps the upper Midwest. The summer and winter ranges seem to coincide, but winter records are lacking from most of the area between the Rockies and the Appalachians. Throughout the eastern part of its range *M. leibii* has always been considered a rare bat. The few summer records are mostly accidentals; in the Northeast it is mainly encountered during hibernation.

Habitat: Little is known concerning the habitat of *M. leibii*. In summer it at least occasionally inhabits buildings. Small maternity colonies have been reported from beneath the wall-paper of an abandoned house in California (Koford and Koford, 1948) and behind a sliding door on a barn in Ontario (Hitchcock, 1955). One of us (RWB) encountered one in an outbuilding in Mammoth Cave National Park in May. Tuttle (1964) has found several in summer beneath rock slabs in quarries in Tennessee, and the only specimen from Missouri was taken from beneath a stone on a hillside by Phillip W. Smith, while he was hunting snakes on October 9, 1949. In large areas of the West where this species is common, day roosts are unknown; perhaps they seek shelter in rock crevices or beneath stones. In Nebraska Jones (1964) found them in a barn and beneath the bark of a pine tree. In the badlands of South Dakota one of us (WHD) found several one summer sheltered in crevices formed by erosion of the clay buttes. Caves and mines are the only known winter habitat.

M. *leibii* uses buildings and caves for night roosts. Near Buena Vista, Colorado, we found these bats using an abandoned schoolhouse in a desert flat. We netted eight of them during three hours and saw several others. At Jewel Cave in South Dakota we captured 47 in three hours one night as they were entering the cave.

Behavior: We observed the behavior of this species while netting bats during the summer of 1963. They were found among several other species flying about the entrances of several caves in Mammoth Cave National Park. Their smallness and slow flight made them easy to recognize as they fluttered about. They seemed to detect our net and avoided it, but were easily captured in hand nets. On July 30, 1963, we captured 11 at Dixon Cave and could probably have taken as many more. At this and other nearby caves *M. leibii* were most frequently seen flying in and out of certain crevices and small low passages at the cave entrance. They flew a repeated pattern within a foot or two of the floor, hung up on the wall of the crevice, and then flew again.

This tiny bat is remarkable in that it is the hardiest species inhabiting the caves and mines in eastern North America. It is among the last to move into the caves in fall, seldom appearing before mid-November in Vermont and New York and leaving by March. It is found in drafty open mines and caves, and hangs near the entrance where the temperatures drop below freezing and humidity is relatively low. Its hibernating habits are similar to those of the big brown bat, but the latter, being a larger bat, would be expected to be more tolerant of cold, dry conditions.

In Canada and New England *M. leibii* frequently seeks winter shelter in narrow crevices near the entrance of a cave or mine. Sometimes 50 or more inhabit such a site, packed in so tightly and so deep that they are easily overlooked. In West Virginia caves, they frequently hang in the open.

Some *M. leibii* can often be found hibernating in the cave floor. In Schoolhouse Cave in West Virginia they retreat into cracks in the dry clay. In other caves and mines they have been found beneath stones on the floor. (Davis, 1955; Martin *et al.*, 1966).

Food and Feeding: Apparently this species fills its stomach within a short time since bats with full stomachs have been shot in early evening in Kansas and New Mexico. Stomachs of two specimens from Kansas contained flies (Anthomyidae), a bug (Jassidae), several *Agallia*, one or more *Piesma cinerea*, minute Scarabaeidae, Staphylinidae, and fragments of ants (Cockrum, 1952a).

Reproduction: Little data are available on breeding in this species. Apparently a single young is produced. Nursery colonies of 12 to 20 bats have been reported in buildings (Hitchcock, 1955; Koford and Koford, 1948). A young was present in a California colony as early as May 26, and the young were still unable to fly on June 16. Quay (1948) captured a pregnant female on July 12 in Nebraska. Jones and Genoways (1966) reported embryos of 9 and 11 mm. on June 17 and 24, respectively, in North Dakota.

Migration: In the Mammoth Cave region of Kentucky, *M. leibii* is fairly common in late summer in the flocks of migrating bats. The whereabouts of these individuals at other seasons is unknown. Bailey (1933) first recorded the species there in summer; his winter records for the caves are perhaps in error. His winter specimen of *M. leibii*, still at Mammoth Cave National Park, is a dark *P. subflavus*.

Hitchcock (1955) reported movements of two individuals in Ontario. He banded them in a cave in winter; they were recovered 10 and 12 miles away.

Remarks: This is one of the few bats known to hibernate in caves and mines in the West. Whitlow and Hall (1933) found them hibernating in several mines around Pocatello, Idaho. They also hibernate in caves in South Dakota.

The tolerance of this species for cold, relatively dry places for hibernation is remarkable for so small a bat. There are obviously some interesting problems in temperature regulation and water loss.

Jones and Genoways (1967b) reported that specimens they took in South Dakota in June and July were molting.

M. leibii is a common bat in some areas, especially in South Dakota, western Kansas, and parts of the Southwest. It is remarkable that so little is known of its life history.

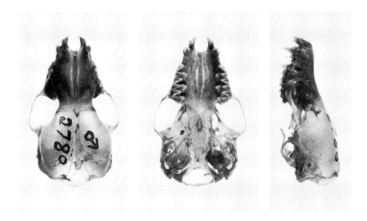

Skull of *Myotis leibii*, x3

Distribution of *Myotis leibii* in the United States

105

LASIONYCTERIS NOCTIVAGANS [Le Conte]

Silver-haired bat

Recognition: Forearm, 37–44 mm.; wingspread, 270–310 mm. A medium sized bat with dark silver-tipped fur. Dorsal surface of interfemoral membrane lightly furred (fig. 57). Ears short, rounded, and naked. Color, usually black, both fur and membranes; some individuals have dark brown, yellowish-tipped fur.

Confusing Species: This animal might be confused with the much larger hoary bat (*Lasiurus cinereus*), which has patches of hair on the ears and wings and is heavily furred on the entire dorsal surface of the interfemoral membrane. The fur is so thick that the membrane is not visible, whereas in *Lasionycteris* it is rather sparse and the membrane easily visible.

Range: Alaska across southern Canada south through all the states except perhaps Florida. Primarily it is a northern species. The young are raised from the northern tier of states northward in Canada nearly to the treeless zone. The southern limits of the breeding range are poorly defined. In the West, it ranges southward in the Rockies probably to New Mexico. Occasional males linger into summer in the Appalachians and along the East Coast south to South Carolina. Males are numerous through June in the mountains of the Southwest, becoming less common as the season progresses.

The winter range is generally from New York City and the Ohio River Valley southward nearly to the Gulf Coast, although there is a winter record from Minnesota. It also winters in the Southwest, and probably in parts of Mexico, although we know of no records from that country. On the West Coast it ranges at least from British Columbia to southern California in winter.

This bat is erratic in abundance, being scarce throughout much of its wide range. The greatest abundance is probably in the northern Rockies, from Wyoming and Idaho north into Canada. It is also rather common in parts of New England and New York. In Arizona and New Mexico it is abundant in May as an apparent transient. It is locally rather common in migration during about a two-week period in May in Illinois and in April in Kentucky and Tennessee. Fall migration is spread over a longer period and the bats seem less common.

Habitat: Lasionycteris noctivagans is a resident of the north woods where it is one of the characteristic animals about woodland ponds and streams. A typical day roost is the space behind a piece of loose bark on a tree. Individuals have also been found in woodpecker holes and a bird's nest. During migration they may be encountered in a wide variety of other shelters. Although they may appear in any kind of building, they favor open sheds, garages, and outbuildings rather than enclosed attics. They frequently rest in a pile of slabs, lumber, railroad ties, or fenceposts, especially when migrating through the prairie country where shelters are scarce.

L. noctivagans hibernates in trees, buildings, rock crevices, and similar protected shelters. Protected crevices in trees probably serve as the usual shelter (fig. 58). Individuals have been found hibernating beneath loose bark in British Columbia (Cowan and Guiguet, 1965) and in a tree in North Carolina (Brimley, 1897). A hibernating bat found in a dead tree felled in Mammoth Cave National Park in January was described to us by the park naturalist and seems surely to have been this species.

They have been found hibernating in skyscrapers, churches, wharf-houses, and hulls of ships in New York (Hamilton, 1943). Frum (1953) found them in buildings in West Virginia in December and March.

Frum (1953) extracted seven from crevices in sandstone cliffs in March in West Virginia. The bats were about 20 inches back in narrow (2 to 4 inches) crevices where they were associated with big brown bats. They were located by probing sticks into crevices until a squeak of a bat was elicited.

Apparently *L. noctivagans* rarely enter limestone caves. There are published records of only six specimens found in winter and spring (Krutzsch, 1966), and the species has not been taken by netting at cave entrances. A sandstone cave in Minnesota yielded one individual in January (Beer, 1956).

The only mines in which this species has been found are the silica mines of southern Illinois, where it is a regular and fairly common winter resident. Several workers have reported it from these mines in recent years. Pearson (1962) examined 35 silica mines during two winters and found 18 silver-haired bats. Numerous silica mines occur across the Ohio River in western Kentucky, but these have not been examined for bats.

Behavior: This species emerges earlier than most and is easily recognized in flight. With the possible exception of the western pipistrelle it is the slowest flying North American bat. It flies slowly and leisurely and sometimes so close to the ground that Hamilton (1943) found that an effective way to collect specimens was to knock them down with a bundle of alder switches. It usually forages over woodland ponds and streams at heights of up to 20 feet and sometimes flies repeatedly over the same circuit during the evening.

The adults usually appear singly but frequently are found in pairs and occasionally in groups of three or four. Because their day roosts are so rarely encountered, no one has studied

57. Silver-haired bat, *Lasionycteris noctivagans*, showing the furred upper surface of the interfemoral membrane.

58. Silver-haired bat, *Lasionycteris noctivagans*, partially concealed in a dead snag.

107

their habits. The most extensive information on the species resulted from a plea to the public in Saskatchewan for bat specimens (Nero, 1957). This species was more often found than any other. Of the 40 records, all but 5 were from August through October, suggesting that only during fall migration do they use shelters where they are likely to be encountered by man.

There is some evidence that *L. noctivagans* may occasionally form nursery colonies. Merriam (1884) found an immense colony in a hollow tree at the edge of Lake Umbagog in the Adirondack Mountains of New York on June 18, 1880. He also found 13 tiny young which he thought to be of this species in a crow's nest. We doubt the accuracy of identification in other old reports of colonial behavior. Snyder (1902) mentioned a colony of about 300 behind a closed blind and clinging to the window casing of a house in Beaver Dam, Wisconsin. Doutt *et al.* (1966) mentioned a report dating from about 1860 of a colony of 10,000 found in a house in Maryland. We can find no reports of colonial behavior within the last 60 years. Therefore, we reserve judgment on possible colonial behavior of this species in its nursery range until there is further information.

Captivity: Silver-haired bats do well in captivity. They will eat banana, bits of raw meat, and insects. Mrs. Philip W. Smith has kept individuals for more than a year on a diet of raw hamburger with occasional drops of a multiple vitamin compound.

Reproduction: Little is known regarding the breeding habits of *L. noctivagans*. Two young are produced, apparently in late June or early July. Bailey (1929) reported embryos from bats taken in Minnesota in late May and early June, and a mother nursing young on July 9.

There is some evidence suggesting a segregation of the sexes in summer in a pattern similar to that of the hoary bat. Only males are found in Arizona, New Mexico, and South Carolina in summer. On the other hand Hamilton (1943) reported that among 85 individuals shot by Merriam in the Adirondack Mountains during summer only 1 was a male.

Migration and Homing: *L. noctivagans* is migratory. Although there are no recoveries of banded individuals, circumstantial evidence for migration is strong. Merriam (1888) described the appearance of *L. noctivagans* at a lighthouse on Mount Desert Rock, a barren spot in the ocean off the coast of Maine, 20 miles from the nearest island and 30 miles from the mainland. The island is not inhabited by bats, but is visited by them every spring and fall. Several specimens captured there about October 1, 1885, were *L. noctivagans*. In many areas where they are unknown in summer, they are fairly common in spring and fall. *L. noctivagans* is a regular and dependable visitor in many areas; observers have noted this in Illinois, Indiana, West Virginia, and Tennessee.

Apparently these bats sometimes migrate in groups. There are several records of groups of weary bats descending upon ships at sea off the Atlantic coast of North America. Such groups usually consist of red bats, but sometimes include *L. noctivagans*. Bird banders along the East Coast occasionally capture bats in their nets. At Cape May, New Jersey, in the fall of 1962 six *L. noctivagans* were taken in one net at one time. This capture suggests that the bats were traveling in a group.

The males resident in the high country in New Mexico in summer apparently have an attachment to their home range. One we netted in June 1966 was recaptured back home a few days later after having been released over 100 miles away.

Remarks: An unusual record is the capture of two of these

bats in mousetraps in southwestern Kansas. In late August Getz (1961) left 36 mousetraps baited with raisins on the floor of an abandoned building. The following June he found the mummified bats. They were caught in closets containing piles of burlap bags and newspapers. Likely the bats stumbled into the traps accidentally, but possibly they were interested in the bait or in insects attracted to it.

In northwestern Saskatchewan, Novakowski (1956) found a family group of *L. noctivagans* living in an abandoned woodpecker hole. He reported that the young were feeding on an accumulation of living dipterous larvae at the bottom of the nest.

A juvenile female specimen was taken at Canyon Island on the Taku River east of Juneau, Alaska, three miles from the British Columbia border, on November 4, 1964. This animal was found roosting in an old gill net hanging in a shed at a fisheries research station. Michael J. McHugh, who collected the specimen, said that snow was about a foot deep, ice an inch or two thick on the beaver ponds in the area, and the Taku River had started to freeze up. The bat was lethargic and apparently in hibernation. The specimen is obviously a juvenile as is evident from the cartilagenous gaps of about one millimeter at the joints of the fingers. This find is unusual so late in the season; perhaps the bat was born late and may have been in hibernation for some time. However the climate in the region is mild, with the first frosts usually in October. The hardiness of the species is attested by the fact that in New Mexico Jones (1965) caught a *L. noctivagans* in a mist net when the temperature was 28° F. (−2° C.).

One species of flea has been recorded from this species (Jackson, 1961), and Ubelaker (1966) recorded a trematode.

We have long been intrigued by Hamilton's (1943) method of collecting *L. noctivagans* with a handful of switches. It seemed incredible to us, having been familiar with the bat

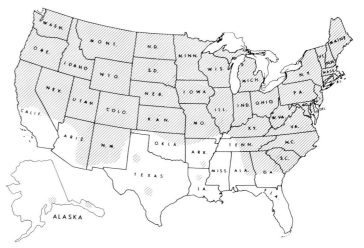

Distribution of *Lasionycteris noctivagans* in the United States

59. Silver-haired bat, *Lasionycteris noctivagans*.

109

only as a migrant where it usually flies at treetop height and does not repeatedly cover the same feeding ground. One of us (WHD) had the opportunity to test the method one summer at a pond near Gorham, New Hampshire. A few minutes after sunset two *L. noctivagans* appeared. They flitted slowly across the pond, repeatedly taking the same path, only occasionally being diverted to catch an insect or to chase one another. At the spot where the bats consistently came over the shore just before turning in flight, a short branch casually swung at them as they passed touched both.

In the winter of 1965 we went to southern Illinois to visit the silica mines in which Pearson (1962) found *L. noctivagans*. We first checked a mine near Elco that consisted of a few hundred feet of passage harboring several *Pipistrellus subflavus* and *Myotis keenii*. At one spot were two *L. noctivagans*; they were hibernating on the wall within three feet of one another.

We wonder why *Lasionycteris* hibernates in the silica mines but so rarely occurs in the limestone caves. Our only reasonable speculation is that the rather soft surface of the walls in these mines is more like the surface of a hollow tree than is limestone.

Skull of *Lasionycteris noctivagans,* x3

PIPISTRELLUS HESPERUS [H. Allen]

Western pipistrelle; canyon bat

Recognition: Forearm, 27–33 mm.; wingspread, 190–215 mm. The smallest bat in the United States. Calcar keeled. Color, usually pale yellow, varying from light gray to reddish brown; membranes dark.

Variation: Six subspecies are currently recognized in the United States:
1) *Pipistrellus hesperus hesperus* (H. Allen)—medium sized; pale yellow; in the major part of the Great Basin.
2) *Pipistrellus hesperus merriami* (Dobson)—darker and brownish; in California.
3) *Pipistrellus hesperus australis* Miller—small sized; drab; in central and southern Arizona.
4) *Pipistrellus hesperus maximus* Hatfield—large sized; gray to drab; in west Texas and adjacent New Mexico.
5) *Pipistrellus hesperus santarosae* Hatfield—large sized; darker; in northern New Mexico and adjacent Colorado.
6) *Pipistrellus hesperus oklahomae* Glass and Morse—large sized; darker and reddish brown; in a small area in Oklahoma and Texas.

The status and distribution of these subspecies has not been fully determined.

Confusing Species: Only *Myotis californicus* and *Myotis leibii* are small enough to be confused with *P. hesperus*. All three are tiny bats with a keeled calcar. The profile, the club-shaped tragus, and the presence of one tiny premolar (*Myotis* has two) behind each upper canine are distinctive.

60. Western pipistrelle, *Pipistrellus hesperus.* The tragus is short and blunt.

Range: The deserts and lowlands of southwestern United States north to Washington. Southward in Mexico to Michoacan and Hidalgo. An apparently isolated population occurs in north-central Texas and adjacent Oklahoma. Known in winter from Nevada, California, Arizona and Texas; limits of winter range unknown.

Habitat: This is a bat of the deserts, at home both in the rocky canyons and the greasewood flats. At elevations below 5,000 feet it is often the most common bat. The favored daytime retreats are rock crevices, and these bats are most abundant where there are rocky canyons, cliffs, or outcroppings. Mines providing narrow crevice retreats are sometimes occupied. Occasional individuals have been found in buildings and behind shutters. Von Blocker (1932) reported finding four *P. hesperus* beneath rocks in southern California and Arizona. Several were found roosting in dense growths of sedge in Nevada (Moore *et al*, 1965).

Only rarely does this species use manmade structures as night roosts, and it is almost never taken by netting mines and caves at night. Krutzsch (1954) found it only occasionally among the numerous bats of a half dozen other species using the Vallecito stage building in California as a night roost, although it was the most abundant bat foraging in the area. Cross (1965) suggested that perhaps it uses the faces of cliffs, but the night roosting sites of this species are essentially unknown.

In winter *P. hesperus* have been found hibernating in mines, caves, and rock crevices in a few scattered localities from Texas to California. They were always found singly and were never numerous.

Behavior: *P. hesperus* emerges much earlier in the evening and remains out later in the morning than other bats. They are often seen in flight before sunset and well after dawn. While it was still quite light one evening Van Gelder and Goodpaster (1952) watched *P. hesperus* flying among hundreds of violet-green swallows. On several occasions they watched a bat and a bird dive apparently at the same insect. Once a swallow drove off a bat when both had gone after the same object.

Evening activity ceases early, however, and *P. hesperus* are rarely taken in a net after 9:30 p.m. except for a flurry of activity near daybreak. An exception to this pattern occurs during the nursing season in mid-July, when lactating females, apparently under stress of water loss, can be captured at waterholes at all hours of the night (Cox, 1965b).

The flight is fluttery and is the slowest and weakest of all our bats. A slight breeze can bring them to a standstill and a stronger wind may send them scurrying for cover. Because of their flight characteristics they are easy to collect by shooting.

P. hesperus is sporadically active throughout the winter in some parts of its range. Cross (1965) found only males active in Arizona in winter, but O'Farrell *et al.* (1967) took both sexes in Nevada throughout the fall and winter. Although they noted a drastic reduction in the number flying on cold days, they netted some at temperatures as low as 34° F. (1° C.). Seven individuals were seen flying one evening when the air temperature varied between 34° and 36° F. (1°–2° C.).

Reproduction: The females give birth to two young in June. Small maternity colonies of up to a dozen bats including the young have been reported in rock crevices on a cliff, but solitary mothers with young have also been found. In Arizona a mother and her babies were found on June 15, and young capable of flight were noted on July 1 (Cross, 1965). On July 13 Koford and Koford (1948) discovered a group of a dozen

P. hesperus, including young and adults of both sexes, behind the window shutters of an adobe house in California.

Remarks: There is some question whether our two pipistrelles should be considered as belonging to the same genus. The bacula are strikingly different (Hamilton, 1949). Also *P. hesperus* has 46 chromosomes, whereas *Pipistrellus subflavus* has 56 (Baker and Patten, 1967). Such differences are not found within other genera of bats.

Over vast areas of flat desert covered almost exclusively with creosote bush (*Larrea*) *P. hesperus* may be the only bat. Driving across these wastelands in the early evening, we have noticed that they appear in scattered groups. Often many miles separate these groups. We have seen them appear over the desert in early evening 20 miles or more from the nearest rocky outcrop and nearly as far from any tree or building. Since in captivity these tiny bats desiccate and quickly perish during the day in the desert if not kept moist, it is unlikely that any could survive the day above ground in the desert flats. A reasonable explanation is that they may occupy the burrows of kangaroo rats, perhaps of the large colonial species such as *Dipodomys spectabilis* and *D. deserti*. We have no evidence to support this theory, but it deserves investigation. The piles of rocks used to anchor the sand at the bases of highway and railroad bridges across dry arroyos afford another possible retreat in some areas. The bridge timbers themselves occasionally give diurnal shelter to some hardy species such as *Tadarida brasiliensis*, *Antrozous pallidus* and *Myotis fortidens*, but probably the tiny *P. hesperus* could not survive there.

In July 1966 we observed the abundance in which *P. hesperus* are sometimes found. We were standing near the head of a shallow canyon in Big Bend National Park, Texas, watching for bats to appear when suddenly the pipistrelles began to fly. Within minutes the air seemed to be filled with them,

Distribution of *Pipistrellus hesperus* in the United States

61. Western pipistrelle, *Pipistrellus hesperus*, from southeastern Arizona.

113

over the canyon floor and up the hillsides. Probably several hundred were seen.

This species does not readily enter a bat net. Although an evening's netting in the low country of the Southwest usually produces several individuals, they are not captured in proportion to their numbers. Their extremely slow flight apparently allows them to avoid the net after detecting it. For each one that is caught many others will be seen to turn away from the net. An effective way to capture them is to drop the upper half of the net over the bat as it approaches. Using this technique Donald Hoffmeister and Wayne Davis caught 70 one evening over a small concrete water tank in Arizona.

It is hard to imagine the remarkably small size of this bat; when in the hand it seems the size of a beetle.

Skull of *Pipistrellus hesperus*, x3

PIPISTRELLUS SUBFLAVUS [F. Cuvier]

Eastern pipistrelle; pipistrelle; pipistrel

Recognition: Forearm, 31–35 mm.; wingspread, 208–258 mm. A small bat, with tricolored fur. The base of the hairs is dark, the middle band lighter, and the tip dark. Anterior third of the interfemoral membrane furred; calcar not keeled. Color, usually yellowish, varying from pale yellow or nearly orange to silvery-gray, chocolate brown, or black.

Variation: Three subspecies are recognized in the United States. *Pipistrellus subflavus subflavus* (F. Cuvier) occupies the major portion of the range. A larger, paler form, *Pipistrellus subflavus clarus* Baker, occurs in the Rio Grande Valley in the vicinity of Del Rio, Texas. *Pipistrellus subflavus floridanus* Davis is a grayish to chocolate brown race in southeastern Georgia and the Florida peninsula. Melanism is common in the Northeast, particularly in Nova Scotia (Bleakney, 1965).

Confusing Species: This species has been confused with some of the smaller *Myotis*, but can easily be recognized by its unique tricolored fur.

Range: Eastern North America from Nova Scotia, Quebec, and Minnesota south to the Gulf; southward through eastern Mexico to Guatemala and Honduras. It is apparently absent from southern Florida and northern New England, but otherwise ranges completely around the Gulf and Atlantic Coasts. In the north, it is unknown from northern Indiana, northeastern Illinois, eastern Wisconsin, and most of Michigan. Summer and winter ranges apparently coincide.

62. Eastern pipistrelle, *Pipistrellus subflavus*.

Habitat: Although the most abundant bat over much of the eastern United States, little is known of its summer daytime roosts. Its appearance at treetops early in the evening suggests that it may roost in foliage. When released during the day *P. subflavus*, unlike *Myotis*, usually takes refuge by hanging on a leaf, where it remains until evening. Findley (1954b) found one hanging in a tree in Mexico. In the Deep South it commonly inhabits clusters of Spanish moss (Jennings, 1958).

All observations suggest that pipistrelles are rarely found in buildings. However, there are authentic records of small maternity colonies in buildings in New York, Pennsylvania, Maryland, Illinois, Indiana, and Kentucky. Such colonies are in open sites where they are exposed to more light than many species would tolerate. A small group in Kentucky was found hanging from the ragged wallpaper of a long-abandoned house from which all windows and doors were missing. Even though such clusters may contain up to about 30 bats, they are silent and leave little or no sign of their presence; consequently they are easily overlooked. Occasionally, *P. subflavus* are found hanging singly in abandoned buildings or beneath porch roofs, especially in spring and fall. Such bats are often in full daylight.

Caves, mines, and rock crevices are used extensively in winter as hibernation sites, and in summer as night roosts.

Behavior: This dainty little bat emerges from its daytime retreat early in the evening. It is a weak flier and so small that it may be mistaken for a large moth. The flight is erratic, and the foraging area is small. Some individuals fly back and forth at treetop level, covering an area so small that they are constantly in view. They are never found foraging in deep woods, nor in open fields unless there are large trees nearby (Davis and Mumford, 1962). Often they forage over watercourses. They usually appear to be solitary, although occasionally in late summer four or five will appear about a single tree.

In late summer, they join the hordes of bats swarming about certain caves in Kentucky and Indiana, where they are among the more common bats taken during August netting operations. The bats seem intent only on entering the cave and rarely give any indication of detecting a mist net. They frequently hit a net with surprising force. It is not at all unusual to take 100 or more individuals at a cave in a single night. Wilson Baker banded nearly 2,000 in two weeks of netting at a cave in Kentucky, a number many times in excess of the bats that hibernate in the cave. One wonders whence so many came and where they go.

Food and Feeding: Little is known of the feeding habits of *P. subflavus*. Lewis (1940) caught one from a large flock of bats feeding on grain moths (*Angomous*) emerging from a corn crib. One of us (RWB) collected two individuals from among a group of about a hundred at dusk on July 24 that were feeding on moths which were emerging in great numbers from a corn crib in eastern Kentucky.

Captivity: We have had little success at keeping *P. subflavus* in captivity. Smith and Parmalee (1954), however, kept one more than a month on a diet of hamburger and mealworms. The animal did not object to handling and became quite tame.

Reproduction: Little is known about reproduction in this species. Jennings (1958) observed copulation in Florida caves during November and Guthrie (1933b) found sperm in the uteri of females taken in Missouri from November 11 to April 30. Data from West Virginia and Kentucky suggest that the young are born during the last two weeks in June and the first

116

week in July. Poole (1938) found a pregnant female in Pennsylvania on July 8. In Florida the young are born in late May and the first three weeks of June (Jennings, 1958). Litter size is normally two, rarely one. As many as four tiny embryos have been reported (Lindsay, 1956b); however, it is unlikely that more than two ever reach term. Wimsatt (1945) found that in this species three or four ova are shed and they usually implant two to each uterine horn. The embryos develop equally for a time, but soon the two implanted medially lag in development and are resorbed.

Growth and Development: The young at birth are remarkably large. A litter of two weighed 1.89 g. (Lane, 1946). The average weight of nine nursing mothers was 5.86 g.; the ratio of fetal weight to maternal weight is about 1:3. The young apparently grow rapidly and can fly within a month (Jennings, 1958).

Since these bats are born later in the season than most, a few youngsters as far south as Kentucky and West Virginia enter hibernation before they lose their dark juvenile pelage or complete their growth. In the Northeast and in Canada this is the usual situation, and all young of the year can be recognized by color and finger bone development. Since growth is curtailed during hibernation, these young generally can be recognized throughout their first hibernating season (Davis, 1963).

Population Dynamics: Davis (1966) studied population dynamics of *P. subflavus* in the caves of West Virginia. Survival is poor during the first year, peaks in the third, and then falls gradually. There are striking differences in survival rates between the sexes (fig. 63). Life tables show about 0.3 percent of the males live to their fifteenth year and that the maximum life span of females is about 10 years.

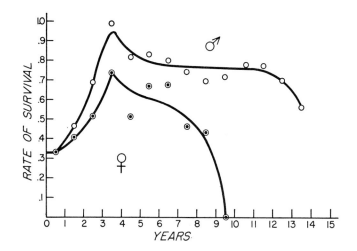

63. Survival rates for *Pipistrellus subflavus* in a West Virginia cave. Points represent the annual survival rates between the years x–1 and x. From the *Journal of Mammalogy.*

Migration: Other than the poorly understood summer swarming and the seasonal movements into and out of caves, little is known of the movements of *P. subflavus.* We have banded about 12,000 over a period of 15 years, but have had few recoveries. These few involve movements of less than 50 miles. Others have reported a few recoveries of individuals banded in caves; the longest known distance traveled is 85 miles (Griffin, 1940).

Hibernation: In winter many *P. subflavus* retreat to caves to hibernate. Like other hibernating bats, they are quite fat when they enter hibernation. Sealander and Young (1955) found that females averaged about a half gram heavier than males.

They inhabit more caves in eastern North America than any other species of bat. Many small caves unsuitable to other species for hibernation contain a few. They hang singly (fig.

117

64. Eastern pipistrelle, *Pipistrellus sub-flavus*, in a Kentucky cave showing the typical hibernating position.

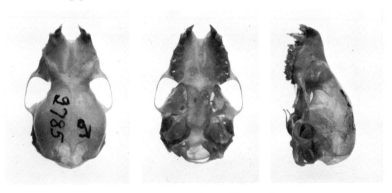

Skull of *Pipistrellus subflavus*, x3

118

65. Hibernating *Pipistrellus subflavus* with tiny droplets of water condensed on the fur.

64) and are scattered throughout the cave, seeming to prefer the warmer locations in protected side passages where they are frequently the only species encountered. In Kentucky they choose a hibernation site within a cave where the temperature is about 52°–55° F. (11°–13° C.) (Hall, 1962; Hassell, 1967). In Florida they hibernate in some caves where the temperature is as high as 58° to 64° F. (14°–18° C.) (Rice, 1957). Numbers in a cave range from a single individual to several hundred.

An individual may occupy a precise spot in a cave on consecutive winters. It usually has several spots in which it hangs, shifting from one to another during the winter. It can always be found at one of these sites. Occasionally, an individual awakens, flies, and returns to the identical spot it left (Hassell, 1967). Although they awaken and move, they do so less frequently than most bats; an individual often remains in one position for weeks. During this time beads of moisture frequently collect on the fur giving the bat a dazzling appearance when a light is flashed on it (fig. 65). Under such conditions the careless observer frequently reports seeing a white bat. Those hanging in drafty sites awaken and move more frequently than others. Females awaken and leave the caves earlier than the males; some males remain in the caves well into June (Sealander, 1956; Davis, 1959a).

P. subflavus appears to be rather hardy, for cave populations do not reach a maximum until December or later in West Virginia, Kentucky, and Arkansas, and in mild winters the cave populations are smaller than during severe ones. The hibernating bats in caves and mines, however, account for no more than a small fraction of the numbers present in summer. Surely they must utilize underground retreats that are inaccessible to man. Davis and Reite (1967) found that in the laboratory, many pipistrelles aroused as the temperature was lowered from 41° to 32° F. (5°–0° C.). Probably those pipistrelles inhabiting the more vulnerable retreats awaken as the weather becomes colder and move into the caves in search of a more stable environment.

Predation: Specific references to predation on this species are almost unknown. A hoary bat is known to have captured and killed one, and one was recovered from the stomach of a frog. Probably these are isolated instances of little significance.

Remarks: Across a large section of the United States *P. subflavus* is by far the most abundant bat. They can be seen in flight at dusk in large numbers, but we can only speculate as to the whereabouts of the bulk of the population on summer days and throughout the winter. The fall swarming and related movements need study. Care of the young needs investigation, as does their growth and development. It seems remarkable that large segments of the natural history of so common an animal remain unknown.

EPTESICUS FUSCUS [Palisot de Beauvois]

Big brown bat; barn bat; house bat

Recognition: Forearm, 42–51 mm.; wingspread, 325–350 mm. Females larger than males. A rather large brown bat with broad nose, a broad rounded tragus, broad wings, and keeled calcar. Color, varying from russet to dark brown.

Variation: Four subspecies are recognized in the United States. *Eptesicus fuscus fuscus* (Palisot de Beauvois) occurs east of the Great Plains except peninsular Florida where a darker race, *Eptesicus fuscus osceola* Rhoads, is found. A pale race, *Eptesicus fuscus pallidus* Young, is found from the western plains through the Rocky Mountains. In the Pacific states the more brightly colored *Eptesicus fuscus bernardinus* Rhoads occurs.

Confusing Species: It is most similar to *Nycticeius humeralis* from which it can be distinguished by its larger size. The only species of *Myotis* that possess a keeled calcar are much smaller.

Range: From Alaska and Canada south through the United States and Mexico to northern South America, including the Caribbean islands. Apparently unknown from southern Florida and much of central Texas. An abundant bat throughout most of its range, but scarce and local in the Deep South and in the far northern states. Summer and winter range identical.

Habitat: E. *fuscus* is closely associated with man and probably is familiar to more people in the United States than is any other species of bat. Favored roosts are in buildings. In summer they form colonies in attics and barns, behind shutters or

66. Bib brown bat, *Eptesicus fuscus.* The worn tips of the upper canines show this bat to be several years old.

unused sliding doors, between expansion joints beneath bridges, or in similar shelters. Cross and Huibregtse (1964) found 20 living in a hollow saguaro cactus in Arizona. Occasionally they use hollow trees. In the region west of the Mississippi River they frequently use rock crevices and sometimes quarry tunnels. In the badlands of South Dakota several scattered individuals and small groups were found hiding behind the peculiar bacon rind formations formed by the erosion of the clay buttes. In Texas Jameson (1959) captured six from cliff swallow nests in September. In winter, they can be found hanging singly or in small groups in buildings, caves, mines, tunnels, quarries, storm sewers, and other similar shelters.

In tunnels of a limestone quarry at Leavenworth, Kansas, Phillips (1966) found that several hundred E. *fuscus* were permanent residents. In spring the females left, apparently seeking warmer spots to raise their young, but the males remained to use the quarry as a summer home. Similar quarries in eastern Nebraska are also used in summer (Jones, 1964), but in the East such places are used only in winter or as night roosts in summer. We have but a single record of two of these bats in a crevice in a rock cliff in Kentucky in summer, and two records from caves in August. All other summer day roosts that have come to our attention in this region are in buildings, bridges, or trees.

Behavior: E. *fuscus* emerges at dusk and flies a steady, nearly straight course at a height of 20–30 feet. Its large size and steady flight makes it readily recognizable. Although at some colonies the bats may begin feeding nearby when they emerge, usually they move off in a steady stream to feeding grounds hundreds of yards away. The flight appears slow, but this may be an illusion due to the bat's large size and slow wing beats.

As with several other species these bats may fly repeatedly over the same course during an evening, with frequent sallies

67. Louver in the belfry of a church in Clay City, Kentucky, occupied in summer by a colony of big brown bats, *Eptesicus fuscus*. The stain at the top indicates where the bats enter and emerge. Such stained areas are often rather conspicuous and betray the usage of a building by bats.

to catch insects. Apparently, some individuals use the same feeding ground each night, for a bat can sometimes be seen following an identical feeding pattern on different nights. If the bat is removed, it may be several nights before another occupies this feeding ground.

After feeding the bat flies to a night roost to rest. Favored night roosts include porches of stucco or brick houses, garages with open doors, or a breezeway. Here it leaves the tell-tale sign of a few droppings each morning. We have frequently been asked how to deal with such a mysterious visitor by an exasperated housewife who rarely is aware of what kind of animal is causing the trouble, for it is never seen. The most likely time to spot such a bat is about an hour after dark. Usually such a single bat is an adult male. The females return to their young after a feeding flight. When the young are on

121

the wing, the group chooses as a night roost the site of the nursery colony or a nearby shelter.

E. fuscus seeks daytime roosts in dark places and is rather intolerant of disturbance. If a group hanging free from a chimney or the rafters of an attic is disturbed, they readily retreat into inaccessible crevices, and they may not use the exposed area again that summer. Handling the bats or disturbing them may cause some to abandon the shelter and move to nearby roosts. On the other hand, repeated handling may cause a colony to become rather tame. A group we studied in Kentucky was handled so frequently that the bats became docile and made little effort to escape or bite as we gathered them for our studies.

Although roosting in attics, this species uses cooler places than do little brown bats and it is not so tolerant of high temperatures. When the temperature in the roost rises above 92°–95° F. (33°–35° C.) the bats move to cooler places or abandon the roost. We have seen several attics in Kentucky where a colony abandoned a building during a hot spell. More frequently, however, they retreat to a cooler part of the house. Spaces in the walls, in a partition between rooms, in crevices at the base of a chimney, or crevices where the roof meets the floor of the attic may be used. If such retreats are not available, they may pass the hottest part of the day in a group on the open floor.

When heat forces the bats to move they frequently encounter man. They may first be noticed squeaking in the walls. If there is a crevice around one of the window frames they may crawl out into a room. Each time there is a heat wave we get several calls from people who have bats in the house. Usually such bats are youngsters which have crawled out of the wall or from a crevice around a fireplace. In one type of house common in Kentucky the space between the inside wall and the outer brick is continuous from attic to basement. In many such houses both young and adult bats appear in the basement during hot weather.

Food and Feeding: E. *fuscus* pursues insects in cleared meadows, among the scattered trees in pastures, along tree-lined village streets, or above the traffic in the middle of a city. It flies a steady course broken by frequent sallies to capture insects.

Hamilton (1933) studied the feeding habits of *E. fuscus* by analyzing droppings obtained from a house in West Virginia in August. From the small amount of identifiable material, he determined the following percentages by frequency of occurrence: Coleoptera, 36.1; Hymenoptera, 26.3; Diptera, 13.2; Plecoptera, 6.5; Ephemerida, 4.6; Hemiptera, 3.4; Trichoptera, 3.2; Neuroptera, 3.2; Mecoptera, 2.7; and Orthoptera, 0.6.

Among the Coleoptera, beetles of the family Scarabaeidae were most frequent, followed by Elateridae, Lampyridae, and Histeridae. Others were a few Carabidae and Hydrophilidae. Hymenoptera were represented by flying ants, braconids, and ichneumonids. Diptera consisted mainly of muscids, but a single wing of a crane fly, *Tipula*, was recognized. Plecoptera of the genus *Isoperla* were frequent. Mayflies, true bugs, caddis flies, lace-wing flies, scorpion flies, and a few orthopterous insects made up the remainder of the identifiable material.

Surprisingly enough, no lepidopterous remains were encountered, although moths make up a major part of the food of many species of bats. Since many of the insects reported by Hamilton are harmful, the feeding habits of the big brown bat, like those of most of our species, are beneficial to man.

Hall (1946) reported an interesting encounter of a big brown bat with a huge beetle. The bat and the beetle, a 60-mm. *Eragates spiculatus*, were found on a road in the evening. Perhaps the bat had captured the large insect in flight and could not carry it. Handley (1956) and Wilson (1958) have reported big brown bats with the head of an ant firmly attached, by the mandibles, to the side of the face. The insects were identified as the winged form of the carpenter ant.

Like other bats, *E. fuscus* is an efficient feeder. Adults can fill the stomach within about an hour. Gould (1955) found an adult accumulated food at a rate of 2.7 g. per hour, but fully grown young did not feed nearly so rapidly. Probably it takes considerable practice for a young bat to learn to capture flying insects by echolocation.

Captivity: Big brown bats adapt best to captivity of all our species. Although they are vicious when first captured and can inflict a painful bite, they soon respond to gentle handling and actually seem to enjoy being stroked on the head. They can be fed mealworms or other insects, or such things as cottage cheese, chopped meat, or banana. They are remarkable in that they eat artificial food without training. If confined in a small space with a dish of food, a bat usually learns to eat by himself within two nights, although prompting him by placing food in the mouth when he tries to bite will make him learn quicker.

When in captivity *E. fuscus* will sometimes kill and eat smaller species of bats.

Reproduction: In Maryland, spermatogenesis occurs in summer, somewhat earlier in adults than in the young of the year. It has ceased in both groups by the middle of October. At this time the tubules of the cauda epididymis are packed with mature spermatozoa (Christian, 1956). Breeding pairs have been seen in a cave from November through March (Mumford, 1958).

Ovulation occurs about the first week in April in Maryland; spermatozoa are present in the female genital tract at this time. Birth occurs about the first of June, a gestation period of about two months. Some yearling females do not produce young.

In Kentucky *E. fuscus* appear in numbers at the maternity colonies near the middle of May, about two or three weeks before the young are born. The colonies vary in size from about 20 to 300 individuals. As parturition approaches the bats become reluctant to fly and spend more time in the roost at night.

Time of parturition is variable with latitude. In Kentucky most young are born during the last week in May and the first week in June. Around San Diego in southern California young are also born in the latter part of May and early June

68. Captive big brown bat, *Eptesicus fuscus*, feeding from a dish of prepared food.

123

69.   Baby big brown bats, *Eptesicus fuscus*, clustered in the attic of a building while their mothers are foraging.   Two adults have already returned and are nursing their young.

(Krutzsch, 1946), but in North Dakota embryos are not yet fully developed in the third week of June (Jones and Genoways, 1966), and pregnant females have been taken in Nebraska in July (Jones, 1964). From the Great Plains to the east each female generally produces two young, but from the eastern edge of the Rocky Mountains westward litter size is nearly always one.

During late pregnancy and when the young are small, adult males are scarce in the maternity roosts. When present, they are usually scattered individuals. At this time most males are solitary or roost in small groups behind window shutters, beneath sign boards, and in other such shelters. As the young mature there is an influx of adult males into the nursery colonies in Kentucky, and for the rest of the season they may be nearly as numerous as adult females.

Care of the Young: We have studied the care of the young in colonies in Kentucky (Davis *et al.*, 1968). The newborn cling tightly to the mother's teats during the day and are sheltered beneath her membranes (fig. 70), clinging so tenaciously that they are difficult to remove without injury. When the mothers leave for the evening's foraging, however, even the smallest youngsters are left behind (fig. 69). We do not know how the mother induces her babies to release their grip.

In Nevada, on consecutive evenings from July 11 to 17, Hall (1946) shot 25 females as they left a crevice near the top of a rock about 80 feet high. Several of these had one small young each clinging to her. Five of six adult females he found using charcoal kilns as night roosts on July 20 in Nevada had one young each. He had been unable to find bats there during daylight, but droppings and insect remains indicated that the site was used as a night roost. This evidence suggests that the bats may carry their young with them while feeding. In Kentucky we found that mothers carried their young outdoors only

while moving them from one roost to another. The fact that eastern *Eptesicus* produce two young per litter may account for this behavioral difference.

When the bats are very young the mothers leave them early in the evening and feed close by, returning within an hour. When an adult enters a cluster of babies each one tries to attach itself to her. The adult crawls over the group, apparently seeking her own. When she finds her babies, she licks them about the face and lips before allowing them to nurse.

The baby bats occasionally fall to the floor. Atlhough some perish there, many are retrieved by their mothers as we discovered when working with a colony which lived high in the rafters of a tobacco barn (Davis *et al.*, 1968). Many dead and dying youngsters were on the floor, and we assumed that

70. Female big brown bat, *Eptesicus fuscus*, at rest in the attic of a building. A baby is tucked beneath each wing.

125

all baby bats which fall from a roost would die. But when a small boy who lived beside the barn told us that he had seen bats come down at night and pick up babies, we decided to investigate. We tagged all live babies we could find on the floor with radioactive tags and returned each to the spot where found. Several days later we found half the tagged bats up in the rafters. The barn was so constructed that they could not have crawled there unassisted.

To investigate the problem further we tagged and released a mother after placing her babies in a tray on the floor. A radiation detector placed next to the tray was wired to record her visits on a chart in another room. Within 15 minutes after bats began to emerge that evening the mother made two trips to the tray and removed her babies.

To test a mother bat's ability to recognize her own baby which has fallen to the floor we captured two mothers with young. One was given a radioactive tag and returned to the colony. Her babies were taken to the laboratory in Lexington and held in a cage with the second mother. The latter's babies were put into the tray beneath the colony. The recorder showed that the tagged mother visited the tray soon after dusk, but she did not retrieve the strange young.

Baby bats that have fallen, or have strayed from the colony, squeak almost continuously. This probably helps the mothers to locate them and is likely important to their survival. By the end of June, when the young are able to fly, the colony becomes silent except for occasional bickering.

Growth and Development: The young are large at birth, weighing nearly 4 g., with a forearm about 18 mm. in length. Growth is rapid; increases in length of the forearm of as much as 2.6 mm. per day were recorded for some individuals, and weight gains of as much as half a gram per day were common among the newborn.

As the young mature they are left alone for longer periods while the mothers range farther and are gone longer on their nightly flights. By mid-June the mothers begin to use night roosts away from the nursery, and about a week later the juveniles are on the wing and join them at the night roosts. By early July all young are able to fly.

In New England many nursery colonies break up as soon as the young are weaned. Harold Hitchcock and Wayne Davis found that many sites were abandoned after the latter part of July in Massachusetts and Connecticut. In Kentucky, however, *Eptesicus* remains in nursery colonies throughout the summer. They leave when cold weather arrives in the fall.

Longevity: Christian (1956) studied tooth wear in *E. fuscus* and concluded that he could accurately determine the age of individuals by wear and by the annual growth rings of dentine. He developed an equation for tooth wear which showed that the teeth could wear down to the rim of the cingulum during a bat's sixth year, and thus six years would be the maximum longevity in Maryland. Since no one has supported Christian's findings with data from bats of known age, and many banded *E. fuscus* are known to have lived far beyond six years, his methods have not been generally accepted. Hitchcock (1965) recorded a bat he banded in Ontario which was found alive 18 years later.

Beer (1955) and Goehring (1958) studied the survival of this species using banding and recapture data. Both found mortality highest during the first year.

Migration: E. fuscus is a rather sedentary species. In Kentucky we have often captured the same individuals using a cave as a night roost in summer that are found hibernating there in winter. Nearly all of the recoveries of banded bats recorded by Beer (1955), Davis *et al.* (1968), and Hitchcock and Davis

126

(unpublished) are of animals recaptured within 30 miles of the banding site. The movement of 142 miles reported by Mumford (1958) is exceptional.

Homing: This species has remarkable homing ability, in spite of the fact that it does not seem to range far afield and thus may be familiar with only a restricted area. Cope *et al.* (1961c) released *E. fuscus* at various distances from the home roost. Those released 20 miles away nearly all returned the same night. Bats taken 40 miles away did not return until the second night, and those taken 100 miles away arrived on the third night. Of bats released 250 miles from home, some returned during the fourth night, and nearly all had returned by the end of the fifth night. Smith and Goodpaster (1958) took 51 adult females and 104 juveniles from a nursery colony in Cincinnati on July 20, 1957, and released them 450 miles to the north. A month later three adults had returned, and after three months four more had appeared. None of the juveniles returned. On August 2, they took 18 bats to western Tennessee, 340 miles southwest of Cincinnati. Fifteen days later two of these, including a juvenile, had returned home.

Hibernation: In late summer *E. fuscus* becomes extremely fat in preparation for the hibernating season. Those captured in September sometimes weigh as much as 30 g., with a third of this weight being fat. That the stored fat is more than adequate for the bat to survive the winter was demonstrated by W. Gene Frum. He once kept two big brown bats hibernating in a box in a refrigerator for nearly a year (fig. 71).

E. fuscus is remarkably hardy. Only during the coldest weather do they retreat into caves, mines, storm sewers, road culverts, basements, burial vaults and other underground shelters. Their stay in such places may be rather short, and a turnover of individuals occurs throughout the winter, even during the coldest weather. In Kentucky a few are found in the caves in autumn and even occasionally in August, but the major influx occurs in November and December. By the middle of March most have left the caves.

Although some bats can always be found in caves and mines during cold weather, the winter quarters of the bulk of the population of this abundant species are unknown. Frum (1953) found them in shallow crevices in sandstone cliffs of West Virginia during March. The findings of Martin *et al.* (1966) that big brown bats sometimes hibernate under rocks on the floor of a mine may also help account for their apparent scarcity in winter. Apparently most of them, however, hibernate in buildings even in the northern part of the range. They have been found thus in Maine, New Hampshire, Minnesota and many more southerly states, and in Canada at Ottawa, Regina, and in British Columbia. The most northern winter record is one found alive in a building at Prince Albert, Saskatchewan, on February 1 (Nero, 1959).

When hibernating in caves *E. fuscus* chooses a site near the entrance where the temperature is rather low and the relative humidity is below 100 percent. Therefore they never become beaded with moisture like *Myotis lucifugus* and *Pipistrellus*

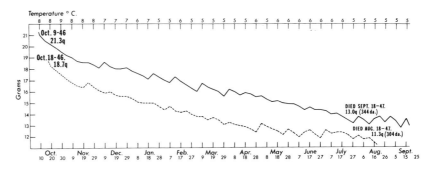

71. Weight changes of two *Eptesicus fuscus* kept hibernating in a box in a refrigerator. (*Courtesy of* W. *Gene Frum*)

subflavus sometimes do. They cannot tolerate such conditions, and soon succumb if kept in a saturated environment in a cold room in the laboratory. They are often found hanging in the open on a cave wall. They seem to prefer a horizontal crevice, however, and they can force themselves into a remarkably small space (fig. 72). A particularly favored locality is the space formed by the partial flaking of layers of rock from the ceiling.

When wintering in mines or caves in northern latitudes, male *E. fuscus* commonly form tight clusters (Rysgaard, 1942; Davis and Hitchcock, 1964; Phillips, 1966), with the females being distributed as singles in the warmer regions.

E. fuscus responds to subfreezing temperature by arousing and remaining active until the temperature rises (Davis and Reite, 1967). They hibernate over a temperature range of about 32°–64° F. (0°–18° C.). The usual pattern for *E. fuscus* seems to be to hibernate in a building where it remains through the winter. If the temperature at the spot it has chosen drops below freezing, the bat arouses and seeks better shelter. During extremely cold weather it is not unusual to see a big brown bat flying outdoors in the city in the daytime, or to find one dead or dying on the ground. Such unfortunate individuals are apparently driven from their hibernation sites by the cold. Rysgaard (1941) found that when drifts from an early snowstorm closed the entrance to a cave in Minnesota on November 11, 1940, over 100 *Eptesicus* died trying to enter the shelter.

A bat in hibernation is a strange creature. When found, the bat is nearly helpless. If put on the ground it extends its wings, flops onto its back, and opens its mouth, all the while making a kissing sound of apparent protest. If it has an opportunity it will bite, and once the jaws have closed the grip is extremely tenacious and it is difficult to pry the animal loose. In the process of arousal, breathing and heart rate increase, temperature rises, and movements become more

72. Big brown bat, *Eptesicus fuscus*, hibernating in a horizontal crevice in Bat Cave, Kentucky.

frequent. Shivering begins, generating still more heat. Within 15 minutes arousal is complete, and the animal is able to fly.

Associates: Eptesicus frequently shares its living quarters with other bats, such as *Tadarida, Antrozous,* and *Myotis yumanensis* in the West, and *M. lucifugus* in the East. The species are usually segregated although we occasionally see a single male *Eptesicus* in a cluster of *M. lucifugus.*

Parasites: Like several of the *Myotis, E. fuscus* is frequently preyed upon by the bloodsucking bug, *Cimex pilosellus.* This insect, a close relative of the bed bug, inhabits the bats' diurnal roost. In nearly every large colony in Kentucky many thousands can be seen crawling on the beams where the bats rest. They stay close to the bats and only rarely appear in the rooms downstairs. These insects are responsible for the popular misconception that bats carry bed bugs. These bugs do not live in the bed clothes and do not molest man. In handling many thousands of bats over the years we have had many *Cimex* crawl off onto us, but only once has one of us been bitten by a bat bug.

E. fuscus is also often parasitized by mites; at least two kinds can usually be found on bats in summer. Sometimes mites become so abundant as to destroy a colony of bats, or drive them from a favored roost. Harold Hitchcock and Wayne Davis saw two instances in Massachusetts where nursery roosts had been recently abandoned; search revealed only a few dead and dying young. The young were emaciated and were heavily infested with mites. Various species of fleas have also been found, and Christian (1956) isolated trypanosomes from the blood. Ubelaker (1966) reported one species of cestode from this bat. Jameson (1959) found nematodes in the intestines and found several species of mites preying on these bats. George and Strandtmann (1960) found a fowl mite on one

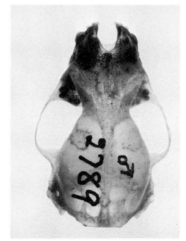 

Skull of *Eptesicus fuscus,* x3

129

in Texas, and Jones and Genoways (1967b) reported ticks on specimens taken in South Dakota.

Predators: Rat snakes, *Elaphe obsoleta*, frequently inhabit the rafters and attics of buildings in rural areas and commonly prey upon big brown bats (Silver, 1928).

Hawks will capture bats when an opportunity arises. On two occasions we have watched sparrow hawks (*Falco sparverius*) capture *E. fuscus*; one took six bats as we banded and released them. Flying more rapidly than the bat, the hawk would overtake and capture it with remarkable ease.

Molt: Jones and Genoways (1967b) described the molt in *E. fuscus* from specimens taken in South Dakota. The annual molt begins in the shoulder region and ventrally in the throat and pectoral areas. Molting spreads so rapidly that lines of molt, such as are often seen in other small mammals, are not evident. Males netted July 22 to 27 had completed molt; most females taken during this time were still molting.

Remarks: Luckens and Davis (1964) reported that these bats are extremely sensitive to DDT in comparison with other mammals. They were about 10 times as sensitive as some laboratory species. Recent work, however, has shown that the effect is influenced by season. A dose 20 times that which is lethal in spring is not lethal in fall. The chlorinated hydrocarbon pesticides are fat soluble and apparently are quickly deposited in the fat when eaten in autumn. The bats are most susceptible to poisoning when they emerge from hibernation with fat reservoirs depleted in the spring.

We need to learn more of the whereabouts of these bats in winter. It is reasonable to suppose that in regions with cold winters most of them hibernate in buildings where they are not often encountered. They exhibit a similar seasonal pattern

of abundance, however, in southern California. In the San Diego region the earliest date Krutzsch (1946) found big brown bats was March 8 and the latest September 21. The colonies may migrate out of the region, hibernate, or break up and scatter for the winter months.

Although several species of bats produce audible sounds while foraging, *E. fuscus* is one of only two species of our vespertilionid bats that commonly utters an audible chatter in flight. The other is *Lasiurus cinereus*. The chatter seems to be a communication between two bats flying close to one another.

Distribution of *Eptesicus fuscus* in the United States

LASIURUS BOREALIS [Müller]

Red bat

Recognition: Forearm, 35–45 mm.; wingspread, 290–332 mm. A medium-sized bat with long pointed wings, short rounded ears, and a heavily furred interfemoral membrane. In flight the tail extends straight out behind. The long tail and interfemoral membrane are distinctive, and this bat can be recognized among *Myotis, Eptesicus* and *Pipistrellus* by its silhouette against the sky. Color, varying from bright orange to yellowbrown. In the East males are usually brighter than females.

Variation: Two subspecies occur in the United States. *Lasiurus borealis borealis* (Müller) occurs throughout the East. *Lasiurus borealis teliotis* (H. Allen) is a brighter, smaller race with shorter ears found in the West.

Confusing Species: Lasiurus cinereus is gray and larger. *Lasiurus ega* and *Lasiurus intermedius* are yellowish, larger, and lack fur on the terminal half of the interfemoral membrane. It is most similar to *Lasiurus seminolus* from which it differs in color, the latter being a deep mahogany brown.

Range: From southern Canada throughout the eastern United States southward through Mexico and Central America; northward in the West through California. Specimens have been taken in British Columbia and Alberta. Winter range roughly the southern half of the United States, extending in the East, from the Ohio River Valley southward and, in the West, along the coast from San Francisco south.

This bat is most abundant in the Midwest and in the east-

73. Family of red bats, *Lasiurus borealis*, in their daytime shelter beneath the leaf of a sycamore tree. The two young are nearly as large as the mother. *(Courtesy of Grady Franklin, Crawfordsville, Indiana,* Journal-Review)

131

central states. In the Ohio River Valley it seems to be out-numbered only by *Pipistrellus subflavus* in summer. The most common summer resident about Champaign, Illinois, Lawrence, Kansas, and Stillwater, Oklahoma, it can probably be found easily wherever there are trees in the prairie and Great Plains states. It is a common breeding species southward into Alabama and South Carolina but is rare in Florida. From the Ohio River Valley northward, it becomes less abundant, being found only locally and uncommonly in Vermont and Minnesota.

Habitat: Summer roosting sites were studied in Iowa by McClure (1942) and Constantine (1966a). The bats spent the daylight hours hanging in the foliage of trees; though any tree that provided suitable shelter was used, they showed some preference for American elms. They usually hung from the petiole of a leaf, but occasionally from a twig or branch. A bat hanging thus is surprisingly well concealed. Hanging by one foot it closely resembles a dead leaf.

In Lewis, Iowa, Constantine (1966a) found the greatest number of bats in fence rows and forest edges. He found a definite preference for the south side of trees and for sites bordered by dense leafy crops such as corn or beans. Roosts were of three general types. Each provided dense shade and cover above and at the sides, but was open below. Usually the bats could be viewed only from beneath. One shelter type was a bowl-shaped canopy consisting of tree branches interlaced with grapevines, providing lush cover and structural rigidity which resisted movement by the wind. Another type was a dense leafy overhang of new, limp, succulent growth. The third shelter type was a dense cluster of older, nonsucculent leaves. Roosts were usually 4–10 feet above ground, except for family clusters which commonly were 10–20 feet high.

Based upon his observations in California, Georgia, and Iowa, Constantine (1966a) listed the following characteristics of roosts of this species and other related lasiurines: protection from view from all directions except below; lack of obstruction beneath allowing the bat to drop downward to begin flight; no lower perches from which predatory birds or mammals could see the bat; dark ground cover minimizing the reflection of sunlight; sufficient neighboring vegetation to break up wind currents and retard the distribution of dust; and location on the south or southwest side of the tree.

In Lewis, Iowa, McClure (1942) estimated the population at about one bat per acre, conjecturing that this concentration resulted from the abundant food supply at street lights; Constantine (1966a), however, found comparatively fewer bats in Lewis than in the surrounding countryside.

Behavior, Summer: L. *borealis* emerges early in the evening. In the hill country of West Virginia and Kentucky they are first seen high in the air where they flutter in slow erratic flight as if in play. After 15–30 minutes, and sometimes considerably longer, they descend and feed from treetop level to within a few feet of the ground. At this time their flight character changes markedly; they fly straight or in wide arcs, the pattern broken occasionally by excursions to capture insects. The flight is swift; Jackson (1961) timed one at 40 miles per hour in level flight.

They forage regularly over the same territory. Davis (1960) observed an individual marked with a torn membrane using the same beat each evening. Another individual foraged nearby. Occasionally the bats encroached upon one another's territory, but without conflict. Jackson (1961) also noted that an individual seemed to cover the same area each evening. He found that they often foraged 600 to 1,000 yards from their day roosts. Layne (1958) noted that red bats seemed to become scarce in mid-May, suggesting that females in advanced

132

pregnancy may be less active or more circumscribed in their evening flights.

We have noticed that when a red bat is shot another moves in to utilize its feeding territory within a few days, and several can be collected from one spot during a summer.

Although this magnificent bat is among the most beautiful of all mammals, its habits are such that few people are familiar with it. The species is solitary and spends the day hidden in the foliage of a tree. Occasionally during June or July a female may fall with her burden of young and become stranded where they can easily be seen. The more brightly colored males, however, are almost never captured or seen except by the bat hunter who must shoot, net, or have the patience to search the foliage of numerous trees to obtain one.

Roost sites are often used by different individuals on different days (Downes, 1964; Constantine, 1966a). Downes collected five in seven days from the underside of a sunflower leaf in Illinois in August. There appeared to be many other suitable roosting sites in the sunflower row, and Downes suspected some kind of communication among the bats regarding the favored site. He found that in captivity one bat will respond to sounds made by another and may thus be attracted to the spot where the other is resting, a behavior pattern also noticed by others. David Easterla told us that he has attracted *L. borealis* to a net by using others as decoys, and Baker and Ward (1967) have used this method to capture red bats in Arkansas.

In August, *L. borealis* joins cave dwelling species swarming at the mouths of certain caves where they can be captured with mist nets. Baker took 60 one night at a cave in Georgia, and we regularly take a dozen or two a night when netting at Dixon and Short caves in Kentucky. The bats enter and fly about in the caves at this season. Where there are small crawlways leading to large rooms, *L. borealis* enters and apparently becomes lost. They hang on the ceiling, where they may remain indefinitely. Myers (1960) found 100 or more in certain rooms of Missouri caves; they ranged from mere skeletons to healthy bats. There is a remote room in Bat Cave, Carter Caves State Park, Kentucky, where we often find three or four red bats hanging from the ceiling in August, but never at any other season. It is interesting to speculate on why they enter caves in August. Since it is the breeding season, it may have something to do with reproductive behavior. Perhaps their remote ancestors were cave dwellers.

Behavior, Winter: Red bats are common winter residents in the Ohio River Valley where temperatures frequently drop far below freezing. Although their roost in winter has not been discovered, they surely hide in trees. Davis and Lidicker (1956) saw them emerging in November from a woodlot in Illinois where there were no underground shelters.

During warm days in winter when the temperature rises to 66° F. or above, *L. borealis* arouse from hibernation and feed. At this season they fly in late afternoon often before sunset. In January 1957, 27 were counted over roads in Mammoth Cave National Park, Kentucky. They fed only a few minutes, and returned to the woods before the chill of evening set in.

This species is well adapted for surviving drastic temperature fluctuations. Whereas those species of bats that winter in the relatively constant environment of underground retreats arouse from hibernation when the environmental temperature rises to 59° F. (15° C.), *L. borealis* remains torpid in the laboratory until the temperature reaches about 68° F. (20° C.) (Davis and Reite, 1967). Davis and Lidicker (1956) found that outdoors the bats became active only on days when temperatures rose to 66° F. (19° C.) or above; however, Lewis (1940) found that in Virginia they flew whenever the temperature rose to 55° F. (13° C.) or above. Thus, they do not arouse unless food, in the form of flying insects, is available. This is an important adaptation, for arousal from hibernation requires expenditure of considerable energy. Probably those bats that become torpid in caves are unable to arouse spontaneously at cave temperatures. Thus *L. borealis* seems to be so adapted to survival outside that it is unable to survive in caves.

The adaptations for survival of *L. borealis* at subfreezing temperatures are both physiological and anatomical. They respond to subfreezing temperatures by increasing the metabolism just enough to maintain the body temperature above the critical low limit of 23° F. (–5° C.) (Reite and Davis, 1966). Since they do not hibernate in caves and thus cannot retreat to a warmer spot, it would be to their disadvantage to arouse at low temperatures, for arousal would use far more energy than regulation during dormancy. The anatomical structure

74. Male red bat, *Lasiurus borealis*, hibernating in a refrigerator. The heavily furred interfemoral membrane covers the wings and ventral surface. The tip of the tail is near the nose, and the right foot can be seen on the forearm.

134

and behavior of the red bat are also specially modified for survival at low temperatures. Except for the ears and parts of the wings the body is almost completely furred. The heavily furred interfemoral membrane and the relatively long tail are significant in heat conservation during hibernation; the bat uses the interfemoral membrane as a blanket (fig. 74). The short rounded ears also help minimize heat loss. That the animal is well adapted for energy conservation at low temperatures is suggested by the heart rate. At 41° F. (5° C.) the heart rate is 10–16 beats per minute, whereas the rates of four common species of bats which hibernate in caves in the eastern United States ranges from 24 to 80 beats per minute at the same temperature (Davis and Reite, 1967).

Food and Feeding: Little is available concerning the food of this species. Evidence has been found of crickets, flies, bugs, beetles, cicadas, and other insects (Hamilton, 1943; Jackson, 1961). The presence of crickets suggests they must take some food from the ground. They commonly feed beneath street lights in towns and occasionally can be seen to alight and capture an insect on a wooden light pole.

Perhaps more than other species *L. borealis* takes advantage of the attraction of insects to lights. The modern fluorescent ultraviolet insect traps attract and occasionally trap red bats. We have obtained more than a dozen specimens from such traps at the University of Kentucky, but have encountered no other species. Wilson (1965) reported several captured in this manner in Indiana.

Lewis (1940) found that in late summer and early fall these bats often congregate in large numbers at dusk about corn cribs to feed upon emerging grain moths (*Angomous*). When a moderate, steady wind is blowing over a moth-infested crib he has seen bats strung out for 200 yards or more, catching moths that were carried by the wind.

75. Multiple exposure of a red bat, *Lasiurus borealis*, in feeding flight. In the center exposure the bat is reaching back in an attempt to catch the moth in its wingtip. *(Courtesy of Frederic A. Webster)*

Captivity: L. borealis adjusts poorly to captivity. In confinement they are obstreperous, belligerent, uncooperative, and sulky. When first caged they thrash about so violently that they often injure the joints in their wings. Although they will quiet down within a short while, they react in the same way to any new disturbance. We have not been able to get them to accept either mealworms or artificial food. When kept caged, their fur becomes wet and matted, they fail to groom themselves, and they die within a few days.

Although we have had little success keeping this species in captivity, some authors report that it does fairly well for a few days or more and can be fed bits of meat, insects, or cottage cheese.

Reproduction: L. borealis breeds in August and September (Hamilton, 1943; Stuewer, 1948; Layne, 1958; Glass 1966). Apparently copulation is initiated in flight; there are several reports of copulating pairs being seen as they fall to the ground. Murphy and Nichols (1913) recounted an observation on two individuals that were seen to join in flight. One made several attempts to alight upon the other. It finally succeeded, and the two remained together about half a minute, flying unsteadily the while, with all four wings beating. Whether or not reproductive activity occurs in winter, as it does in several other species, is unknown.

Apparently the sperm are stored in the uterus through the winter and fertilization occurs in the spring, as is usual in vespertilionid bats. Jackson (1961) estimated a gestation period of 80 to 90 days in Wisconsin. He said the young are born completely hairless, with eyes closed, and weigh about one-half gram each. This weight seems unusually small. One of us (WHD) shot a specimen containing three embryos each 23 mm. in crown to rump length; such embryos would weigh considerably more than half a gram.

Counts of embryos from 45 specimens of the eastern race show a single individual with one embryo, 4 with 2 embryos, 24 with 3, and 16 with 4, for an average of 3.2 embryos per bat (Cockrum, 1955; Layne, 1958; Jennings, 1958).

Parturition occurs in the latter part of May and early June in southern Illinois (Layne, 1958), and at about the same time in Florida (Jennings, 1958). In Iowa the young are born in June and early July (McClure, 1942). The number of young in a litter ranges from 1 to 4 and averages about 2.3 (McClure, 1942; Constantine, 1966a). This is less than the average number of 3.2 embryos. Discrepancies could be due to intra-uterine mortality and resorption, or high mortality among the young. Blue jays persistently prey on these bats and likely take a heavy toll of young.

Care of the Young: The mother bat hangs during the day with her young, but she does not support the entire weight of the family. Each young clasps the mother with its wings but hangs from a twig or leaf by one or both feet (Johnson, 1932). In the evening the mother leaves the young behind as she forages for food.

Young bats have been found clinging to their mothers in Iowa at various times from June 28 to August 24, but many families had dispersed as early as July 17 (McClure, 1942). The growing young were observed exercising every hour of the day. They stretched their wings, wiggled, swung, yawned, washed themselves, and licked their mother's face (Johnson, 1932; McClure, 1942). When the air temperature rose above 90° F. (32° C.) the bats cooled themselves by hanging stretched to full length, with the wings slightly drooped. At any disturbance they contracted into bundles. In August, family clusters under observation disappeared one by one (McClure, 1942).

Occasionally a red bat is shot in the evening while carrying one or two young (e.g., Golley, 1966). Probably in such instances bats are moving their young from one roost to another, as is known to occur in many species. Unfortunately, such observations have led numerous authors (e.g., Poole, 1932; Hamilton, 1943; Burt, 1954; Schwartz and Schwartz, 1959; Doutt *et al.*, 1966; Peterson, 1966) to the conclusion that the mother bat carries her brood while feeding. Peterson said they cling to her in flight until their combined weight exceeds hers. Schwartz and Schwartz said that a female is known to have carried in flight four young whose combined weight exceeded her own. We know of no basis for these statements, and we suspect that they are erroneous. *L. borealis* detects flying insects by echolocation and captures them in flight with a wingtip or occasionally the interfemoral membrane. It is doubtful whether a bat could perform this feat with young clinging to her.

Growth and Development: No data are available concerning growth rates. Hamilton (1943) implies that the young are weaned at one month of age, and Jackson (1961) said that they become able to fly at an age of five or six weeks. Probably these figures are estimates. Our estimate is that they fly at three to four weeks and are weaned at five to six weeks of age. Jones *et al.* (1967) reported that in Kansas, where young are born in late May and in June, the first flying young were shot the last of June.

Migration: This species is generally considered to be highly migratory. Several accounts detail their arrival, sometimes in groups of 100 or more, aboard ship 100 miles or so off the Atlantic coast in autumn. Migration patterns are unknown, however, and there are few records of movements of individual bats.

At San Francisco *L. borealis* is resident through the winter

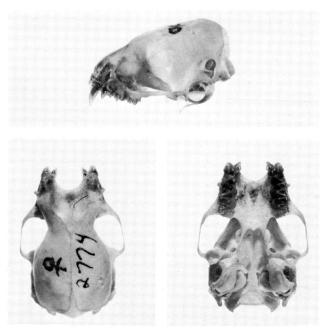

Skull of *Lasiurus borealis*, x3

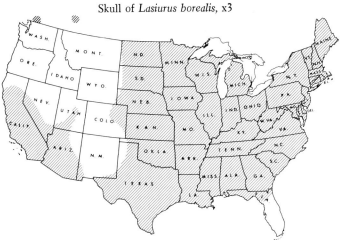

Distribution of *Lasiurus borealis* in the United States

137

from September to May but is absent in summer (Orr, 1950b). About 70 miles to the northeast, in Yolo County, it is absent in winter but appears in February or March (Constantine, 1959). In the eastern United States there is probably a general southward movement in fall. A specimen we banded in central Kentucky in August was later found dead in the Texas Panhandle. Circumstances suggest it may have been carried by a truck hauling grain from the Texas coast. There are several reports of these bats among the thousands of migrating birds killed by striking the Empire State Building and various television towers.

Late fall and winter records from West Virginia to Missouri are all males (Davis and Lidicker, 1956), as are all specimens taken in southeastern Arkansas in winter (Baker and Ward, 1967). At Urbana, Illinois, the earliest spring records include both sexes (Davis and Lidicker, 1956). In Florida 73 of 101 adults taken were females (Jennings, 1958). Jones *et al.* (1967) suggested that eastern Kansas, where *L. borealis* is abundant

76. Dead red bat, *Lasiurus borealis,* impaled on the top strand of a barbed wire fence in Illinois. *(Courtesy of Stephen Humphrey)*

in summer, is primarily a nursery area, with the population consisting almost entirely of adult females and their young. Grinnell (1918) thought that the males in California migrate to the higher altitudes to spend the summer. These data suggest differential migration, and different summer and winter ranges for the sexes. A thorough analysis of data available in collections would clarify the situation.

Predation and Accidents: L. borealis falls victim to a variety of predators and accidents. Opossums, roadrunners, sharp-shinned hawks, sparrow hawks, and great horned owls are known to feed on them, but blue jays are perhaps the most important predators (Hoffmeister and Downes, 1964). Jays are probably particularly destructive of the young (Allan, 1947; Elwell, 1962). There are numerous reports of this species, as well as *L. cinereus,* being impaled on the barbs of a wire fence. In nearly every instance a barb of the top strand of wire pierced the interfemoral membrane (fig. 76). Red bats sometimes are found entangled in ripe burdock. Koestner (1942) gathered 15 red bats entrapped in oil on a 500-foot stretch of road in Illinois in September. The road was heavily oiled, and probably a migrating group mistook it for water.

Remarks: Hall (1955) recounted how a family of red bats was mistaken for a peach. While picking peaches a person grasped the bat and her three partly grown young; their yellowish color flecked with white caused the mistake. Hall observed the group of bats himself and noted that the resemblance to a ripe peach was indeed remarkable.

The western race of the red bat is known occasionally to congregate during migration. In August Constantine (1959) found a cluster of 3 and a group of about 15 in an apricot orchard in California. Grinnell (1918) reported one taken from among many of its kind in a tree in Fresno in April.

Orr (1950b) reported up to four occupying a clump of *Sparmannia africana* through the winter in San Francisco.

Quay and Miller (1955) reported an erythrocyte count of 17.63×10^6 cells per mm^3. in a male taken in summer, and Dunaway and Lewis (1965) found an average of 19.61×10^6 in five individuals. These numbers are considerably higher than those found in other species of bats and are about four times as great as in man. This may represent an adaptation to the environmental stresses to which red bats are exposed. Dunaway and Lewis (1965) suggested that perhaps the hemapoietic system of *L. borealis* has evolved in response to the severe metabolic demands that arise during cold weather.

Jackson (1961) found that parasites include fleas, bat bugs, trematodes, cestodes, and a protozoan.

LASIURUS SEMINOLUS [Rhoads]
Seminole bat; mahogany bat

Recognition: Forearm, 35–45 mm.; wingspread, about 300 mm. A medium-sized bat with long, pointed wings and short, rounded ears. Interfemoral membrane heavily furred dorsally. Color deep mahogany, sometimes tipped with silver. Sexes similar.

Confusing Species: It appears identical to *Lasiurus borealis*, except for color; the latter is red or yellowish. *Lasiurus cinereus* is gray and larger. *Lasiurus intermedius* and *Lasiurus ega* are yellowish, larger, and lack fur on the posterior half of the interfemoral membrane.

Range: In summer, from the southern tip of North Carolina along the coast through Texas into Mexico. Distribution nearly coincides with that of Spanish moss, *Tillandsia usneoides*. In August, a few wander northward; they have been taken in Oklahoma, Arkansas, Pennsylvania, and New York. It winters in the Deep South; northern limits unknown.

Habitat: The interior of the clumps of Spanish moss which festoon the trees of the Deep South is the favored roost of *L. seminolus* during most of the year. Jennings (1958) took 69 seminole bats from moss plants in Florida, finding them in all months except July, August, and September. He found but few litters in the Spanish moss, and suggested that they do not rear their young there as exclusively as does *L. intermedius*.

Constantine (1958b) observed seminole bats at their roosts

77. Seminole bat, *Lasiurus seminolus.*

Distribution of *Lasiurus seminolus* in the United States

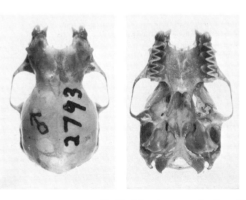

Skull of *Lasiurus seminolus,* x3

78. Ventral view of a seminole bat, *Lasiurus seminolus,* asleep in a grape-vine.

in their natural habitat in southwestern Georgia. He located 23 bats at roosting spots. Most were found on the southwest side of trees and all but one inhabited the interior of a moss clump. Bats were found in February, March and April, but none was located in May or June. Inhabited clumps of Spanish moss were hanging over ground covered with dead leaves, which minimized reflected sunlight. The area beneath the bat was always clear of limbs, and the occupied tree usually bordered a clearing. The height of the roosts was from 3½ to 15 feet above the ground. The bats were always solitary, but different individuals sometimes occupied the same clump on different days. They were also found at roosts later occupied by *L. borealis* and *L. intermedius*. Why they chose these particular spots is difficult to understand, for there were many moss clumps available in situations which seemed identical to the observer.

Behavior: In a large part of the South this is the most abundant bat seen flying in the evening. They may be seen at all seasons, even on warm evenings in mid-winter. Constantine (1958b) found that they did not arouse and fly until the air temperature rose to about 70° F. (21° C.). One individual did not fly when the air temperature rose to 65° F. (18° C.) at dusk, and another failed to fly after the temperature rose to 66° F. (19° C.). Jennings (1958) noted that they rarely flew when the temperature was below 64° F. (18° C.).

L. seminolus emerges early in the evening from its daytime roost and usually feeds at treetop level, some 20–45 feet above ground. The flight is direct and usually rather swift. Harper (1927) said that in the Okefenokee Swamp they forage over watercourses, pine barrens, clearings, and to a lesser extent over prairies and hammocks.

Food and Feeding: *L. seminolus* feeds on insects which it captures on the wing around and in the tree canopy. One was observed feeding on insects attracted to the flower spikes of a cabbage palm, *Sabal palmetto*. It circled continuously, but each time it passed the palm it landed for a few seconds on a horizontal frond and quickly captured an insect. On several occasions these bats have been noted flying repeatedly into gaps in the tree canopy where they fed on swarms of hovering insects. They have been seen catching insects at street lights (Jennings, 1958). On a late afternoon in December, Sherman (1935) shot one that held in its teeth a struggling cricket, *Gryllus assimilis*; apparently they occasionally feed on the ground, for this is a flightless cricket. Hamilton (1943) said that they eat various species of Homoptera, Diptera, and Coleoptera.

Captivity: Constantine (1958b) kept a *L. seminolus* in captivity for a short time. It ate cooked liver, boiled egg, and crickets and drank readily from a dish. In the evening the bat flew about in the building where it was kept and occasionally flew along the floor, dragging its chin on the shiny surface as if to drink, apparently mistaking the smooth floor for a pond. We have noted similar behavior in several species of captive bats and it has also been reported by Griffin (1958).

Reproduction: Jennings (1958) believes most births occur before the second week of June in Florida. All of 26 females shot in Alachua and Levy counties on June 7 and 8 had already given birth. Large embryos were found from May 21 to June 18. Counts from 21 pregnant females showed one with a single embryo, one with 2, 9 with 3, and 10 with 4 embryos for an average of 3.3.

Population Dynamics: Males made up only 38 percent of the 588 *L. seminolus* collected in Florida. Jennings believes this is due to higher mortality among males. Using tooth wear, he separated the sample into five age classes. The sexes were nearly equal in the two youngest age groups, but females predominated heavily in the older three.

Migration: Barkalow (1948) studied *L. seminolus* and *L. borealis* at Auburn, Alabama, over a period of several years and concluded that *L. seminolus* in the northern part of the breeding range in Alabama makes a definite shift southward in fall and winter. He found the two species equally abundant in spring and summer, but no *L. seminolus* in winter when a few *L. borealis* were seen on warm days. The fact that the latter arouse and fly at lower temperatures could also account for his winter observations.

L. seminolus, like several other species, apparently wanders extensively after the young are weaned, as indicated by late summer records outside the breeding range.

Remarks: The remarkable similarity between *L. seminolus* and *L. borealis* poses a difficult problem concerning the taxonomy of the two forms. Although most authorities agree that they probably represent two species, no one has yet been able to demonstrate any visible difference between them other than color. Clearly they are not subspecies, since the breeding ranges of the two overlap broadly and the forms do not intergrade. The possibility that the two are simply color phases has not been disproved, although it seems unlikely, since the two forms occupy distinctive ranges and mixed litters have not been found. Writers discussing the problem (Howell, 1921; Barkalow, 1948; Coleman, 1950; Davis, 1957; Jennings, 1958) all agree that intermediate forms are unknown. Koopman *et al.* (1957) studying the closely related insular form,

Lasiurus minor, in the Bahamas, found that these bats ranged in color from that typical of *L. borealis* to the color of *L. seminolus*, and included some intermediates. They said that on the mainland intermediates between the latter two forms certainly occur, but they cited no specimens to support this statement. We have never seen an intermediate specimen. Alleged intermediates which we have examined were female *L. borealis* which can be matched for color in any extensive collection of this species from the eastern United States. All *L. seminolus* that we have seen are readily recognizable and show little resemblance in color to *L. borealis*.

Although Spanish moss provides an excellent day roost for this species, as well as pipistrelles and yellow bats, it is sometimes responsible for tragedy to the inhabitants. Dunaway (1960) found an individual which had been strangled by several strands of Spanish moss twisted tightly around its neck. It was found dead beneath a sweet gum tree in South Carolina.

Seminole bats are abundant in the Deep South. Being familiar with the species and having shot them in Louisiana, Georgia, and Florida, we thought it would be rather easy to capture one alive. However, it developed that they were difficult to net because they never flew near the ground. One August night in Florida we stretched four nets among the trees, over a pond, and over a bayou, but caught no bats. Next night the nets were raised to about 10 feet with bamboo fishing poles, but the bats still flew over them. Finally one pole was attached to a chimney on the roof of a house and the other to a nearby tree branch, with a net stretched between them, high above the roof. An hour after dark we caught a specimen. Holes in the net next morning indicated that two other bats had been caught but chewed out.

Macrotus waterhousii,
Leaf-nosed bat

Mormoops megalophylla,
Leaf-chinned bat

Leptonycteris nivalis,
Mexican long-tongued bat

Choeronycteris mexicana,
Hog-nosed bat

Leptonycteris sanborni,
Sanborn's long-tongued bat

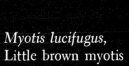

Myotis lucifugus,
Little brown myotis

Myotis grisescens,
Gray myotis

Myotis austroriparius,
Southeastern myotis

Myotis occultus,
Arizona myotis

Myotis velifer,
Cave myotis

Myotis auriculus,
Mexican long-eared myotis

Myotis keenii,
Keen's myotis

Myotis thysanodes,
Fringed myotis

Myotis evotis,
Long-eared myotis

Myotis sodalis,
Indiana myotis

Myotis volans,
Long-legged myotis

Myotis leibii,
Small-footed myotis

Lasionycteris noctivagans,
Silver-haired bat

Lasiurus seminolus,
Seminole bat

Pipistrellus subflavus,
Eastern pipistrelle

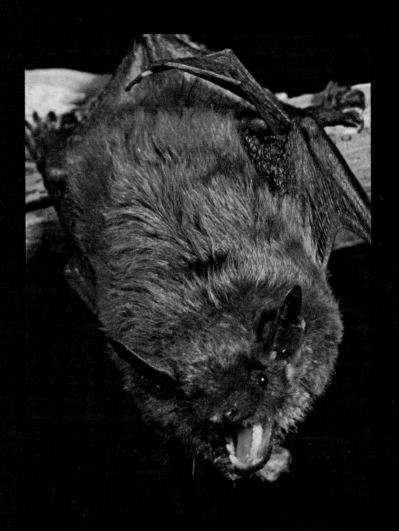

Eptesicus fuscus,
Big brown bat

Lasiurus borealis,
Red bat, male

Lasiurus borealis,
Red bat, female

Lasiurus cinereus,
Hoary bat

Lasiurus intermedius,
Northern yellow bat

Nycticeius humeralis,
Evening bat

Lasiurus ega,
Southern yellow bat

Euderma maculatum,
Spotted bat

Plecotus rafinesquii,
Rafinesque's big-eared bat

Plecotus townsendii,
Western big-eared bat

Plecotus phyllotis,
Allen's big-eared bat

Antrozous pallidus,
Desert pallid bat

Tadarida femorosacca,
Pocketed free-tailed bat

Tadarida macrotis,
Big free-tailed bat

Eumops perotis,
Western mastiff bat

Tadarida brasiliensis,
Brazilian free-tailed bat

Eumops underwoodi
Underwood's mastiff bat

Eumops glaucinus,
Wagner's mastiff bat

LASIURUS CINEREUS [Palisot de Beauvois]
Hoary bat

79. Hoary bat, *Lasiurus cinereus*, in Arizona.

Recognition: Forearm, 46–58 mm.; wingspread, 380–410 mm. A large, dark-colored, heavily furred bat. Dorsal surface of interfemoral membrane completely furred. Ears are relatively short and rounded and edged with black. Tips of many hairs are white, giving an overall frosted, hoary appearance.

Variation: Two subspecies occur in the United States. *Lasiurus cinereus cinereus* (Palisot de Beauvois) shows remarkably little variation across North America. A smaller, more reddish race, *Lasiurus cinereus semotus* (H. Allen), is restricted to several of the Hawaiian Islands.

Confusing Species: This species is not easily confused with any other American bat. The only other one resembling it is the much smaller silver-haired bat, *Lasionycteris noctivagans*, which lacks fur on the feet, ears, and underside of the wings.

Range: This is the most widespread of all our bats. It probably occurs in all 50 states, although it has not yet been recorded from Alaska. It ranges from Hawaii, the tundra of Southampton Island, Iceland and the Orkney Islands, southward through Central and South America to Chile, Argentina, and Uruguay. There are also records from Bermuda and the Dominican Republic.

The hoary bat is rare throughout most of the eastern United States, becoming more common in the prairie states. Records are scarce in the northern Rockies but more frequent in the Pacific northwest. Only in southern California, Arizona, and

143

New Mexico is it a common animal, and its occurrence in these regions is seasonal.

The breeding range is across Canada and the north central and northeastern United States, south at least to Kansas and Kentucky, perhaps to Arkansas, Louisiana, and Georgia. It winters in southern California, southeastern United States, and probably much of Mexico. December records from Michigan, Connecticut, and New York, and a January record from Indiana suggest some may winter even farther north than *Lasiurus borealis*.

Habitat: L. cinereus spends the summer days concealed in the foliage of trees. They choose a leafy site well covered above but open from beneath, generally 10–15 feet above the ground (Constantine, 1966a) and usually at the edge of a clearing. There is an unusual record of a specimen found in a woodpecker hole high in a tree in British Columbia (Cowan and Guiguet, 1965). In late summer they sometimes wander into caves; many of these never find their way out (Myers, 1960).

Because it almost never enters houses, spends the daylight hours well concealed, and is generally rare, this magnificent bat is seldom encountered by man.

Behavior: The flight is swift and more direct than that of the smaller bats. Its flight pattern and great size make it readily identifiable on the wing anywhere in the United States except where the largest free-tailed bats occur.

The hoary bat generally emerges late in the evening. In the Southwest where it is abundant during June, we never saw one in flight except in the light of our headlamps. In some instances, however, they emerge before dark. Like L. borealis they sometimes awaken and fly during late afternoon on warm days in winter. There seems also to be a tendency toward early flight during migration (Dalquest, 1943; Hall, 1946). We have shot these bats at dusk in April and May in the East.

Except for *Eptesicus fuscus*, this is the only one of our vespertilionid bats which regularly utters an audible chattering sound during flight. Although we have often heard them chattering as they approached our nets, they sometimes came in silently.

Food and Feeding: Almost nothing is known of the feeding habits of this species. Poole (1932) reported finding remains of a large bug and a mosquito in the stomach of one shot in Pennsylvania. Dalquest (1953) watched one chasing a large moth. He noted that the stomach contents of hoary bats he examined were not as finely ground as in the smaller bats. Whitaker (1967) found grass and a snakeskin in the alimentary canal of one collected in Indiana in winter. Perhaps hoary bats occasionally feed on their smaller relatives. Bishop (1947) saw one attacking a pipistrelle in New York, and one was seen to pursue a western pipistrelle in California (Orr, 1950a).

Captivity: This species generally does poorly in captivity. However, Jackson (1961) gave an account of one which was kept for six weeks and became tame. It was fed live mealworms, moths and beetles. Rollin Baker once kept a hoary bat in captivity for two weeks. Dead mice which were cut open and given it were devoured.

Reproduction: Available data indicate that in every case litter size is two. Parturition dates probably range from the middle of May into early July (Gottschang, 1966; Provost and Kirkpatrick, 1952).

The mother gives birth to her young while hanging in the leafy shelter of her daytime retreat. A newborn young is blind and has a forearm length of 18–19 mm. Its skin is brown, darker on the body than on the wings, and lighter beneath.

144

The throat and head are pale, approaching buffish, and the hind feet and thumbs are nearly black. The fur covering the dorsal surface is prominent and is noticeably tipped with white (Munyer, 1967).

Care of the Young: After birth the young cling tightly to the mother through the day, but are left clinging to a twig or leaf while she forages at night. The family generally occupies the same roost, but after disturbance the mother may move her babies to a new location.

Poole (1932) shot a hoary bat in the evening as she was carrying her young in flight. They weighed 5.25 g. each. Their eyes were unopened and he judged the babies to be less than a week old.

Like *L. borealis*, this bat sometimes comes to the attention of man when the female and her young fall from a day roost. Unable to fly with the two large youngsters, the female is nearly helpless on the ground. Two of the three records from Lexington, Kentucky, are of such family groups, and finds of this sort are frequent in other areas.

McClure (1942) studied a family of hoary bats in Lewis, Iowa, during the summer of 1940. An adult was first noticed clinging to the limb of a Norway spruce on May 13; the roost was occupied thereafter almost every day. She gave birth to two young about June 12. On July 9 the group was missing; probably the young could fly by then. On July 10 all three had returned, but two days later they were gone. Constantine (1966a) noted that two youngsters were still suckling and incapable of efficient flight on July 30.

Migration: *L. cinereus* is one of our most accomplished migrants. Like many species of birds they move in waves. Waves of migrants have been noted at Cape Cod in August and September (Miller, 1897a), in California in August, Sep-

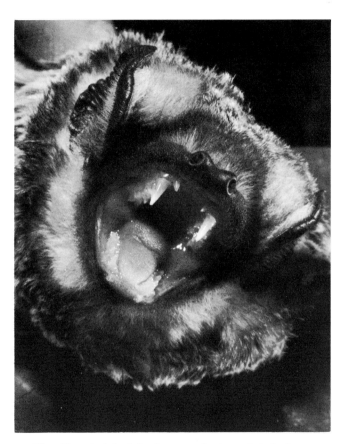

80. Characteristic defensive pose of a hoary bat, *Lasiurus cinereus.*

145

tember, and May (Tenaza, 1966; Vaughan, 1954), in Nevada in August (Hall, 1946), and in New Mexico in May and June (Findley and Jones, 1964).

Miller (1897a) watched bats from the lighthouse on the sandy point of Cape Cod from the last week of August through the middle of September. He saw numerous *L. cinereus, L. borealis*, and *Lasionycteris noctivagans* about the lighthouse and shot several. Since the spot is unfavorable for tree bats, they were probably migrants.

Tenaza (1966) observed migrants on South Farallon Island about 30 miles west of San Francisco. There were only three small trees, and bats which found themselves on the island at daybreak had little choice of roosting sites and were easily located. Observations were made daily from August 30 to September 8. The number of bats fluctuated from none on three days to 18 and 21 on others. This suggests migratory waves of bats visiting the island. Tenaza also noted a tendency of the bats to collect in certain areas in the trees. Most were hanging in groups of two to seven, the individuals being a few inches apart. Ordinarily *L. cinereus* at their day roosts are solitary except when with young.

Vaughan (1954) caught males with a wire stretched over a pond in southern California in May. On the evening of May 25, 1951, they were especially abundant and he caught 22. He caught only a few on several subsequent nights.

Hall (1946) described a flight seen in late afternoon of August 28, 1932, in Nevada. The bats were flying among cottonwood trees and the total number was estimated as 200–300. The two collected were males.

Findley and Jones (1964) noted migratory waves in May and June in New Mexico. On the nights of May 13 and 14, 1960, they netted 48 hoary bats at Glenwood. The largest numbers were captured during June, and very few were taken in August and September despite intensive netting. Mumford netted 35 on June 24, 1962, near Portal in the Chiracahua Mountains of Arizona. We netted 59 at the same locality on June 18, 1966.

The sexes are apparently segregated throughout most of the summer range, and in some areas during spring migration. Adult males are extremely rare or absent in the nursery range of the eastern and central United States and across the prairie provinces of Canada. The males are essentially limited to the western states at this time (Findley and Jones, 1964; Dalquest, 1943), but both sexes occur in the Black Hills of South Dakota in summer (Jones and Genoways, 1967b).

In New Mexico the females move through, apparently going north, in April and May. Findley and Jones captured 32 pregnant females in two nights in the middle of May. By June the females had left the region. All the more than 200 *L. cinereus* netted there during June were males.

Both sexes occur in southern California during spring migration. Vaughan and Krutzsch (1954) suggested that an altitudinal separation exists there, with the males moving through the foothills and mountains and the females in the lowlands and coastal valleys.

In autumn the sexes are found together. Tenaza (1966) found both sexes on South Farallon Island in the early fall. In New Mexico, there are several records of each sex in September and October but no migratory waves or peaks like those in spring have been discovered (Findley and Jones, 1964).

Although strong circumstantial evidence for migration of this species is abundant, we as yet have no direct evidence of specific movements or migration paths or patterns. Few individuals have been banded and we know of no recoveries.

Remarks: This is the only species of bat to have reached the Hawaiian Islands where it is known from Hawaii, Kauai, and

Oahu. Nixon Wilson says that there are no recent records from Oahu, but the bat is still very common on Hawaii. A Honolulu newspaper recently reported a bat captured on Maui.

The bats have evidently been on the island for a long time; the population constitutes a well defined geographic race. P. Quentin Tomich, of the Hawaii Department of Health, once showed us a series of these bats which he had collected. Although their close relationship to *L. cinereus* of North America is evident, obvious differences occur. Many are more reddish than any found on the continent, although some individuals from Hawaii match some from the mainland.

Baldwin (1950) studied the Hawaiian bat over a period of 11 years. He found them during all seasons, and although they ranged from sea level to 13,200 feet, they were noted most frequently below 4,000 feet elevation. Bats were seen in both dry and wet areas with yearly rainfall averages of from 20 to 90 inches. They were not found in the dense rain forests, apparently preferring a habitat of open or mixed character. Open bodies of water or trees did not seem to be essential. In the middle uplands they were noted in partly wooded places where openings such as pastures or lava flows interrupted the forest. Occasionally they flew over sparsely vegetated or barren deserts, such as parts of the Kau Desert and the summit area of Mauna Loa.

Ordinarily they appeared after the sun had set or gone behind the mountains. Five were seen between 3:00 and 5:30, near the mouth of Waipio Valley, on November 17, 1948. The sun set about five o'clock. In flight the tail was curved forward under the body. This contrasts with the behavior of *L. borealis* which holds the tail straight in flight, except when capturing an insect.

The only data available on reproduction of the Hawaiian race are from reproductive tracts of two females. One taken in May had two fetuses; the other, in November, had none.

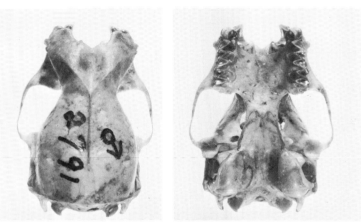

Skull of *Lasiurus cinereus*, x3

Distribution of *Lasiurus cinereus* in the United States

The Hawaiian bat was first introduced to science by Gray (1862) at a meeting of the Zoological Society of London. He read a letter from W. H. Pease of Honolulu, dated November 20, 1861, which stated that he was sending a specimen and skull of the bat found in the Islands. He said that it was the only mammal indigenous to the Islands and was quite a curiosity to the natives, very few of whom had ever seen one. Gray did not describe the animal as new; he compared it with *L. cinereus* from Chile and recognized it as being the same species. He noted that the bat was interesting in that it showed a similarity in the fauna of the Islands to that of the western coast of South America.

The occurrence of this bat in Hawaii poses some interesting questions: how and why did it alone of the bats establish itself in the Islands? This large bat is a powerful flier and apparently an accomplished migrant; if any bat could get there it should be this species. Its wanderings are so extensive that it is difficult to determine what marginal records are within its normal range and which are accidentals. Surely the four records from the southwest coast of Iceland in October and December, and the single record from the Orkney Islands in September are of migrants which had gone astray. The pregnant animal found on June 17 at Southampton Island, Northwest Territories, likely was beyond its normal summer range. The island is typical tundra, over 500 miles north of the tree line. The fact that the natives there had never seen a bat indicates that its occurrence was unusual. However, there is an additional record of this species seen in the Northwest Territories by Seton on July 12, 1907 (Hitchcock, 1943).

Hoary bats occur in the Bermuda Islands at least in spring and fall. Van Gelder and Wingate (1961) suggested that these records resulted from the influence of storms, implying that the Bermudas are not within the normal range. A specimen was taken in the Dominican Republic in March and perhaps some individuals winter in the Caribbean (Findley and Jones, 1964). Netting in Cuba during the winter might produce interesting results.

L. cinereus with its larger size and more luxuriant fur seems better adapted to withstand the cold than its close relative, *L. borealis*, which apparently winters in trees as far north as the Ohio River Valley. Unfortunately, the rarity of hoary bats makes winter observations scarce. One was seen flying at midday in a Pennsylvania forest during a February thaw (Hamilton, 1943). There is apparently little useful information regarding the two December records from the northern states (Allen, 1962). The only report of apparent hibernation concerns an individual found in a squirrel nest in Georgia (Neill, 1952). Although no date was given, the bat was said to be "apparently numbed by the cold, and could only buzz loudly and show its teeth."

The scarcity of this species may be more apparent than real, for it usually takes to the wing much later at night than other species, and mist netting has shown it to be rather common in areas where it was previously unknown. Baker and Ward (1967) captured 14, including 4 in one night, by netting at night over ponds in southeastern Arkansas in July and August. It was unknown from the Chiracahua Mountains of Arizona before mist netting was begun there in 1955 (Cockrum and Ordway, 1959), yet we took more hoary bats than any other species while netting there in June 1966. We banded 201 bats in Arizona and New Mexico during this month, and E. Lendell Cockrum and his students at the University of Arizona have banded many in recent years.

L. cinereus is easy to net. The lasiurines rarely give any indication of being aware of a net, whereas most bats detect and avoid it more frequently than not. When catching these beautiful animals over water in Arizona, our lights would frequently reveal one as it made passes over the net and across the pond. We could predict with some confidence that the bat would soon hit the net and we would get ready, for if a hoary bat bounces off the net into the water, he pauses but a few seconds in obvious surprise before he launches himself with a single mighty thrust of the wings against the water.

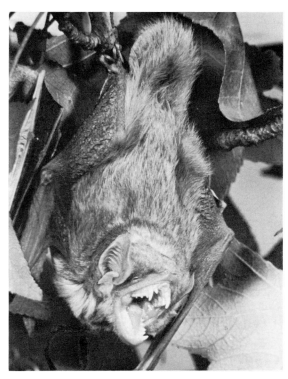

81. Yellow bat, *Lasiurus intermedius.* The yellow bats have more pointed ears than the other lasiurines.

LASIURUS INTERMEDIUS H. Allen

Northern yellow bat; eastern yellow bat

Recognition: Forearm, 45–56 mm.; wingspread, 350–390 mm. A large bat with long wings, short ears, and an interfemoral membrane furred on the anterior half of the dorsal surface. Color variable, but generally yellowish, ranging from yellowish orange through yellow brown to nearly gray; tips of hairs often gray or brown.

Variation: Two subspecies are recognized in the United States. *Lasiurus intermedius intermedius* H. Allen is known from the lower Rio Grande Valley. A smaller, less brightly colored race, *Lasiurus intermedius floridanus* (Miller) occurs in the Southeast. Geographic variation in color and size is seen in this race when specimens from Louisiana and Florida are compared.

For many years the two subspecies in the United States were considered separate species. Hall and Jones (1961) found them to be only subspecifically distinct.

Confusing Species: This large yellow bat could not easily be confused with any other species occupying its range within the United States. The eastern pipistrelle is much smaller. *Lasiurus borealis* is smaller with ears more rounded, is usually more brightly colored, and lacks yellow hues. In southern Texas the similar southern yellow bat, *Lasiurus ega*, may occur; however, in this region a large race of *L. intermedius* occurs (forearm 51–56 mm.), and the two species could be separated on the basis of size.

Distribution of *Lasiurus intermedius* in the United States

82. Yellow bat, *Lasiurus intermedius*, from Louisiana.

150

Range: Lasiurus intermedius floridanus occurs in the southeastern United States from southeastern Virginia along the coast to eastern Texas and inland as far as Austin. There is a record of an apparently accidental autumn wanderer from New Jersey. *Lasiurus i. intermedius* ranges from extreme southern Texas through the lowlands of eastern Mexico to Honduras, and up the west coast as far as the Mexican state of Sinaloa.

The distribution of the eastern race nearly coincides with that of Spanish moss, *Tillandsia usneoides,* in which the animal lives. On the East Coast the distribution pattern of this bat remains obscure. North of South Carolina it is known from only two specimens—one from Norfolk, Virginia, and one from Westfield, New Jersey. The New Jersey specimen, an adult male captured flying in a garage on the night of October 16, 1964, was surely a transient far beyond its normal range. The one from Norfolk, however, contained three embryos and was found hanging in a tree on May 8, a time at which bats are not known to wander beyond their normal breeding range. In Florida it is known from all parts of the state except the Everglades and the Keys. It is one of the few species to occupy the coastal ridge down to Miami. Apparently, it is a permanent resident through its range.

The southern race, *L. i. intermedius,* is known from the United States only in the lower Rio Grande Valley, where it has been found in the tall palms from April to November (Davis, 1960). There is a gap of about 250 miles of nearly treeless country between the known ranges of the two races; this area may be unsuitable for the species.

Habitat: In the United States this species is closely associated with Spanish moss in which it roosts and bears its young. The yellow bat is abundant in the highlands of central Florida from Pinellas to Highlands counties where orange groves and pastures dominate the landscape. In much of this area it is the most abundant bat, inhabiting the stands of long-leaf pine and turkey oak. A single oak, festooned with Spanish moss, may harbor several of these bats. It is not unusual to see a flight of them emerging from a grove of moss-draped trees in the evening. Many have been captured by professional moss gatherers (Jennings, 1958). A worker once gathered about 20 yellow bats, including mothers and young, from a grove of live oaks less than an acre in extent. More than 30 additional bats escaped, many of them carrying young.

In Veracruz, Mexico, *L. intermedius* has been found in groups hidden among dried corn stalks hanging from the sides of large open tobacco sheds. On July 22, 1955, about 45 were flushed from one such shed and 5 from another; they emerged singly or in groups of as many as 8. Most of them occupied the row of stalks nearest the roof, and only the south and east sides were used. The 15 specimens collected indicated that these were nursery colonies (Baker and Dickerman, 1956).

In the lower Rio Grande Valley, groups of these bats are reported to live among the lower dead leaves of palm trees, where their presence is betrayed by their droppings on the ground and their noisy bickering during the day (Davis, 1960). The existence of 59 specimens of this species from Brownsville, Texas, (Miller, 1897b) suggests that an early collector may have encountered a colony.

Behavior: The species was studied extensively in Florida by Jennings (1958), and most of our information about its life history comes from that source.

In Florida this bat characteristically forages 15–20 feet above the ground over open areas with few shrubs and only scattered tree clumps, or along the forest edge. Grassy areas such as airports, open pastures, golf courses, and lake edges are favored.

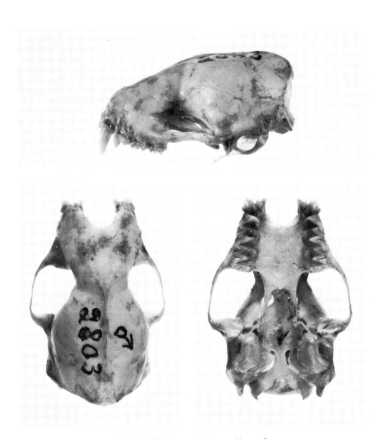

Skull of *Lasiurus intermedius,* x3

The bats are never abundant unless such open grassy areas are near the roosts.

In June, July, and August when the young are on the wing, *L. intermedius* form evening feeding aggregations. As many as 108 females and flying young have been shot in such a concentration area in a single evening, and several groups of 20–50 bats have been taken.

The sexes are segregated during a major part of the year in Florida, and adult males rarely appear in the feeding aggregations. Only 9 were among 130 yellow bats shot near Tampa in July 1953, and none was among the 231 taken in Pinellas County in July 1961. Probably the males are solitary and scattered at this season.

Apparently males congregate in winter. During two evenings in February 1956, 17 males were shot in Jefferson County, Florida, where U. S. Highway 98 crosses the Aucilla River. Just west of the river a dozen or more tall palms stand in the right of way of the road, apparently the only such trees for many miles. Perhaps the male yellow bats hibernate in these palms and emerge on warm evenings.

Reproduction: The extent of the mating season is unknown. In Florida males have enlarged epididymides in July and are reproductively active at least until mid-February. A copulating pair was captured when they fell on a road on November 23, 1957, and females taken in mid-December contained many sperm in the uteri.

Counts of embryos in the Florida race show eight females with 3 each and five with 4, for an average litter size of 3.4. Parturition ranges from about the last week of May through most of June. Newborn young were taken in mid-June, but some young could fly at that time. One young bat was shot while foraging on July 3, but another taken from a litter on July 20 had only milk in its stomach. Newborn young have a forearm length of about 16 mm. and weigh about 3 g.

Litter sizes of eight bats of the Florida race show 2 litters of 2 young and 6 of 3, for an average of 2.8. Young of the year made up 74 percent of the 89 yellow bats shot among nursery aggregations in Florida in August and September, a proportion which indicates a surviving litter size of about 2.8 at this time. Thus the mortality rate among the young seems lower than in *L. borealis* which also has a large litter size; however, Jennings' (1958) sample may be biased, for young bats are easier to shoot.

Davis (1960), referring to the race in the lower Rio Grande Valley, said that the litter size is usually two and that the young are born in May and June. He gave no evidence to support the statement. The only data we have found on reproduction in this race concerns a specimen taken three miles north of Mazatlan, in the Mexican state of Sinaloa. This animal, found roosting in a coco palm on June 30, 1962, carried two embryos measuring 25 mm. in crown–rump length (Loomis and Jones, 1964).

Care of the Young: As with other bats it is doubtful if the mother ever carries her young while feeding. No attached young were found on any of 84 lactating females shot while feeding in Florida. Mothers of three captive litters, confined to a screened porch for observation, left their young sleeping quietly in the Spanish moss when they flew at dusk. When disturbed during the day, however, all carried their young as they flew. This also happened frequently when mothers were flushed in the wild (Jennings, 1958).

Remarks: These bats are large enough to carry transmitters for radiotelemetry, which could provide information on the movements of individual bats. Information is also needed on the winter groups of males and the winter whereabouts of the females. This species is somewhat colonial, especially the females during the nursing season. Although the adults do not cluster, there is a tendency for a number of them to roost in the same shelter. More information is needed on group behavior.

In August of 1965 we attempted to capture L. *intermedius* near Freeport, Florida, where we saw one on each of several evenings. It flew above the treetops, usually made a single pass, and never lingered to feed with the L. *seminolus*. Because of the consistently high flight of the bats, we caught none in three nights. Finally we mounted a net on top of a house, and stretched it high above the roof. As darkness approached one of us stood beside the house with a long cane pole. With the butt of the pole firmly on the ground, the tip was swung vigorously from side to side, creating a swishing sound. Such noise seems to have some attraction for bats. Within a matter of seconds after the swishing began, a yellow bat crashed into the net and appeared to drop securely into a pocket. Although we reached the net within a few seconds, the bat had somehow escaped. A L. *seminolus* was captured later that night, but the L. *intermedius* apparently did not return. The only yellow bat we have handled alive was obtained from Richard K. LaVal who sent us one from Louisiana. He has found places near Baton Rouge where he can consistently net a yellow bat or two.

LASIURUS EGA [Gervais]
Southern yellow bat; western yellow bat

Recognition: Forearm, 45–48 mm.; wingspread, 335–355 mm. A rather large bat with gray-tipped yellow fur, long wings, short ears, and with the dorsal surface of the interfemoral membrane furred on the anterior half.

Variation: Several subspecies are recognized but only *Lasiurus ega xanthinus* (Thomas) is known from the United States. For nomenclature of this species see Handley (1960).

83. *Lasiurus ega,* in Cave Creek Canyon, Portal, Arizona.

153

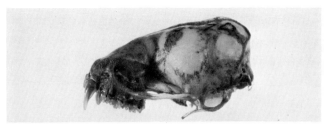

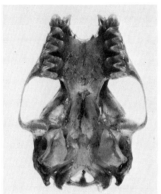

Skull of *Lasiurus ega*, x3

84. *Lasiurus ega* asleep.

Distribution of *Lasiurus ega* in the United States

154

Confusing Species: Quite similar to the larger Lasiurus inter-medius from which it is geographically separated in the United States. In southern Texas, the only place in the United States where the two might occur together, a large race (forearm 51–57 mm.) of L. intermedius occurs. It is also similar to Lasiurus borealis, which has a reddish or orange cast to the fur and has more rounded ears. Similar in color to Antrozous pallidus, which has much larger ears, and to the tiny Pipistrellus hesperus, which is much smaller.

Range: South America, from Uruguay and Argentina through Central America and tropical Mexico into southern California, Arizona, and extreme southwestern New Mexico. In eastern Mexico it ranges as far north as the border states of Tamaulipas and Coahuila and may some day be found in Texas. It is a permanent resident in the United States. It has been taken in Arizona during nine different months.

Habitat: Little is known regarding the habitat. Like other lasiurines it roosts by day in leafy vegetation. In New Mexico one was found roosting in a hackberry branch overhanging a road; the roosting site was 14 feet above the ground and well concealed from above. At dusk two other bats thought to be this species took flight from horizontal limbs of sycamores overhanging the road. These roosts were about 15 feet above the ground and 75 feet apart.

In Guadelupe Canyon, New Mexico, these bats have been taken in nets over water holes in an intermittent stream. In Cave Creek Canyon near Portal in the Chiracahua Mountains of Arizona, we encountered them in a similar situation during June 1966. They occurred here at an altitudinal range of 5,000 to 5,800 feet.

In Tucson they apparently hibernate among the dead fronds of the Washington fan palms.

Behavior: In San Luis Potosí, Mexico, Dalquest (1953) shot a L. ega which emerged at dusk from a grove of large cypress trees and flew slowly and steadily across a clearing. He also noted that those netted at night struck the nets at high speed. The stomachs of some netted two hours after dark were crammed with insect remains. One male shot in flight in New Mexico was flying in a straight line with slow wing beats about 75 feet above the ground (Mumford and Zimmerman, 1963).

Reproduction: Three pregnant females taken in New Mexico indicate that the litter size is two, and that parturition occurs about the second week of June. Four females netted over the Rio Cuchijaqui in southern Sonora on June 22, 1966, were lactating.

Remarks: This bat is known in the United States chiefly from the cities of Tucson and Phoenix. The first record in this country was an adult female collected while flying in the day-time at Palm Springs, California, on November 3, 1945. The species was next reported from Tucson where Cockrum (1961) obtained specimens in January and February 1960. These were captured by a crew of gardeners at the University of Arizona who were trimming dead palm fronds. The bats were hanging among these fronds. Five or six bats were seen and two adult females were captured and preserved. These bats have since been found to be fairly common residents of Tucson.

It was next noted in New Mexico where Mumford and Zimmerman (1963) captured eight specimens in Guadalupe Canyon in the extreme southwestern corner of the state.

Constantine (1966b) reported 10 specimens from Phoenix and suburbs and 1 from Yuma, collected during spring and fall months from 1960 through 1963. All were obtained by county health departments, and all those from the Phoenix area were either dead or dying when found.

This bat seems to be extending its range in the United States. On June 4, 1966, we netted a male over the swimming pool at the Southwest Research Station in the Chiracahua Mountains of Arizona and later saw two others momentarily in our nets over nearby Cave Creek. Yellow bats had never been encountered in the Chiracahua Mountains before, although the swimming pool and Cave Creek had been netted extensively (every night during one summer) by many workers during the past 10 years.

The pattern of appearance of this species in other parts of Arizona also suggests recent invasion. Extensive bat work had been in progress for several years at the University of Arizona before *L. ega* was first encountered there in 1960. If it is extending its range, one might next expect it in the cottonwood canyons of southern Nevada and southwestern Utah.

That this species may be migratory, in at least part of its range, is suggested by the capture of a specimen in late summer when it flew aboard a ship 208 miles off the coast of Argentina (Van Deusen, 1961).

85. Evening bat, *Nycticeius humeralis*, from Texas. The short rounded tragus distinguishes this species from all the *Myotis*.

NYCTICEIUS HUMERALIS [Rafinesque]

Evening bat; twilight bat

Recognition: Forearm, 33–39 mm.; wingspread, 260–280 mm. Females larger than males. A rather small brown bat, lacking distinctive external features. Calcar not keeled. Tragus short, curved, and rounded. The skull is broad, especially anteriorly. There are but two upper incisors.

Variation: Two races have been described from the United States. *Nycticeius humeralis humeralis* (Rafinesque) occupies most of the ranges of this species. A smaller, paler, more yellow-brown race, *Nycticeius humeralis subtropicalis* Schwartz occurs in subtropical Florida.

Confusing Species: This rather nondescript species can be readily separated from all other brown bats by the fact that it has but two upper incisors; all other brown bats have four. It looks like a small edition of the big brown bat, *Eptesicus fuscus,* but can be distinguished from it on the basis of size. It bears a superficial resemblance to *Myotis lucifugus* with which it has often been confused. The short curved, rounded tragus separates it from all eastern *Myotis.*

Range: Southeastern United States, from southern Pennsylvania and the eastern tip of West Virginia, south along the coast and in the piedmont to the Gulf Coast, including all of Florida except the Keys; south in Mexico to Veracruz. It ranges northward in the central states to Nebraska, central Iowa, southern Michigan, and Ontario and eastward to central Ohio. It is absent or extremely scarce in the western piedmont of the Appalachians in Kentucky, Ohio, and West Virginia. The winter range is unknown, although a few specimens have been taken in Florida in February (Jennings, 1958).

Habitat: N. *humeralis* inhabits buildings and cavities in trees in summer. Maternity colonies in houses often consist of hundreds of individuals. Smaller colonies have been found behind the loose bark of dead pines and in hollow cypress trees. Three adult females were taken from Spanish moss hanging from cypress trees bordering a lake in central Florida (Jennings, 1958). Winter habitat is completely unknown. Bats of this species accumulate large reserves of fat in autumn, sufficient for either hibernation or a long migration.

Behavior: N. *humeralis* emerges early and flies a slow and steady course. It is readily recognizable in flight by an experienced observer.

It is one of the very few bats which almost never enters caves, although it sometimes joins the bats swarming about certain entrances in late summer. We have captured six of these bats among the many thousands of bats netted during August just outside the entrance to Dixon Cave in Mammoth Cave National Park. Easterla (1965a) reported that Myers took a juvenile male *Nycticeius humeralis* in Bat Cave, Pulaski County, Missouri on August 19, 1957. We know of no other record of this species having been found in a cave.

In the southeastern states *Tadarida brasiliensis* and N. *humeralis* commonly inhabit the same building; the two usually form separate colonies but are sometimes intermingled.

Reproduction: The young are born in nursery colonies where females sometimes congregate in the hundreds. In Florida, Louisiana, and Alabama parturition occurs from the middle of May to mid-June.

Skull of *Nycticeius humeralis*, x3

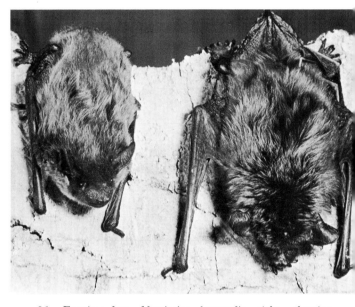

86. Evening bat, *Nycticeius humeralis*, right, showing superficial resemblance to the larger big brown bat, *Eptesicus fuscus*.

Distribution of *Nycticeius humeralis* in the United States

The usual litter size is two. A summary of data on embryo counts in various parts of the range shows 52 females with two each, 4 with one, 1 with three, and 1 with four. The one with three was taken in Florida in late May when the embryos were well developed, with forearm measurements of 7 mm. (Jennings, 1958). Perhaps three young would have been born to this bat. The one with four embryos was shot on May 12 in Alabama by Barkalow (1948), who did not give the size of the embryos. It is doubtful, however, if such a litter would have been delivered. In some species of bats the number of ova shed regularly outnumber the embryos that survive to parturition (Wimsatt, 1945).

Scant information is available on reproduction in the northern part of the range. Easterla (1965a) shot six pregnant evening bats in Missouri during the first week in June. Kunz (1965) took a lactating female on July 24 in Nebraska. Four pregnant females that we shot near Urbana, Illinois, during the last three days in May had embryos ranging from 7 to 13 mm.

The sexual cycle in the male has not been studied. Presumably spermatogenesis occurs in late summer. Baker and Ward (1967) found the testes enlarged in males taken in southeastern Arkansas in the latter part of August; they noted that the young of the year had testes as large as the adults, a fact which suggests that males may breed during their first year.

Growth and Development: Jones (1967) described birth and development in captive *N. humeralis*. As with most other species of bats, birth is by breech presentation. Births took from 3 to 114 minutes and most litters were dropped during the afternoon. The mothers ate the placentae and umbilical cords within 35 to 70 minutes after delivery. Placentae were eaten first and the cords then eaten to within 2 or 3 mm. of the navel area.

After the young are born they grasp a nipple within about five to eight minutes, clinging to it tenaciously. The newborn are pink, except for slight dark pigmentation on the feet, membranes, ears, and lips; their skin is so transparent that the viscera can be seen. A few hairs are present on the feet and back, and vibrissae are evident. Immediately after birth the bats begin to squeak. Within 24 hours the eyes open and heavy skin pigmentation appears.

The deciduous dentition is complete at birth. The permanent canines begin to break through at seven days and by four weeks the permanent dentition is completed.

At birth the ears are folded, but become erect within 24 to 36 hours. For the first two weeks, while the mother is at rest, the young remain attached to the nipples and are covered by her membranes. During the third week they become able to fly and at three weeks they can negotiate turns, land, and hang from the walls and ceiling of a room. They scamper freely about when disturbed, but hang adjacent to the mother when at rest. At this age they first show an interest in food by smelling and licking portions of insect larvae. By four weeks they are taking food and water presented to them in captivity. The young cease nursing at six to nine weeks.

Growth is rapid. The forearm grows from about 14 mm. at birth to the nearly adult range of 28–32 mm. within 30 days. As in many other species of bats the females are larger than males.

Captivity: This species takes to captivity fairly well. Gates (1941) fed them a mixture of eggs, cheese, and chopped mealworms and gave them water and milk to drink. Jones (1967) captured pregnant females, succeeded in keeping them in the laboratory, and raised 14 litters of young. He fed the bats mealworms by hand; only two adults ever learned to pick them up from the floor of the cage.

Movements: Apparently evening bats abandon the nursery colonies in the fall, although observations on this point are limited. Baker and Ward (1967) found only 3 torpid specimens in a building in Arkansas on March 21 where over 1,000 were present in August and where they were still plentiful in September. Perhaps they migrate, but the few recoveries among those banded by James Cope and his students in Indiana are insufficient to establish a pattern.

N. *humeralis* has the ability to return home after displacement. Cope and Humphrey (1967) found that many of the adults and a few juveniles returned to a nursery colony in Indiana after having been released 96 miles away.

Remarks: The distribution of this species is rather peculiar. Although generally southern, it ranges extensively through the Midwest. It can be seen flying about the campus of the University of Illinois on most summer evenings, and in many neighboring localities it is exceeded in numbers only by *Lasiurus borealis.*

In Kentucky we consider this bat to be rather scarce; it is definitely less common than in Indiana and Illinois. In spite of our intensive work with summer bat colonies, we know of no colonies of this species in Kentucky. We have seen but one specimen from the Lexington region and none from the hill country east of Lexington.

Throughout the southern coastal states this is one of the most common bats. It is found about the towns and also in areas far from human habitation. In the vast Everglades region in Florida it is the only bat known, being found anywhere that a few cypress trees occur. Considering its relative abundance remarkably little is known about this species. Careful observations of any phase of its life history would be of value.

87. Spotted bat, *Euderma maculatum.*

EUDERMA MACULATUM [J. A. Allen]

Spotted bat; pinto bat

Recognition: Forearm, 48–51 mm.; wingspread, unknown. A rather large bat with striking markings. Dorsal surface black with three large white spots, two in the shoulder region and one on the rump. Ears are larger than those of any other American bat. The markings are so distinctive that it could not be confused with any other species.

Range: Western North America. It is most frequently encountered in California, Arizona, New Mexico, southern Colorado, and southern Utah, with scattered records from other states, and it may be expected occasionally throughout the western United States. Several specimens have been netted in the Mexican state of Durango. The abundance and pattern of distribution are not yet understood. Winter range unknown.

Habitat: E. maculatum is one of the rarest species of bats in the United States. Little of its life history is known. Before 1958 there were only 16 known specimens in collections; these were all encountered accidentally, mostly under circumstances which gave little clue to the habits. During the last few years some collectors have succeeded in capturing specimens in mist nets, and a little information concerning the habitat has accumulated.

During June and July the spotted bat is a resident of the ponderosa pine region of the western highlands. David Easterla, however, has evidence suggesting that it prefers the cracks and crevices of high cliffs and canyons. Most specimens that have been netted have come from 6,000–8,000 feet elevation in New Mexico, Colorado, and Utah. In late summer and autumn the bats apparently wander to lower elevations. Several early records are from lowland deserts.

Behavior: E. maculatum is a late flyer like its big-eared relatives, *Plecotus.* Nearly all of the more than two dozen that have been captured in recent years have struck a net after midnight. An exception is the one taken by Constantine (1961a) at 8:38 p.m. Unlike many species *Euderma* does not readily chew a net. Nets left unattended overnight are badly chewed by bats such as *Eptesicus fuscus*, and few bats are left to reward the collector. However, several spotted bats have been found next morning in nets left unattended after midnight.

While feeding, these bats produce a loud, high pitched call, said to be even louder than that of *Plecotus phyllotis* with which it frequently forages. Those who are familiar with them can recognize the two species by their calls.

Euderma carries its ears erect only when alert, just preparatory to flight. In flight, the ears project forward. At other times they lie along the back and are slightly curled. Constantine (1961a) found that one bat kept its ears folded while torpid in a refrigerator.

Food: Studies of fecal material (Ross, 1961b) and stomach contents (Easterla, 1965b) of several spotted bats netted in New Mexico and Utah suggest that these bats feed entirely upon moths. In the laboratory Constantine (1961a) induced one to eat mealworms. Others fed in captivity have taken cottage cheese and flies (Handley, 1959). This bat adjusts poorly to captivity; none has yet been kept longer than three weeks.

Reproduction: Almost nothing is known about reproduction

161

88. *Euderma maculatum* from New Mexico.

89. Spotted bat, *Euderma maculatum*, entangled in a mist net. (*Courtesy of David A. Easterla*)

Distribution of *Euderma maculatum* in the United States

162

in this species. The males that have been taken have not been examined for the presence of sperm. Constantine (1961a) reported that a male which died in captivity on August 27 had testes which measured 4 by 2 mm.; Easterla (1965b) netted a male in Utah on August 21 which had testes 7 x 3 mm. Findley and Jones (1965) took lactating females in New Mexico on June 23, 30, and July 1. Mike Bogan netted one there on July 9. Easterla (1965b) reported that females he netted in Utah on August 10, 15, and 18 were lactating. The meager evidence available suggests that a single young is produced.

Remarks: *E. maculatum* is rather passive when handled and like the related *Plecotus* does not bite readily. It is usually gentle, but an exception was reported by Constantine (1961a).

Of the half dozen or more localities where the species has been netted, the best known is in Catron County, New Mexico, where Clyde Jones captured five adults on the night of June 23, 1960. The site is a stock pond in a clearing surrounded by a pure stand of ponderosa pine on the flat top of a mountain above the Willow Creek Ranger Station in the Gila National Forest. Since Jones reported his remarkable night, many hopeful bat collectors have netted at this pond. Findley and Negus captured two in 1963, but no other spotted bats have yet been taken there. During June 1966 we visited the area and netted this tank and several other water holes in the vicinity for three nights without success. In Durango, Mexico, three specimens have been netted at one locality in May, but in-

Skull of *Euderma maculatum*, x3

tensive efforts there during June have failed to yield additional ones (Gardner, 1965). Much further research is necessary before the distribution, patterns of movement, and natural history of this species can be understood.

If one wants to see the elusive and beautiful spotted bat, the available evidence suggests that he should stretch a net across a waterhole in the Upper Sonoran or Transition Life Zone in one of the southwestern states and plan to tend it all night. The netting site should be over the only water source for miles around and should be within a few miles of trees.

PLECOTUS TOWNSENDII [Cooper]

Western big-eared bat; Townsend's big-eared bat; lump-nosed bat; long-eared bat

Recognition: Forearm, 39–48 mm.; wingspread, 297–320 mm.; males smaller than females. A medium-sized bat with large ears, measuring more than an inch in length. Two large lumps appear on the dorso-lateral surface of the snout. Color brown, varying from a pale brown to nearly black; the underparts are brown.

Variation: Several subspecies have been described. *Plecotus townsendii townsendii* (Cooper) is a dark race found in the Pacific Northwest. *Plecotus townsendii pallescens* Miller is a pale race occupying desert areas. Other races include *Plecotus townsendii ingens* Handley, and *Plecotus townsendii virginianus* Handley. For distribution of the several geographic races, see Handley (1959).

Confusing Species: The several big-eared bats of the United States are readily distinguishable. *Antrozous pallidus* has somewhat shorter, broader ears, is pale yellowish, has a larger forearm, and lacks the lumps on the nose. *Euderma maculatum* has three spectacular white spots on a black dorsum and enormous ears (40–45 mm.). *Macrotus waterhousii* has a nose leaf. *Plecotus phyllotis* has a pair of unique lappets protruding from the base of the ears forward over the forehead. *Plecotus rafinesquii* is the only other species in the United States with glandular lumps on the nose. It is easily separated from *P. townsendii* by its whitish rather than tan underparts, gray

90. *Plecotus townsendii* from a cave in Lee County, Kentucky.

164

rather than brown dorsal fur, long hairs on the toes, and bicuspid upper incisors.

Range: Most abundant along the West Coast and in the Southwest, but ranging throughout much of western North America from British Columbia, Idaho, southern Montana, and the Black Hills of South Dakota, south across western Texas through Mexico to Oaxaca, and east to the edge of the Edwards Plateau.

Isolated populations occur in the gypsum cave region of Kansas, Oklahoma, and Texas; a small section of the Ozarks in Missouri, Arkansas, and Oklahoma; parts of five counties in east-central Kentucky (one reported from Carter County by Handley [1959] was probably not this species); two caves in Tazewell County in southwestern Virginia; and a small area of five counties in eastern West Virginia and two neighboring counties in Virginia.

In the gypsum cave region the species is still rather common, but the continued existence of the more eastern populations is tenuous. In the Ozarks it is scarce. No colonies are known in this region; there are but few scattered records from several caves. In Kentucky a colony of nearly 1,000 was discovered recently in a remote cave in Lee County (Rippy and Harvey, 1965), and banded individuals from this group have been reported from several neighboring counties. This may be the only population in the state. A group of about 300 still survived in a cave in western Virginia as late as 1963 (Holsinger, 1963). In West Virginia the species is still rather abundant in certain caves. The center of distribution there is Pendleton County, where it has been found in at least 15 caves. The distribution in this region has been studied by Conrad (1961). The bats seem to be abandoning more caves each year, apparently as a result of ever increasing human disturbance as spelunking becomes more popular. The species

seems destined to perish in the eastern United States unless the caves it uses receive protection. It may not be too late to save the eastern population, for as recently as 1962 a nursery colony of over 1,000 survived in a remote portion of a popular West Virginia cave (Hall, 1963b) and the colony in Kentucky remains intact.

This species is found at all seasons throughout its range. Altitudinal limits are from sea level to 9,600 feet.

Habitat: Although seldom abundant, this species is widespread in North America and occupies a variety of habitats. Most typical are the arid western desert scrub, piñon-juniper, and pine forest regions; it is apparently absent from extreme desert regions. As with several other species, there is a dark race which inhabits the humid coastal region of the Pacific Northwest. In the eastern part of the range, this species is generally associated with caves, cliffs, and rock ledges in well drained, oak-hickory forests; however, a large colony occurs in a cave in a beech-maple-hemlock association on the moist western slope of the Appalachians in Tucker County, West Virginia.

P. townsendii is a cave dwelling species. In the eastern part of the range it seems restricted to caves as day roosts except for occasional records of transients and accidentals found in buildings. In the West, it is perhaps the most characteristic bat of caves and abandoned mine tunnels, scattered individuals and small colonies being found in more such shelters than any other species of bat. It may be found in such retreats at any season and, indeed, is the only species that can regularly be found hibernating in fair numbers in western caves and mines.

Only on the West Coast and in the higher forested regions of the West is *P. townsendii* a regular resident of buildings. In parts of California nursery colonies are most frequently encountered in the attics of buildings, although they also occur in mines in the same region (Dalquest, 1947b; Pearson, et al., 1952). In arid regions buildings are seldom used as day roosts. Likely the bats would encounter a serious problem of water loss during the hot day.

Like many other species in the western United States, *P. townsendii* regularly uses open buildings as night roosts, and bat collectors often capture them in such places where there are no bats by day. An old building on the south rim of the Grand Canyon is such a site. During the summer of 1954 one of us (WHD) camped at the abandoned Hearst Ranch in Grand Canyon National Park with a field party collecting mammals. Late one night a bat was noticed flying about in a shell of a building which contained but one room and had all windows and doors missing. The bat was knocked down with a burlap bag. At frequent intervals until midnight on this and other nights, bats were collected this way. Several species of *Myotis* were taken, but *P. townsendii* was most numerous; 13 of them were captured. Bats first appeared in the building about an hour after dark. We took five additional specimens of *P. townsendii* elsewhere in the Park in a similar manner. These bats were trapped when they flew into an open loft of a barn. These 18 specimens represent the only records of this species from the Park (Hoffmeister, 1955). Pearson *et al.* (1952) and various other workers have also noted the frequent use of buildings for night roosting by *P. townsendii*.

Graham (1966) detailed the occurrence of *P. townsendii* in the natural limestone caves of California based upon extensive observations over more than a decade. No bats were ever found in 83 percent of the caves, and in the remainder their presence was irregular. *P. townsendii* were found in 40 caves and constituted 88 percent of all observations of bats in caves. Prior to 1963 several nursery colonies were known, but apparently none remains in California caves today. Abandonment was caused by increasing disturbance by people. Some long established roosts were vacated. Graham chronicled the shifting of one colony to ever more inaccessible regions of one cave before the cave was finally abandoned in 1961. He said that with cave exploration becoming ever more popular *Plecotus* may soon disappear entirely from the natural caves of California.

Behavior: In summer this species forms nursery colonies, but the males are usually solitary. Both sexes sometimes occur in a summer roost although not usually clustering together. In the West colonies range in size from a dozen to about 200 individuals, but in the East colonies of 1,000 or more are known. The bats prefer an area with dim light near the zone of total darkness in a cave or mine. Apparently they never crawl away from the spot where they land, and thus the clusters are always in places easily reached by flying.

P. townsendii never enter cracks or crevices, but hang from an open ceiling. Dalquest (1947b) noted that they frequently hang by one foot. At rest the ears lie back along the neck where they may coil slightly. The posterior portion of the ear is wrinkled, rather accordion-like, and there is also some lateral contraction. At the least disturbance the bat is alerted and the ears become erect.

The summer colonies do not go into daily torpor. When one intrudes upon their roost and flashes a light on the cluster, the bats immediately become excited. They seem to stare at the light, with ears erect and continuously moving, perhaps to find the intruder also by echo-location. Since the bats are tightly clustered, the mass of moving ears is a memorable sight. If one approaches too closely or shines a light upon the cluster for more than a few seconds, the entire group is likely to take flight.

Although nursery colonies prefer the edge of the lighted

zone in a cave, disturbance will cause the entire group to move to a remote section or to leave the cave entirely. Pearson *et al.* (1952) found that banding the young at night after all adults had left to feed apparently caused the colony to move. During the same night that 75 young were banded, the adults returned, picked up their young, and moved to another roost 1.3 miles away.

Nearly all observers who have studied this species at its summer roosts agree that it is a late flier which begins foraging only after darkness. Like several other species they exhibit a light sampling behavior as evening approaches (Handley, 1959). Individuals fly to the entrance, turn back into the cave, and then hang up for a few minutes before sampling the light again (Twente, 1955a).

Because of their late flight, the big-eared bats (*Plecotus* and *Euderma*) are rarely seen foraging in the evening, even in areas where they are common. Few exceptions are known. Krutzsch and Heppenstall (1955) reported one *P. townsendii* that was shot in Utah as it foraged in the early twilight, and Bailey (1936) shot two in one evening in Oregon as the bats circled about the edge of a forest. Handley (1959) quoted from Vernon Bailey's field notes that near Sundance, Wyoming, these bats were the earliest seen in the evening. He said that when they first appeared there was enough light to see their long ears. Bailey also noted that *P. townsendii* emerged early at Yellowstone National Park. Hamilton (1943) reported watching them leave a West Virginia cave at dusk and soar to several hundred feet in the sky; however, we could not confirm this finding with observations at caves in West Virginia and Kentucky.

Early emergence is apparently unusual in this species and needs further investigation. Does it occur only under special conditions such as just after birth of the young, on dry or windy days when the bats are thirsty, on cool or overcast days, or early or late in the season? The answers to these questions await further study.

Flight: The big-eared bats are among the most versatile in flight of our insectivorous species. After release in a room, the flight of *P. townsendii* varies from swift darting movements to slow deliberate moves to hovering as the bat inspects the room from floor to ceiling. Many kinds of bats when freed in a room repeatedly circle close to the ceiling and may even fail to discover an open window.

In flight the wing beats are deep and smooth, often alternating with short glides (Handley, 1959). Usually the head is bent downward and the body forms a smooth curve from chin to tip of tail. The ears, pointed forward almost parallel to the plane of the body, are scarcely noticeable. In slow flight, the head is not depressed and the ears are vertical and conspicuous. Sometimes flight is silent, but at times the wings create a relatively noisy flutter.

Like other bats, when *P. townsendii* alights on a wall or ceiling it swoops up from below, the wings fold, and with great agility it flips over and immediately grasps a foothold.

Dalquest (1947b) and three other persons, all with butterfly nets, spent several hours trying to capture *P. townsendii* in a building and concluded that these bats see well, are swift in flight, are agile dodgers, and have an excellent sense for danger. Dalquest noted, and we can confirm, that even when cornered at the end of a narrow mine tunnel they are difficult to capture and readily slip by people who are almost obliterating the passageway.

P. townsendii are not often taken in mist nets. Perhaps their unusually cautious flight and possibly an especially keen echo-location system allow them to detect and avoid the nets more readily than do most other species. Handley (1959) found but a single report of one having been taken in a mist net.

167

Cockrum and Ordway (1959) operated nets all summer over water within a mile or so of nursery colonies of *P. townsendii* without capturing any. In an attempt to capture some they put a net across the entrance to a cave before the bats emerged. They observed that the bats repeatedly flew right up to the net and turned back into the cave; only a few young were captured.

Cockrum and Cross (1964), however, reported 20 *P. townsendii* netted in 1958 at night over the south fork of Cave Creek, in the same area studied by Cockrum and Ordway. During June 1966 we captured several in mist nets set over this stream. All were adults, and we noted that they struck the net hard, giving no suggestion of having detected it. We also netted one as it entered a mine at night in Arizona and one entering a cave in Kentucky. Many species are readily taken in nets as they enter a mine, but the same species detect and refuse to enter a net if it is blocking their exit.

Food and Feeding: Hamilton (1943) reported that all specimens he had examined contained only the remains of Lepidoptera. Perhaps this species feeds entirely on moths.

Captivity: *P. townsendii* is difficult to maintain in captivity. Donald R. Griffin and his colleagues, who have been particularly interested in working on echo-location in big-eared bats, have been successful in keeping many species of bats healthy in the laboratory, but their *P. townsendii* generally die within a week or so.

Pearson *et al.* (1952) kept big-eared bats in captivity with limited success. It was difficult to get the bats to feed themselves, and pregnant ones, even when eating well, aborted or resorbed their embryos. Most could be induced to eat within a day or so by pushing decapitated mealworms into their mouths. Once they learned to take mealworms, they could be hand fed and would take as many as 40 mealworms daily. Some individuals eventually learned to eat mealworms out of a dish, but most did not. Self feeding was encouraged by stringing mealworms on a wire along the sides of the cage. The bats that had been taught to feed themselves and were kept in a cage large enough to allow them to fly survived most successfully.

Reproduction: The most thorough study done on reproduction of a North American bat is that of Pearson *et al.* (1952) on *P. townsendii*. This work was done in California and may not be applicable throughout the range of the species. Although their findings may not apply to other species of vespertilionid bats, they expose several fallacies concerning reproduction in bats, and this paper should be studied carefully by anyone interested in this subject. The following account is based primarily upon it.

MALE. *The cycle of the testis:* 1. Young males. During July and August the testes of bats two to three months old are usually slightly smaller than those of adults. They can be readily identified in sectioned material by the large amount of interstitial tissue and by the absence or scarcity of mitotic and meiotic activity in tubules. The testes of the young gradually enlarge through the summer, reaching maximum size between late August and October, when the adult testes are largest. Maximum size of the young testis is 6 mm. (about 15 mg.), whereas the adult testis reaches 13 mm. (377 mg.). The young testis has some meiotic activity near the end of the period of enlargement, and at least some individuals produce a few sperm. However, because sperm are so few and the accessory sex glands remain small, males in their first year are almost certainly sterile.

2. Adult males. The adult testes in summer are characterized by proportionally less interstitial tissue than in the young. After mid-August, primary spermatocytes appear and the testes enlarge. In September the meiotic divisions and spermiogenesis occur within less than three weeks, and the tubules become exhausted, containing practically no spermatogenic stages in October. At that time most mature sperm have moved into the epididymis, and the tubules begin a dramatic shrinkage. This results in the testes decreasing to about one twenty-fifth their former volume as the sperm appear in the epididymides. Thus, the peak of testis size is passed before the animal becomes fertile. The testes remain quiescent throughout the winter while the animal is reproductively active. Spermatogenesis begins anew in April.

The cycle in the epididymis: The epididymides of the young males are poorly developed during their first year and do not project conspicuously into the interfemoral membrane as they do in the adults. They sometimes contain a few sperm until November. The adult epididymides are frequently larger than the testes during the winter and always project conspicuously into the interfemoral membrane. They shrink gradually through the winter, and by the end of April are indistinguishable from those of the young. Since they are packed with sperm in the fall, this decrease probably results from release of sperm in copulation during this period, and perhaps gradual leakage of sperm as can happen in the absence of copulation. No evidence of phagocytosis of sperm in the epididymis was seen, even in specimens taken as late as May.

The cycle in the accessory glands: During autumn the ampullary and prostate glands enlarge, attaining maximum size at the beginning of the breeding season in October and November. They remain large throughout the winter, despite regression of the testes at this time. The accessories of the adults are conspicuously larger than those of the young

throughout the winter, but regress to about the same size in April.

The interstitial cells of the testis: The production of androgens by the interstitial cells of the testes generally causes development of the accessory glands and sexual activity in mammals. Enlargement of the accessories and the beginning of sexual activity in *P. townsendii* at the time the testes are shrinking is unusual. In experiments involving castrated bats and with other work involving histochemical tests, Pearson *et al.* showed that the shrunken testes, with their regressed interstitial cells, produce androgens. Perhaps the androgenic activity of the brown fat discovered by Krutzsch and Wells (1960) is also involved in the winter sexual activity. The endocrine relationship among testes, accessories, and sexual behavior of *P. townsendii* is not the same as in other mammals and deserves further study.

Copulation: Most breeding occurs in the winter roosts, although some females are inseminated before they arrive. No breeding occurs during September, but all females are inseminated during the first three weeks in October. Females only four months old mate as early as adults, although young males probably do not breed during their first year. Repeated mating occurs, with the peak of copulatory activity ranging from November to February. No firm vaginal plug is formed following copulation as happens in some individuals of *M. lucifugus*.

In precopulatory behavior observed in the laboratory, the male approached a female while making a twittering sound and vigorously rubbed his snout over her face, neck, forearms, and ventral surface. He seemed to be making use of the large nose glands, which apparently were responsible for the strong odor noticed.

The only copulation observed by Pearson *et al.* occurred high on the ceiling of a cave in November. The female was completely torpid. This situation has been reported for *Myotis lucifugus*, and we have noticed it with *Pipistrellus subflavus* and many times in *Myotis sodalis*. Apparently mating with a torpid female occurs frequently among bats in winter.

FEMALE. *Growth of the follicle:* In October, as much as six months before ovulation occurs, the follicle destined to release the next egg is well developed. Follicles in late summer are seldom larger than 250 micra in diameter but in late September, before copulation, they expand to between 250 and 340 micra. After copulation the follicle which will rupture in the spring is easily recognized; it is larger than the others, and the cells forming the cumulus oophorus fill most of the follicle. This large cumulus and consequent small antrum are characteristic of the ripening follicle in bats. Such follicles are never found in females which have not copulated. The dominant follicle grows little if any during much of the winter, but enlargement occurs before April.

Maturation of the follicle and subsequent ovulation in *P. townsendii* may depend upon the stimulus of copulation, even though it is administered several months prior to ovulation. The two ovaries are equally active, although implantation nearly always (49 of 50) occurs in the right horn of the uterus.

Ovulation in *P. townsendii* is similar to that described for *M. lucifugus* by Wimsatt (1944b). The entire ball of cells making up the cumulus oophorus surrounds the ovum as it enters the oviduct, but these cells are shed during early passage. The second meiotic spindle has formed when the ovum enters the oviduct, and fertilization occurs in the upper part of the tract. Cleavage begins in the middle portion, and an embryo of 6–11 blastomeres enters the uterus.

Ovulation: In California ovulation occurs primarily during March, but ranges from late February into April. The bats ovulate in the winter quarters or soon after they leave. Many females do not join nursery colonies until some time after ovulation and fertilization. Apparently during early pregnancy the tendency to organize into colonies is not so great as later, for many have been found roosting in places which are not used by nursery colonies and where bats in late pregnancy or with young have never been found. Nursery colonies reach full size in late April or May.

Apparently there is a period in autumn and early winter during which ovulation will not readily occur, for individuals taken from hibernation in December and kept in a warm room for several weeks failed to ovulate. The basic reproductive time of these bats may well be spring. Perhaps the long survival of sperm and the fact that unreceptive females can be inseminated while torpid has advanced the time of copulation.

Survival of spermatozoa: As with other species of hibernating bats, the spermatozoa have remarkable longevity. In the male they retain motility for at least six months after they reach the epididymides and abundant spermatozoa were found in the uteri of females after isolation in a cold room for 108 days. In specimens removed from hibernation and kept at room temperature, spermatozoa were found in all that had not yet ovulated at the time they were examined; these included some that were kept at room temperature for 26 days. Spermatozoa quickly disappear from the female reproductive tract, however, after ovulation occurs.

Gestation: Duration of pregnancy varies widely and is probably dependent upon climatic conditions and temperatures at the roosting site. In California Pearson *et al.* calculated gestation periods of from 56 to 100 days in different colonies and different years. Probably the major cause of such diversity is variation in the amount of daily torpor during early pregnancy. A cold spell in March, just after ovulation, could delay development considerably. Pregnancy proceeds at a more regular rate after the nursery clusters form and high metabolism is maintained.

170

Parturition: In the single delivery observed by Pearson *et al.* a captive *P. townsendii* suspended herself from the wire top of her cage by feet and thumbs. The membranes of wings and tail formed a spacious basket into which the young was born. As in most bats the presentation was breech. The fluids and afterbirth were consumed by the mother, and within a few minutes the young attached to a nipple and was hanging by its feet from the top of the cage but still enfolded by the mother's membranes. The mother retained her position at the top of the cage for more than half an hour after birth.

After parturition the right horn of the uterus regresses to a resting stage in two or three weeks, but it never shrinks to the original small size. Adults which have produced young can be separated from the young and the nonparturant adults throughout the winter by the condition of the uterus.

Dates of birth: Most of the young in central California are born in late May and early June. Dates vary considerably in different colonies and different years. Probably the variability is due to a number of factors; bats in a colony may come from different hibernation sites, may arrive at different times, and may vary in age. Yearlings generally give birth several days later than older bats.

Dalquest (1947b) found most females accompanied by newborn young in a colony in central California on May 7; Hall (1946) said the young are born in late June in Nevada; and Cowan and Guiguet (1965) found that birth occurs in mid-July in British Columbia.

Limited data are available on parturition in the eastern population. Mohr (1933) found many bats each carrying a single young in a cave in Virginia in late June. One gravid female carried a fetus which weighed 2.6 g. and surely was near term. A maternity colony we examined in a cave in Pendleton County, West Virginia, on July 9, 1949, contained young of several sizes, some of which could fly.

Pearson *et al.* estimated birth dates in California, Nevada, and Arizona from embryo size fitted to curves for embryo growth that they had developed. They calculated birth dates ranging from April 19 in central California to July 22 in Arizona. However, since rate of development may vary so greatly with environmental and behavioral factors, such estimates are probably not reliable.

Reproductive failure: Studies at California nursery colonies showed that at least 5.5 percent of the bats were neither pregnant nor lactating. This is a minimum value for reproductive failure inasmuch as some bats pregnant at the time of examination may have later reabsorbed or aborted their embryos. Another source of error is the probability that many nonpregnant females never join the nursery colonies and thus would not be counted. Several such females were found in May and June hanging alone in places not used by nursery colonies.

Nine of fifteen nonproductive females whose ages were known were yearlings. As these made up 26 percent of the yearlings whose reproductive behavior was known, apparently reproductive failure is more common among the young females than among adults.

Of 16 nonproductive females examined, 2 were resorbing embryos and 4 had either resorbed or lost their young. Only 1 of the 13 in which the ovaries were examined had failed to ovulate.

Lactation: The single pair of mammae are pectoral and nearly lateral, as in most species of bats. Tiny nipples, about one-half mm. in length are characteristic of young and nonparous females; mothers always have larger nipples. Thus nipple size can be used throughout the winter to separate productive adults from the young and the nonparous.

The nipples begin to enlarge at the time of implantation of the embryo in spring and reach a maximum length of about 3 mm. at parturition or shortly thereafter. Mammary tissue becomes apparent when the fetus is about 7 mm. in crown–rump measurement. It enlarges to cover an area as great as 12 x 17 mm. when the young is a month old. Lactation ceases gradually, and even in autumn, after mammary tissue has all but disappeared, a small drop of fluid can often be squeezed from each nipple.

Care of the Young: During the day each young bat clings to its mother. When adults leave the roost at night to feed, they leave the young behind in clusters and do not return before midnight. By comparison of band numbers on successive visits to a maternity colony, Pearson *et al.* found that in every case each mother carried the same young as before; upon returning from feeding she selected the individual she left in the cluster.

Pearson *et al.* studied the mother-young relationship in a colony in a mine on June 5, 1949. Banded adults were released at the rear of the tunnel, and their banded young (from 1 to 18 days old) were placed on the floor just 10 feet from the entrance where the observers sat. All but one of the young immediately crawled to the sides of the tunnel where they formed clusters. Many babies made audible squeaks which attracted the mothers; clusters of young which were not squeaking were not approached by the adults. A mother would fly back and forth several times in front of a cluster. Then she would land and crawl about over the group of babies as though searching for her own. After selecting a baby, she would cover it with her body and wings, apparently encouraging it to attach itself to her, and fly off with it. Although the squeaking seems important in attracting the mother, she uses some other sense, perhaps smell, to locate the particular baby she seeks. In each of six times females were watched selecting a baby from among the clusters, they first made contact with one or two other babies which they

rejected. That each picked the same young she had previously carried was determined by subsequently checking the band numbers.

Some mothers that were released returned to where the young were being banded as if seeking their lost babies and retrieved young that had been placed on the ground within a few feet of the observers. Females carrying young were not attracted to squeaking babies. No bats showed interest in their unattached young when placed in a cage with them. However, this is also true with many kinds of bats and other mammals.

Growth and Development: Ten newborn ranged from 2.1 to 2.7 g. (average 2.4) and had forearm measurements of 16–18 mm. (average 16.6). Crown–rump length of the term embryo is about 24 mm., and the total length from tip of nose to tip of tail is about 35 mm.

Pearson *et al.* described the newborn *P. townsendii* as a grotesque creature. The large ears flop over the unopened eyes, and the disproportionately large feet and thumbs give the young a spider-like appearance. The dried umbilical cord may remain attached for a day or two. The pink naked body becomes covered with short gray hair within the first four days.

Within a few hours of birth the young are able to squeak, and at seven days they can make the squawking noise of the disturbed adult. When separated from its mother a baby will climb a nearby object and either hang quietly or utter a series of chirps.

The young grow rapidly and within a month of their birth are almost full grown. During the first two weeks the forearm lengthens about 1.2 mm. per day. The young can fly when about three weeks old but are still dependent upon the mother. One 42-day-old bat, as large as its mother and a

172

skillful flier, had a stomach full of milk and no insect fragments. By six weeks some leave the roost at night with the
adults. The young are weaned at about two months.

Nursery colonies start to disperse in August about the time
the young are weaned. Adults that have lost their young
leave earlier than lactating females. Young males tend to
leave earlier than young females.

Population Density: Pearson *et al.* (1952) estimated the
population density of *P. townsendii* on Santa Cruz Island,
about 20 miles off the California coast, as about one bat per
310 acres. These bats shared the island with at least equal
numbers of *Antrozous pallidus* and with *Myotis californicus.*
Rough estimates of the density on the mainland were similar.

Pearson *et al.* speculated on the possible factors limiting the
population of this bat which seems to be nowhere abundant.
The shortage of suitable summer roosting sites with adequate
feeding territory seemed the most significant factor.

How new nursery colonies become established is not known
for this or any other bat. Pearson *et al.* noted that if a satisfactory roost becomes available near an established colony, the
colony does not divide to make use of both; the entire colony
uses one or the other, or alternates between the two. If a
cluster is necessary for raising the young, a single female could
not establish a new colony; a group would have to adopt the
new residence. In other vertebrate animals studied, the
young tend to disperse to new territory and the old to retain
the home area. From the limited evidence available for bats
they apparently do not follow this pattern.

Population Dynamics: Pearson *et al.* (1952) found wide
variation in sex ratios among hibernating populations in California. In one region 69 percent were males; in another, 31
percent. Among the newborn the sexes were equal. Rippy

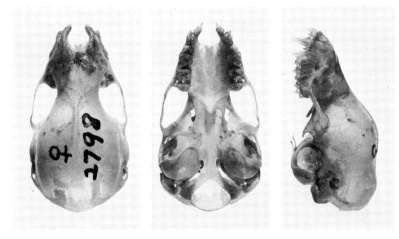

Skull of *Plecotus townsendii,* x3

Distribution of *Plecotus townsendii* in the United States

173

and Harvey (1965) found as many males as females in a cluster of 850 hibernating in a Kentucky cave. Hamilton (1943) found a cluster in a cave in West Virginia in August consisting entirely of males.

Pearson *et al.* suspected a higher mortality among the females but were unable to confirm this by banding returns.

Pearson *et al.* studied population structure and survival of the females by banding in nursery colonies. They postulated that a colony of 100 females produces about 45 young females in a season. Only about half of these survive and return to the colonies, but about 80 percent of the adults return. Thus about 20 female bats are added to the colony per 100 adult females present each year and the adults survive at a rate of about 80 percent a year. These percentages would suffice to maintain a colony at a constant size, and this condition obtained in the colonies studied. Assuming an equal mortality for adults of all age classes, Pearson *et al.* constructed the following theoretical age structure for a colony of 100 female *P. townsendii*:

Age in Years:	1	2	3	4	5	6	7	8	9	10	11	12	13	14	15	16	17	18	19
Number of Individuals:	20	16	13	10	8	7	5	4	3	3	2	2	1	1	1	1	1	1	1

Although the assumption of an equal mortality rate is probably not valid for this or any other mammal (see Caughley, 1966), this table probably gives a reasonably accurate estimate of the age structure over most of the range (see Davis, 1966).

Migration and Homing: P. townsendii readily moves from one roost to another, but it probably does not perform major migrations. The longest movement recorded by Pearson *et al.* (1952) among the 1,500 they banded in California was a 20-mile journey by a young male. We have recorded several movements of up to 40 miles in Kentucky and West Virginia. Cockrum (1956a) took 54 individuals from a cave in Arizona in May and released them 28 miles away. Four were later recaptured at the home cave.

Hibernation: P. townsendii hibernate throughout their range in caves and mines where temperatures are 55° F. (12° C.) or less, but generally above freezing. They have been found hibernating in environmental temperatures as low as 28.5° F. (–2° C.). In the western part of the range the bats usually hang singly or in small groups in the cooler air near the entrance of a mine. They readily awaken and move, apparently in response to temperature changes. Pearson *et al.* (1952) found that at least 17 of 56 torpid bats aroused during a single winter night and moved to other spots within the mine. They also noted that the population wintering in mine tunnels changed continually, with new bats present on each visit and many banded ones absent. At different times in the winter the bats sought different parts of the tunnels. In November they were in the warm deep parts where the temperature was 55° F. (13° C.). In December and January the bats were in the well-ventilated parts of the tunnels, where the temperature was 33° F. (0.5° C.). The females tended to roost in cooler places than males. Whitlow and Hall (1933) prevented one from moving by caging it along with two *Myotis leibii* at the spot where they were found in an Idaho mine. During a month of colder weather all perished.

Where *P. townsendii* hibernate in caves in northern California Pearson *et al.* (1952) found that the bats began to arrive in late October and the colony reached maximum size by January. The females tended to arrive earlier in the fall and remained later in the spring than did the males. Small numbers of bats, predominantly males, continued to arrive and depart from the caves throughout the winter. Most of the colony left the caves by April.

Occasional individuals hibernate in buildings (Dalquest, 1947). One female apparently remained torpid in one spot in a building for six weeks during the winter (Pearson *et al.*, 1952).

The males choose warmer hibernating sites, awaken more often, and seem generally more active in winter than females. In west-central California some individuals remain active all winter and occasionally appear at night roosts in buildings. A night roosting individual was captured repeatedly through the winter when temperatures at the time of capture ranged from 37° to 57° F. (3°–14° C.). Numerous records of other individuals at the night roosts, including some females, indicate that winter activity is not unusual in this region.

The source of energy for such winter activity is unknown. Flying insects are scarce at low temperatures, and Pearson *et al.* suggested that fat stores are probably not sufficient to sustain the activity. Adult males they examined from mines in December contained no stored fat.

In Idaho Whitlow and Hall (1933) found that fat amounted to 17 percent of the weight of *P. townsendii* hibernating in mines in November and December. They noted weight loss of about 20 percent from February to May. Pearson *et al.* (1952) noted that throughout the winter the young contained more subcutaneous fat than did adults. In other species of bats, fat is more abundant in adults.

We have noticed, as have several other workers, that *P. townsendii* banded in one cave often moves to another, even in the coldest weather. How much of such movement is due to the disturbance has not been ascertained.

In Kentucky and West Virginia *P. townsendii* sometimes hibernates in clusters of several hundred to a thousand or more. One such colony in Kentucky contains about twice as many bats in winter as in summer. The winter group is 50 percent male, whereas the summer group is a nursery colony. In several caves in eastern Kentucky *P. townsendii* can be found with *P. rafinesquii* in winter. This is the only region where the two species are known to occupy the same caves.

In Tucker County, West Virginia, one of us (WHD) observed a colony of about 1,000 *P. townsendii* over several winters. The clusters always occupied the same spot on the ceiling not far from the entrance, and about 20 feet above a stream in the cave. Several solitary individuals could usually be found hibernating in various parts of this huge cave system. A summer colony of several hundred bats occupied another entrance to the cave.

Hibernating *P. townsendii* seem almost as intolerant of disturbance as the summer groups. Twente (1955b) noted that those banded in Kansas caves in winter left the caverns for weeks or months, and many never returned. One of us (WHD) noted the same behavior in West Virginia and had the unique opportunity of discovering what happened to 1 of the 24 banded in October in a Tucker County cave. Two months later a single bat was found hibernating in a small fissure in the cliff beside the large Cave Mountain Cave in Pendleton County; it was one of this group, having traveled at least 25 miles and crossed two major ranges of the Appalachian Mountains.

In hibernation the ears are coiled like a ram's horn and lie tightly against the neck (fig. 91). The thin tragus remains erect, and at first glance may be mistaken for an ear. The fingers are spread so that the wings effectively cover the ventral surface of the body, the tail and interfemoral membrane are extended anteriorly covering the venter and parts of the wings, and the body hairs are erect (fig. 92). In this position, the bat is practically enveloped with a layer of dead air, effectively insulating itself. The ears can be coiled inde-

91. Two big-eared bats, *Plecotus townsendii*, hibernating in a Kentucky cave. The ears are coiled back and lie pressed against the body. An erect tragus can be seen extending from each of three ears.

92. Side view of the same bats shown in fig. 91. The wings cover the ventral surface of the body.

pendently, and often a bat is seen with one ear erect and the other coiled.

As with other species of hibernating bats, once the process of awakening is initiated, the body temperature rises rather rapidly. Twente (1955a) measured the temperature rise as about 1° F. (0.6° C.) per minute until the bats were able to fly well at 82°–86° F. (28°–30° C.).

William Z. Lidicker and Wayne Davis once observed the rectal temperature rise in a torpid *P. townsendii* they removed from a refrigerator. The rise was steady until the temperature was above 68° F. (20° C.) when the bat became able to move about. Then temperature rise was often in sudden jumps of several tenths of a degree. These sudden rises in body temperature were always followed immediately by strenuous muscular effort, such as an attempt to fly. By watching the needle on the temperature gauge, one could predict such activity.

Temperature: Pearson *et al.* (1952) found that most *P. townsendii* were lethargic at air temperatures below 62° F. (17° C.) and Dalquest (1947b) reported that when he placed active individuals in a refrigerator at 40° F. (4.5° C.) all became lethargic within 20 minutes. In contrast, we found this species and *P. rafinesquii* more resistant to cooling than any other hibernating species. We once put one of each species in a cigar box in a refrigerator at 46° F. (8° C.). We looked at them several times during the next few hours and they were always active.

This is one of the bats which form tight clusters. The function of the cluster has been studied and speculated upon by several workers. In summer the cluster seems to function in heat conservation, maintaining a high temperature conducive to rapid growth of the young. Adults in the colony are usually awake and maintain a high body temperature. That this is due to clustering is suggested by the finding that a lactating female with young kept in a cage at 70° F. (21° C.) showed a drop in body temperature. Her young grew much more slowly than young in the wild (Pearson *et al.*, 1952).

All our bats which inhabit caves and mines by day in summer form tight clusters and do not drop into daytime lethargy as do many other bats. Handley (1959) suggests high temperatures of the clusters aid in digestion and assimilation of food, and Pearson *et al.* (1952) believe that gestation, lactation, and other reproductive processes may be facilitated by the higher temperatures.

The function of winter clusters seems to be to stabilize body temperature against external changes. Twente (1955a) found that the temperature of a cluster approached that of the substrate, whereas that of an individual was more influenced by the air temperature, which may differ from that of the rock by several degrees. Handley (1959) said that the winter cluster protects the bats from heat rather than cold. Probably the cluster minimizes changes in either direction.

Pearson *et al.* (1952) found a cluster of *P. townsendii* hibernating where the air temperature was 30° F. (–1° C.) but temperature within the cluster was 32° F. (0° C.). Many bats were hibernating within a few inches of icicles. Davis and Reite (1967) have shown that several species of bats, when faced with sub-freezing temperatures, respond with a compensatory increase in metabolism. Certainly clustering could decrease the energy expenditure required to maintain the temperature gradient.

Parasites: Winged parasitic flies of the family Streblidae are common on this species throughout its range. These rather large yellow insects are quite conspicuous and can be found on the bats at all seasons. They are abundant; a half dozen can sometimes be found on a single bat. Wingless parasitic flies, family Nycteribiidae, commonly found on western bats, have been reported on *P. townsendii* from the western part of its range. Mites have been reported on specimens from western North America and from Oklahoma. A protozoan parasite has been found in the blood of a specimen from California (Handley, 1959).

Molt: Molt generally occurs in August when the young lose their dark juvenile pelage, and the adults undergo their single annual molt. New hairs appear on some individuals as early as June and July. The molt is general, rather than patterned, with new hair appearing at the same time on all parts of the body.

Remarks: In handling this species we have noted a behavior unique among all bats with which we are familiar. When put into a handling cage they congregate at the bottom, piling on one another so tightly that many may smother. Because of this behavior only a few can be handled at one time in an ordinary gathering cage. Most species of bats persistently climb the sides of a cage in an attempt to escape or to attain the highest roost.

   This is a gentle bat. Only occasional individuals attempt to bite and they are never as vicious as many species. They are generally silent, but some individuals utter a few shrill notes when handled. A high-pitched twittering has been reported as commonly heard in the summer roosts (Grinnell, 1918).

93. Rafinesque's big-eared bat, *Plecotus rafinesquii.*

178

PLECOTUS RAFINESQUII [Lesson]

Rafinesque's big-eared bat; eastern big-eared bat; southeastern big-eared bat; eastern lump-nosed bat

Recognition: Forearm, 40–46 mm.; wingspread, 265–301 mm.; males smaller than females. A medium-sized bat with large ears measuring more than an inch in length. Two large lumps occur on the dorso-lateral surface of the snout. The first upper incisors are bicuspid. Color, gray above and nearly white below. Basal portion of the hairs black, strongly contrasting with the tips.

Variation: Two subspecies are recognized. *Plecotus rafinesquii refinesquii* (Lesson) occurs in the Ohio River Valley. A darker race, *Plecotus rafinesquii macrotis* LeConte, is found east and south of the Appalachians, westward along the Gulf Coast.

Confusing Species: Within the range of *P. rafinesquii*, only *Plecotus townsendii* is similar. *P. rafinesquii* is easily distinguished by its nearly white underparts, strongly bicolored fur, long hairs which project beyond the toes (fig. 94), and the noticeably bicuspid first upper incisor.

Range: Southeastern United States from the Dismal Swamp in Virginia south and west through the coastal states to eastern Texas. Known from southeastern Oklahoma and western and southern Arkansas up the Mississippi River Valley to southern Illinois, southern Indiana, and western Kentucky. Apparently isolated populations occur in southern Ohio, eastern Kentucky, and central West Virginia. A single individual has been taken near West Lafayette, Indiana. These bats are permanent residents throughout the range.

Habitat: This is a bat of the forested regions of the South. In summer it is most frequently encountered in buildings where females form nursery colonies of from half dozen to several dozen adults. Males are generally solitary during the nursing season and can be found in buildings, crevices behind loose bark, and in hollow trees. Nursery colonies in caves are exceptional but are known in Kentucky and Tennessee.

Although they sometimes inhabit dark attics of occupied houses, they prefer a badly dilapidated building where the rooms are partially lighted. This species and the eastern pipistrelle choose more open and lighted day roosts than other kinds of bats. Both species commonly hang in the open in plain sight. In spite of this, however, they are easily overlooked, for they leave scant sign of their presence.

In the northern part of the range *P. rafinesquii* hibernates in caves and in similar shelters. Several mines in southern Illinois each shelter an individual or two upon occasion

94. Foot of *Plecotus rafinesquii*, left, and *P. townsendii*.

179

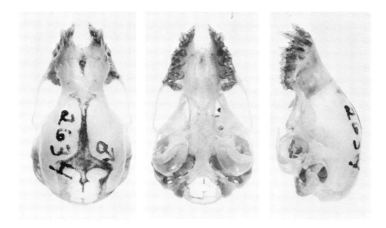

Skull of *Plecotus rafinesquii*, x3

Distribution of *Plecotus rafinesquii*

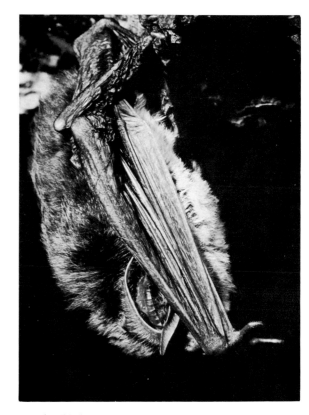

95. *Plecotus rafinesquii* hibernating. The large coiled ear is partially hidden by a wing, but the erect tragus is conspicuous.

(Pearson, 1962). A similar situation obtains in a few limestone caves in Indiana, Ohio, Kentucky, Tennessee, and Alabama, but one can explore hundreds of caves in these states without finding a single *P. rafinesquii*. Two caves in eastern Kentucky contain colonies of about 100 each, and scattered individuals of this species and *P. townsendii* can be found in numerous small caves in the same general area. Two sandstone caves in the wooded, rugged bluff country of central West Virginia occasionally harbor *P. rafinesquii*, but it is unknown in the extensive limestone caverns of Virginia and West Virginia.

The single specimen from West Lafayette, Indiana, probably represents a straggler somewhat beyond the normal range, for it was found in a highway culvert which had been checked for bats 42 times over three winters (Wilson, 1960).

An unusual shelter used primarily in winter has been described by Hoffmeister and Goodpaster (1962)—an abandoned open cistern near Reelfoot Lake, Tennessee. As many as 64 have been found at one time. Banding has shown considerable turnover during late winter and early spring, with many bats leaving and new ones arriving.

P. rafinesquii is a hardy bat. In the northern part of its range, hibernating individuals are usually found just beyond the twilight zone of caves and mines, often within less than 100 feet of the entrance. They apparently awaken frequently and move throughout the winter.

Behavior: In summer when approached at rest, *P. rafinesquii* is immediately alerted and begins to wave its ears, apparently trying to keep track of the intruder by echos from him or the sounds he produces. The bat also gives the impression that it is peering intently at the observer.

In a rather large nursery colony in a cave in Kentucky, Hall (1963a) noted that the bats were active and began to fly almost immediately. They made a rather loud sound, different from any other bat he had ever heard. He described it as a low, hoarse bark, rather like a small dog.

Once put to flight, *P. rafinesquii* is remarkably agile and difficult to catch. We have spent considerable time with limited success in trying to catch them with a hand net in the confines of small rooms.

When released in a room this bat moves swiftly throughout the entire room, apparently seeking an escape route. The flight varies from swift to nearly hovering. Unlike most bats they will fly near the floor, into corners, and behind furniture, as well as near the ceiling. Hahn (1908) noted that a *P. rafinesquii*, when attempting to escape from a room in which it had been flying for 10 or 15 minutes, repeatedly flew against the windows. It returned to the same point time and again, striking the pane when the window was closed or the wire screen, if the window was open. Usually it struck with considerable force and fell to the sill, but immediately got up and repeated the performance. Although we found this behavior common in *Myotis*, our *Plecotus* seemed much more cautious in flight and seldom crashed into a window.

Like its close relatives, *P. rafinesquii* emerges late in the evening; there are no records of its foraging at twilight. At a camp in Breathitt County, Kentucky, where a colony occupies several buildings, we have often shot other bats in the narrow valley, but never *Plecotus*. On the bay at Freeport, Florida, an outbuilding used regularly as a day roost by one or two of these bats was watched for several evenings; the bats did not emerge until after dark.

Reproduction: Little information is available concerning reproduction in this species. Breeding probably occurs in fall and winter. An adult male was found in a nursery colony in mid-July (Baker and Ward, 1967). Enlarged testes were noted in Kentucky in late August (Hall, 1963a) and in North

Carolina in January (Handley, 1959). A single young is produced after the nursery colonies form in the spring. The young apparently are born in late May or early June in the northern part of the range and about the middle of May in Louisiana.

The young shed their milk dentition by mid-July and reach full size and assume adult pelage by August or early September (Handley, 1959).

Care of Young: Barkalow (1966) said that when the young are born they are carried by their mothers during feeding flights until they become too heavy to transport, at which time they are left hanging in the nursery while the mother goes in search of food. He presented no evidence for this statement. Most bats will carry their small young in flight when frightened from the roost, and many species will move them to an alternate roost after disturbance, but probably no bats commonly carry their young on feeding flights.

Molt: Molt occurs from July and August in South Carolina and Alabama to September in Tennessee. In the young, molt begins on the head, neck, and underparts and proceeds posteriorly. In two adults examined, molt appeared on all parts of the body at the same time (Handley, 1959).

Remarks: This is one of the least known of our bats. Much that has been written about it is based upon inferences from what is known of other species. It is nowhere abundant, but is readily available for study at many localities.

96. *Plecotus phyllotis* from the mountains of New Mexico.

PLECOTUS PHYLLOTIS [J. A. Allen]

Allen's big-eared bat

Recognition: Forearm, 43–49 mm.; wingspread, 310–350 mm. A rather large bat with enormous ears, a broad (4–5 mm. at widest point) tragus, and a unique pair of lappets projecting from the median bases of the ears anteriorly over the top of the snout. There is a rather conspicuous tuft of light colored hairs at the posterior base of each ear. Color varies from light tan to nearly black. Underparts only slightly paler than upperparts. Bases of hairs black.

Confusing Species: This species is readily distinguished from all other big-eared bats by the lappets projecting from the ears over the snout.

Range: The central highlands of Mexico from the Distrito Federal, San Luis Potosí, Tamaulipas, and Durango northward into New Mexico and Arizona. Known in the United States from west-central New Mexico across Arizona to the Colorado River Valley, mostly at higher elevations. Additional collecting will probably reveal a more extensive range including parts of several other states. Winter range unknown.

Habitat: P. phyllotis inhabits the forested areas of the montane Southwest. In pine-oak forested canyons and the coniferous forests of the mountains from about 5,000 to 8,500 feet, it is one of the most common bats. It is a late flier, rarely seen except by the bat collector who erects a net across a woodland pool and has the patience to keep it in operation far into the night.

Commissaris (1961) described a day roost of this species in Arizona—an open-fronted cave about 800 feet wide and 100 feet deep in a canyon. Part of the roof had fallen, leaving a pile of boulders and rubble about 100 feet deep on the floor of the cave. In interconnected spaces and passageways among these boulders about 30 P. phyllotis and several *Plecotus townsendii* and *Myotis thysanodes* were found on August 23, 1958.

Cockrum and Musgrove (1964a) discovered P. phyllotis in a series of mines located in the Lower Sonoran Life Zone in northwestern Arizona, not far from the Colorado River. The bats were abundant, forming clusters of up to 97 individuals. These were maternity colonies, with no adult males, and they occupied the mines at least from early April to the last of September. This is the first record of this species outside forested areas, although Gardner (1965) has taken several from a sparsely wooded arroyo in the Upper Sonoran Life Zone in Mexico.

Behavior: P. phyllotis apparently leaves the roost only after darkness is complete. Cockrum and Cross (1964) caught them most frequently about 1½ to 2 hours after sunset.

They generally fly about 30 feet above ground and reveal their presence by loud calls which they emit at about one second intervals.

The flight has been described as rapid (Commissaris, 1961), as relatively slow (Jones, 1961) and as "light" (Hayward and Johnson, 1961). It seems to us that they fly more slowly than the molossids, but are somewhat swifter than most other bats. When released in a room, their flight, like that of other *Plecotus*, may be described as exploratory. It consists of swift, direct movements from one place to another, interspersed with slower flights and by occasional near hoverings, as if the bat were carefully seeking an exit.

When at rest the huge ears lie along the back. They are

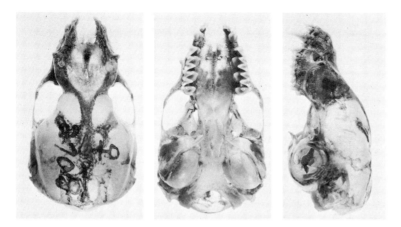

Skull of *Plecotus phyllotis*, x3

Distribution of *Plecotus phyllotis* in the United States

97. *Plecotus phyllotis.*

erected only when the bat becomes alert and ready to fly. When put in hibernation, the ears coil in the ram's horn appearance so characteristic of *Plecotus*.

Reproduction: The only known maternity colonies consist of a dozen or more females in rock shelters and mines. The scant evidence available suggests parturition dates probably ranging from the first three weeks in June in the southern part of the range to the last three weeks and into July in the northern part. A single young is produced.

Jones (1961) found no mature sperm in two males taken in New Mexico on June 20. No other information is available on the reproductive cycle in the male.

Remarks: Considering the striking appearance and relative abundance of this bat, it seems most unusual that it remained unknown in the United States for so long. The species was first described in 1916 from a specimen taken in Mexico in 1878. E. Lendell Cockrum in 1955 was first to capture one in the United States, and this was the only one from this country among the three specimens available when Handley (1959) revised the American *Plecotus*. Its absence among early collections is all the more remarkable when one considers that many mammal collectors have worked in Arizona during the past century and that the species has recently been found in mines and caves. Such sites have long been favored by bat collectors; possibly *P. phyllotis* has only recently adopted these habitats.

The major reason for the abundance of this bat in later collections is the recent adoption of the mist net for collecting bats in the United States. Late flying bats, like *P. phyllotis* and *Euderma maculatum*, are almost unknown to the collector with a gun (one *P. phyllotis* has been shot in flight), but are now rather routinely taken in mist nets.

This leads to an important point of common knowledge among bat collectors: different collecting methods (shooting, netting, picking from day roosts and from night roosts) commonly yield different species of bats in the same locality. With the use of the mist net, so new yet so productive, surely there must be much yet to learn about distribution of bats in the United States. Extensive netting in this country has been done only in Arizona and New Mexico. We would not be at all surprised if in the next few years the range of *P. phyllotis* is found to include parts of Texas, California, Nevada, Utah, and Colorado.

Possibly the distribution of this species is in flux. The colony described by Commissaris (1961) has been revisited three times, including the same month a year after the original find, and the bats have never been seen again. In Cave Creek Canyon, near Portal, Arizona, where *P. phyllotis* has been found commonly in recent years by E. Lendell Cockrum and his students, we failed to catch any during June 1966, although we ran nets nightly over the same pools where others have taken them. We heard only one.

Our major experience with this bat was in the area studied by Jones (1961) in Catron County, New Mexico. On June 25, 1966, we joined Robert J. Baker there and netted several over the tank in the ponderosa pine forest on the mountain top where Jones had found them in 1960. Next day we visited nearby Iron Mesa Lake, which lies 1½ miles by trail up the mountain from the Willow Creek Ranger Station. This beautiful woodland pond looked so attractive to us that we stretched a half dozen nets over various parts of the water. As evening approached a steady rain began, but bats appeared in good numbers. We caught several *Myotis*—M. *volans*, M. *occultus*, M. *evotis*, and a single M. *thysanodes*—as well as several *Eptesicus fuscus*, *Lasionycteris noctivagans*, and *Lasiurus cinereus*. Then at 9:00 p.m., after the last twilight was gone, *P. phyllotis* began to appear, and they became more numerous as the night progressed. Their loud distinctive calls were heard continually from 10:00 until we left the area at midnight. The calls are evenly spaced about a second apart as the bats are cruising. These sounds are similar to those of *Tadarida macrotis* and *E. maculatum*. Often as many as four could be heard at one time. They generally flew about 30 feet above the ground, and only occasionally did one come down to the net. We left the nets in place when we retired and upon returning the next morning we found 15 bats in our badly shredded nets. Six were *P. phyllotis*, more than any other species. All were lactating females.

While running traps and collecting small mammals at night with dust shot in the Grand Canyon throughout the summer of 1954, one of us (WHD) was continually intrigued by the intense evenly spaced calls of occasional bats flying overhead. These were often heard at several places on the South Rim among the pines and also over the open sagebrush flats in the western part of the Park. In the field notes is the suggestion that these were probably *P. townsendii*. At that time, this was the only species known to emerge so late, and none of the early flying bats made such calls. It now seems likely these bats may have been *P. phyllotis*. Although the species has not been taken there, it likely is a common resident of Grand Canyon National Park.

Like their near relatives, these bats are generally docile. They do not struggle in a net and make little attempt to chew out. When handled they rarely bite and react only with a few hoarse notes.

98. Desert pallid bat, *Antrozous pallidus*. The shape of the snout is distinctive in this species.

ANTROZOUS PALLIDUS [Le Conte]

Desert pallid bat

Recognition: Forearm, 48–60 mm.; wingspread, 360–390 mm.; females larger than males. A large pale bat with big ears, large eyes, broad wings. The ears are widely separated and more than half as broad as long. Color above, light yellow, the hairs tipped with brown or gray. Underparts pale creamy, almost white, not bicolored.

Variation: Four subspecies are recognized in the United States. *Antrozous pallidus pallidus* (Le Conte) occupies most of the southwest. *Antrozous pallidus pacificus* Merriam is a large, dark race which occurs on the West Coast. The intermediate *Antrozous pallidus cantwelli* Bailey ranges east of the Cascades in the Pacific Northwest. A small area in Kansas and Oklahoma is occupied by *Antrozous pallidus bunkeri* Hibbard.

Confusing Species: This species is not readily confused with any of the other big-eared bats. *Macrotus waterhousii* is similar in appearance but has a conspicuous noseleaf and gray fur. In *Plecotus townsendii* and *Plecotus phyllotis* the dorsal fur is darker at the base than at the tips; the reverse is true of *Antrozous.*

Range: The southwestern deserts and semiarid lands from Queretaro in the central plateau of Mexico, north through California and east of the coast range in Oregon and Washington, to southern British Columbia; in the lower elevations in parts of Nevada, Utah, Colorado and in Arizona and New Mexico; the panhandles of Oklahoma and Texas, and all of trans-Pecos Texas eastward into the Edwards Plateau. Apparently disjunct populations occur in the gypsum cave region of southern Kansas and adjacent Oklahoma and in the Wichita Mountains of Oklahoma. It is probably a permanent resident in most of its range, having been found in winter from northern California to Kansas.

Habitat: A. *pallidus* is one of the commonest species at lower elevations throughout the Southwest. Its favored habitat is the rocky outcrop regions where the dominant vegetation consists of scattered desert scrub such as mesquite and cat's-claw, although it commonly ranges up into the forested oak and pine regions. It becomes scarce and local above 6,000 feet. Summer daytime roosts most commonly are in rock crevices and buildings, less frequently in mines, caves, and hollow trees. In an abandoned barn in California a nursery colony was once found roosting in piles of burlap sacks (Beck and Rudd, 1960). Colonies are small, generally from a dozen to 100 individuals.

These bats choose a daytime roosting site where they can retreat out of sight and wedge themselves into a tight crevice. They are intolerant of disturbance and may abandon a roost when molested, not to return for years. They also often shift about among daytime roosts without apparent provocation. Perhaps this is a result of seasonal temperature changes, for this bat, in spite of being a desert dweller, is intolerant of temperatures above 100°–104° F. (38°–40° C.) (Licht and Leitner, 1967a).

Night roosts are in open shelters readily accessible by flight. Where the same shelter serves as both day and night roosts, the bats hang from the rafters or a similar exposed place at night. Favored night roosts include rock shelters, open buildings, porches, highway bridges, and mines. Night roosts in buildings are frequently a source of annoyance to man. Orr (1954) described instances where their excrement fouled hay

187

in a barn and a car in a garage. The open porch of a ranch house less than a year old was used as a night roost by a group of these bats. When Orr visited the locality one evening, nine bats were resting on the beams supporting the roof. The beams had been creosoted recently, and an electric light had been left burning on the porch all evening; neither seemed to discourage the bats.

By mid-September the young are nearly indistinguishable from adults, but the colonies are still intact. By the middle of October, however, colonies in California begin to disperse into smaller groups. At this time they may be found in many sites where they do not occur in summer.

Eben McMillan (in Orr, 1954) made a series of interesting observations in autumn at a ranch in California. Pallid bats were not seen about the ranch during spring and summer of 1948, but in the latter part of October they began to use some of the buildings for night roosts. Each morning numerous fresh droppings and insect fragments were found on the floor beneath the beams where the bats rested. After the middle of November bats were no longer seen. In 1949 they appeared during the second week in October. Each evening McMillan placed clean sacks beneath the roosts. After October 25, there was a gradual decrease in the number of nightly droppings until November 1, when there were but two droppings, and none were found during the rest of the year.

Little is known about this bat in winter throughout most of its range. It is not known to perform long migrations, apparently wintering within a few miles of its summer home. In Kansas a population of about 200, which inhabited an abandoned barn in summer, hibernated in winter in a crevice in the ceiling of a cave about four miles away; they were destroyed in 1964 by vandals. A. pallidus is known to hibernate in a building at the University of Arizona, and a few have been taken from hibernation in mines in Nevada (Hall, 1946).

Orr (1954) listed a few scattered occurrences in winter from California, including one found beneath a piece of damp canvas on a building in a redwood forest. Beck and Rudd (1960) noted that a schoolhouse in California where they studied a nursery colony was used in winter, but they did not indicate by how many bats.

As with many other species of bats, especially in the West, A. pallidus seems scarce in winter. The hibernation sites of the major part of the population remain unknown.

Hibernation: A. pallidus probably hibernate throughout much of their range. They readily go into hibernation when put into a refrigerator and can be kept for three to four months without apparent ill effects (Orr, 1958). Orr (1954) studied weight changes in several groups kept in a refrigerated room at about 40° F. (4.5° C.) and recorded an average weight loss of 0.2 percent per day. Breathing rate ranged from 0 to 52 breaths per minute. The longest period of apnea was four minutes.

Orr also made observations on the accumulation of fat. Bats were probably at minimum adult weight when they arrived at the summer colonies in spring. Males weighed about 20 g. at that time, soon increased to about 25 g. and retained this weight through the summer. Fat deposition occurred in late summer; males averaged 29 g. in October.

These weights were considerably greater than weights of bats studied by Chew and White (1960) in a California colony (average 15.8 g.) and those from Texas (Herreid, 1961c) where adult females averaged only 18.9 g. in July.

Bats in the laboratory, fed mealworms ad libidum, maintained nearly constant weight from late May through August 7, although daily consumption of food increased from 3.5 to 4.5 g. during this period. From August 14 to September 23 weights climbed steeply, from an average of 28.3 g. to 38.6 g.

while food consumption averaged 4.7 g. (Orr, 1954). There must be some interesting metabolic changes occurring in bats in August when the time comes to deposit fat preparatory to hibernation. Elucidation of these problems might be helpful in understanding some of the problems of obesity in man.

Behavior: On cool days and in the early morning Orr (1954) found that A. *pallidus* were silent and motionless unless disturbed. If one was prodded, it opened its mouth and produced a buzzing sound. Movements were slow and only after several minutes of disturbance would the bats become active enough to fly.

On warm days, however, the bats were frequently heard squabbling from 100 feet away. If an intruder reached into an inhabited crevice, the bats gave numerous intimidation and squabble notes and retreated into the innermost recesses of the roost. They were very alert at such times, with heads raised and frequently mouths open. If further disturbed, some individuals moved rapidly to the entrance and took flight.

When captured and handled, these bats bite viciously. While squabbling in an active colony, they frequently bite one another when vocal warning fails to discourage an annoyer.

A. *pallidus* emerges fairly late in the evening. In California Orr noted that the first bats emerged 47 minutes after sunset in June when the light intensity was less than 0.1 foot candle. In the morning the last pallid bat was seen flying 51 minutes before sunrise when the light was still less than 0.1 foot candle. In Kansas pallid bats emerge when light intensity is 0.5 to 2.0 foot candles (Twente, 1955a).

Upon leaving the roost the bats generally fly about three or four feet above the ground as they head for the nearest water or feeding ground. Within a half hour after emergence some individuals appear at night roosts, and mothers begin returning to their young. At the night roosts and where small young are resting, adults come and go throughout the night. In the roosts every bat is alert, ready to take flight if alarmed.

O'Farrell *et al.* (1967) found an occasional A. *pallidus* during a study of winter bat flight in Nevada. The bats were netted when air temperatures were as low as 36° F. (2° C.). Winter activity of this species seemed erratic and infrequent, however, for it was a common bat in summer. It is possible that only a few of the summer residents remained in winter.

Voice: Orr (1954) described several different sounds which apparently have different functions. One he called the "intimidation" note. It is a loud insect-like buzz that is uttered when a bat is frightened, angered, or annoyed. These sounds are produced at a rate of about three to five per second, with the mouth half open and the teeth bared. Disturbance of a roosting colony during the day results in one or more bats making this sound.

The "squabble" note consists of a series of high-pitched, dry, rasping, thin double notes lasting up to one second. This sound is produced with the mouth open and the teeth bared. It appears to be a sign of irritation and anger, uttered by individuals which are being crowded or molested by others. The squabbling sounds led Orr to the discovery of several colonies.

The "directive" call consists of one to five rapidly repeated notes. The notes are single, clear, resonant, and high pitched. Orr said the call was reminiscent of the sound made by a power line with a short circuit. This call is usually given as soon as the bat emerges in the evening. The call may be frequently heard at night in areas where these bats are abundant. Once when Orr was releasing bats in the daytime he heard this note after they disappeared from sight in a rock crevice; they were answered by other bats being released. The calls seemed to serve as a means of directing the latter to the crevice. On another occasion he noted in the laboratory that the directive notes produced by one bat apparently enabled another to find it.

The directive note of the very young is a high-pitched, bird-like chirp which is produced from the moment of birth. This chirp is sounded whenever a mother leaves her young and continues monotonously until she rejoins it. The frequency of these chirps increases from about two or three per second during the first day of postnatal life to five per second by the tenth day. At about 12 days this chirp is replaced by a directive call similar to that of the adults.

A sound Orr described as a "chittering" was heard occasionally; each note was high pitched, of about one-half second duration, and repeated three or four times with half-second intervals between. It was thought to be a note of contentment.

"Plaintive" notes, apparently associated with pain, were uttered by females in labor. These were loud, harsh, gutteral double notes repeated three or four times, each note having a duration or about two seconds. They were uttered with the mouth open, the lips drawn back, and the eyes partly closed.

On occasion, as the bats groomed themselves they produced a nonvocal, explosive nasal sound. This apparently was the result of a sudden release of air through the nasal passages, and Orr suggested that it may serve as a means of dislodging loose hairs that adhere to the nose.

Finally, Orr described faint clicks heard as bats flew near him. Surely these must have been the ticklaute, that portion of the echo-location calls of bats which is faintly audible to the human ear (Griffin, 1958). These can be heard in nearly any echo-locating bat if it passes close to the observer.

Flight: Flight of the pallid bat is rather noisy, with considerable fluttering. It is less agile and lacks the maneuverability of the smaller species and the leaf-nosed bats. The flight seems slow, but this is partly an illusion due to the large size and slow wing beats. Natural flight speed is unknown. Hayward and Davis (1964) timed flights in a hallway, but speeds of bats indoors are not comparable to those in natural flyways (Mueller, 1965). *Tadarida brasiliensis*, a small molossid which frequently shares day roosts with *Antrozous*, is much swifter. Orr noted that they easily outdistanced A. *pallidus* upon emerging in the evening.

In the laboratory Orr noted that pallid bats occasionally hovered momentarily when flying close to the floor and that flight sometimes included gliding for short distances. He recorded 10–11 wing beats per second, considerably slower than the 15 recorded by Griffin (1946) for smaller eastern species.

On vertical surfaces A. *pallidus* usually alight head up, grasping the surface with the claws on their thumbs and feet. They then assume the inverted position of a resting bat by releasing all holds except one foot, allowing the body to swing downward. Although many other species will sometimes alight head upward when preparing to enter a crevice above them, they usually alight with the head down when coming to rest on a vertical surface.

Food and Feeding: This species has one of the most unique feeding habits of any North American bat. Little, if any, of their food is captured in flight; their prey is taken primarily from the ground. Perhaps their low flight and rather large eyes are adaptations for this type of feeding.

Nelson (1918) captured a pallid bat that had alighted on the ground in an apple orchard in northern Arizona. The bat was so engrossed in eating a flightless Jerusalem cricket (*Stenopelmatus fuscus*) it had found that Nelson was able to capture it by hand. Burt (1934) watched pallid bats foraging on a lawn in Nevada where they alighted to capture June beetles (*Polyphylla*). Twente (1955a) reported similar behavior in Kansas.

There are several reports of these bats being caught in mousetraps. Davis (1960) captured one in a trap set beneath a mesquite bush in such a position that the bat must have crawled over the ground to reach it. Most collectors of small mammals who have trapped extensively in the North American deserts have caught A. *pallidus* in mousetraps. Probably the bats are attracted to insects feeding on the bait.

Apparently pallid bats also forage among the foliage of trees. Hall (1946) noted several instances of these bats being taken at night in trees where they apparently had alighted to obtain insects. On July 5, 1966, we obtained evidence suggesting that pallid bats feed in the inflorescence of agave. We netted 22 individuals over a pond in Big Bend National Park. All but two of them were heavily covered with pollen, which was particularly noticeable on both surfaces of the wings. It was well scattered over the body surface except the top of the head and neck. Since the known pollen feeder, *Leptonycteris nivalis*, captured at the same time, had pollen primarily on the head, neck, and shoulders, it seems likely that the *Antrozous* were not feeding upon the pollen or nectar. Most likely they were alighting on the large inflorescences to forage for insects among the flowers.

Food items most frequently used by A. *pallidus* seem to be Jerusalem crickets, grasshoppers, scorpions, June beetles, and ground beetles. In captivity they will eat lizards and other bats (Engler, 1943). Although this may have been due to confinement, perhaps they attack most any small creature encountered while feeding. Ross (1961b) compiled an impressive list of prey taken by *Antrozous*.

Captivity: A. *pallidus* do quite well in captivity. Orr (1958) found that they adjusted better than any other species he has kept. They quickly learned to take food from a pan, and most individuals became gentle after a few days of handling. Some individuals learned to respond to their caretaker and anticipated feeding. Various foods have been found acceptable. Ramage (1947) fed them fly pupae. Orr (1958) used mealworms supplemented with vitamin drops and succeeded in raising young from birth and keeping them healthy for several years. Al Beck told us that he finds canned dog food an adequate diet.

Reproduction: Reproduction has not been studied as carefully as other aspects of the life history. Much of the information comes from Orr's (1954) observations on captive bats.

The testes attain maximum size in late August and Sep-

99. *Antrozous pallidus* in flight. (*Courtesy of Robert T. Orr*)

tember, but mating does not begin until the latter part of October, after the summer colonies have disbanded. Breeding probably occurs sporadically throughout the winter, at least until the latter part of February. As with several other species of bats, live sperm can be retained in the uterus of the female through the winter and fertilize ova as they are released. A female which Orr isolated in an outdoor flight cage on December 29 gave birth about May 21, some five months later. This exceeds considerably the gestation period, which Orr estimated as 53–71 days.

An individual which Orr removed from a cold room on December 5 and kept in a heated greenhouse gave birth on February 26 and reared its young successfully. However, ovulation in California usually occurs during the first two weeks of April.

Maternity colonies generally begin to form in early April in California. Beck and Rudd (1960) reported that except for an occasional yearling, males are absent from the maternity clusters. In Nevada Hall (1946) noted that the sexes separate in spring before the young are born, and at the time of parturition the males have formed separate clusters, sometimes in the same building. This agrees with Dalquest's (1947b) finding of a cluster of 60 males in a building on July 8, 1945. An occasional lactating female may be found with the males in June and July.

Orr, however, presented ample documentation that males are frequently found in the nursery colonies, both when the females are pregnant and when they have young. Often the males outnumbered the females. He concluded that in California, summer colonies may be composed of adults of both sexes, and that either sex may predominate. Although Orr said that adults were captured at random, it is not clear whether or not the adult males were actually a part of the cluster of nursing females. In most species of bats in which adult males are found in maternity colonies, it has been observed that they are generally separated from the nursing groups.

Most young are born during the first half of June, but parturition dates in California range at least from May 10 to June 23. Beck and Rudd (1960) found young in late April, and Twente (1955a) said that most young were born in late June and early July in Kansas.

Two is the usual number of young, but a single baby is produced in about 20 percent of the births. There are no records of three young, but three embryos have been recorded. Wimsatt (1945) has shown that multiple ovulation and resorption of excess embryos is common in some bats, but this has not been studied in *Antrozous*. In all members of the Kansas population examined the embryo number and litter size was two (Twente, 1955a).

During labor the female hangs upright with the uropatagium curled ventrally to form a basket which receives the young. Labor varies from a few minutes to nearly two hours. When twins are produced the time between births varies from 12 to 65 minutes. The females respire rapidly during this time and frequently utter notes of pain during contractions. Birth is by breech presentation. The rump and tail emerge first with the uropatagium folded over the ventral part of the body. As soon as the feet emerge the baby assists in the birth by pushing against the mother's body. The female often severs the umbilical cord with her teeth and eats the placenta when it is expelled. Orr noted that females which did not eat the placentae refused to accept their young, and either killed them by biting or allowed them to fall and perish. Thus in this species eating the placenta may be the factor which determines the mother-young specificity. *Antrozous*, like most other bats, nurse only their own young which they can recognize among a cluster (Twente, 1955a).

Care of the Young: The mother licks the young thoroughly during and immediately after birth. The newborn then climbs to the mammary glands using thumbs, feet, and mouth to grasp the mother's fur and pull itself along; the female assists by nuzzling the young. After the young becomes attached to a nipple, the mother envelops it with her wing. The young clings tightly to a nipple and is difficult to remove without injury. Babies weigh about 2.9 to 3.3 g. at birth and have a forearm length of about 17–18 mm.

Until they are about two weeks old, the young hang onto their mother's nipples during the day. Thereafter the mother shields them with her wings until they become too large for this arrangement.

Twente (1955a) said that the females apparently carry their young when they go out to feed for the first evening or two, and Davis (1960) reported that the female apparently carries her family on her forays until they are nearly half grown. Twente gives no evidence supporting his statement, and Davis' conclusion seems to be based upon his capturing a female carrying two young that were one-third grown as she attempted to escape from a nursery colony he had discovered in a hollow cypress tree in Nuevo Leon, Mexico.

Although all species of bats with which we are familiar will carry their small young in flight when they are flushed from a roost, we do not consider this evidence that they carry them during their normal foraging flights. Because of the problems involved in echo-locating flying insects and capturing them with the wingtips or in the membranes, it seems unlikely that any insectivorous bat normally carries its young when feeding. Although many writers have said that bats carry their small young while feeding, we know of no evidence to support such allegations. Bats shot in flight while carrying young could have been moving them from one roost to another, an activity which is common. *A. pallidus* feeds upon the ground and

conceivably could take her young along. Adequate evidence is not available to decide the question.

In Kansas, when bats went out to feed they left their young at the roost (Twente, 1955a). Upon returning mother bats inspected the young and selected their own. When very young, the babies were scattered over the wall, but as they grew older they began to form clusters.

Development: Apparently pallid bats mature more slowly than most other species. At birth the eyes are closed, the ears are folded tightly against the sides of the head, and the skin is pink and appears naked. On the fourth day scattered hairs can barely be seen, and by the tenth day scanty fur is clearly evident on most of the upper parts of the body.

The eyes open between the eighth and tenth days, and the ears become erect about the same time. The young begin to exhibit fear at 10 days by withdrawing from a disturbance and producing the intimidation buzz.

Distribution of *Antrozous pallidus* in the United States

193

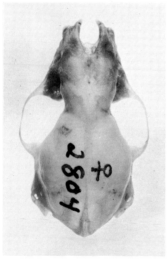
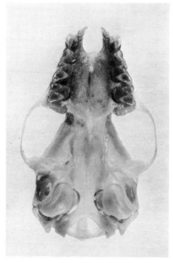

Skull of *Antrozous pallidus*, x3

When the bats are 18 days old, short scanty pelage is present on all upper parts of the body except between the shoulders. The skin has darkened wherever hair is present and the flight membranes have become somewhat grayish.

By the time the young are 24 days old the fur is dense and long enough to obscure the skin except between the shoulders. As in most other species the color of the dorsal pelage is darker than that of adults. By the 34th day the light basal parts of the hairs on the dorsum become evident.

The young can fly well at six weeks; probably flight begins earlier. Captive bats at this age began eating mealworms, although they continued to nurse for several more weeks until the females discouraged this by withdrawing and threatening them when they approached.

By the time the young has attained adult size in late summer, pelage is indistinguishable from that of adults. By September Orr was unable to recognize young in the field.

Dentition: There are 22 deciduous and 28 permanent teeth. The canines are the first to erupt in the embryo. They are followed shortly by the incisors; this is the dental condition at birth. Premolars usually appear about the third to fifth day of postnatal life, but are sometimes present at birth. By the early part of the second week the deciduous teeth are fully grown.

Eruption of the permanent teeth generally precedes the loss of the deciduous ones. The various permanent teeth erupt in the age interval of 3–5 weeks, whereas the deciduous components are lost between 2 and 10 weeks.

Migration: Little information is available on migration of this species. They seem rather sedentary and probably do not move far between summer and winter homes. Evidence shows some autumnal wanderings, as in other species of bats, but the distances involved are as yet unknown. R. Davis (1966) reported a bat banded at a summer roost and recovered 17 miles west in early spring; this suggests migration between summer and winter roosts. He also reported two 19-mile journeys from one night roost to another.

Homing: A. *pallidus* is capable of homing from several miles, but is not as adept at homing over long distances as many other species. R. Davis (1966) recorded one which returned from 108 miles within eight months, but few taken more than 60 miles away were ever found to have returned.

Davis and Cockrum (1962) recorded a female which returned from eight releases, all in different directions at distances of 21 to 68 miles. R. Davis (1966) cited this as evidence that this bat can orient toward home from unfamiliar territory. However, the bat may have been familiar with the entire area.

Parasites: The bat bug *Cimex pilosellus* is seldom found on pallid bats. The nycteribiid fly *Basilia antrozoi* is rather common, with most individuals carrying a few in spring and summer. The flea *Myodopsylloides palposa* is scarce. Like several other species of western bats, A. *pallidus* is often heavily infested with ticks. Mites are found on the flight membranes of nearly all individuals; these have been identified as of the genera *Spinturnix* and *Steatonyssus* (Orr, 1954). Orr also found (1958) sarcoptic mites which produced open lesions on membranes of the bats. A new genus and species of bat chigger has recently been described from A. *pallidus* (Vercammen-Grandjean and Watkins, 1966).

Odor: Pallid bats emit a characteristic faintly skunk-like odor. Orr (1954) noted that sometimes this odor could be detected 15 feet from the entrance to a roosting crevice. The odor arises from secretions of glands on the muzzle. Depressions occur on

100. Typical habitat of *Antrozous pallidus* in Arizona. A colony of these bats occupies a crevice in the ceiling of the rock shelter shown near the center of the picture.

101. Face of *Antrozous pallidus*, showing the odor-producing glands on the muzzle. (*Courtesy of Robert T. Orr*)

the surface of each gland. A bristle lies in the center of each depression, and each bristle is surrounded by about five smaller hairs (fig. 101). When a bat is disturbed, numerous tiny droplets exude within a few seconds, and the odor becomes much stronger. When the glands of a freshly killed bat are cut, the odor becomes intense. Likely the secretion serves as a defense mechanism, since the glands are most active when the bats are alarmed. Perhaps the odor produced by the muzzle glands tends to repel predators. The structure of these glands has been described by Walton and Siegel (1966).

Molt: The single molt occurs during the summer, usually in June and July. New pelage first appears between the shoulders and mid-ventrally at the base of the neck. With the appearance of the first new hair, the skin of the back becomes dark. Following this, new hair is soon seen from the crown to the lower back and on the ventral parts of the head and body. New hair grows more rapidly on the mid-dorsal surface than elsewhere. The old fur falls out when the new fur in that area has grown to half its normal length. In a captive individual Orr noted that molt was essentially completed within 13 days.

Remarks: In June 1966 we observed the behavior of a colony of A. *pallidus* at Tonto National Monument in Arizona. The bats occupied a crevice in the top of a rock shelter housing the ruins of primitive Indian dwellings (fig. 100). Mastiff bats were reported to inhabit this shelter, and in an unsuccessful attempt to catch one we set up a net and stayed with it all night. Pallid bats were active throughout the night. Several times they alighted on the ground with an audible flutter of wings, crawled about for a short time, and noisily took flight again. Perhaps they were foraging for the small scorpions that were most abundant at night in the shelter and along the trail.

We have noticed that this is one of the few bats that can be identified in flight after dark. When netting bats in Texas, we could readily recognize A. *pallidus* when we caught sight of one in the beam of a light flashed over the pond. The pale color, large size, and relatively slow flight are distinctive.

The Molossidae

TADARIDA BRASILIENSIS [I. Geof. St.-Hilaire]

Brazilian free-tailed bat; Mexican free-tailed bat; guano bat; free-tailed bat

Recognition: Forearm, 36–46 mm.; wingspread, 290–325 mm. A rather small bat with long narrow wings. The lower half of the tail is free from the interfemoral membrane. The ears almost meet in the midline but are not joined. Hairs as long as the foot protrude from the toes. Color dark brown or dark gray. Individuals in some caves have been bleached by ammonia fumes to an abnormal pale brown. Hair nearly uniform in color from base to tip; white at the extreme basal portion in some individuals. Scattered white hairs are commonly found; large patches of white fur occur on occasional individuals.

Variation: Two subspecies occur in the United States. *Tadarida brasiliensis cynocephala* (Le Conte) is found in the Southeast west to Texas, and the smaller *Tadarida brasiliensis mexicana* (Saussure) occupies the rest of the range. White fur on the throat giving the appearance of whiskers is common in some populations in Oklahoma, but this feature apparently occurs rarely throughout the rest of the range (Glass, 1954).

The *Tadarida* of the southeastern United States had been considered a separate species until Schwartz (1955) decided that it differed only subspecifically from the western form. However, the two differ ecologically. *T. b. cynocephala* dwells in buildings, never uses caves, and is apparently nonmigratory.

102. Brazilian free-tailed bat, *Tadarida brasiliensis.*

197

103. Foot of *Tadarida brasiliensis*. The exceedingly long stiff hairs are characteristic of our molossid bats.

104. The ears of *Tadarida brasiliensis* are not attached at the midline.

198

T. b. mexicana in Texas dwells primarily in caves and is highly migratory. It is suspected that mating of this latter population takes place in Mexico, and thus the two forms could not interbreed where the ranges meet in east Texas. Werner (1966) found that one form has facial sweat glands and the other does not. Davis (1960) treated the two as separate species. In his key he separates them on the basis of geography and average length of the tibia. *T. brasiliensis* on the West Coast also differs ecologically from those of central Texas and Oklahoma in that it never uses caves and is apparently nonmigratory. Behavioral characteristics intergrade between these regions, however. These two populations have not been considered subspecifically distinct.

Confusing Species: This is the smallest of our free-tailed bats; only *Tadarida femorosacca* is small enough to be confused with it. *T. brasiliensis* is the only species of *Tadarida* in the United States in which the ears are not joined at the midline. It is also the only one in which the hair is of uniform color; in *T. femorosacca* and *Tadarida macrotis* the basal half of each hair is white.

Range: Tropical America from northern South America and the Caribbean Islands through Central America northward. In the United States nursery colonies occur at lower elevations throughout California, across southern Nevada and southern Utah, Arizona, New Mexico, Texas, and parts of Oklahoma, and across the Southeast to Charleston, South Carolina. As with the other powerfully flying molossid bats this species is likely to appear outside its usual range after the young are weaned. There are records from Atlanta, Georgia, and southern Ohio. Records from throughout Kansas probably represent autumn wanderers from the great colonies in Oklahoma caves. A pregnant female taken in Lincoln, Nebraska, in June perhaps was a lost migrant, but may represent a local breeding population. Two other specimens have been taken from that city in August.

In the Far West the winter range is essentially the same as the summer range. Winter specimens are known from Oregon, California, Nevada, and Utah. In mid-continent nearly all migrate southward in the fall, although a few winter in Arizona and southern Texas. Winter range of the gulf population is not known, but at least a few winter in southern Louisiana, Georgia, Florida, and South Carolina.

Habitat: The habitat differs in various parts of the United States. On the West Coast and in the Southeast it inhabits buildings; in Texas, Oklahoma, New Mexico, and Arizona it is primarily a cave bat. It is one of the most gregarious of bats, colonial at all seasons. Maternity colonies of a thousand or more inhabit buildings in the Southeast and in California. Several million occupy Carlsbad Caverns in summer, and even larger nursery colonies occur in caves in Arizona, Texas, and Mexico. In spite of its great abundance, only a small percentage of the available caves and mines are used. This species seems local in abundance and spotty in distribution throughout much of the central part of its range. Large colonies are known in 13 caves in Texas, 5 in Oklahoma, and 1 each in New Mexico, Arizona, and Nevada.

In the West *T. brasiliensis* is most characteristic of the Lower and Upper Sonoran life zones. It commonly ranges into the Transition Zone and occasionally wanders into the mountains at least to 9,200 feet. In the Southeast little habitat preference has yet been defined. Jennings (1958) found it to be an abundant bat in Florida and suspects that nearly every town in the state harbors one or more colonies. Hamilton (1941) noted bats he thought to be *Tadarida* roosting among the dead leaves of a palm in Florida in April. Moor *et al.*

(1965) found *T. brasiliensis* roosting among a thick growth of sedges in Nevada on April 9.

Behavior: *T. brasiliensis* hangs in great clusters which blanket huge areas of the walls and ceiling of their retreat (fig. 105). In our experience these clusters consist of a single layer, but Krutzsch (1955a) found a colony in which the bats clung one upon another, forming several layers.

Krutzsch (1955a) described the activity of a colony of *T. brasiliensis* in a church in San Marcos, California. The daily behavior seemed to be influenced by temperature. On warm days activity began in the morning but on cool days the bats remained quiet and inactive. When the bats were awake, they kept up an incessant squeaking and chattering, which could be heard a considerable distance from the roost, and continually scrambled about and crawled over one another. Late in the afternoon most bats became quiescent, arousing again shortly before sunset. On foggy or cloudy evenings they began taking wing before sunset, but on clear evenings emergence started shortly after sunset. They left at a rate of about 300 per hour until most of the 1,000 adults were gone. Except for a few which were seen nursing young, most bats were absent between 11:00 and 4:00 o'clock, when the return flight began. By 5:00 a.m. most bats were back in the roost.

Flight: The great flights of millions of *T. brasiliensis* leaving a cave sound like the roar of a white-water river and appear as a dark cloud visible for many miles.

At the Texas caves the flights usually start at about 15 minutes after sunset and about 10 minutes earlier on cloudy days (Herreid and Davis, 1966). Two distinct flight patterns occur. Commonly the bats leave the cave and spread out in several directions, acting individually, with little group integrity. Then there is the spectacular rapid exodus of a

199

105. Part of the nursery colony of over ten million *Tadarida brasiliensis* in an Arizona cave. (Courtesy of Bruce Hayward)

serpentine undulating column of bats which stretches for many miles across the sky (fig. 106). The stream of bats is shaped like an undulating tube with a diameter of about 30 feet. The column slopes gradually upward to a height of about 500 feet where it divides into small flocks of bats. When viewed from a distance, the dark column of bats resembles a cloud of smoke, which may account for the fact that many guano caves are called smoke holes. When the bats emerge in the serpentine pattern, they nearly always begin to depart before sunset.

Bats leave the cave at speeds of up to about 35 miles per hour. As they get into the open sky they increase velocity. Davis *et al.* (1962), following a column of bats in a helicopter at a speed of more than 40 miles per hour, noted that the bats were outdistancing them; they estimated a top speed of at least 60 miles per hour. At the largest colonies the exodus lasts several hours with bats still emerging long after others have started to return. In caves inhabited by the largest populations there may not be opportunity for all bats to emerge every night. At three nursery colonies in Texas, in caves which have relatively small entrances, Herreid and Davis (1966), using data on estimated rate and duration of exodus concluded that in a population of a million bats each could leave the cave only every fourth or fifth night. Since these caves contained about 4, 6, and 10 million bats (Davis *et al.*, 1962), an individual could leave the cave only a few times each season. Obviously, something is wrong with their conclusion. Eads *et al.* (1957), studying the flights at the same Texas caves, concluded that the majority of the bats leave the caves every evening during the warmer months.

The return flights at the Texas caves were described by Davis *et al.* (1962). The pattern of numbers and flow density were essentially the reverse of the exodus. Influx began with the sporadic appearance of small groups as early as 11:00 p.m. and gradually built up into a continuous stream of fluctuating density about two hours before sunrise, reaching the peak of speed and density less than half an hour before dawn. By sunrise the flights were usually over.

The first incoming bats seemed to approach the cave leisurely, often in a long glide. As the density of flight increased, the angle of approach became steeper. By the time the incoming stream became continuous, the bats were actually dropping out of the sky into the cave entrance. Each bat seemed to perform a rapid series of free falls with closed wings, with abrupt, brief, openings to control speed and direction. The brief braking action produced a characteristic flutter, giving rise to an eerie staccato sound as the rain of bats hurtled into the cave. Davis *et al.* (1962) estimated that the speed of the free falling bats must have commonly exceeded 80 miles

106. *Tadarida brasiliensis* leaving an Arizona cave. (*Courtesy of Bruce Hayward*)

201

per hour, although Edgerton *et al.* (1966) estimated a velocity of about 34 miles per hour for similar free falling bats at Carlsbad Caverns, based upon calculations made from a photograph.

In Texas, where buildings are used primarily during migration by small (average 50) groups of bats, Davis *et al.* (1962) described flight patterns. Bats usually left a roost in groups, or having left singly, soon formed groups. These groups of a few to several dozen bats formed upward spiraling, loose clusters near the roost. When 50–100 feet above the roost the cluster suddenly moved off laterally. In some cases the bats emerged in a steady stream, forming an undulating, twisting rope of bats. These flights ascended gradually to about 100 feet, where they broke up into small clusters that moved off in various directions.

Bats began returning to the roost within 1½ to 2½ hours after the first had left, almost always arriving in groups. By this time the roost was often empty, with no bats flying in the vicinity. The returning bats appeared suddenly, forming a circular pattern as they approached the entrance. Each bat usually made 5–15 passes before entering the roost. At heavily used roosts, returning groups appeared at intervals all night, with the late comers crowding about in circular approach patterns as dawn neared.

Davis *et al.* (1962) described an interesting and unusual flight pattern in some groups of bats taken from buildings and released in the daytime. Although many such groups behaved like bats leaving the roosts in evening, several groups climbed almost straight up in a spiraling cluster. Even when watched with binoculars, they disappeared from sight, while still climbing, at an estimated height of over 10,000 feet.

Food and Feeding: T. *brasiliensis* feeds almost exclusively on small moths (Storer, 1926a; Ross, 1961b), and probably all food is captured while the bats are on the wing. Most insects taken are 5–9 mm. in length. Since it is established that most insectivorous bats use the interfemoral membrane in capturing prey (Webster and Griffin, 1962), the short membrane of this species apparently poses a problem. However, in flight the calcars are pointed backward, extending the membrane almost to the tip of the tail (Edgerton *et al.*, 1966).

Krutzsch (1955a) described the feeding behavior of this species based on observations at several localities in southern California. The bats appeared on the wing before sunset. Their long narrow wings and straight, rapid flight made them easily distinguishable from other species of bats. Foraging routes were at various heights. Sometimes the bats were seen hunting 15–30 feet above ground, where quick changes of direction apparently marked the pursuit of insects. Elsewhere the bats were first seen over 100 feet above the ground, descending as darkness increased until they were feeding among the top branches of live oaks. At still another locality they were seen flying low over an open meadow.

Unlike most other species of bats T. *brasiliensis* rarely uses night roosts. Krutzsch (1955a) found them only occasionally among the many other species that frequent night resting stations. However, his observations from evening until daylight at a nursery colony showed that most individuals were away from dusk until dawn. Glass (1958b) noted that Alabaster Cavern in Oklahoma is used as a night roost by T. *brasiliensis* throughout the summer.

Davis *et al.* (1962) estimated the average nightly consumption of insects at 1.0 g. per bat. This is less than 10 percent of the body weight and is probably much too low. Herreid (1967a) found that T. *brasiliensis* maintained a far higher metabolism during the day than *Myotis lucifugus* which consumes insects equal to about one-third its body weight within a half hour (Gould, 1955, 1959).

202

Based upon the figure of 1.0 g. of insects per bat per night, Davis *et al.* (1962) estimated that *T. brasiliensis* consumes about 6,600 tons of insects per year in Texas. A more realistic figure for the nightly consumption per bat would at least triple this value.

At Carlsbad Caverns the bats travel about 40 miles to reach their feeding area along the Pecos River. How far a colony of several million bats disperses to feed at night is not known. Davis *et al.* (1962) believe that they do not go much beyond 50 miles.

Reproduction: The great colonies of *T. brasiliensis* are nurseries where the females congregate to bear and raise their young. Some males are always present. They arrive earlier in the spring and are more erratic in numbers. Probably they are more nomadic than females. However, it is difficult to obtain representative samples for determining sex ratios because the sexes sometimes partially segregate within the roost. Twente (1956) found that the adult males in a maternity colony in Oklahoma were mostly in the younger age classes, but Perry (1965) found no difference in the age distribution between the sexes in the same cave.

Males tend to gather in certain caves near some maternity colonies. Eads *et al.* (1957) found that 80 percent of the 400 bats they examined in Beaver Creek Cave, Texas, on July 6, 1955, were males, and Perry (1965) found a population in Merrihew Cave, Oklahoma, that was made up predominantly of males throughout the summers of 1963 and 1964.

Krutzsch (1955a) found the sexes together throughout the year in California, but noted that fewer adult males were in the colonies when the young were being reared. Adult males seem to be widely distributed during summer; perhaps they dwell mostly in small colonies at this time. E. Lendell Cockrum captures as many males as females when netting over water

holes in Arizona. We found only males in Big Bend National Park, Texas, on July 5, 1966. Some adult males apparently remain in Mexico all summer, where small colonies are found in the highlands and central tropics (Villa and Cockrum, 1962; Long and Kamensky, 1967).

Spermatogenesis begins in September and continues throughout the winter in Florida (Sherman, 1937). Mature sperm first appear in the testes in late January but are not in the epididymides at that time. The males are sexually active only from February until April; breeding occurs in February and March. Ovulation takes place in the latter part of March. Gestation is about 77–84 days in Florida and was estimated as 100 days in California by Krutzsch (1955a). The peak of parturition occurred between June 3 and 11 one year and June 15–17 another, in Florida. In Texas birth peaks were June 8 and June 19 on different years (Davis *et al.*, 1962). In Oklahoma young are born during the last part of June and first part of July (Twente, 1956; Glass, 1958; Perry, 1965) and in southern California Krutzsch (1955a) said most young are born by mid-July.

A single young is produced in the right horn of the uterus. Krutzsch (1955a) found occasional females containing two embryos, and Sherman (1937) found one with an embryo in the left horn. Davis *et al.* (1962) found not a single fetus in the left horn of over 2,000 reproductive tracts examined in Texas.

Birth dates within any colony are not nearly so variable as among vespertilionids. In a Texas colony in 1958, two-thirds of all births occurred within 5 days, and 90 percent within a 15-day period.

Yearling females returning to the Oklahoma caves in spring are pregnant (Glass, 1959). This contrasts to the vespertilionids in which many yearlings are nonparous, and those that are pregnant bear their young much later than older females, thus giving rise to the wide variation of parturition dates within a colony (Davis and Hitchcock, 1965).

If many yearling female *T. brasiliensis* are nonparous, they must not join the nursery colonies. Davis *et al.* (1962) reported that virtually all female bats coming north to Texas bear young every year. However, in Florida Jennings (1958) found that eight percent of 120 females examined in summer showed no evidence of breeding activity.

At term the embryo is about 25 mm. in crown to rump length, has a forearm of about 18 mm., and weighs about 2.7 g., nearly one fourth the weight of a nonpregnant female. The babies are blind and naked at birth.

As with most other species of bats, the young is born in breech presentation. Sherman (1937) watched a captive female give birth. The mother hung head down and did not receive the baby in the interfemoral membrane as do the vespertilionids. The young emerged in less than two minutes. After all but the head was free the mother scratched the amnion to shreds with the claws of her feet. Davis *et al.* (1962), observing parturition in Texas caves, noted that the mothers clung to the ceiling with their feet, but sometimes with feet and thumbs. Several were seen to assist birth by pulling at the baby with their teeth. A birth which they observed in a captive bat took about one hour.

Sherman noted that the placenta remained attached to the young by the cord from eight hours to two days. The dried cord finally breaks and the placenta falls. He noted hundreds of young in the colony with placentae attached. Apparently in the Texas colonies the mothers sometimes consume the placentae, for Davis *et al.* (1962) found afterbirth tissue in the stomachs of several females.

Care of the Young: During the day the young cling together in large masses at roosting sites separate from the adults. In some cases millions of babies are packed together in continuous sheets covering large areas of a cave ceiling where they continually are moving about, squeaking and crawling over one another.

The mothers leave the young behind when they emerge to feed. They carry the young only to move them from one place to another, especially after a colony has been disturbed. Krutzsch (1955a) found that at least some mothers returned to the colony during the night and fed the young; adult females were found in the building at midnight, and the young with them had stomachs distended with milk.

T. brasiliensis is a prolific producer of milk. Nursing females returning to a cave in the morning contain so much milk that it oozes out with the least handling. Average weight of the mammae in this condition is about 0.8 g. or 8 percent of the average body weight of the adult. Based upon apparent milk loads in the mothers, Davis *et al.* (1962) postulated that the bats may nurse twice during the day, once in the morning and again after mid-afternoon. They estimated the average milk consumption by a baby at 0.85 g. per day.

No one has studied mother-young relationships in this species, but the scant evidence available suggests the mother does not recognize her own young among the millions of others in the Texas cave. Davis *et al.* (1962) found that a mother would accept and nurse any baby. When a lactating bat was held in a cluster of babies, she was immediately swarmed over by them, and made no attempt to reject the first babies to find her nipples. They suggested that every mother venturing into the nursery area is suckled by the first two babies to find her mammae and that no mother selects the young. If this is true, the superabundance of milk would be important for survival of the young. The abundance of milk leads to some parasitism; a few adult females have been found with milk in their stomachs.

Growth and Development: Short (1961) studied growth and development of *T. brasiliensis* in Davis Cave, Texas, during 1958. The work was based upon a study of samples with ages estimated on the basis of time from the estimated average birth date. He presented graphs which gave an estimate of weight and forearm length versus age. From measurements in utero he also graphed the relationship between embryo size and time until birth.

He noted that about 20 percent of the young flushed from the ceiling at Davis Cave on July 13, 1958, and about 80 percent flushed on July 21. Since 86 percent of the young had been born between June 3 and June 16, apparently they first take flight at about five weeks of age. This is later than vespertilionids, most of which can fly within three weeks after birth. Perhaps development is slower in *T. brasiliensis*, but molossids, with their narrow pointed wings, have difficulty launching when compared to vespertilionids; they may require more development for flight.

Herreid (1967b) studied mortality of the young in a Texas cave by gathering and counting the fallen babies at intervals throughout the day. He calculated that during their first two months of life only 1.3 percent perish.

Longevity: Survival has been studied, and age-class tables prepared by Davis *et al.* (1962) and by Perry (1965). Unfortunately, their calculations are based upon aging techniques of questionable accuracy. Davis *et al.* (1962), as well as Jennings (1958), separated the bats into arbitrary groups based upon tooth wear. However, none of the groups could be assigned an age in years. Perry (1965) aged his bats by weight of the eye lens. He assumed that the weight increases each year throughout life, an assumption that has not been validated for these animals. Individual bats could not be aged accurately because of wide overlap of lens weight in known aged bats.

Davis *et al.* calculated the maximum survival for female *T. brasiliensis* as 15 years, but assumed constant death rates for each year class, an assumption which has been found invalid for bats and for every other mammal yet studied (Davis, 1966; Caughley, 1966). Perry suggested that population turnover is complete in seven or eight years. Reliable data on longevity and age structure of *T. brasiliensis* apparently await further studies.

Populations: Population estimates for *T. brasiliensis* have been made by various writers for many colonies and several areas. Davis *et al.* (1962) estimated the total populations found in Texas caves in 1957 as at least 100 million distributed in millions, as follows: Bracken, 20; Nye, 10; James, 6; Davis, 4; Goodrich, 14–18; Rucker, 12–14; Frio, 10–14; Fern, 8–12; Devils Sink Hole, 6–10; Valdena Sink, 4; and Webb, Wilson, and Y-O Ranch caves less than 0.6 each.

In Oklahoma Perry (1965) estimated the peak population in 1963 at 6,960,000, distributed in millions among the caves

Distribution of *Tadarida brasiliensis* in the United States

205

as follows: Reed, 4; Vickery, 1.4; Selman's, 0.8; Conner's, 0.7; and Merrihew, 0.06. He thought the population was about one million less than in 1962. Twente (1956) estimated the highest population that he found at anytime during 1953 in Merrihew Cave at over 100,000, but noted striking fluctuations throughout the summer.

At Carlsbad Caverns the population has been estimated from as high as 8,700,000 in June of 1936 (Allen, 1962) to a present low of 250,000 (Edgerton *et al.*, 1966).

The great colony which has recently been discovered in Eagle Creek Cave in Arizona has been estimated to contain more than 10 million bats (Villa and Cockrum, 1962). Cockrum has told us that he thinks there may actually be more than twice that number.

In Florida, where *T. brasiliensis* apparently never enters caves, large colonies are found in buildings. Sherman (1937) estimated a colony in Gainesville at 10,000. Jennings (1958) found colonies of 50,000 individuals to be common and said that some may be much larger. He suggested that *T. brasiliensis* may be the most abundant bat in the state.

Migration: T. brasiliensis performs an annual migration which covers many hundreds of miles. Almost the entire population that inhabits Texas, Oklahoma, New Mexico, and Arizona in summer spends the winter in Mexico. Many thousands of these bats have been banded in recent years by various workers, and recoveries of banded bats have made it possible to piece together the migratory pattern. Papers describing these movements include Villa (1956a), Glass (1958b; 1959), Short *et al.* (1960), Davis *et al.* (1962) and Villa and Cockrum (1962).

A few *T. brasiliensis* winter in Arizona and southern Texas. Large winter populations occur in caves in the border states of Sonora, Nuevo Leon, and Tamaulipas and southward in caves and buildings through central and tropical Mexico. One banded at Calsbad Caverns on September 18, 1952, was recovered on November 25, 1952, over 800 miles to the south in Jalisco. A female which Glass banded as a baby in Oklahoma on July 7, 1963, was recaptured at Estación Tamuin, San Luis Potosí, on November 14 of that year. This bat traveled from Oklahoma about 1,000 miles into the lowland tropics south of the Tropic of Cancer. Numerous other banding recoveries document shorter movements.

In central Mexico *T. brasiliensis* is rare or absent from February through September. The numbers increase gradually during October, and from November to early January many large populations occur. By late January the numbers are decreasing, and in spring and summer only small colonies, generally made up of males, occur in the area.

In the Texas bat caves the first few thousand arrivals appear in late February. Numbers increase steadily during March and April as many transients bound for other caves to the north arrive. Apparently the bats travel in large flocks. At about midnight on April 22, 1958, Davis *et al.* (1962), observed several million bats hurtle down out of the sky into Frio Cave within a space of 10 minutes. This was a season when there were yet few *T. brasiliensis* in Texas, and Frio Cave had only a few dozen. The observers concluded that this was probably the arrival of a flight of migrants from the south.

In May the summer resident population is present in Texas, and the population remains rather stable through June and July when the young are being raised. After the young are weaned the adults begin deserting the caves. During August and September, both adults and young wander widely and are likely to be encountered many miles from the nursery cave. During October populations in the Texas caves fluctuate widely, possibly because of migrants from the north. By December the caves of the United States are essentially deserted by *T. brasiliensis*.

In Oklahoma these bats appear in the nursery caves during the first week of April. The population builds up steadily until all adults have arrived in time for the young to be born in June and July. By the end of October all are gone.

In Arizona transient populations appear in the low desert mine tunnels in late March and early April, and by late June many maternity colonies exist in the state. By late September these colonies begin to break up, and after October few individuals remain.

Homing: Like other bats, *T. brasiliensis* is capable of returning after having been released many miles from the roost. R. Davis (1966) released bats at various distances up to 328 miles. At the greatest distance 2 of 13 females returned to a roost at St. David, Arizona, after having been released at Kingman, Arizona. Although the distance is considerable, this performance is not especially remarkable, for *T. brasiliensis* might be expected to be familiar with extensive areas.

Hibernation: The extent of hibernation in *T. brasiliensis* is not clear, although in some parts of their range in the United States they are regular winter residents. In Oregon, Jewett (1955) found a building containing a colony of these bats in February, and Hardy (1941) reported that they often hibernate in houses in Utah. Hall (1946) mentioned specimens taken in Nevada in January and February. In California, Grinnell (1918) described a building in which large numbers of these bats spent the winters; Benson (1947b) also noted hibernating *T. brasiliensis* in the state.

Krutzsch (1955a) said that the colony which he studied in California abandoned the building in winter. Philip Leitner has been accumulating data for several years and finds that large numbers winter in California.

In the Southeast, Sherman (1937) found that of 10,000 bats

Skull of *Tadarida brasiliensis,* x3

in a building in Gainesville, Florida, only a few hundred remained in winter. Jennings (1958) reported that most breeding roosts in Florida were deserted during cold weather, but that sometimes a small remnant of the colony remained to hibernate in a protected crevice. At Thomasville, Georgia, one of us searched for this species in February in three buildings known to harbor summer colonies; several dozen inactive bats were present in one. At Charleston, South Carolina, at the northeastern edge of the known range, *T. brasiliensis* is a permanent resident; they have been shot in flight on warm days in January (Golley, 1966).

When placed in a refrigerator, *T. brasiliensis* readily enters torpor. However, Orr (1958) found that they rarely survived more than 3–4 weeks, and never more than 6 weeks, under conditions where *Antrozous* and *Myotis* remained healthy for 3–4 months.

Herreid (1963a) tested the ability of *T. brasiliensis* to hibernate by placing 20 bats in a room at 41° F. (5° C.). They survived from 17 to 95 days and had an average weight loss at death of 18 percent. Relative humidity was 60 percent. A small wet cloth was provided, but no drinking water was available. Some species of bats dehydrate quickly when hibernating at humidities as low as 80 percent (Kayser, 1961), and although they can regain most lost water by arousal and drinking (Kayser, 1961; Kallen, 1964), they soon perish if free water is not available. Herreid (1963c) found the relative humidity in a Texas cave colony of *T. brasiliensis* ranged from 88 to 96 percent. Optimal conditions for hibernating *T. brasiliensis* remain unknown.

T. brasiliensis, like the hibernating vespertilionids, deposits considerable fat during late summer or fall. The average weight of adult females in October is 15.2 g.; in April, 11.5 g. (Twente, 1956).

Temperature: T. brasiliensis often selects hot attics as roosts. Krutzsch (1955) recorded body temperatures of young bats in a cluster as high as 108° F. (42° C.) at a room temperature of 95° F. (35° C.). Herreid (1967a) found in the laboratory that the young could withstand slightly higher temperatures than adults. Licht and Leitner (1967a) observed a colony in a crevice between rafters in a barn in California. At the spot inhabited by the bats the temperature sometimes climbed above 104° F. (40° C.) in the afternoon. Whenever this happened the bats avoided the temperature extreme by temporarily moving down the rafter a few inches (fig. 107). Henshaw (1960) found that as temperature rises at Bracken Cave, Texas, many bats hang in the twilight zone of the entrance to escape the heat.

Twente (1956) found that the bats generally selected the warmer parts of a cavern and that the activity of many individuals in a cluster caused the temperature of the cluster to be higher than that of the environment. When bats hung singly, their body temperature was about the same as the environment. In the spring when the highest temperature in the cave was about 50° F. (10° C.), the bats formed tight hibernating clusters and did not leave the cave to feed for several days.

Herreid (1963b, 1963c, 1963d, 1967a) studied the responses of *T. brasiliensis* to temperature changes in a cave and in the laboratory. In the cave, the bats generally maintained a high body temperature, but in the laboratory body temperature seemed dependent upon the environment. He found an inverse relationship between the number of bats in a container and metabolism of the individual. The implication is that the larger the colony, the less the energy expenditure per bat to maintain a given temperature. High temperatures are essential for the rapid growth of young bats.

107. Response of *Tadarida brasiliensis* living in a building in California to excessive heat. In the morning the bats are nearly concealed in crevices (A). As the temperature rises, the bats move down away from the hot roof (B). (*Courtesy of Paul Licht and Philip Leitner*)

Associated Species: *T. brasiliensis* is often found in association with other species of bats. In Texas and Oklahoma they nearly always occur with *Myotis velifer.* The two species usually cluster separately but occasionally are mixed. Mixed groups are frequently encountered at temporary roosts during migration, sometimes in unusual retreats such as the cliff swallow nests noted by Buchanan (1958). Farther west they often share roosts in buildings with *Antrozous pallidus, Eptesicus fuscus* and *Myotis yumanensis.* In the Southeast they are frequently found with *Nycticeius humeralis* and less often with *Myotis austroriparius.* At least 11 species of bats have been found to share roosts with *T. brasiliensis* in the United States.

Parasites and Disease: Eads *et al.* (1957), Jameson (1959), George and Strandtmann (1960), and Strandtmann (1962) listed the many species of parasites they found on *T. brasiliensis* in southwestern caves. The mites *Ichoronyssus robustipes* and *Nycteriglyphus bifolium* were most abundant; at least five other species have been recorded. The flea *Sternopsylla texana* was common, and another species of flea was found occasionally. Three species of ticks were found in the caves. The giant bat bug *Primicimex cavernis* was found in Nye Cave. A parasitic fly, *Trichobius major*, which feeds primarily on *M. velifer*, also attacks *Tadarida.* Internal parasites included various species of cestodes, trematodes, and nematodes. Cain (1966) has listed the helminth parasites.

Many *T. brasiliensis* have been found to test positively for rabies. However, it is unlikely that more than a minute percentage of these ever transmit the disease. Like other bats, it seems to usually recover from an infection. No evidence of other epizootic diseases has been found.

Predation: The great colonies of *T. brasiliensis* attract numerous predators which feed upon the bats. Great horned owls

209

(*Bubo virginianus*) and barn owls (*Tyto alba*) live in small cave entrances and prey extensively on bats. Red-tailed hawks (*Buteo jamaicensis*), Cooper's hawks (*Accipter cooperi*), peregrin falcons (*Falco peregrinus*), sparrow hawks (*Falco sparverius*), and Mississippi kites (*Ictinia mississippiensis*) feed upon free-tailed bats.

Among predatory mammals, raccoons (*Procyon lotor*) seem to be the most important. These abundant animals range throughout the caves and feed heavily upon *Tadarida*. Opossums (*Didelphis marsupialis*) and skunks (*Mephitis mephitis*) also enter the caves and feed upon fallen bats.

Rat snakes (*Elaphe guttata* and *E. obsoleta*) are highly successful predators on the bats. They are excellent climbers and find their way to ceiling crevices which harbor bats. Sometimes several of these snakes inhabit a bat cave. Coachwhips (*Masticophis flagellum* and *M. taeniatus*) also inhabit

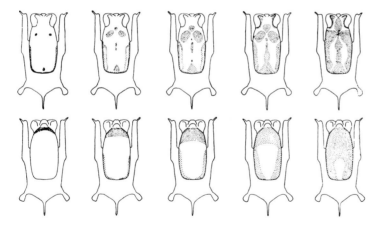

108. Molt pattern of *Tadarida brasiliensis mexicana*. Upper row, dorsal view. Lower row, ventral view. The fresh pelage appears in stippled areas. Early stages are at left, later stages at right. The dorsal surface is almost completed before molt begins on the ventral. (*Courtesy of Denny G. Constantine, from the* Journal of Mammalogy)

the caves and feed upon the bats. Eads *et al.* (1957) saw four individuals in Bracken Cave in one day. The snakes showed no fear of man, coming right up to devour bats which were being released. A copperhead (*Agkistrodon contortrix*) found in a cave entrance by Davis *et al.* (1962) contained bat remains. Herreid (1960b) saw a roadrunner (*Geococcyx californianus*) picking up young bats from the floor of a cave entrance.

Odor: Although all bat colonies develop a musty odor, the molossids produce a pungent smell characteristic of the group, and a free-tail colony site can be readily recognized even when not inhabited. Krutzsch (1955a) noted that one can often detect the odor of a colony from several hundred feet away. While the odor is not unpleasant, it is quite penetrating and will remain for several weeks in a bag in which bats have been kept. Herreid (1960a) noted that in November and December there is a difference in odor between the sexes.

Molt: Constantine (1957) described molt in *T. brasiliensis*. There is a single annual molt. Adult males mostly molt during July and adult females during August. The molt pattern is shown in figure 108.

Remarks: *T. brasiliensis* does not readily adapt to captivity. However, Krutzsch and Sulkin (1958) have developed a laboratory care program for this species. Workers at the Public Health Service Laboratory at University Park, New Mexico, have also had success in rearing these animals in captivity.

In most of the caves which harbor great colonies of *T. brasiliensis* in the United States the guano is harvested and sold as fertilizer. At Bracken Cave, Texas, where 20 million adult *Tadarida* and their young live in summer, about 60 tons of guano are harvested each year. The guano is removed during

December and January when the bats are not present. It is a considerable source of income to the owner of the cave.

Herreid (1959a) reported sexual dimorphism in the teeth of *T. brasiliensis*, the males having larger upper canines. This is probably a reflection of the finding of Schwartz (1955) that the skulls of males are larger than those of the females. Evidence available from many species of bats from the United States suggests the generalization that in molossids the males average larger than the females, whereas in the vespertilionid bats the females average larger than males.

A visit to one of the huge colonies of *T. brasiliensis* is a memorable experience. The bats are always alert, and the disturbance of the intruder's lights causes them to peel off from the great clusters in rapidly increasing numbers until the cave is filled with hordes of milling bats. The floor and the walls of the cave soon seem to be crawling with them, and they collide with the observer in ever increasing numbers. They cling to him and crawl upward to reach a high point from which to launch into flight. A writhing mound of bats quickly accumulates and, although they make no effort to bite, one gets the feeling that he may be smothered by the animals as he sinks deeper into the loose and sometimes soggy guano which covers the cave floor. The caves are oppressively hot during summer when the bat populations are at a maximum, the humidity is very high, and there is almost no air movement. Ammonia from the urine and decaying guano is sufficiently concentrated to cause irritation to the eyes and nasal passages. Indeed, concentrations above the level of human tolerance have been measured (Mitchell, 1965; Studier, 1966).

Several other factors contribute to the excitement of visiting the large colonies of *T. brasiliensis*. Mites exist in such numbers in some caves that they seem to cover every available surface. They quickly move to cover the additional surface

109. Dead *Tadarida brasiliensis* impaled on the spines of a cactus. Such accidents are not uncommon where cacti occur near the entrance to certain nursery caves. (*Courtesy of David A. Easterla*)

presented by a human visitor. The carnivorous beetles *Dermestes carnivorous* are abundant in the guano where they feed upon fallen bats, both dead and alive. Although they apparently will feed upon bat guano, they prefer flesh and can skeletonize a bat within hours. They do not hesitate to bite people, although they rarely bother a person on the move.

Venomous snakes, especially rattlesnakes of various species, are an additional concern. They commonly seek shelter in the entrances of caves and mines in the Southwest.

No one should enter a cave housing an active colony of *T. brasiliensis* unless he has been immunized against rabies. Although one is not likely to be bitten, even when bats are crawling all over him, rabies is a hazard in these caves. In recent years a bat research worker and another individual died of rabies after entering the Texas bat caves, although neither was known to have been bitten by any animal. Constantine (1962) reported that several species of carnivorous mammals kept caged in one of these caves contracted rabies, apparently via airborne virus.

110. *Tadarida femorosacca* showing the ears are joined at the midline.

TADARIDA FEMOROSACCA [Merriam]

Pocketed free-tailed bat

Recognition: Forearm, 44–50 mm.; wingspread, 330–360 mm. A bat of medium size with long narrow wings and tail protruding free from the interfemoral membrane for nearly an inch, or about half its length. Ears joined at the base. Hairs as long as the foot protrude from the toes. The membranous femoral pocket for which this species was named is not readily noticed and occurs in other species of free-tailed bats. Color, dark brown to gray both above and below, but basal half of the hairs nearly white.

Confusing Species: Similar to *Tadarida brasiliensis* which can readily be recognized by the fact that its ears do not quite join at the midline; in *T. femorosacca* the ears are clearly joined (fig. 110). All other free-tailed bats presently known from the United States are considerably larger than *T. femorosacca* with forearm measurements exceeding 55 mm. in the adults.

Range: Arid lowlands of the Southwest from southern California and New Mexico southward in Mexico through Baja California and along the West Coast through Sonora, Durango, and Jalisco at least to Michoacan. In the United States it has been recorded from a dozen localities in California and Arizona, from Carlsbad Caverns in New Mexico, and the Big Bend region of Texas. The use of mist nets at suitable localities will probably show a more extensive distribution in the United States. Dates of collections and observations suggest that it is a permanent resident where found.

Habitat: *T. femorosacca* is an inhabitant of the southwestern deserts where it is usually associated with high cliffs and rugged rock outcroppings in the crevices of which it finds shelter by day. Some have adopted manmade shelters. Colonies are small, usually less than a hundred individuals, but they carry on a great deal of squeaking during the day, and may thus draw attention to their hiding place.

Behavior: Krutzsch (1944b) observed a colony of these bats which inhabited a crevice in a cliff on a southwest facing slope in Palm Canyon, Borrego Valley, San Diego County, California. When emerging in the evening each bat dropped 4–5 feet before taking wing. It then flew in a wide arc over the opposite rim of the canyon and circled above the cliffs on both sides. The bats left in groups of twos and threes over a period of a half hour. The colony size was estimated at 50–60 bats.

This species leaves the roost late in the evening, usually well after dark. From June through December Gould (1961) studied emergence of a colony which lives beneath the roofing tiles of the chemistry building at the University of Arizona in Tucson. He stated that emergence always began after solar radiation reached zero, and the average emergence time was 45 minutes after the zero point.

As the bats take flight from their roost in the evening they produce loud, high-pitched calls. Calls sometimes continue while the bats are in flight. As with other free-tailed bats the flight is swift and lacks the fluttering characteristic of many vespertilionids.

Benson (1940) captured 11 *T. femorosacca* by stretching wires just above the surface of a small shallow pond near Alamos, Sonora. The bats were drinking from this pond late at night. They flew swiftly and made distinctly audible whistling and fluttering sounds with their wings. Occasionally they squeaked and chattered shrilly. In drinking the bats would hit the surface of the water hard while in flight and

213

Distribution of *Tadarida femorosacca* in the United States

Skull of *Tadarida femorosacca*, x3

111. *Tadarida femorosacca* from Sonora, Mexico.

214

scoop up a mouthful of water. Those which struck a wire and fell into the water never were able to rise from the surface as some species do, but rather swam to shore after a moment's surprised hesitation.

Reproduction: Apparently a single young is produced. Two of four females examined by Benson (1940) in southern Sonora on April 24 each contained a single embryo. Gould (1961) said that parturition occurred at Tucson during late June and early July. Adult females netted in Arizona on August 25 were still lactating (Cockrum and Musgrove, 1965).

Remarks: Our experience with this species is rather limited. On June 22, 1966, Robert J. Baker led us to a locality near Alamos, Sonora, where this bat is rather common. Nets were placed across the Rio Cuchijaqui, and we captured about a half dozen of this along with 19 other species of bats. *T. femorosacca* seems to be a permanent resident at this site, as Baker has also taken them there in November.

In June 1966 we visited the old Mormon church in Eden, Graham County, Arizona at the suggestion of Russell Davis, to search for *Macrotis waterhousii*. This abandoned church is an unusual structure in that it has a belfry which is readily available to bats and is constructed with mortar giving it a cave-like inner surface. Evidence indicated that this open belfry was heavily used by bats as a night roost. Among the droppings we found three skeletons of bats. One was *Macrotus*, one was *Myotis velifer*, and one was *T. femorosacca*.

This species is sometimes preyed upon by the California lyre snake, *Trimorphodon vandenburghi*. Krutzsch (1944a) captured a snake that had recently eaten a *T. femorosacca* in a crevice occupied by the bats.

TADARIDA MACROTIS [Gray]
Big free-tailed bat

Recognition: Forearm, 58–64 mm.; wingspread, 417–436 mm. A rather large bat with the tail extending free an inch or more beyond the interfemoral membrane. The ears are large, extending well beyond the end of the rostrum when laid forward, and are joined basally in the midline. Color varies from a light reddish brown to dark brown or black; the fur is glossy. The hair is bicolored, the basal portion being nearly white.

Confusing Species: *Tadarida brasiliensis* is smaller and the ears are not joined. *Tadarida femorosacca* is smaller. *Eumops perotis* and *Eumops underwoodi* are both larger. It is most similar to the slightly larger *Eumops glaucinus*, but in the United States this latter species is restricted to southern Florida, whereas *T. macrotis* is found only in the West.

Range: From northern South America and the Caribbean Islands northward into the western United States. Local but common as a breeding bat in Big Bend National Park, Texas, and at localities in New Mexico and Arizona. It breeds in northern New Mexico, and summer records from southwestern Utah suggest a breeding population there. Young specimens from Nevada and California (Hall, 1946) show that it also breeds there, but records from these states are scarce.

Records of accidentals are widely distributed over western North America. This bat is a powerful flier, and after the young are weaned individuals may appear hundreds of miles beyond what seems to be the normal range; there are fall records from Iowa and British Columbia.

Distribution of *Tadarida macrotis* in the United States

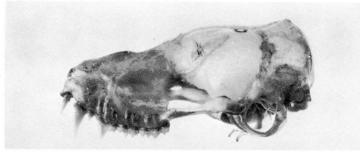

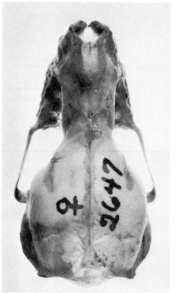

Skull of *Tadarida macrotis*, x3

112.   Big free-tailed bat, *Tadarida macrotis*.

216

There are winter records from San Diego, as well as Yuma, Arizona, and Sinton, Texas. The northern limits of its winter range are yet to be determined.

Habitat: This species is primarily an inhabitant of rugged, rocky country. The bats apparently spend the day in crevices in rock cliffs; however, only one day roost is presently known in the United States.

Until the advent of the mist net, *T. macrotis* was thought to be very scarce in the United States. Like other molossids it is readily captured in nets, and one who tends a net over the right waterhole may expect to take several. At Ghost Ranch in northern New Mexico, Constantine (1961a) netted 47 in August and September. Cockrum and Ordway (1959) netted 56 over the swimming pool at the Southwestern Research Station in the Chiricahua Mountains at Portal, Arizona, during the summer of 1955.

In spite of its local abundance, this species is not found in many places where the habitat seems suitable. It also is unpredictable in abundance. Only three were taken at the Southwestern Research Station when nets were in operation over the swimming pool throughout the summer of 1958 (Cockrum and Cross, 1964), and we captured only one while netting over the pool throughout June 1966.

Borell (1939) described a colony of *T. macrotis* which he found on May 7, 1937, in the Chisos Mountains in what is now Big Bend National Park. The bats occupied a horizontal crevice about 20 feet long and 6 inches wide on the side of a cliff some 40 feet above a talus slope. At the base of the cliff and extending the full length of the crevice was a pile of guano 3–4 feet wide and up to 6 inches deep. The fecal pellets were 5–6 mm. long and 2–3 mm. in diameter. Borell fired shots into various parts of the crevice and collected 10 bats. All were female *T. macrotis*; eight were pregnant.

The next evening Borell returned to the site to watch the bats emerge. They began to appear late, 40 minutes after pipistrelles began to forage. The bats left in small groups during a period of about 15 minutes, and Borell counted about 130. The swish of their rapid flight as they took wing was noticeable, but it was too dark to determine the direction in which they flew. Borell suggested that a reason this bat was so rare in collections is that it forages only after it is too late to see to shoot them.

Reproduction: Litter size is one. That they form nursery colonies is indicated by the report of Borell (1939) and the concentrations of adult females found by Cockrum and Ordway (1959), Constantine (1961), and Gardner (1965). Those shot by Borell contained embryos measuring 12–14 mm., suggesting that they were not yet near term on May 7. One from the Chiricahua Mountains taken on May 29 contained a 23 mm. embryo. In Durango, Mexico, eight females netted June 8 and 10 contained embryos measuring 22–25 mm. Apparently the young are born during June.

Constantine (1961a) found that all but 3 of 30 adult females he netted between August 14 and September 17 in northern New Mexico were still lactating.

Remarks: When foraging *T. macrotis* usually emits a loud piercing chatter. We noticed this the night of June 4, 1966, when netting at the Southwestern Research Station. At 8:45 p.m. a pair of bats appeared over the net. They flew rapidly, constantly uttering a sharp piercing note. The sound was similar to the note of a flying squirrel, but louder and more piercing. After the chattering bats had passed over the pool several times, one struck the net and was caught. It was a male *T. macrotis*. Constantine (1961a) noted that it does not always chatter in flight.

On the night of July 5, 1966, we netted bats over a sewage settling pond in the Chisos Mountains in Big Bend National Park. Many times during the evening we heard a loud chattering as several bats flew overhead, but none of them ever came down to the level of the net. We suspect that they were *T. macrotis* but are not sure, since several other bats including *Eumops*, *Euderma*, and *Plecotus phyllotis* make similar loud, piercing calls.

We found this species easy to handle. They are not particularly vicious, although if handled somewhat roughly, they protest vocally and open the mouth widely in a threatening gesture. Like other molossids they make no attempt to fly when confined in a small room. Molossids, with their long pointed wings, are swift fliers but limited in maneuverability and have more difficulty in launching themselves than our other bats. If forced to fly in a rather small room, they usually crash into a wall.

Husson (1962) showed that the correct name for this species is *Tadarida macrotis*. It has been called *Tadarida molossa* in recent literature.

Borell (1939) found *T. macrotis* parasitized by bat bugs and fleas.

113. In the United States *Eumops perotis* is our largest bat and *Pipistrellus hesperus* the smallest.

EUMOPS PEROTIS [Schinz]

Western mastiff bat; greater mastiff bat

Recognition: Forearm, 72–82 mm.; wingspread, 530–570 mm. A very large bat with long narrow wings; large ears joined at the midline, running forward instead of erect, nearly concealing the eyes, and extending beyond the nose. Distal half of tail free from the interfemoral membrane. Color, dark gray or brownish gray, somewhat lighter below. Hair bicolor, being nearly white at the base.

Variation: Several subspecies are recognized, but only *Eumops perotis californicus* (Merriam) occurs in the United States.

Confusing Species: E. perotis is our largest native bat and can readily be separated from most other free-tailed and mastiff bats by size alone. It is most similar to *Eumops underwoodi* from which it can be separated by its larger size (the *E. underwoodi* in the United States have foreams which measure less than 72 mm.), darker color, and lack of long guard hairs on the rump. The ears are longer, measuring about 40 mm. from the notch (about 30 mm. in *E. underwoodi*); they extend beyond the nose when laid foreward, and are joined at the midline.

Range: This species has a most unusual distribution consisting of three widely separated populations. One occupies South America from Argentina to Lima, Peru, and northern Brazil. A second population is found in Cuba. The third ranges from California to Texas and across northern Mexico from Sonora to Coahuila. In the United States it ranges from San Francisco Bay across southern California, southern Nevada, and the southern half of Arizona. It also occurs in the Big Bend region of Texas east at least to Pumpville, Val Verde County. It probably occurs across New Mexico but apparently has not been taken in that state. There are unconfirmed reports of *E. perotis* in Lake County, California, north of San Francisco. *E. perotis* is apparently a permanent resident throughout its range in the United States.

Habitat: This species is a resident of the Lower and Upper Sonoran life zones of the arid Southwest. It prefers the rugged rocky canyons and cliffs where crevices provide its favored daytime retreats. It has adapted to manmade shelters and is now found in such cities as Tucson and Los Angeles. In California nearly as many day roosts are known in buildings as in natural crevices. Colonies are small, nearly always less than 100.

The sheltered crevices occupied by a colony of *Eumops* can usually be easily recognized by the massive urine stains on the cliff below and the droppings, which are larger than those of other bats.

This bat is so large and its wings so narrow that it has some difficulty in taking flight, and all regularly used roosts are in situations which allow the bats a vertical drop of about 10 or more feet for launching into flight.

In the daytime roosts *E. perotis* prefer to retreat far back into a tight rock crevice. In a building they also generally prefer to crowd into crevices, but occasionally they may be found hanging from a rafter in the open (Howell, 1920a). Probably they move out into the open in response to excess heat. Because of a reluctance to fly they are easy to capture in an accessible roost.

Vaughan (1959) made extensive observations on *E. perotis* in California where he located 22 roosting sites. Eight of these were inhabited by colonies; the remainder housed single individuals or groups of two or three.

Roost sites were in crevices in vertical cliffs. Crevices used were all more than a foot deep and at least two inches wide. Larger crevices with slit-like openings several feet long were preferred; colonies were usually found in crevices that were 10 or more feet deep. Since granitic and consolidated sandstones flake upon weathering and form deep crevices, *E. perotis* was found most commonly in broken terrain where extensive exposures of these rocks occur.

The roosting sites had several characteristics in common. All had moderately large openings that could be entered from below. Openings were always at least two inches wide, or nearly twice the thickness of the bats' bodies, enabling the bats to enter easily and quickly. Entrances were horizontal and faced downward so that the bats could leave the roost by simply dropping out. All roosts were crevices that became narrow enough at some point to enable the bats to wedge themselves tightly into the interior of the retreat. Roosts were high above the ground and had unobstructed approaches. A drop of 20 feet or more from the crevice was usually available.

Behavior: Vaughan's observations showed that the bats entered a roost in the morning by swooping up into the entrance from below, grasping the rock surface with thumbs and feet, and crawling into the crevice. The maneuver was carried out so rapidly that the bats just seemed to disappear into the crevice. After entering each bat crawled rapidly into the remote recesses of the retreat. The bats crawled with remarkable speed until both the dorsum and venter came into contact with the rock surface. Then each bat turned around, and in an upside-down position, wedged itself into the crevice by reaching upward with its feet and pulling itself into the crevice. They wedge themselves so tightly that sometimes animals shot and killed do not fall from their crevice. When the bat crawls the tail sticks up into the air at about a 45° angle. It probably serves as a tactile organ when the bat is in a crevice.

In colonial roosts *E. perotis* moves about at any time of the day, but is most active in early morning and late afternoon when it is rather vocal. In the morning they are in the deepest parts of the crevice, but in the afternoon some may move nearer the entrance. Individuals which roost alone are quiet during the day.

Krutzsch (1955c) described a daily rhythm of activity at a colony in a series of crevices on a cliff in San Diego County, California, which he observed for several years. The bats were inactive in the early morning hours, and did not squeak or crawl about until the sun had warmed the rocks. Usually on clear days the bats became active between 10:00 and 10:30 a.m. On foggy, or cloudy and cool days, bats remained inactive until afternoon. In becoming active first one bat would squeak followed quickly by several others. The squeaking would continue undiminished, and soon bats could be seen moving about. Activity lessened considerably after 4:00 p.m. The bats would then hang motionless, with the only audible sounds being low chirping calls. This period of quiescence continued almost until, and sometimes after, sunset, when the bats again became active. The bats emerged only after complete darkness; then they left singly at intervals of several minutes. It was more than an hour and a half before all had left. The bats did not return to this roost at least until after midnight.

These observations are considerably different from those of Cox (1965a) who studied two maternity colonies in Arizona in July and August. The bats left individually after dark, but most were gone within an interval of a few minutes. At one roost activity continued throughout the night, with bats returning, leaving and flying about the roost. At both roosts when the bats returned for the day they came in almost simultaneously, at a rate so rapid that Cox could not count them. Since these were maternity colonies, the behavior of the adults was probably influenced by the young. With other species of bats it has been noted that the adults return to their young at night, but after weaning will use night roosts elsewhere.

Foraging and Flight: A colony of *E. perotis* becomes increasingly active as darkness approaches. The bats move to the mouth of the crevice, chatter loudly and emit a peculiar, loud, smacking noise. Then as each bat launches itself, it utters a series of high-pitched cries. In launching, the bat drops from the crevice and gives several powerful strokes of the wings as it falls rapidly. It dives 10–20 feet at a roughly 45° angle before it pulls up in a wide arc into level flight. Vaughan (1959) noted that at some colonies most bats would drop 20–25 feet in launching themselves. In the locations where little space was available they would drop only 5–10 feet and then pull sharply upward.

Vaughan found that this species was unable to maintain flight after launching from a table top. Individuals thrown 15 feet into the air would take flight, but bats thrown half that distance could not. He concluded that five or six feet from the ground is the minimum height from which *E. perotis* can launch itself into sustained flight.

After a bat leaves the roost it climbs high in wide circles. Vaughan watched two individuals which left a roost early enough to be seen. They could be observed with binoculars until they disappeared at an estimated 1,000 feet above ground and their cries could be heard for some time after they were out of sight. Vaughan says that they can be heard clearly when flying about 1,000 feet overhead and that one can make a rough estimate of their altitude by the intensity of the sound. In southern California he often heard them when

114. Western mastiff bat, *Eumops perotis*.

221

they were flying so high as to be barely audible; he estimated such bats to be as much as 2,000 feet overhead. At other localities he found that they regularly foraged at 100 to 200 feet above ground. Apparently they normally forage at considerable heights, generally higher over rugged country than over lowland valleys.

Cockrum (1960b) noted when a mastiff bat flew down a canyon with high cliffs on either side the calls and echos could be heard at least a quarter of a mile away. Like our other species of *Eumops,* the calls are so loud and distinctive that they can be easily recognized once one is familiar with them. E. Lendell Cockrum told us that he frequently hears these bats at night over Tucson, Arizona.

Bad weather does not seem to inhibit the foraging of *E. perotis,* for Vaughan (1959) has heard them flying on rainy nights and even during a thunderstorm. Activity seemed to be limited on foggy nights.

The foraging range of *E. perotis* apparently is extensive. Vaughan (1959) has heard them many times flying over the desert flats several miles from the nearest likely roosting sites. In the Mohave Desert they were heard foraging 15 miles from the nearest hills. Although suitable roosts are rather scattered, the wide foraging area makes the distribution of these bats continuous across southern California late at night.

This species has an exceptionally long foraging period. They seldom use night roosts like other kinds of bats, and only occasionally do individuals return at night to the daytime roost to rest (see Cockrum, 1960b). Vaughan (1959) noticed that their cries could be heard overhead at all hours of the night and that they did not seem to have activity peaks like other bats. He estimated an activity period of 6½ hours per night. Because this species is large and feeds extensively upon Hymenoptera (Ross, 1961b) at high altitudes, it probably takes a long time to obtain a meal.

These bats generally begin leaving the roost about an hour after sunset. By 90 minutes after sunset most are gone. Females with young in the roost occasionally return during the night and stay in the roost for a short time. Activity at the roost peaks between 2:30 and 3:00 a.m. when most bats return.

While flying in the open, *E. perotis* emits a high-pitched, piercing cry every two or three seconds. As the bat approaches and enters the roosting crevice, the sounds increase in frequency until they blend together into a high buzz (Vaughan, 1959; Cockrum, 1960b). This may be a case of a bat producing echo-locating sounds audible to the human ear.

The flight is strong and fast, more direct, and less erratic than that of most bats. When the bats are in flight, the wings make a sharp swishing sound that can be heard up to about 100 feet. Using these sounds, Vaughan (1959) estimated four wing beats per second during level flight.

Like other kinds of bats returning to the roost in the morning, *E. perotis* usually makes several passes at the entrance before entering, but the behavior of this species is rather spectacular as the bats dive repeatedly at the colony site. A dive is always begun with a sudden increase in the rate of the cries being produced by a passing bat. Then, with the cries merging into a continuous buzz, the bat dives at high speed toward a point below the crevice, pulls sharply upward just before reaching the cliff, and makes a half loop as it veers off to the side to avoid crashing into the cliff. At the bottom of the dive the wings are spread suddenly, the membranes producing a loud swishing sound like canvas being lashed in the air (Vaughan, 1959).

Food: Ross (1961b) studied the stomach contents of four *E. perotis* and droppings from beneath a roost in Arizona. He found that these great bats were feeding on rather small insects, more than half of which were Hymenoptera. The list of insect fragments and the percentages of the total number of specimens found includes: Odonata: Aeshnoidea, 1; Orthoptera: Acrididae, 10; Hemiptera: Miridae, 10; Coleoptera: Scarabaeidae, *Cremastocheilus* sp., 1, Tenebrionidae 5, Curculionidae 5; Lepidoptera: moths 10; Hymenoptera: Halictidae 36, Formicidae 12, Megachilidae 5, Anthophoridae 5.

Reproduction: In California Howell (1920a) and Krutzsch (1955c) have found the sexes together throughout the year. At a large maternity colony in Arizona an adult male was found in late August, and at a site used by a small nursery colony, a single adult male was the only bat present on August 18 (Cockrum, 1960b). Data are not available on the sex composition of the colonies when the young are small.

Breeding probably occurs in early spring. Testes of the adult males are small and have not descended in the fall. They are enlarged and descended in March but have regressed in some individuals by the middle of April (Cockrum, 1960b).

Time of ovulation and length of the gestation period are unknown. Parturition dates vary more extensively in this species than any other bat in the United States. Embryos 18 mm. in crown–rump length were found as early as April 6 (Krutzsch, 1955c), and 15 young estimated at 1–3 weeks old were seen in a colony on June 16 (Howell and Little, 1924). Juveniles nearly ready to fly and small naked young were found together on July 18 in California (Krutzsch, 1955c), and a female gave birth on August 10 in Arizona (Cockrum, 1960b). We have a juvenile specimen taken from the attic of a church in Azusa, California, on November 11, 1952. This animal was very young, with cartilaginous gaps of about 2 mm. at the finger joints. Although nothing is known of growth rates in *E. perotis*, it seems unlikely that such a bat could be more than about two months old.

A single young per female is ordinarily produced. Krutzsch (1955c) noted a female carrying two embryos on April 10. One was 20 mm. in crown–rump length and the other 15 mm. It is not known if two young are ever produced; supernumerary embryos are commonly resorbed in bats, but it seems unlikely that one this size would be.

The young are born naked except for some tactile hairs on the feet and face. One newborn observed by Krutzsch had its eyes unopened but one which Cockrum observed was born with its eyes open.

Movements: Apparently *E. perotis*, like many other species of bats, will move about among alternate daytime roosts. Krutzsch (1955c) observed the utilization by these bats of three crevices on the face of a cliff. They used only those portions of the crevices which were 15 feet or more above ground. They showed no preference between vertical and horizontal openings, but never used shallow crevices which extended only

Distribution of *Eumops perotis* in the United States

a foot or two into the cliff. The colony would shift freely among the main roost and two other crevices. Sometimes the main roost would be deserted except for the young, with the adult bats found in the other crevices. When the young were unable to fly the adults always returned to them within 24 hours. After the young were independent the colony often shifted from one site to another without apparent provocation. Such shifting is probably influenced by temperature and other local conditions as well as by human disturbance.

Most roosts are not occupied year around. Howell (1920a) found E. perotis at all seasons, but in different roosts. The colony studied by Krutzsch was present from April through October. Leitner (1966), however, studied a colony in the attic of a building in Glendora, California, and found the bats present at all seasons. Probably local microclimatic conditions at the roost determine whether or not it will be used all year.

Numerous records of single bats being taken at obviously temporary roosting sites in fall and winter suggest that dispersal of the summer colonies is common. We know nothing about the extent of movements and have no data on possible seasonal migrations.

Temperature Regulation: Leitner (1966) studied temperature regulation in *E. perotis* in the laboratory and at a large colony in southern California throughout the year. He found that the bats maintained high body temperatures during the day from March through October. During December, January, and February, however, the bats entered a daily torpor, even when kept in the laboratory at room temperatures. They remained in torpor from early morning until late afternoon or evening, when they aroused spontaneously.

At the natural roost, the attic of a heated building, the bats were always in daily torpor from December through February, but they regularly aroused at night and left their roost to feed. Only on nights when the temperature at dusk was below 41° F. (5° C.) did the bats fail to emerge.

In laboratory experiments Leitner (1966) found that *E. perotis* maintained a high body temperature when exposed to air temperatures over the range of 32°–104° F. (0°–40° C.). The neutral temperature for the species seems to be 86° F. (30° C.), for metabolism, as measured by oxygen consumption, heart rate, and shivering, increased at temperatures above and below this point.

Leitner's findings conflict with those of Krutzsch (1955c), who found that individuals placed in a refrigerator at 50° F. (10° C.) quickly became dormant and remained inactive until aroused by removal to higher temperatures 10 days later. Perhaps these responses are due to seasonal differences, but unfortunately neither author mentioned the dates or seasons at which the work was done. A single juvenile which one of us put into a refrigerator in the middle of November readily went into torpor.

The resting body temperature of 93°–95° F. (34°–35° C.) in *E. perotis* is somewhat lower than the body temperatures maintained by most mammals. Leitner found that when the air temperature was increased above 86° F. (30° C.) the body temperature increased. Body temperature was always higher than the ambient temperature, and the animals apparently could not regulate their temperature by cooling. They could tolerate ambient temperatures of 100°–102° F. (38°–39° C.) without undue heat stress.

Odor: This species has a penetrating odor, stronger than that of most other bats. This seems to be due, in part at least, to the secretions of a peculiar dermal gland on the throat just anterior to the sternum. This gland is present in all individuals including the newborn, but is inconspicuous and poorly developed in females. In males its development is seasonal and probably related to reproduction. The gland is most active in early spring when it measures 11–14 mm. across and 4–5 mm. in depth. It makes a thick swelling about a rather large opening from which exudes a slimy oily secretion of strong odor. Howell (1920a) found the gland active in only one individual taken in early December. Glands were most active in March, but by the middle of April had greatly subsided. Other species of *Eumops* also have such glands (fig. 119).

Associates: E. *perotis* frequently shares the same attic or rock crevice with other species of bats, but apparently they do not cluster with the smaller species. *Eptesicus fuscus*, *Antrozous pallidus*, and *Tadarida brasiliensis* often share their abode. There is one record of the rare *Tadarida femorosacca* living in a rock crevice with E. *perotis*.

Remarks: All our molossids, with their long narrow wings, are swift fliers with poor maneuverability, but E. *perotis* because of their larger size have greater problems than the others. When released in a small room they refuse to fly, even when thrown into the air. In a large room they seem unable to execute a complete circle and often crash into a wall when forced to fly. In spite of this, colonies are sometimes found in attics of houses where the bats gain entrance and exit through the louvers of a ventilator. It has not been reported how the bats get from the roosting site to the ventilator when they exit from such buildings; probably they crawl. Howell (1920a) once found 18 of these bats that had died in the attic of a house because the ventilator at their end of the building had been plugged and the bats could not or would not go to the other ventilator.

Although some individuals can launch themselves into flight from the ground (Little, 1920), most seem unable to do so.

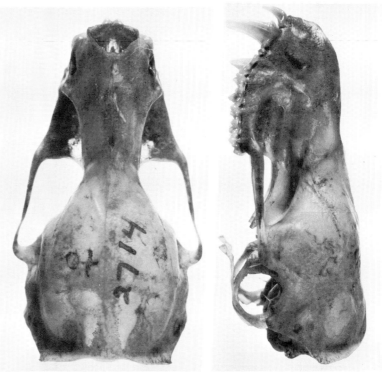

Skull of *Eumops perotis*, x3

225

115. A rock shelter which harbors a colony of *Eumops perotis* in Eagle Creek Canyon, Arizona. The poles support a net set to capture bats.

To observe this we released two lactating females on July 1 by placing them on the ground. The bats had been captured two nights before and seemed healthy. They had just been handled and were active when released in mid-afternoon. They were released individually by placing them on a gravel drive in an open area. The first one tried 6–8 times to launch itself, all the while crawling rapidly toward a large oak tree 100 feet away. When it reached the tree, it swiftly climbed the trunk and disappeared. When the second bat was released it immediately ran to one of the observers and climbed his trouser leg. When replaced on the ground, it started at once toward someone else. When he moved away, the bat headed toward a third person. After we all moved out of the area the bat headed straight for the oak tree. We caught it just before it reached the tree and threw it high into the air. It flew high in a wide half circle and alighted in the foliage of a distant tree.

We had some difficulty obtaining specimens of *E. perotis* to photograph. Since the known roosts in Arizona are in nearly inaccessible crevices in high cliffs, we decided to try to get one in California where many roosts have been found in buildings. However, Luther Little told us that all the colonies he had known have been destroyed, and Charles McLaughlin said that specimens have rarely been brought to the Los Angeles County Museum in recent years. We talked with several other Californians who work with bats, and none knew where we could obtain a *E. perotis*. Roy Johnson told us about the ones he found at Tonto National Monument in Arizona. We visited there, and spent a night at the ruins with a net stretched below the crevice in the rock shelter where the bats had been found. At this time the crevice was occupied by a nursery colony of *A. pallidus* and we neither saw nor heard *Eumops*.

We next decided to try Cockrum's locality on Eagle Creek in Arizona. Here the bats are in a crevice at the top of a rock shelter about 50 feet above the ground. Since the bats drop about 10 feet in launching themselves, we decided to set the nets about 40 feet high to catch them. We bought several lengths of different sizes of conduit, and set out to build a net pole by fitting them together. We made two poles, each of which was 28 feet long.

The rock shelter is about 60 feet across at the front, just right for our 60-foot nets. We could climb the cliff on both sides far enough easily to get the nets up to 40 feet. We put two nets together to make a wider surface and erected it (fig. 115). The arrangement was surprisingly successful. When darkness arrived the first *Eumops* emerged and struck the net. It became entangled, and uttered a stream of the loudest vocal protest we have ever heard from a bat. This continued until we had lowered the net and removed the bat. We had just got the net up again when the second bat emerged, and she, too, was caught. While we were removing this bat another emerged and flew down the canyon. We got the net up again and soon caught the fourth bat which emerged. We could probably have caught nearly the entire colony, but we closed up our nets rather than disturb the nursery colony any more than necessary.

When first captured they were quite pugnacious and bit viciously, but they quickly became docile after handling. Like all other molossids we have handled, they were cooperative and good subjects for photography.

E. perotis apparently never detects a mist net and is readily taken in one. This great bat is never taken over the little woodland ponds that are often so productive for netting other species of bats, however. Apparently it prefers a large pool in the open with plenty of open space for the approach.

Krutzsch (1955c) recorded the ectoparasite *Hesperoctenes eumops* from one of two bats examined.

116. The long guard hairs on the rump are distinctive of *Eumops underwoodi.*

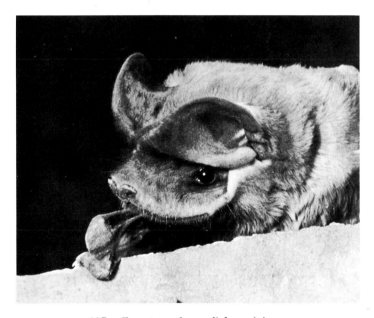

117. *Eumops underwoodi* from Arizona.

EUMOPS UNDERWOODI Goodwin

Underwood's mastiff bat

Recognition: Forearm, 65–77 mm.; wingspread, 500–540 mm. A large bat with long narrow wings, ears meeting at the midline, and the distal half of the tail free from the interfemoral membrane. A few long guard hairs on the rump extend 7–10 mm. beyond the rest of the fur (fig. 116). Color, a rich, dark brown above, somewhat grayish below. Fur bicolor, lighter at the base.

Variation: Two subspecies are known. The race that occurs in the United States is *Eumops underwoodi sonoriensis* Benson.

Confusing Species: Superficially similar to all of our other free-tailed bats but much larger than *Tadarida brasiliensis* and *Tadarida femorosacca. Tadarida macrotis* is somewhat smaller, with wingspread considerably less, and weighs generally less than 30 g. rather than more than 40 g. *Eumops glaucinus* is similar to *E. underwoodi,* but smaller and darker, and within the United States these two species are widely separated geographically.

    E. underwoodi is most similar to *Eumops perotis.* The latter is slightly larger and has much longer ears, measuring about 40 mm. from the notch and reaching beyond the nose when laid forward. In *E. underwoodi* the ears are about 30 mm. long and just reach the end of the nose when laid forward. In the United States, the two species can be separated on the basis of forearm length; *E. underwoodi* has a forearm less than 72 mm. in length, but a Mexican race is larger. *E. perotis* lacks long bristle-like hairs like those that protrude from the rump of *E. underwoodi.*

Range: In the United States this species is known from only four localities within about 20 miles of one another in the vicinity of the Baboquivari Mountains in Pima County, Arizona. From here, it extends southward through Sonora and the western parts of Mexico, mostly in the arid lowlands, through parts of Colima, Michoacan, Morelos, and Chiapas, into Honduras. Winter distribution and limits of the range are unknown.

Habitat: Little is known about the habitat of *E. underwoodi.* Most specimens have been taken in mist nets set over waterholes in the desert. Benson (1947a) captured 15 with wires stretched over water in Sonora.

A locality in Arizona which has produced more specimens of this species than all other localities together is a pond behind an earthen dam in a fairly flat mesquite desert at 4,000 feet elevation six miles from the nearest low mountain range. This tank is two miles east of Sasabe, Arizona, and only a few hundred yards north of the Mexican border.

Reproduction: Apparently the single young is born in late June or in July. A specimen we have from Sasabe, which was taken on June 19, 1966, contained a single embryo which measured 30 mm. in crown–rump length. Seven of the eight females taken there on July 16 were lactating, and the other carried a 39 mm. embryo which surely was near term (Cockrum and Gardner, 1960). A female gave birth on July 5 to a normal young which was raised successfully in captivity (Constantine, 1961b).

Remarks: Constantine found these bats were amenable to

118. *Eumops underwoodi* in a defensive pose. In spite of the ferocious appearance this is a rather gentle bat.

229

Distribution of *Eumops underwoodi* in the United States

119. Adult male *Eumops underwoodi* showing an active gular gland.

Skull of *Eumops underwoodi*, x3

captivity after he trained them to eat mealworms. The one which was born in captivity was still doing well when we visited the Public Health Service Laboratory at University Park, New Mexico, in June 1966. The animal is remarkably tame; it squeaks to attract attention, scampers across its cage to meet visitors, jumps onto a hand and runs up an arm whenever it has the opportunity, and squeaks when company leaves.

Apparently *E. underwoodi* is common at the tank east of Sasabe, Arizona, although the location of the diurnal roost remains unknown. Nineteen specimens captured there have been reported in the literature (Cockrum and Gardner, 1960). On June 19, 1966, Robert Baker and Bryan Glass visited the locality and erected several nets over the pond. When they quit netting at midnight with 20 adult *E. underwoodi*, including both sexes, bats were still flying over the tank as evident from their piercing calls.

The presence of mastiff bats in an area can be detected by listening for their characteristic high-pitched "peeps" produced several times a minute in flight. Observers have noted that the calls of *E. underwoodi* are more intense than those of *E. perotis*. They are so intense as to actually hurt the ears of the observer standing close by when the bats are flying. Constantine (1961b) noted that the sounds seemed to increase in frequency and intensity as the bats approached a pond where he was netting. Robert Baker told us that they do not always call when approaching.

Despite their great size and formidable dentition they seem rather gentle, and we found them easy to handle in captivity.

EUMOPS GLAUCINUS [Wagner]
Wagner's mastiff bat

Recognition: Forearm, 57–66 mm.; wingspread, about 470 mm. A large bat with long narrow wings and with the tail protruding free from the interfemoral membrane for about half its length. Ears joined at the midline. Color dark gray, nearly black; slightly paler below. Fur glossy, hairs sharply bicolor, white at the basal half.

Variation: No subspecies of this bat have been described, but the Florida population probably represents an undescribed race. Individuals are considerably larger than those from Central America, with forearms measuring 64–66 mm., whereas the latter measure 57–61 mm., and the skulls are noticeably different.

Confusing Species: The only other free-tailed bat in Florida is *Tadarida brasiliensis*, which is much smaller than *E. glaucinus*. The *E. glaucinus* in Florida are large bats with forearm greater than 60 mm., whereas the forearm of *T. brasiliensis* is less than 50 mm.

Range: From Ecuador and Brazil through northern South America and Central America into central Mexico at least as far north as Yucatan, Morelos, and Colima. Also on the islands of Cuba and Jamaica and into extreme southeastern Florida. In the United States, known only from the cities of Miami and Fort Lauderdale and from the suburbs of Miami. It is a permanent resident.

Habitat: Most of the information about *E. glaucinus* in the

120. *Eumops glaucinus* from Miami, Florida.

Distribution of *Eumops glaucinus* in the United States

232

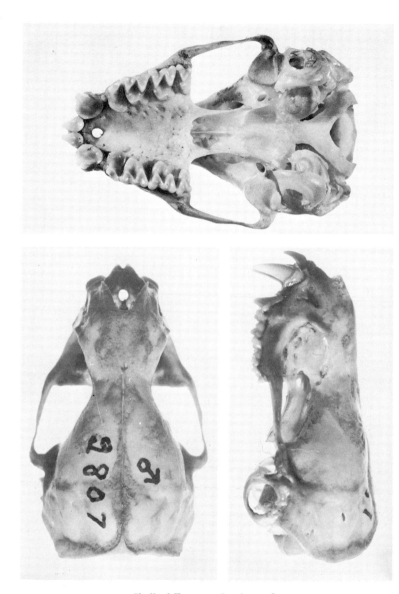

Skull of *Eumops glaucinus*, x3

United States comes to us from Gordon Hubbell of the Crandon Park Zoo in Miami, who has made observations on these bats for several years and has kindly supplied us with his notes.

Hubbell says that the favorite roosting place for *E. glaucinus* is under the Cuban tiles which are used as roofing material extensively in certain Miami areas, especially in Coral Gables. For this reason many of the specimens which have been collected have come from the Coral Gables area.

Behavior: This bat leaves its roost after dark and flies high where it is seldom seen. It has a very loud, piercing call, and once a person recognizes this call, he can easily pick it out from the other nighttime sounds of the city. Hubbell hears these bats flying overhead while driving his car in heavy traffic in downtown Miami.

Hubbell has searched for these bats in the evenings on rooftops and in wooded areas, and noticed that they seldom fly below 30 feet. From within 10 feet of one in flight he could not perceive any noise from the wing beats, as can be heard in some other species of bats.

Reproduction: Apparently the young are born in June and July. A female aborted a fetus on July 5, eight days after she had been captured. Two young estimated to be about two weeks old were brought to the Crandon Park Zoo in June. One was captured by a girl in Fort Lauderdale, who reported that the mother bat had thee babies clinging to her and seemed unable to fly with the weight of the babies. This is a most unusual observation since our molossid bats normally produce but one young per litter. We remain skeptical of this interesting report until further data on litter size in this species are available.

121. *Eumops glaucinus.*

233

Remarks: Little is known about this bat. It is considered a rare species throughout most of its range, and perhaps it is as common in Miami, Florida, as anywhere.

When first reported from the United States on the basis of a single specimen captured in 1936, it was thought that perhaps this individual had been accidently imported by boat, but numerous recent records indicate that a considerable population of these bats inhabits southern Florida.

Jennings (1958) reported 20 specimens from Florida, but was able to get little information concerning the species there. Most specimens were injured or young individuals which were accidently encountered in situations suggesting that they were not in their normal retreats.

On the average about two *E. glaucinus* per year are brought to the Crandon Park Zoo in Miami. Most are injured when received and seldom live more than a few days. One adult female was kept for a month on a diet of raw ground beef, vitamins, and water. Hubbell has found his captive specimens capable of taking flight from a flat surface. They fly faster than smaller bats and cannot maneuver as well in small spaces.

In Panama, Tyson (1964) found *E. glaucinus* in a church and in the attic of a house. In the house a colony of about 10 was found living adjacent to the tin roof, where specimens were captured by hand in August. In Colima, Mexico, specimens have been taken in August, October, and March.

A Guide to the Study of Bats

Although much can be learned about bats' feeding behavior, flight, activity patterns, and the like from systematic observation of bats on their foraging flights, a detailed knowledge of their life history requires locating their diurnal roosts. One thing, however, should be borne in mind from the outset: many species will not tolerate disturbance. With bat populations decreasing at an alarming rate in America, anyone studying bats should therefore make every effort to avoid disturbing the colonies and to encourage the conservation of these unique and interesting mammals.

Finding Bats: The difficulty of locating the day roost varies greatly among the forty species in America. As a general rule the larger the colony the easier it is to locate. The great colonies of *Tadarida brasiliensis* in the Southwest, where caves are occupied by many millions of bats, are widely known. At the other extreme are the roosts of *Pipistrellus subflavus*, the most abundant bat in much of the eastern United States, which usually spends the summer days hanging individually or in groups of a mother and her young among the foliage of the tree tops and which consequently is virtually impossible to locate. In between are the numerous species living in colonies ranging in size from a dozen to over a thousand individuals; with patience these can usually be found by using the habitat information given for each species. Churches, homes, barns, warehouses—any of these may harbor a colony of bats. Bats nearly always reveal their presence by external signs—droppings on the ground beneath their entrance holes, a brown stained

122. The attic of this house shelters a maternity colony of bats. The bats enter through the small hole at the apex. The dark stain beneath the opening and the spattering of fecal material on the wall are characteristic and betray the presence of bats.

area around the entrance, and spatterings on the wall below (fig. 122). In churches bats often enter through the louvers of the belfry and leave droppings plainly visible on the concrete stoop at the front door. Out of a dozen churches usually at least one will house a colony of bats. In one Kentucky village all six churches are inhabitated, and in New England Harold Hitchcock claims that the holy smell associated with so many of the old churches is a direct product of bat colonies.

Often on private homes the spattering of bat fecal material on a painted wall is noticeable from the street and easily recognized by an experienced observer. Window shutters also often serve as day roosts, especially for transients in migration and for males which frequently take refuge there during the nursery season. In exceptionally hot weather entire colonies sometimes abandon an attic and take up residence behind shutters. Shutters on brick houses, where the bats can obtain good footing, are especially likely spots.

Another effective way to find bats is to watch for their emergence. One of us once located seven colonies in a Vermont village simply by strolling along the streets one evening. Some of these were found by hearing the bats squeaking, for most colonial bats usually become vocal an hour or two before they leave their roosts to forage.

Local inquiry can produce excellent results. Based upon extensive experience with this method in New England, Harold Hitchcock and Wayne Davis concluded that older people are the best sources of information about bat colonies. Inquiry among the group of elderly men outside almost any county courthouse in summer is nearly always productive; however, women seem somewhat more likely than men to be aware of bat colonies. The postmistress of a small town seems always to know who has bats.

Once a bat colony in a house has been located, one should inquire there about others. People who have bats are likely to know who else has them, and they are usually pleased to tell of others in their area who are similarly blessed with the furry residents.

Newspaper publicity or advertisement can be effective in locating bats. Publicity is easily obtained; any work being done with bats seems newsworthy, and a reporter can usually be induced to include a statement that bats are needed. A phone number is far more effective than an address. Psychology can be useful in a newspaper story. To locate bats in the Albany, New York, region, Hitchcock and Davis planted stories in the paper implying that bats were locally scarce. The response was excellent; numerous people wrote that *they* had bats.

A classified advertisement in a newspaper is most effective if it states that bats are needed for research purposes, and will be removed free. However, the method is not very useful for finding colonies where the bats can be studied for extensive periods. Unfortunately people who have bats in the house nearly always want to get rid of them.

In the West, summer colonies of bats are frequently found in abandoned mines, in caves, and in rock crevices. In the East, with the exception of a few species, summer populations do not use such places for daytime roosts. Hibernating bats can be found in winter in most caves, quarries, and mine tunnels in the eastern United States. Such bats should not be disturbed any more than necessary, since these hibernating aggregations often represent the total summer population from extensive areas and are highly vulnerable at this time. If one needs bats for experimental purposes he should obtain them from summer colonies in buildings. The species found in buildings are generally widespread and abundant, and reasonable harvesting of these will have no appreciable effect on the species.

When checking a likely site for a summer colony, one should

examine the ground or floor for droppings. Fecal matter from most of our bats is easily recognized because it consists mostly of chitinous insect remains. Frequently droppings are found where no bats are seen. This means that the bats are hiding in crevices, they have left for the season, a former colony site has been abandoned, or the bats use the shelter at night only. Night roosting is common among most bats and they can be found at night in many shelters where they are absent during the day. Most mines and caves have some night traffic of bats.

After locating a colony of bats one should take care to minimize disturbance. Bats are sensitive and many will desert a roost after being molested. If bats need to be removed for study, avoid taking more than are needed. Most of our bats produce but one young per year and careful conservation is needed to maintain a population.

The solitary bats are difficult to find, and even the common ones are seldom seen except when foraging. Most encounters with *Lasiurus* and *Lasionycteris* in the daytime are accidental, and attempts to locate these bats in their day roosts are so unproductive as to seem a waste of time. However, in favorable localities some can be found. In parts of the Midwest, where *Lasiurus borealis* is abundant, foliage suitable for cover in the in the daytime is restricted to streambanks, fencerows, and the vicinity of houses. A careful inspection of the foliage in such places can turn up some bats. In Florida, where solitary bats roost in Spanish moss, bats can be secured from professional moss gatherers.

Capturing and Handling Bats: Many effective methods of catching bats have been devised. Shooting in the evening with a shotgun or with .22 caliber dust shot is an old method which is still useful occasionally for obtaining specimens. When flying about in a night roost such as a mine or building, bats can often be collected by knocking them down with a jacket or burlap bag or with a branched stick. The latter can sometimes be used to collect weak flying species when they are foraging low overhead. Some species which feed close to the surface of a stream or pond can occasionally be knocked into the water with a branched stick. All these methods are of limited usefulness since they usually kill and mutilate the bats.

Hibernating bats can be captured easily by hand or, when beyond reach, with a long pole with a small bag or net on the end. We use a 16-foot fiber glass fishing pole which telescopes to a manageable length for transporting. It is tipped with a small wire hoop supporting a plastic bag.

In many summer colonies bats can be captured by hand. Gloves should be worn to guard against bites and the attendant possibility of rabies. Collecting is most successful in the morning when the bats are least active. In buildings which shelter diurnal colonies, a pair of long forceps is often useful for extracting them from crevices. Active bats in inaccessible crevices can sometimes be driven out with tear gas or insecticide bombs, but this generally should be avoided, for it is harmful to the bats.

A dipnet is useful for catching bats. The handle should be easily detachable; when working in buildings, one often needs a net without a handle. Sometimes a widemouthed net is desirable; one a yard or more wide is effective for catching bats in a cave or mine, or where they are leaving an accessible colony site.

If the exit holes from a colony are not too numerous, traps can sometimes be extremely effective. A good trap can be built by taping a cloth sleeve to a wire cage and fastening it over the exit with thumb tacks or tape (fig. 123). Since bats are reluctant to enter a trap, all exits not covered with traps must be plugged. For some kinds of bats a very simple trap is effective. A large cardboard box set just beneath an exit will sometimes capture big brown bats. This species drops a few feet when launching itself and the bats fall into the box from which they can be retrieved if grabbed while they are still bewildered. Such a trap might also be effective on molossids, which have greater difficulty launching themselves.

A small wire, fishing line, or cord stretched about two inches above the surface of water has been used to catch bats. The bats strike the wire, fall into the water, and swim to shore, where they can be gathered. This method is effective for molossids and for some heavy-bodied bats such as *Eptesicus fuscus* and *Antrozous pallidus*. Most species of small bats seldom fall into the water, and those few which do readily take off from the surface.

Where foraging bats can be seen abundantly, a dried fruit of the common burdock (*Arctium minus*) can be used to catch a few specimens. The bur should be fastened to a fine thread and dangled where the bats are feeding. A bat will sometimes catch the bur which sticks to its wing membrane. A trout fly will also work but is not so effective as a bur. The burs can also be used to capture bats as they emerge from a hole in a building.

A bat trap was designed by Constantine (1958a) to capture bats from the great flights at Carlsbad Caverns and other caves in the Southwest. This trap is effective on free-tailed bats in these caves, but is of limited use for catching other types of bats. As modified by Cockrum and his group at the University of Arizona, this trap consists of a square frame several feet on a side with a series of pegs two inches apart along two opposite sides. A monofilament nylon fishing line is stretched from the pegs across the frame in such a way as to make parallel lines two inches apart. The square is suspended in the cave mouth with the lines vertical, and a plastic sleeve funneling into a cage is arranged beneath it. The bats fly into the lines, and slide down them into the

123. Trap built to capture *Myotis lucifugus*. Fecal spatterings are evident on the wall beside the trap. (*Courtesy of Franklin Vikan, the Fosston, Minnesota,* Thirteen Towns)

238

funnel and cage. The funnel and cage should be readily separable, so that bats can be quickly released if too many are caught.

By far the most interesting development in bat catching is the Japanese mist net (fig. 124). Made for snaring birds, these nets have come into wide usage by bird banders in the United States in recent years, but when properly used, they are equally effective for catching bats. Indeed, a greater variety of species can be taken with nets than by any other method, and some late flying species can rarely be taken except by this means. Mist nets, however, are illegal in many states, and permits must be obtained for their use.

Proper use of the nets is a skill that requires considerable experience. If possible, one who plans to use them should first go afield with an experienced netter. A few general hints on how and where to use a net may be helpful for the beginner. Never set a mist net where large numbers of bats will be caught. A cave occupied by many bats or an attic with a large colony should be avoided. It is difficult for the beginner to extract a bat from a net, and given enough time, some bats will become so entangled that they can hardly be freed without injuring the bat or cutting the net. With experience, a person can learn to remove bats from a net at a rate of several per minute.

Nets set outside should nearly always be put over water and placed at an angle to the usual flight path. In netting a pond, put the net across the center whenever feasible. Have it within a few inches of the surface so that bats cannot readily fly under it. When netting a stream choose a pool, preferably where the trees come down to form a canopy, making it inconvenient for bats to fly over the net. Most species can detect a net and many bats avoid it if they can easily do so.

One of the best places to net is at the entrance to a cave or mine. Bat traffic occurs in nearly all such shelters at night

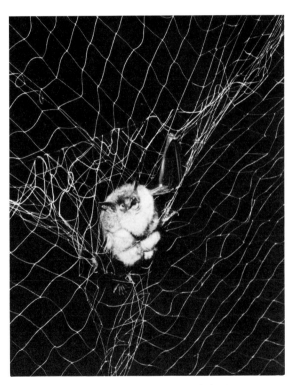

124. *Myotis lucifugus* entangled in a Japanese mist net. These nets are very effective for catching bats.

in summer. If a mine is occupied by a diurnal colony, these bats can sometimes be shut in temporarily by blocking the passage with a cloth or plastic sheet while other species are being netted at the entrance. A mine used by one species is likely to be attractive to others. An excellent way to net a small entrance is to place two nets forming a narrow V with the apex inside the mine. Bats funnelling in along the nets usually are forced into one of them. If the entrance is too high to cover, place a net in it anyway. If bats are flying about some will likely be caught. We have had successful netting at some Kentucky caves with entrances much too large to cover.

When capturing bats, one needs a gathering cage of some sort. A simple, effective one is a cloth bag. A bag 6 x 12 inches will hold a dozen bats and a bag the size of a pillowcase will hold a hundred or so. Overcrowding should be avoided as it will cause some to suffocate. In the Southwest where bats will die within minutes after being taken from their moist cool roost on a hot dry day, a cloth bag has an advantage over other containers in that it can be kept wet and cool. Disadvantages of the cloth bags are that bats are hard to handle without some escaping, and they sometimes chew out.

A widely used gathering cage invented by Donald Griffin is made from a cylinder of 1/8-inch mesh hardware cloth, a one-foot length of furnace pipe, and a furnace pipe cap. The cap serves as a floor, the hardware cloth cylinder is soldered to it and the length of pipe soldered to this, forming a sleeve at the top (fig. 125). Bats climb the sides as high as they can on the hardware cloth, but are stopped by the smooth furnace pipe. The top is open and bats are easily added or removed. Disadvantages are that the cage is easily tipped over, it is rather cumbersome, and some bats can fly out through the open top. This type of cage is not satisfactory for *Lasiurus* which flop around and injure their wings.

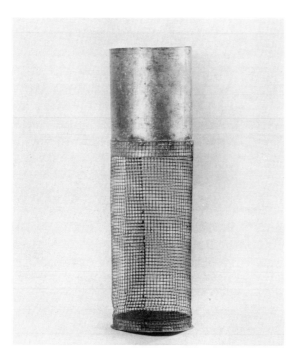

125. Gathering cage for holding live bats.

240

Richard Myers invented a useful collapsible cage which can be made from a piece of ¼-inch mesh nylon fish net, a heavy wire, plywood, bolts, a rope, and an inner tube from a truck tire (fig. 126). Bats are thrust through the slit rubber top. Such a cage holds up to about 300 active bats without difficulty. The large porous bottom makes this cage especially desirable for working with hibernating bats. More than 100 torpid bats can be distributed in the cage with no danger of suffocation. This cage is also useful when netting bats outdoors, for it can be hung from a tree branch. A disadvantage is that it must be suspended, and a suitable place to hang it sometimes is not available. Also the bats eventually chew through the netting.

A gathering cage satisfactory for handling up to 100 active bats is easily made from a five quart oil can and a cloth bag. The ends of the can are removed, and the resulting open cylinder is suspended from one end by a cord, and a bag is fastened around the outside of the other end. Bats are easily dropped in or removed, but most species cannot fly out.

For handling large numbers of bats plastic garbage cans are useful. Line the inside with hardware cloth so that bats can disperse themselves, and cut a hole in the center of the lid. Ventilator holes can be drilled into the sides and bottom, but be sure that they are so small (less than ¼ inch) that bats cannot push a folded wing through them.

Another important item for working with bats is a light. Of the many we have tried the best by far is the Wheat lamp. Although this equipment, including a charger for the battery, is expensive, it will apparently last indefinitely and is so superior to other lights that it is recommended for any project requiring long hours of work in darkness. These lamps may be obtained from mining equipment suppliers. Headlamps powered by dry cells and carbide lamps may also be used.

126. Myers holding cage for bats.

241

127. Group of bats, *Myotis sodalis*, many of which have been banded in a study of migration.

128. Bands issued by the United States Fish and Wildlife Service for use on bats.

129. *Pipistrellus subflavus* marked with colored parakeet bands for individual recognition at a distance.

Marking Bats: Many aspects of the behavior of bats can be studied without special equipment. These include such things as emergence and retiring time, foraging, activity in the roost, activity of the young, hibernation, and seasonal changes in the colonies. Most studies of bats in their natural environment, however, require that individuals be marked for future recognition.

Bat bands, similar to those put on birds, can be placed on the forearm to study migration and other aspects of life history such as longevity and population dynamics (fig. 127). In the United States about 30 active banders tag nearly 100,000 bats each year. Bands are provided by the United States Fish and Wildlife Service, Washington, D. C., and are available free to any qualified investigator who has a project for which they are needed (fig. 128).

Although any number of bats can be marked individually with numbered bands, a disadvantage for some types of studies is that each bat must be handled to identify it. For a study of natural waking periods Hassell (1967) used plastic parakeet bands of different colors. By using combinations of bands of several colors he marked hundreds of bats and could identify an individual without disturbing it (fig. 129).

Several workers have studied cluster integrity in hibernating bats by lightly touching their ears with paint. This can be done without arousing the bats, whereas banding cannot.

Radioactive tags have played a useful part in several studies. Punt and van Nieuwenhoven (1957) used them to show that populations of bats hibernating in European caves are larger than they appear because some individuals retreat out of sight in crevices. Cope *et al.* (1961b) used radioactive gold in homing experiments to determine when the bats arrived at the roost. They were able to detect bats in the walls of a building where they could not be seen. We have found radioactive cobalt to be more useful than gold because of its longer

243

half-life. A tiny piece of Co⁶⁰ alloy wire is placed in the bat by putting the wire in a large hypodermic needle, inserting the needle beneath the skin, and pushing the tag out with a wire plunger. We used these tags to determine mother-young relationships in *Eptesicus fuscus*. By feeding the audio output of a survey meter into a stripchart recorder, a continuous record of the activity of a tagged bat can be obtained. Hassell (1967) used this method to study arousal frequency in hibernating bats.

Tracking Bats: An electric eye can be used to ascertain activity inside a roost or at an exit. For example if big brown bats hibernating in a building leave to drink occasionally, their movements could be established. A counter should be attached to the electric eye. Time can be established with a strip chart recorder. We have used a tiny mercury cell and minute pinlite bulb in an attempt to determine the feeding range of individual bats. The bats carried such lights easily (fig. 130). The method should be useful in sparsely settled regions where lights are scarce; there were too many extraneous lights where we worked.

Radio tracking seems ideal for studies of feeding range and homing, but transmitters of sufficient range are still too cumbersome for small bats to carry. Donald R. Griffin and his group have been quite successful in using radio tracking to study homing of the large bat, *Phyllostomus hastatus*, in Trinidad (Williams *et al.*, 1966a; 1966b).

Transporting Bats: Nearly everyone who works with bats is likely sometime to need to ship or receive them. They are easily transported if done with reasonable care.

Bats should be shipped by air express. Postal regulations do not cover bats and their acceptance in the United States mail depends upon the interpretation made by each local

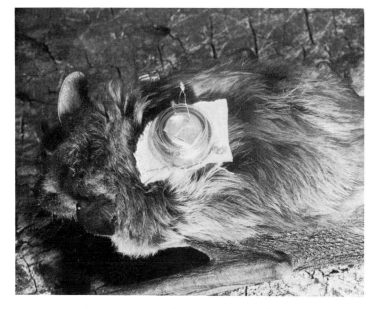

130. Big brown bat, *Eptesicus fuscus*, with a battery powered pinlight attached for study of foraging flight patterns.

postmaster. An opinion we solicited from the Post Office Department is that live bats are not mailable.

It is important to have bats in good condition when they are put into the shipping container. If possible, plan to collect them so they can be shipped without delay. Avoid weekend delivery unless the recipient is notified to pick them up at the airport.

If bats must be kept overnight before shipping, all should be stored in a refrigerator except the Phyllostomatidae; these ship poorly and should not be kept overnight. The humidity in a refrigerator is too low for hibernating bats, but this problem is easily remedied. Offer each bat a drink and then put it in a box which can be closed, and place it in the refrigerator; a cigar box is ideal. Place a heavy object on the box to prevent escape. Do not be concerned about suffocation; 8 to 10 small bats can be kept in a cigar box and have adequate oxygen. Allow about an hour for the bats to settle, and introduce a small flat dish of water to each box. This provides drinking water and raises the humidity. Temperature is not critical, so long as it is above freezing.

A shipping container should be fairly tight; wire cages are generally not satisfactory. A light metal bucket with a compression lid is suitable. Punch a few small holes for ventilation. They should not be more than 2–3 mm. in diameter, for if too large, a bat may get a wing through. Avoid putting too many bats in a container. A half a dozen small bats can be shipped in a gallon bucket.

Bats can withstand a wider temperature range than most small animals, and adverse temperatures are seldom a factor in shipping them. If temperature extremes are expected, use a styrofoam cooler as a container. Water loss, however, is likely to be critical; the large surface of the wings and interfemoral membrane can cause excess evaporation. Two or three moist, but not wet, paper towels should be placed in the cage. Wet the towels and squeeze them. Avoid using scraps of cloth that are not hemmed; bats tangle in loose threads. If the bats are active offer each a drink of water before packing.

If bats must be transported across a desert by car, place them in a wet cloth bag and never allow it to dry. In some instances this may necessitate wetting the bag every 15 to 30 minutes. We have kept fragile species alive and well during a full day's travel across the Sonoran desert in this manner.

Keeping Bats in Captivity: Bats vary in their adaptability to captivity, both among species and individually. A few species adapt readily, but some have never been successfully kept. The majority are in between; with proper conditions, and considerable patience, they can be established under laboratory conditions.

Breeding colonies have not been established for any native bats. Orr has reared *Antrozous pallidus* from birth in the laboratory and workers at the Southwest Rabies Investigation Laboratory have had some success in raising baby *Tadarida brasiliensis*. However, complete life cycles or sustaining colonies have not yet been established. The tropical vampire readily breeds in captivity and several laboratory colonies exist.

Food: Bats have been induced to take many types of food. Those most likely to be accepted include banana, cottage cheese, and raw hamburger. The food must be placed in the open mouth.

Such foods suffice only temporarily. Most bats soon develop diarrhea and die unless adequate roughage is available. Two rather standard diets have been developed and nearly every laboratory which keeps bats uses one or the other. One diet consists of live mealworms (the larvae of a flour beetle *Tenebrio molitor*). These are available from suppliers of pet food and fish bait. The other is a mixture developed by Ernest P.

245

Walker. It consists of equal parts of ripe banana, yolk of boiled egg, cream cheese, and mealworms. The insects are finely ground and mixed with the other ingredients. The final mixture is commonly known as glop. The formula has undergone several modifications. A common mixture consists of banana, canned dog food, dry curd cottage cheese, and ground insects.

Insects can be obtained in quantity from the various light traps which have recently become popular. We store gallons of them in a freezer for use during the winter. In making food we use roughly equal parts but manipulate quantities to obtain a food of firm consistency; it should not be watery. The food is stored in plastic containers in a freezer. The size of the packages depends upon the number of bats to be fed; once thawed the food will keep about a week in a refrigerator.

Care: Bats should be housed individually in small containers while they are learning to feed in captivity. It is important to have them close to food and to avoid having gluttonous individuals take all the food. Cylindrical cardboard pint ice cream cartons are used as cages at the Southwest Rabies Investigation Laboratories at Las Cruces, New Mexico. The top of the lid is removed and replaced with window screen from which the bat suspends itself. Food and water are placed in the bottom of the container.

We use wide-mouthed gallon jars as cages. A cheap grade of 15 cm. filter paper is placed in the bottom and a bat is introduced. After allowing an hour for the bat to settle, we add some food and a Syracuse watchglass. A little water is put into the watchglass with a wash bottle. If too much water is added, the bottom of the cage will soon become wet and soggy. Since most larger bats cannot fly out of such a container, a cover may not be needed.

The cages should be cleaned daily. In addition to the general desirability of cleanliness in the care of animals, this helps keep down the mite population. If mites become a problem (they are easily seen crawling on the bats and in the cage) they can be controlled by applying a commercial pesticide recommended for mites. Orr (1958) bathed bats in warm water containing tincture of green soap to control mites.

If bats lose fur or begin to lose their sleek appearance, add a few drops of a multiple vitamin preparation to the food. If they develop sores on the bottoms of the feet, fix a screen so they can hang head downward.

Of all bats we have tried to keep in the laboratory, the big brown bat, *Eptesicus fuscus*, is by far the easiest to maintain. Most individuals will eat artificial food during their first night in captivity; after the third night virtually all are feeding. They also will do nicely on mealworms (larvae or adults) and learn to feed themselves after a few hand feedings.

Another species which does well in captivity is *Antrozous pallidus*. Orr (1958) found these the easiest to keep of all species he studied. Many took mealworms the first night, and few had to be hand fed more than two or three days.

Few other species of native bats take readily to captivity. Most require patience or special conditions, or both, for successful laboratory adaptation. Both types of food should be tried. To hand feed a bat place it on a table and put a hand over it in such a way that only the head protrudes. Hold a bite of food with forceps and agitate the bat. When the mouth is opened in threat, insert the food. The bat will bite, but probably not chew. Move the food slightly or further agitate the bat. If it does not then eat, return it to the cage and try again next day. Bats are less likely to eat the day they are captured than on the following evening. Several workers never attempt to feed bats until they have been caged a day or two.

Try keeping some bats at a temperature higher than ordinary room temperature. *Myotis lucifugus*, the common little brown bat, did notoriously poorly in the laboratory until Stones (1965) kept them at the temperatures normally encountered in their attic roosts. He found that they did nicely at 92° F. (33° C.) and learned to eat mealworms by themselves after one or two feedings by hand.

The nectar eating bats (*Leptonycteris* and *Choeronycteris*) can be fed sweetened water or be induced to feed from flowers containing nectar. However, they generally do not do well in captivity and die in a few days.

Photographing Bats: Almost any camera can be used to photograph bats, provided that it will work sufficiently close to the subject to get a sizable image and has a sufficiently sharp lens. A 35 mm. single lens reflex camera, with bellows, and a short mount lens of about 105–150 mm. focal length seems most desirable. The lens is more convenient if automatic, but a preset diaphragm works admirably; it takes merely a quick twist to set it. The lens should stop down to at least f22 because this opening will frequently be needed in close-ups with electronic flash.

There are some inherent advantages in a larger format, at least up to 2¼ x 2¼ inches. However, we consider the advantages to be outweighed by the fact that the larger format cameras are heavier, bulkier, usually slower to operate, and film costs are higher.

Nearly any of the modern 35 mm. single lens reflex cameras are suitable for photographing bats. We normally use Nikon F and Nikkormat bodies interchangeably on a bellows with a short mount Nikkor-Q 135 mm. f4 lens. A tripod is indispensable.

Choice of film is largely a matter of personal preference. We use Ektachrome X because its color fidelity is good and its speed is a convenient one. Most of our close-ups are shot at f16 or usually f22, and our black and white work, using Panatomic X, is shot at the same settings. We normally process our own films, and can certainly get faster service than can be had commercially. Speed in processing is important, since most bats do not take well to captivity; it is desirable to see results while specimens are still fresh and alert.

Being creatures of the night, bats do not react well to the intensity of light necessary for close-up photographs. Therefore some type of flash is required. Although flash bulbs are adequate, the best choice for reasons of convenience and overall economy is electronic flash. Usually three lights are used, a main one near the camera, a fill-in at an angle to one side, and the third as a back-light. Generally, the main light, near the camera, is moved forward and back with the camera and serves to compensate more or less automatically for variations in f stop due to bellows draw. Fill-in and back lights are usually 3–4 feet from the subject, depending on the subject and the output of the unit.

With a little imagination the photographer can select a setting that matches the animal's habitat—an old rough board for a species common in buildings, a rock for a cave dweller, a branch or slab for a tree bat. Backgrounds should be constructed at a convenient height on a movable stand.

A common technique to keep a small animal still for photographic purposes is to chill it. This will work for bats; however, the resulting pictures reflect no life or personality. Occasionally this technique will afford a particularly patient and alert photographer some good pictures. When a chilled bat is placed in an appropriate setting at room temperature, it will usually become alert in about half an hour, and, if undisturbed, will sometimes remain in place for several seconds, long enough for a few exposures. At times even a fresh-caught bat, especially the phyllostomids and molossids, when first set down will remain there, looking alert. The photographer can then shoot as he pleases, shifting lights and camera, and rotating the background and bat for various angles.

When the animal is set in place, cupping the hands about it until it quiets is advisable. When the hands are removed, the bat usually flies or has fallen asleep. If asleep, it can be teased awake with a small brush, by blowing on it, snapping the fingers, or some other means. Upon awakening it may afford an opportunity for an exposure. If it flies, it must be recaptured and the whole process repeated. Sooner or later, it will remain in position long enough for one or more exposures. Sometimes a particularly exasperating bat can be calmed by giving it a drink of water or by letting it fly about freely for several minutes.

Patience and gentleness are the keys. Be persistent and don't hurt the bat. Sooner or later it will cooperate.

Obviously, such a technique can be used only in a room where the animal can easily be recaptured. We like a rather small room, but for color work it is important that the walls be white or at least some light, neutral shade.

A person working alone has difficulty photographing bats. It is better to have one person manipulate lights and camera, while another handles the bat. Gloves are desirable when handling bats; some, particularly the larger species, can inflict nasty bites.

Bats seem to respond to the characteristics of their handler. One who is gentle, firm, and absolutely without fear of bats can elicit the desired response in much less time than one who does not possess these characteristics. We are at a loss to explain this phenomenon, but it exists in many species.

The photography of bat skulls presents some interesting challenges. Most photographs of skulls are taken with a black background. This is readily accomplished by placing the skulls on a glass shelf above a piece of black velvet. The same technique, using a white card in lieu of the velvet gives a light background; however, it is difficult to obtain a white background with this technique and still retain medium contrast and good detail in the skull itself.

Our personal choice of backgrounds for skull photographs is white, which can be obtained by trans-illuminating the background. We find tracing paper works well; ordinary typewriter bond seems too nearly opaque, but this is a function of the back light. Experimentation is needed to ascertain the best light placement and intensity to give a proper lighting ratio between background and subject. Caution must be used to avoid degrading the image by an over lighted background.

We have found a tiny dab of children's play putty works well between the skull and the glass shelf to hold the skull at the desired angle. It is advisable to light the skulls from both anterior and posterior aspect, with the lights placed slightly dorsal in lateral views to increase contrast between the usually light teeth and the light background.

De la Torre and Dysart (1966) devised a technique of applying soluble gray paint to the teeth to improve contrast. If carefully applied, the paint works well. We did not use the technique because we had difficulty getting a sufficiently even coat of paint.

We photographed bat skulls at a 1-1 ratio, using a Micro-Nikkor f3.5 mm. lens with an M-ring in a Nikkormat or Nikon F camera. Lighting was by electronic flash, both subject and trans-illuminated background. Our lighting was such that the flash exposure at f45 on Panatomic X film, developed in 1-1 D76, at 68° F. for 8 minutes gave negatives of the density we prefer. The photographs could just as well have been done with floods and/or spots, but we found flash much cooler, simpler, and easier to use.

Saving Specimens: For various reasons it may be desirable to save specimens of bats. A bat collected beyond the known range of the species should be saved as should specimens of questionable identity. A person may be interested in determining what kinds of bats occur in a particular region and may need to save representatives of each species.

The easiest way to preserve a bat is in liquid. Make a cut through the skin and muscle on the belly, exposing the intestines. Make a label by cutting a piece of good quality paper about ½ x 2½ inches. Write firmly with lead pencil (some permanent inks are satisfactory but many inks will wash out) the date collected and the exact locality in latitude and longitude or with reference to a town or other landmark readily found on a map, or both. Other worthwhile data which should be included are: measurements, sex, collector's name, a collection number, elevation of the collecting site above sea level, and any data concerning the habitat or circumstances of collection. Tie the label firmly to the bat and drop into a preservative. A preservative can be made by diluting 37–40 percent formaldehyde obtainable at a drug store. Use nine parts water to one part of the formaldehyde. Ethyl alcohol (70%) is also a good preservative.

Another method of preserving bats is to make museum study skins. This requires more time and some skill. We give a brief description of the method here. A person who is interested in making study specimens of animals should carefully study the booklet entitled "Collecting and Preparing Study Specimens of Vertebrates" by E. Raymond Hall (1962), Miscellaneous Publication number 30 of the University of Kansas Museum of Natural History. This booklet is available for 50 cents from the Museum and should be studied by anyone interested in making study specimens. Minimum equipment for preparation of a study specimen includes labels for skin and skull, pen and waterproof ink or lead pencil, millimeter rule, needle and thread, pliers, no. 22 wire, forceps, scalpel or razor blade, small pointed scissors, cotton, saw-dust from the sanding of a new hardwood floor or white corn meal, tooth brush, pins, and fiberboard.

Measurements of the bat should be taken carefully and listed in order on the label as follows: Total length from tip of snout to tip of the tail (fig. 131-A); length of the tail (fig. 131-B); length of the foot from base of heel to tip of the longest claw (fig. 131-C); and length of the ear from the notch (fig. 131-D). Wingspread is also a useful measurement. Other measurements which may be useful in identifying a bat, or studying variation may be taken at any time from the dried specimen.

String the label with a heavy white button and carpet thread (no. 8 or 12) and tie an overhand knot about one inch from the label. Then tie the label firmly around the ankle. Mark the skull tag as shown in figure 131-L. Mark both sides firmly with a lead pencil. Many so-called permanent inks do not survive the treatments involved in skull cleaning. Number all specimens consecutively, and keep a notebook containing all the information about each specimen as well as field observations and notes.

With razor blade, scalpel, or scissors make an incision through the skin on the belly (fig. 131-E). Pile on some sawdust (fig. 131-F). Always work in plenty of sawdust to avoid getting blood and fat on the fur. Using forceps, work the skin away from the body. When the base of the tail is encountered grasp it with forceps and pull it out (fig. 131-G). When the legs appear snip them close to the body, leaving tibia and femur with the skin (fig. 131-H). Then work the skin up over the body (fig. 131-I). Avoid pulling the skin, for it stretches easily. When the wings are reached, grasp the humeri and break or cut them close to the body (fig. 131-J). Work the skin forward and use a razor blade or scalpel to free the ears, eyes and lips, always cutting as close to the body as possible (fig. 131-K).

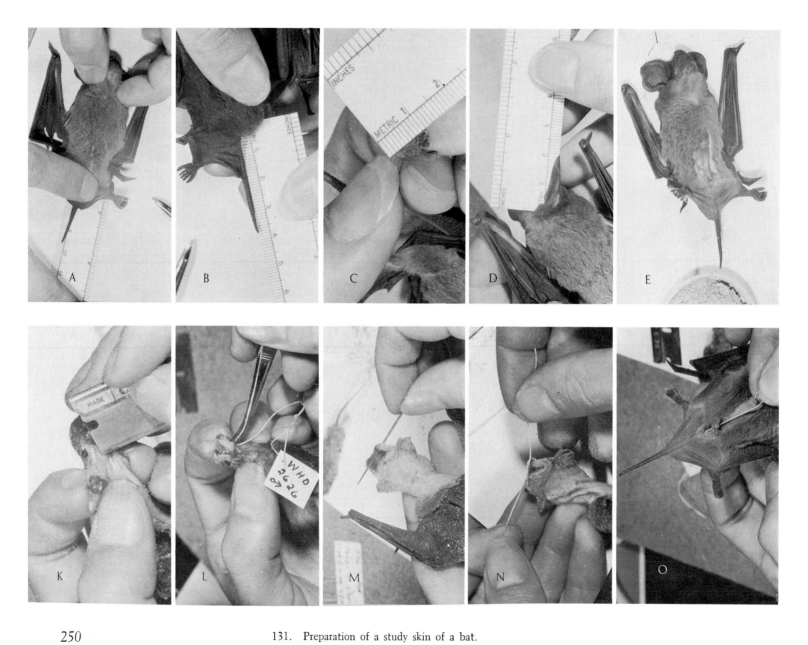

131. Preparation of a study skin of a bat.

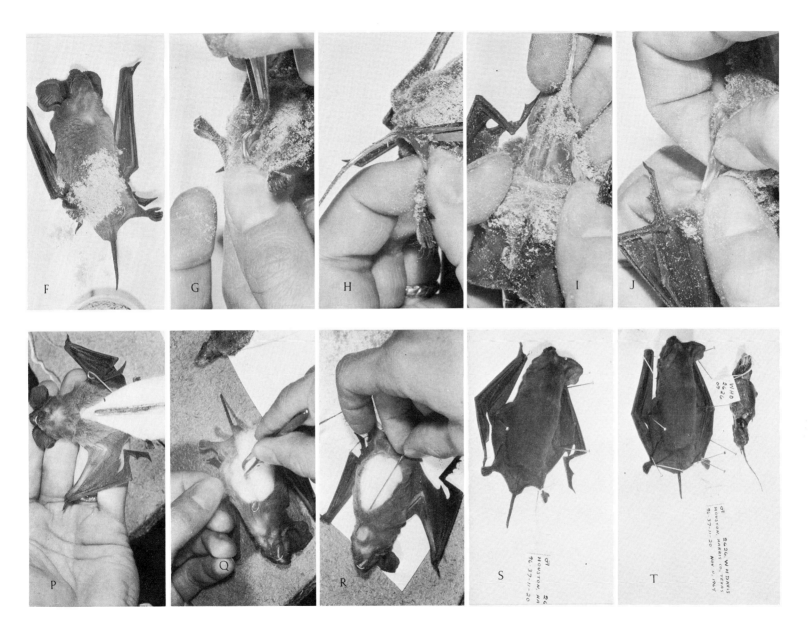

When the skin is free, wash the sawdust from the carcass (it inhibits the cleaning process), and attach the skull tag around the lower jaw as shown in figure 131-L. With the skin inside out, apply sawdust liberally to the hide especially working it into the regions where the limbs were severed. If fat is present, be sure that it is thoroughly absorbed. If the skin has dried, dab it with water and then apply sawdust. With a little practice one can finish skins before excessive drying occurs.

With the needle and thread make one stitch across the upper lips (fig. 131-M) and then through the lower lip. Tie the ends of the thread firmly (fig. 131-N). Turn the skin right side out. With pliers stretch a wire until it breaks. Number 22 wire can be used for all small bats, but the larger 20 is desirable for many species, and even 18 for the largest molossids. Insert the wire into the tail (fig. 131-O). Be sure the broken end goes in as it is smooth and rounded and inserts easily. Work the wire to the tip of the tail.

Fold a piece of cotton to form a body and insert it with forceps (fig. 131-P). Put the tail wire over the body, and using forceps, work the cotton under the skin (fig. 131-Q). Sew up the bat, beginning at the anterior end of the incision (fig. 131-R). If the specimen is a male, be sure the penis is not hidden; the nearly microscopic penis bone is useful in identifying some species.

Clean the fur with sawdust and toothbrush. If blood spots are present, they can be removed by spotting with cold water and drying with sawdust. Finally, shape the body with fingers and tooth brush and pin it on a piece of fiberboard as shown in figure 131-S,T. Start with pins at the wrists and work posteriorly.

After the specimens are dried the skin and skull should be deposited in a museum which has a permanent curatorial staff. The skull will be cleaned and cared for at the museum.

If not adequately cared for, skins are soon destroyed by insects. Some collectors apply various poisons to skins during preparation to inhibit insect activity, but these do not prevent damage. Specimens can be kept adequately for a while by storing them in nearly airtight containers with moth flakes.

Study Collections: There are many good collections of bats in the United States at various museums and universities, and the person interested in these animals would find it profitable to visit one of these. Although the research collections are not open to the public, anyone with a genuine interest who wishes to examine some specimens is welcomed. He should ask to see one of the curators of the research collection of mammals and explain his interests and desires to him. When possible, arrangements should be made prior to the visit.

There are excellent collections of bats at the American Museum of Natural History, New York; the Museum of Comparative Zoology, Harvard University, Cambridge, Massachusetts; the Academy of Natural Sciences of Philadelphia; the United States National Museum, Washington; the University of Michigan Museum of Zoology, Ann Arbor; the University of Illinois Museum of Natural History, Urbana; the Chicago Natural History Museum; the University of Minnesota Museum of Natural History, Minneapolis; the University of Kansas Museum of Natural History, Lawrence; Texas A. and M. University, Department of Wildlife Science, College Station; the University of New Mexico Museum of Southwestern Biology, Albuquerque; the University of Arizona Department of Zoology, Tucson; the Los Angeles County Museum; and the University of California Museum of Vertebrate Zoology, Berkeley. In Canada there are good collections at the Royal Ontario Museum, Toronto; the National Museum, Ottawa; and the University of British Columbia, Vancouver. There is a good collection at the National

University of Mexico, in Mexico City. In addition to these, many other institutions, especially state and provincial universities, have collections of various quality.

Literature: The scientific literature on bats is scattered in numerous journals and books. However, a substantial part of the important papers in this field appear in the *Journal of Mammalogy*. This journal, published by the American Society of Mammalogists, probably contains more papers on bats than any other journal in the world. Anyone with a serious and lasting interest in bats or other mammals should join the society. To join one should contact the Secretary-Treasurer, whose name and address appear in every issue of the *Journal*.

Bat Research News, a quarterly newsletter, is produced by the authors and distributed at cost to those interested in bats. It consists mainly of news of bats, bat research, and bat research workers. It can be obtained by writing to the Department of Zoology, University of Kentucky, Lexington.

Glossary of Scientific Names

alascensis (ăl-a-sĕn′-sis), belonging to Alaska
Antrozous (ăn-tro-zo′-us), cave animal
apache (a-pă′-chee), a proper name—Apache
auriculus (au-rick′-u-lus), the external ear
australis (aus-trā′-lis), of the south; southern
austroriparius (aus′-tro-ri-par′-i-us), frequenting southern stream
   banks
bernardinus (ber′-nar-dee′-nus), a proper name—Bernardino
borealis (bor-e-ā′-lis), of the north; northern
brasiliensis (bră-zil′-i-ĕn′-sis), belonging to Brazil
brevis (brĕ′-vis), short
bunkeri (bun′-ker-i′), a proper name—Bunker
californicus (cal-i-for′-ni-cus), a proper name—California
cantwelli (cant′-well-i′), a proper name—Cantwell
carissima (ca-riss′-i-ma), dearest
caurinus (cau-rīn′-us), of the northwest wind; northwestern
Choeronycteris (ker′-o-nick′-ter-is), nocturnal pig
ciliolabrum (sil′-ĭ-olā′-brum), hairy lips
cinereus (sĭ-near′-e-us), ash-colored
clarus (clăr′-us), clear; brilliant; shining
cynocephala (sī′-no-seph′-a-la), dog head
ega (ē′-ga), a proper name—Ega
Enchisthenes (en-kis′-the-nees), spear palm
Eptesicus (ep-tess′-i-cus), flying
Euderma (you-derm′-a), good skin
Eumops (you′-mops′), good bat
evotis (e-vōt′-is), good ear
femorosacca (fem′-or-o-sac′-ka), a sack on the thigh
floridanus (flor-i-dā′-nus), a proper name—Florida
fortidens (fort′-ĭ-dens′), gate teeth (opening)
fuscus (fus′-cus), brown
gatesi (gate′-sī′), a proper name—Gates
glaucinus (glau-sīn′-us), silvery; gray; gleaming
grisescens (gri-ses′-sens), beginning to gray
hartii (hart′-ĭ-ī′), a proper name—Hart
hesperus (hes′-per-us), the land of the west; western; evening

humeralis (hume-er-al′-is), pertaining to the humerus
incautus (in-cau′-tus), heedless; improvident
ingens (in′-gens′), great; remarkable; large
interior (in-tier′-i-or), internal; inside
intermedius (in-ter-mĕd′-i-us), intermediate; occupying the middle
keenii (keen-i-i′), a proper name—Keen
Lasionycteris (la′-zi-o-nick′-ter-is), hairy and nocturnal
Lasiurus (la-zi-your′-us), hairy tail
Leptonycteris (lep-tow-nick′-ter-is), slender and nocturnal
longicrus (lon′-ji-crus), long leg; long thigh
lucifugus (lu-ci′-fu-gus), fleeing light
macrotis (ma-cro′-tis), large ear
Macrotus (ma-cro′-tus), large ear
maculatum (ma-cu-la′-tum), spotted
maximus (max′-i-mus), large
megalophylla (meg-a-lo-phil′-a), large leaves
melanorhinus (me-lan′-or-rine′-us), black nose
merriami (mer-ri-aim′-ī), a proper name—Merriam
mexicana (mex-i-cān′-a), a proper name—Mexico
micronyx (my-krŏ-nicks), little claw
molossus (mo-loss′-us), mastiff
Mormoops (mor-mo′-ops), monster bat
mumfordi (mum′-ford-ī), a proper name—Mumford
Myotis (my-o′-tis), mouse ear
nivalis (ni-val′-is), snowy
noctivagans (noc-ti′-va-gans′), night wandering
Nycticeius (nick-tee′-see-us), night hunter
occultus (o-cult′-us), hidden; obscure
oklahomae (ok-la-hom′-ee), a proper name—Oklahoma
osceola (os-see-ol′-a), a proper name—Osceola
oxalis (ox-al′-is), sharp; pointed
pacificus (pa-ci′-fi-cus), a proper name—Pacific
pahasapensis (pa-ha-sa-pen′-sis), belonging to Paha Sapa (the Sioux name for the Black Hills)

pallescens (pal-es′-cens), pale; wan
pallidus (pal′-id-us), pale
perotis (per-o′-tis), maimed ear
phasma (fas′-ma′), an apparition; a monster
phyllotis (fil-oat′-is), leaf ear
Pipistrellus (pĭ′-pĭ-strel′-lus), a bat
Plecotus (ple-coat′-us), twisted ear
rafinesquii (raf-in-es′-kae-ī), a proper name—Rafinesque
rufescens (ru-fes′-cens), reddening; becoming red
sanborni (san′-born-ī), a proper name—Sanborn
santarosae (san′-ta-ro′-sae), a proper name—Santa Rosa
saturatus (sat′-ur-a′-tus), filled
seminolus (sem′-i-no′-lus), a proper name—Seminole
semotus (se-mote′-us), separated; distant
sociabilis (so-see-ab′-i-lis), passive companionship
sodalis (so-dal′-is), a comrade
sonoriensis (so-no′-ri-en′-sis), belonging to Sonora
stephensi (ste′-vens-i′), a proper name—Stephens
subflavus (sub-fla′-vus), somewhat yellow
subtropicalis (sub-trop′-i-cal′-is), subtropical
subulatus (sub-u-late′-us), provided with an awl
Tadarida (ta-da′-ri-da), withered toad
teliotis (te-li-oat′-is), web ear
thysanodes (thigh′-san-o′-dees), with a thing like a fringe
townsendii (town-sen′-dĭ-i′), a proper name—Townsend
underwoodi (un′-der-wood-i′), a proper name—Underwood
velifer (vel′-i-fer), bearing a veil
virginianus (vir-gin′-i-a′-nus), a proper name—Virginia
volans (vo′-lans′), flying
waterhousii (wa-ter-house′-i-i′), a proper name—Waterhouse
xanthinus (zan-thyn′-us), yellowish
yumanensis (you′-ma-nen′-sis), belonging to Yuma (Arizona)

Bibliography

Albright, R.
  1959   Bat banding at Oregon caves. Murrelet 40:26-27.

Alcorn, J. R.
  1944   Notes on the winter occurrence of bats in Nevada. J. Mamm. 25:308-10.

Allan, P. F.
  1947   Blue jay attacks red bats. J. Mamm. 28:180.

Allen, A. A.
  1921   Banding bats. J. Mamm. 2:53-57.

Allen, G. M.
  1921   Bats from New Mexico and Arizona. J. Mamm. 3:156-61.
  1962   Bats. Dover, New York. 368 pp.

Alvarez, T.
  1963   The Recent Mammals of Tamaulipas, Mexico. Univ. Kansas Publ., Mus. Nat. Hist. 14:363-473.

Alvarez T., and C. E. Aviña
  1964   Nuevos registros en Mexico de la Familia Molossidae. Rev. Soc. Mex. Hist. Nat. 25:243-54.

Alvarez-Lomeli, B., B. Villa-R, and W. A. Wimsatt
  1964   Contribucion al conocimiento de la epidemiologia de la rabia en algunos murcielagos de la Republica Mexicana. Boletin del Instituto de Estudios Medicos y Biologicos 22:387-92.

Anderson, K.
  1917   On the determination of age in bats. J. Bombay Nat. Hist. Soc. 25:249-59.

Anderson, R. M.
  1948   Methods of collecting and preserving vertebrate animals. Natl. Mus. Canada Bull. 69. 162 pp.

Anderson, S.
  1961   Mammals of Mesa Verde National Park, Colorado. Univ. Kansas Publ., Mus. Nat. Hist. 14:29-67.

Anderson, S., and C. E. Nelson
  1965   A systematic revision of Macrotus (Chiroptera). Amer. Mus. Novitates No. 2212.

Axtell, R. W.
  1961   An additional record for the bat Tadarida molossa from Trans-Pecos Texas. S. W. Nat. 6:52-53.
  1962   An easternmost record for the bat Choeronycteris mexicana from Coahuila, Mexico. S. W. Nat. 7:76.

Bailey, B.
  1929   Mammals of Sherburne County, Minnesota. J. Mamm. 10:153-64.

Bailey, V.
  1926   A biological survey of North Dakota. The mammals. N. Amer. Fauna No. 49. 226 pp.
  1931   The mammals of New Mexico. N. Amer. Fauna No. 53. 412 pp.
  1933   Cave life of Kentucky. Amer. Midl. Nat. 14:385-635.
  1936   The mammals and life zones of Oregon. N. Amer. Fauna No. 55. 416 pp.

Baker, J. K.
  1962   Notes on the Myotis of the Carlsbad Caverns. J. Mamm. 43:427-28.

Baker, J. K., and P. F. Spangle
  1962   Some observations on the flight habits of Mexican free-tail bats. S. W. Nat. 7:76-77.

Baker, R. H.
  1954   A hoary bat from northwestern Kansas. Trans. Kansas Acad. Sci. 57:196.

Baker, R. H. (*continued*):

1955   A new species of bat (genus *Myotis*) from Coahuila, Mexico. Proc. Biol. Soc. Washington 68:165-66.

1956a   Mammals of Coahuila, Mexico. Univ. Kansas Publ., Mus. Nat. Hist. 9:125-335.

1956b   *Eumops underwoodi sonoriensis* in Arizona. J. Mamm. 37:111-12.

1964   *Myotis lucifugus lucifugus* (LeConte) and *Pipistrellus hesperus maximus* Hatfield in Knox County, new to northcentral Texas. S. W. Nat. 9:205.

1967   A new subspecies of pallid bat (Chiroptera: Vespertilionidae) from northeastern Mexico. S. W. Nat. 12:329-30.

Baker, R. H., and R. W. Dickerman

1956   Daytime roost of the yellow bat in Veracruz. J. Mamm. 37:443.

Baker, R. H., and J. K. Greer

1962   Mammals of the Mexican state of Durango. Michigan State Univ. Publ. Mus. 2:29-154.

Baker, R. H., and C. J. Phillips

1965   Mammals from El Nevado De Colima, Mexico. J. Mamm. 46:691.

Baker, R. H., and H. J. Stains

1955   A new long-eared *Myotis* (*Myotis evotis*) from northeastern Mexico. Univ. of Kansas Publ., Mus. Nat. Hist. 9:81-84.

Baker, R. J., and L. Christianson

1966   Notes on bats from Sonora, Mexico. S. W. Nat. 11:296-312.

Baker, R. J., and E. L. Cockrum

1966   Geographic and ecological range of the long-nosed bats, *Leptonycteris*. J. Mamm. 47:329-31.

Baker, R. J., and J. L. Patten

1967   Karyotypes and karyotypic variation of North American vespertilionid bats. J. Mamm. 48:270-86.

Baker, R. J., and C. M. Ward

1967   Distribution of bats in southeastern Arkansas. J. Mamm. 48:130-32.

Baker, W. W.

1967   *Myotis leibii leibii* in Georgia. J. Mamm. 48:142.

Baldwin, P. H.

1950   Occurrence and behavior of the Hawaiian bat. J. Mamm. 31:455-56.

Banks, R. C.

1965   The bats of Anza-Borrego Desert State Park, San Diego County, California. Report to California Div. of Beaches and Parks. 30 pp.

Banks, R. C., and C. Parrish

1965   Additional records of *Choeronycteris mexicana* from Southern California and Baja California. Bull. So. California Acad. Sci. 64:163-64.

Barbour, R. W.

1951   The mammals of Big Black Mountain, Harlan County, Kentucky. J. Mamm. 32:100-10.

1957   Some additional mammal records from Kentucky. J. Mamm. 38:140-41.

1963   Some additional bat records from Kentucky. J. Mamm. 44:122-23.

Barbour, R. W., and C. H. Ernst

1968   Forearm length and wingspread of *Myotis sodalis*. Trans. Kentucky Acad. Sci. In press.

Barbour, R. W., W. H. Davis, and M. D. Hassell

1966   The need of vision in homing by *Myotis sodalis*. J. Mamm. 47:356-57.

Barbour, T.

1936   *Eumops* in Florida. J. Mamm. 17:414.

Barkalow, F. S., Jr.

1939   The LeConte free-tailed bat in Alabama. J. Mamm. 20:370.

1948 The status of the seminole bat, *Lasiurus seminolus* (Rhoads). J. Mamm. 29:415-16.

1966 Rafinesque's big-eared bat. Wildl. North Carolina. Jan., 14-15.

Barkalow, F. S., Jr., and D. A. Adams
1955 The seminole bat, *Lasiurus seminolus*, in North Carolina. J. Mamm. 36:453-54.

Barkalow, F. S., Jr., and J. B. Funderburg, Jr.
1960 Probable breeding and additional records of the seminole bat in North Carolina. J. Mann. 41:394-95.

Barr, T. C., Jr., and R. M. Norton
1965 Predation on cave bats by the pilot black snake. J. Mamm. 46:672.

Beatty, L. D.
1955 The leafchin bat in Arizona. J. Mamm. 36:290.

Beck, A. J., and R. L. Rudd
1960 Nursery colonies in the pallid bat. J. Mamm. 41:266-67.

Beer, J. R.
1954 A record of the hoary bat from a cave. J. Mamm. 35:116.

1955 Survival and movements of banded big brown bats. J. Mamm. 36:242-48.

1956 A record of a silver-haired bat in a cave. J. Mamm. 37:282.

Beer, J. R., and A. G. Richards
1956 Hibernation of the big brown bat. J. Mamm. 37:31-41.

Bell, J. F.
1959 Transmission of rabies to laboratory animals by bite of a naturally infected bat. Science 129:1490-91.

Bell, J. F., D. L. Lodmell, G. J. Moore, and G. H. Raymond
1966 Rabies virus isolation from a bat in Montana in midwinter. Pub. Health Repts. 81:761-62.

Bell, J. F., G. J. Moore, G. H. Raymond, and C. E. Tibbs
1962 Characteristics of rabies in bats in Montana. Amer. J. Pub. Health 52:1293-301.

Bels, L.
1952 Fifteen years of bat banding in the Netherlands. Publ. Natuurh. Genootschap Limburg. 99 pp.

Benedict, F. A.
1957 Hair structure as a generic character in bats. Univ. of California, Publ. Zool. 59:285-548.

Benson, S. B.
1940 Notes on the pocketed free-tail bat. J. Mamm. 21:26-29.

1947a Description of a mastiff bat (genus *Eumops*) from Sonora, Mexico. Proc. Biol. Soc. Washington 60:133-34.

1947b Comments on migration and hibernation in *Tadarida mexicana*. J. Mamm. 28:407-408.

Bishop, S. C.
1947 Curious behavior of a hoary bat. J. Mamm. 28:293-94.

Blair, W. F.
1952a Bats of the Edwards Plateau in Central Texas. Texas J. Sci. 4:95-98.

1952b Mammals of the Tamaulipan Biotic Province in Texas. Texas J. Sci. 4:230-50.

Bleakney, J. S.
1965 First specimens of eastern pipistrelle from Nova Scotia. J. Mamm. 46:528-29.

Bole, B. P., Jr.
1943 *Myotis austroriparius* in Tennessee. J. Mamm. 24:403.

Booth, E. S.
1965 A bat die off in Mexico. J. Mamm. 46:333-34.

Borell, A. E.
1937 A new method of collecting bats. J. Mamm. 18:478-80.

Borell, A. E. (*continued*):

1939 A colony of rare free-tailed bats. J. Mamm. 20:65-66.

1942 Feeding habit of the pallid bat. J. Mamm. 23:337.

Borell, A. E., and R. Ellis

1934 Mammals of the Ruby Mountains region of north-eastern Nevada. J. Mamm. 15:12-44.

Bradley, W. G., G. T. Austin, and M. O'Farrell

1965 *Lasionycteris noctivagans, Lasiurus cinereus* and *Tadarida molossa* in Clark County, Nevada. S. W. Nat. 10:220.

Bradley, W. G., and R. A. Mauer

1965 A collection of bats from Chihuahua, Mexico. S. W. Nat. 10:74-75.

Bradley, W. G., and M. J. O'Farrell

1967 The mastiff bat, *Eumops perotis*, in southern Nevada. J. Mamm. 48:672.

Bradshaw, G. V. R.

1962 Reproductive cycle of the California leaf-nosed bat, *Macrotus californicus*. Science 136:645-46.

Bradshaw, G. V. R., and A. Ross

1961 Ectoparasites of Arizona bats. J. Arizona Acad. Sci. 1:109-12.

Brandon, R. A.

1961 Observations of young keen bats. J. Mamm. 42:400-401.

Brimley, C. S.

1897 An incomplete list of the mammals of Bertie County, North Carolina. Amer. Nat. 31:237-39.

Buchanan, O. M.

1958 *Tadarida* and *Myotis* occupying cliff swallow nests. J. Mamm. 39:434-35.

Burt, W. H.

1934 Mammals of southern Nevada. Trans. San Diego Soc. Nat. Hist. 7:375-427.

1938 Faunal relationships and geographic distribution of mammals in Sonora, Mexico. Univ. Michigan Misc. Publ. 39:7-77.

1939 The Rafinesque bat in Michigan. J. Mamm. 20:103.

1952 A field guide to the mammals. Houghton Mifflin Co., Boston. 200 pp.

1954 The mammals of Michigan. Univ. Michigan Press, Ann Arbor. 288 pp.

1957 Mammals of the Great Lakes Region. Univ. Michigan Press, Ann Arbor. 246 pp.

Cagle, F. R.

1950 A Texas colony of bats, *Tadarida mexicana*. J. Mamm. 31:400-402.

Cagle, F. R., and L. Cockrum

1943 Notes on a summer colony of *Myotis lucifugus lucifugus*. J. Mamm. 24:474-92.

Cahalane, V. H.

1932 Large brown bat in Michigan. J. Mamm. 13:70-71.

Cain, G. D.

1966 Helminth parasites of bats from Carlsbad Caverns, New Mexico. J. Parasitol. 52:351-58.

Campbell, B.

1931 Bats on the Colorado Desert. J. Mamm. 12:430.

1934 Notes on bats collected in Arizona during the summer of 1933. J. Mamm. 15:241-42.

Carter, D. C., R. H. Pine, and W. B. Davis

1966 Notes on middle American bats. S. W. Nat. 11:488-99.

Carter, T. D.

1950 On the migration of the red bat *Lasiurus borealis borealis*. J. Mamm. 31:349-50.

Caughley, G.

1966 Mortality patterns in mammals. Ecology 47:906-18.

Chermock, R. L., and J. S. White

1953 *Myotis keenii septentrionalis*, a new bat for Alabama. J. Alabama Acad. Sci. 25:24.

Chew, R. M., and H. E. White
  1960   Evaporative water losses of the pallid bat. J. Mamm. 41:452-58.

Christian, J. J.
  1956   The natural history of a summer aggregation of the big brown bat, *Eptesicus fuscus fuscus*. Amer. Midl. Nat. 55:66-95.

Cockrum, E. L.
  1952a   Mammals of Kansas. Univ. Kansas Publ., Mus. Nat. Hist. 7:1-303.
  1952b   The big free-tailed bat in Oklahoma. J. Mamm. 33:492.
  1955   Reproduction in North American bats. Trans. Kansas Acad. Sci. 58:487-511.
  1956a   Homing, movements and longevity of bats. J. Mamm. 37:48-57.
  1956b   The pocketed free-tail bat, *Tadarida femorosacca*, in in Arizona. J. Mamm. 37:282-83.
  1960a   The recent mammals of Arizona: Their taxonomy and distribution. Univ. Arizona Press, Tucson. 276 pp.
  1960b   Distribution, habitat and habits of the mastiff bat, *Eumops perotis*, in North America. J. Arizona Acad. Sci. 1:79-84.
  1961   Southern yellow bat from Arizona. J. Mamm. 42:97.
  1964   Cave myotis, *Myotis velifer*, from southern Nevada. J. Mamm. 45:636-37.

Cockrum, E. L., and S. P. Cross
  1964   Time of bat activity over water holes. J. Mamm. 45:635-36; Addendum: 46:356.

Cockrum, E. L., and A. L. Gardner
  1960   Underwood's mastiff bat in Arizona. J. Mamm. 41:510-11.

Cockrum, E. L., and B. Hayward
  1968   Natural history of the long-nosed bat, *Leptonycteris nivalis* (Saussure)—Chiroptera, Phyllostomatidae. Amer. Mus. Novitates. In press.

Cockrum, E. L., and B. F. Musgrove
  1964a   Additional records of the Mexican big-eared bat, *Ple-cotus phyllotis* (Allen), from Arizona. J. Mamm. 45:472-74.
  1964b   Cave myotis, *Myotis velifer*, from southern Nevada. J. Mamm. 45:636-37.
  1965   Extension of known range of the pocketed free-tailed bat. J. Mamm. 46:509.

Cockrum, E. L., and E. Ordway
  1959   Bats of the Chiricahua Mountains, Cochise County, Arizona. Amer. Mus. Novitates. No. 1938.

Cohen, E.
  1942   *Myotis keenii septentrionalis* (Trouessart) in Maryland. J. Mamm. 23:96.

Coleman, R. H.
  1940   *Dasypterus floridanus* in South Carolina. J. Mamm. 21:90.
  1950   The status of *Lasiurus borealis seminolus* (Rhoads). J. Mamm. 31:190-92.

Commissaris, L. R.
  1959   Notes on the yuma myotis in New Mexico. J. Mamm. 40:441-42.
  1961   The Mexican big-eared bat in Arizona. J. Mamm. 42:61-65.

Conrad, L. G.
  1961   Distribution and speciation problems concerning the long-eared bat, *Plecotus townsendii virginianus*. D. C. Speleograph 17:49-52.

Constantine, D. G.
  1948   Great bat colonies attract predators. Bull. Natl. Speleolog. Soc. 10:100.
  1952   A program for maintaining the free-tail bat in captivity. J. Mamm. 33:395-97.
  1957   Color variation and molt in *Tadarida brasiliensis* and *Myotis velifer*. J. Mamm. 38:461-66.
  1958a   An automatic bat-collecting device. J. Wildlife Management 22:17-22.
  1958b   Ecological observations on lasiurine bats in Georgia. J. Mamm. 39:64-70.

Constantine, D. G. (*continued*):

1958c   *Tadarida femorosacca* and *Tadarida molossa* at Carlsbad Caverns, New Mexico. J. Mamm. 39:293.

1958d   Color variation and molt in *Mormoops megalophylla*. J. Mamm. 39:344-47.

1958e   Bleaching of hair pigment in bats by the atmosphere in caves. J. Mamm. 39:513-20.

1959   Ecological observations on lasiurine bats in the North Bay area of California. J. Mamm. 40:13-15.

1961a   Spotted bat and big free-tailed bat in northern New Mexico. S. W. Nat. 6:92-97.

1961b   Locality records and notes on western bats. J. Mamm. 42:404-405.

1962   Rabies transmission by nonbite route. Pub. Health Repts. 77:287-89.

1966a   Ecological observations on lasiurine bats in Iowa. J. Mamm. 47:34-41.

1966b   New bat locality records from Oaxaca, Arizona and Colorado. J. Mamm. 47:125-26.

1967   Activity patterns of the Mexican free-tailed bat. Univ. New Mexico Publ. Biol. No. 7. 79 pp.

Cope, J. B., W. Baker, and J. Confer

1961a   Breeding colonies of four species of bats of Indiana. Proc. Indiana Acad. Sci. 70:262-66.

Cope, J. B., E. Churchwell, and K. Koontz

1961b   A method of tagging bats with radioactive Gold-198 in homing experiments. Proc. Indiana Acad. Sci. 70:267-69.

Cope, J. B., K. Koontz, and E. Churchwell

1961c   Notes on homing of two species of bats, *Myotis lucifugus* and *Eptesicus fuscus*. Proc. Indiana Acad. Sci. 70:270-74.

Cope, J. B., and S. R. Humphrey

1967   Homing experiments with the evening bat *Nycticeius humeralis*. J. Mamm. 48:136.

Cowan, I. McT.

1945   Notes and observations. Canadian Field-Nat. 59:149.

Cowan, I. McT., and C. J. Guiguet

1965   The mammals of British Columbia. British Columbia Provincial Mus. 11:1-141.

Cox, T. J.

1965a   Behavior of the mastiff bat. J. Mamm. 46:687-88.

1965b   Seasonal change in the behavior of the western pipistrelle because of lactation. J. Mamm. 46:703.

Crain, J. L., and R. L. Packard

1966   Notes on mammals from Washington Parish, Louisiana. J. Mamm. 47:323-25.

Cressman, L. S.

1938   Two new Oregon localities for two races of pale bats. J. Mamm. 19:248-49.

Cronan, J. M., and A. Brooks

1962   The mammals of Rhode Island. Wildlife Pamphlet No. 6. Rhode Island Div. of Fish & Game. 133 pp.

Cross, S. P.

1965   Roosting habits of *Pipistrellus hesperus*. J. Mamm. 46:270-79.

Cross, S. P., and W. Huibregtse

1964   Unusual roosting site of *Eptesicus fuscus*. J. Mamm. 45:628.

Cutter, W. L.

1959   The hoary bat in the panhandle of Texas. J. Mamm. 40:442.

Dalland, J.

1965   Hearing sensitivity in bats. Science 150:1185-86.

Dalquest, W. W.

1938   Bats in the state of Washington. J. Mamm. 19:211-13.

1943   Seasonal distribution of the hoary bat along the Pacific Coast. Murrelet 24:21-24.

1946   The daytime retreat of a California mastiff bat. J. Mamm. 27:87-88.

1947a   Notes on the natural history of the bat, *Myotis yuman-*

Dalquest, W. W. (*continued*):

ensis, in California, with a description of a new race. Amer. Midl. Nat. 38:224-47.

1947b   Notes on the natural history of the bat *Corynorhinus rafinesquii* in California. J. Mamm. 28:17-30.

1948   Mammals of Washington. Univ. Kansas Publ., Mus. Nat. Hist. 2:1-444.

1953   Mammals of the Mexican state of San Luis Potosi. Louisiana State Univ. Press, Baton Rouge. 229 pp.

1954   Netting bats in tropical Mexico. Trans. Kansas Acad. Sci. 57:1-10.

Dalquest, W. W., and M. C. Ramage

1946   Notes on the long-legged bat (*Myotis volans*) at Old Fort Tejon and vicinity, California. J. Mamm. 27:60-63.

Davis, R.

1966   Homing performance and homing ability in bats. Ecol. Monographs 36:201-37.

Davis, R., and E. L. Cockrum

1962   Repeating homing exhibited by a female pallid bat. Science 137:1-2.

1963   Bridges utilized as day-roosts by bats. J. Mamm. 44:428-30.

Davis, R. B., C. F. Herreid II, and H. L. Short

1962   Mexican free-tailed bats in Texas. Ecol. Monographs. 32:311-46.

Davis, W. B.

1939   The recent mammals of Idaho. Caxton Printers, Ltd., Caldwell. 400 pp.

1944a   Status of *Myotis subulatus* in Texas. J. Mamm. 25:201.

1944b   Notes on Mexican mammals. J. Mamm. 25:370-403.

1960   The mammals of Texas. Game and Fish Commission, Austin. 252 pp.

1966   Review of South American bats of the genus *Eptesicus*. S. W. Nat. 11:245-74.

Davis, W. B., and D. C. Carter

1962a   Notes on Central American bats with description of a new subspecies of *Mormoops*. S. W. Nat. 7:64-74.

1962b   Review of the genus *Leptonycteris* (Mammalia: Chiroptera). Proc. Biol. Soc. Washington 75:193-98.

Davis, W. B., and R. J. Russell

1954   Mammals of the Mexican state of Morelos. J. Mamm. 35:63-80.

Davis, W. H.

1955   *Myotis subulatus leibii* in unusual situations. J. Mamm. 36:130.

1957   The status of the seminole bat, *Lasiurus seminolus* (Rhoads). Proc. Biol. Soc. Washington 70:181.

1959a   Disproportionate sex ratios in hibernating bats. J. Mamm. 40:16-19.

1959b   Taxonomy of the eastern pipistrel. J. Mamm. 40:521-31.

1963   Aging bats in winter. Trans. Kentucky Acad. Sci. 24:28-30.

1964a   Winter awakening patterns in the bats *Myotis lucifugus* and *Pipistrellus subflavus*. J. Mamm. 45:645-47.

1964b   Fall swarming of bats at Dixon Cave, Kentucky. Bull. Natl. Speleolog. Soc. 26:82-83.

1966   Population dynamics of the bat *Pipistrellus subflavus*. J. Mamm. 47:383-96.

1967   A *Myotis lucifugus* with two young. Bat Research News 8:3.

Davis, W. H., and R. W. Barbour

1965   The use of vision in flight by the bat, *Myotis sodalis*. Amer. Midl. Nat. 74:497-99.

Davis, W. H., R. W. Barbour, and M. D. Hassell

1968   Colony behavior of the big brown bat *Eptesicus fuscus*. J. Mamm. 49: in press.

Davis, W. H., M. J. Cawein, M. D. Hassell, and E. J. Lappat

1967   Winter and summer circulatory changes in refrigerated and active bats, *Myotis lucifugus*. J. Mamm. 48:132-34.

Davis, W. H., and J. W. Hardin

1967   Homing in *Lasionycteris noctivagans*. J. Mamm. 48:323.

Davis, W. H., M. D. Hassell, and C. L. Rippy
  1965   Maternity colonies of the bat *Myotis l. lucifugus* in Kentucky. Amer. Midl. Nat. 73:161-65.

Davis, W. H., M. D. Hassell and C. L. Rippy
  1965   *Myotis leibii leibii* in Kentucky. J. Mamm. 46:683-84.

Davis, W. H., and H. B. Hitchcock
  1964   Notes on sex ratios of hibernating bats. J. Mamm. 45:475-76.
  1965   Biology and migration of the bat, *Myotis lucifugus*, in New England. J. Mamm. 46:296-313.

Davis, W. H., and W. Z. Lidicker, Jr.
  1955   *Myotis subulatus leibii* in Missouri. J. Mamm. 36:288-89.
  1956   Winter range of the red bat, *Lasiurus borealis*. J. Mamm. 37:280-81.

Davis, W. H., W. Z. Lidicker, Jr., and J. A. Sealander, Jr.
  1955   *Myotis austroriparius* in Arkansas. J. Mamm. 36:288.

Davis, W. H., and M. M. Luckens
  1966   Use of big brown bats *(Eptesicus fuscus)* in biomedical research. Lab. Anim. Care 16:224-27.

Davis, W. H., and R. E. Mumford
  1962   Ecological notes on the bat *Pipistrellus subflavus*. Amer. Midl. Nat. 68:294-98.

Davis, W. H., and O. B. Reite
  1967   Responses of bats from temperate regions to changes in ambient temperature. Biol. Bull. 132:320-28.

Dean, W. D., K. T. Maddy, E. L. Cockrum, and H. G. Crecelius
  1960   Rabies in insectivorous bats in Arizona. Arizona Med. 17:69-77.

DeBlase, A. F., and J. B. Cope
  1967   An Indiana bat impaled on barbed wire. Amer. Midl. Nat. 77:238.

DeBlase, A. F., S. R. Humphrey, and K. S. Drury
  1965   Cave flooding and mortality in bats in Wind Cave Kentucky. J. Mamm. 46:96.

DeCoursey, G., and P. J. DeCoursey
  1964   Adaptive aspects of activity rhythms in bats. Biol. Bull. 126:14-27.

Dickerman, R. W.
  1960   Range extension of *Tadarida femorosacca* in Arizona. J. Mamm. 41:265-66.

Douglas, C. L.
  1967   New records of mammals from Mesa Verde National Park, Colorado. J. Mamm. 48:322-23.

Doutt, J. K., C. A. Heppenstall, and J. E. Guilday
  1966   Mammals of Pennsylvania. Pennsylvania Game Commission, Harrisburg. 273 pp.

Downes, W. L., Jr.
  1964   Unusual roosting behavior in red bats. J. Mamm. 45:143-44.

Downing, S. C.
  1961   Sharp-shinned hawk preys on red bat. J. Mamm. 42:540.

Dunaway, P. B.
  1960   Seminole bat strangled by Spanish moss. J. Mamm. 41:400.

Dunaway, P. B., and L. L. Lewis
  1965   Taxonomic relation of erythrocyte count, mean corpuscular volume, and body-weight in mammals. Nature 205:481-84.

Dunning, D. C., and K. D. Roeder
  1965   Moth sounds and insect-catching behavior of bats. Science 147:173-74.

Durrant, S. D.
  1952   Mammals of Utah. Univ. Kansas Publ., Mus. Nat. Hist. 6:1-549.

Durrant, S. D., and W. H. Behle
  1938   A second record of *Tadarida* from Utah. J. Mamm. 19:500.

Durrant, S. D., and H. W. Setzer
1943   Notes on *Tadarida macrotis* in Utah. J. Mamm. 24: 501.

Dymond, J. R.
1936   Life history notes and growth studies on the little brown bat, *Myotis lucifugus lucifugus*. Canadian Field-Nat. 50:114-16.

Eads, R. B., J. S. Wiseman, J. E. Grimes, and G. C. Menzies
1955   Wildlife Rabies in Texas. Publ. Health Repts. 70:995-1000.

Eads, R. B., J. S. Wiseman, and G. C. Menzies
1957   Observations concerning the Mexican free-tailed bat, *Tadarida mexicana* in Texas. Texas J. Sci. 9:227-42.

Easterla, D. A.
1965a   A nursery colony of evening bats in southern Missouri. J. Mamm. 46:498.
1965b   The spotted bat in Utah. J. Mamm. 46:665-68.
1966   Yuma myotis and fringed myotis in southern Utah. J. Mamm. 47:350-51.
1967   Black rat snake preys upon gray myotis and winter observations of red bats. Amer. Midl. Nat. 77:527-28.

Easterla, D. A., and L. C. Watkins
1967   Silver-haired bat in southwestern Iowa. J. Mamm. 48:327.

Edgerton, H. E., R. F. Spangle, and J. K. Baker
1966   Mexican free tail bats: Photography. Science 153:201-203.

Elwell, A. S.
1962   Blue jay preys on young bats. J. Mamm. 43:434.

Emmons, C. W., P. D. Klite, G. M. Baer, and W. B. Hill, Jr.
1966   Isolation of *Histoplasma capsulatum* from bats in the United States. Amer. J. Epidemiol. 84:103-109.

Engels, W. L.
1936   Distribution of races of the brown bat (*Eptesicus*) in western North America. Amer. Midl. Nat. 17:653-60.

Engler, C. H.
1943   Carnivorous activities of big brown and pallid bat. J. Mamm. 24:96-97.

Fargo, W. G.
1929   Bats of Indian Key, Tampa Bay, Florida. J. Mamm. 10:203-205.

Fenton, M. B.
1966   *Myotis sodalis* in caves near Watertown, New York. J. Mamm. 47:526.

Findley, J. S.
1954a   Reproduction in two species of *Myotis* in Jackson Hole, Wyoming. J. Mamm. 35:434.
1954b   Tree roosting of the eastern pipistrelle. J. Mamm. 35:433.
1960   Identity of the long-eared *Myotis* of the southwest and Mexico. J. Mamm. 41:16-20.

Findley, J. S., and C. Jones
1961   New United States record of the Mexican big-eared bat. J. Mamm. 42:92.
1964   Seasonal distribution of the hoary bat. J. Mamm. 45:461-70.
1965   Comments on spotted bats. J. Mamm. 46:679-80.
1967   Taxonomic relationships of bats of the species *Myotis fortidens*, *M. lucifugus* and *M. occultus*. J. Mamm. 48:429-44.

Fitch, J. H.
1966   Weight loss and temperature response in three species of bats in Marshall County, Kansas. Search, Univ. Kansas Publs. 6:17-24.

Fleharty, E. D., and J. D. Farney
1965   A second locality record for *Myotis keenii* (Merriam) in Kansas. Trans. Kansas Acad. Sci. 68:200.

Folk, G. E., Jr.
1940   Shift of population among hibernating bats. J. Mamm. 21:306-15.

Frum, W. G.

1946 Abnormality in dentition of *Myotis lucifugus*. J. Mamm. 27:176.

1948 *Corynorhinus macrotis*, big-eared bat, in West Virginia. J. Mamm. 29:418.

1953 Silver-haired bat, *Lasionycteris noctivagans*, in West Virginia. J. Mamm. 34:499-500.

Gardner, A. L.

1962 Bat records from the Mexican states of Colima and Nayarit. J. Mamm. 43:102-103.

1965 New bat records from the Mexican state of Durango. Proc. Western Found. Vert. Zool. 1:101-106.

Gates, W. H.

1936 Keeping bats in captivity. J. Mamm. 17:268-73.

1937 Notes on the big brown bat. J. Mamm. 18:97-98.

1941 A few notes on the evening bat, *Nycticeius humeralis* (Rafinesque). J. Mamm. 22:53-56.

George, J. E., and R. W. Strandtmann

1960 New records of ectoparasites on bats in west Texas. S. W. Nat. 5:228-29.

Gerberg, E. J., and F. C. Goble

1941 Two unusual records of Mallophaga from bats. J. Mamm. 22:454.

Getz, L. L.

1961 New locality records of some Kansas mammals. J. Mamm. 42:282-83.

Gifford, C. E., and D. R. Griffin

1960 Notes on homing and migratory behavior of bats. Ecology 41:378-81.

Girard, K. F., H. B. Hitchcock, G. Edsall, and R. A. MacCready

1965 Rabies in bats in southern New England. New England J. Med. 272:75-80.

Glass, B. P.

1953 Variation in the lower incisors of the Mexican freetail bat, *Tadarida mexicana* (Saussure). Proc. Oklahoma Acad. Sci. 34:73-74.

1954 Aberrant coloration in *Tadarida mexicana*. Amer. Midl. Nat. 52:400-402.

1956 Effectiveness of Japanese mist nets for securing bats in temperate latitudes. S. W. Nat. 1:136-38.

1958a The seminole bat in Oklahoma. J. Mamm. 39:587.

1958b Returns of Mexican freetail bats banded in Oklahoma. J. Mamm. 39:435-37.

1959 Additional returns from free-tailed bats banded in Oklahoma. J. Mamm. 40:542-45.

1961 Two noteworthy records of bats for Oklahoma. S. W. Nat. 6:200-201.

1966 Some notes on reproduction in the red bat, *Lasiurus borealis*. Proc. Oklahoma Acad. Sci. 46:40-41.

Glass, B. P., and R. J. Baker

1965 *Vespertilio subulatus* Say, 1823: Proposed supression under the plenary powers (Mammalia, Chiroptera). Bull. Zool. Nomencl. 22:204-205.

Glass, B. P., and R. C. Moore

1959 A new pipistrel from Oklahoma and Texas. J. Mamm. 40:531-34.

Glass, B. P., and C. M. Ward

1959 Bats of the genus *Myotis* from Oklahoma. J. Mamm. 40:194-201.

Goehring, H. H.

1955 Observations on hoary bats in a storm. J. Mamm. 36:130-31.

1958 A six year study of big brown bat survival. Proc. Minnesota Acad. Sci. 26:222-24.

Golley, F. B.

1962 Mammals of Georgia. Univ. Ga. Press, Athens. 218 pp.

1966 South Carolina mammals. Charleston Museum, Charleston. 181 pp.

Goodpaster, W., and D. F. Hoffmeister

1950 Bats as prey for mink in Kentucky cave. J. Mamm. 31:457.

Goodpaster, W., and D. F. Hoffmeister (*continued*):
1952   Notes on the mammals of western Tennessee. J. Mamm. 33:362-71.

Goslin, R.
1964   The gray bat, *Myotis grisescens* Howell, from Bat Cave, Carter County, Kentucky. Ohio J. Sci. 64:63.

Gottschang, J. L.
1966   Occurrence of the hoary bat (*Lasiurus cinereus*) in Ohio. Ohio J. Sci. 66:527-29.

Gould, E.
1955   The feeding efficiency of insectivorous bats. J. Mamm. 36:399-407.
1959   Further studies on the feeding efficiency of bats. J. Mamm. 40:149-50.

Gould, P. J.
1961   Emergence time of *Tadarida* in relation to light intensity. J. Mamm. 42:405-407.

Graham, R. E.
1966   Observations on the roosting habits of the big-eared bat, *Plecotus townsendii*, in California limestone caves. Cave Notes 8:17-22.

Gray, J. E.
1862   Notice of a species of *Lasiurus* sent from the Sandwich Islands by Mr. W. H. Pease. Proc. Zool. Soc. London 33:143.

Griffin, D. R.
1934   Marking bats. J. Mamm. 15:202-207.
1936   Bat banding. J. Mamm. 17:235-39.
1940   Migrations of New England bats. Bull. Mus. Comp. Zool. 86:217-46.
1945   Travels of banded cave bats. J. Mamm. 26:15-23.
1946   Mystery mammals of the twilight. Natl. Geographic Mag. 90:117-34.
1950   Acoustic location of insect prey by bats. Anat. Rec. 111:32-33.
1953   Bat sounds under natural conditions, with evidence for the echolocation of insect prey. J. Exp. Zool. 123:435-66.
1958   Listening in the dark. Yale Press, New Haven, 413 pp.

Griffin, D. R., J. H. Friend, and F. A. Webster
1965   Target discrimination by the echolocation of bats. J. Exp. Zool. 158:155-68.

Griffin, D. R., and R. Galambos
1941   The sensory basis of obstacle avoidance by flying bats. J. Exp. Zool. 86:481-506.

Griffin, D. R., and H. B. Hitchcock
1965   Probable 24-year longevity record for *Myotis lucifugus*. J. Mamm. 46:332.

Griffin, D. R., and A. Novick
1955   Acoustic orientation of neotropical bats. J. Exp. Zool. 130:251-300.

Griffin, D. R., and J. H. Welsh
1937   Activity rhythms in bats under constant external conditions. J. Mamm. 18:337-42.

Grinnell, H. W.
1918   A synopsis of the bats of California. Univ. California Publ. Zool. 17:223-404.

Gunderson, H. L., and J. R. Beer
1953   The mammals of Minnesota. Univ. Minnesota Press, Minneapolis. 190 pp.

Guthrie, M. J.
1933a   Notes on the seasonal movements and habits of some cave bats. J. Mamm. 14:1-19.
1933b   The reproductive cycles of some cave bats. J. Mamm. 14:199-216.

Guthrie, M. J., and K. R. Jeffers
1938   Growth of follicles in the ovaries of the bat *Myotis lucifugus lucifugus*. Anat. Rec. 71:477-96.

Haagner, A. K.
1921   Red bat at sea. J. Mamm. 2:36.

Hahn, W. L.

1908　Some habits and sensory adaptations of cave-inhabiting bats. Biol. Bull. 15:135-93.

Hall, E. R.

1939　The spotted bat in Kern County, California. J. Mamm. 20:103.

1946　Mammals of Nevada. Univ. California Press, Berkeley. 710 pp.

1955　Handbook of mammals of Kansas. Univ. Kansas Mus. Nat. Hist. Misc. Publ. No. 7. 303 pp.

1962　Collecting and preparing study specimens of vertebrates. Univ. Kansas Mus. Nat. Hist. Misc. Publ. No. 30. 46 pp.

1965　Names of species of North American mammals north of Mexico. Univ. Kansas Publ., Mus. Nat. Hist. 43: 1-16.

Hall, E. R., and W. W. Dalquest

1950　A synopsis of the American bats of the genus *Pipistrellus*. Univ. Kansas Publ., Mus. Nat. Hist. 1:591-602.

1963　The mammals of Veracruz. Univ. Kansas Publ., Mus. Nat. Hist. 14:165-362.

Hall, E. R., and J. K. Jones, Jr.

1961　North American yellow bats, "*Dasypterus*," and a list of the named kinds of the genus *Lasiurus* Gray. Univ. Kansas Publ., Mus. Nat. Hist. 14:73-98.

Hall, E. R., and K. R. Kelson

1959　The mammals of North America. Vol. 1. Ronald Press, New York. 546 pp.

Hall, E. R., and B. Villa

1949　An annotated check list of the mammals of Michoacan, Mexico. Univ. Kansas Publ., Mus Nat. Hist. 1:431-72.

Hall, J. S.

1961　*Myotis austroriparius* in central Kentucky. J. Mamm. 42:399-400.

1962　A life history and taxonomic study of the Indiana bat, *Myotis sodalis*. Reading Public Mus. and Art Gallery, Sci. Publ. 12:1-68.

1963a　Notes on *Plecotus rafinesquii* in central Kentucky. J. Mamm. 44:119-20.

1963b　*Plecotus* in West Virginia. Bat Banding News 4:21.

Hall, J. S., and C. H. Blewett

1964　Bat remains in owl pellets from Missouri. J. Mamm. 45:303-304.

Hall, J. S., R. J. Cloutier, and D. R. Griffin

1957　Longevity records and notes on tooth wear of bats. J. Mamm. 38:407-409.

Hall, J. S., and N. Wilson

1966　Seasonal populations and movements of the gray bat in the Kentucky area. Amer. Midl. Nat. 75:317-24.

Halloran, A. F., and B. P. Glass

1964　Additional mammal notes from the Wichita Mountains Region of Oklahoma. Proc. Oklahoma Acad. Sci. 44:56-58.

Hamilton, W. J., Jr.

1930　Notes on the mammals of Breathitt County, Kentucky. J. Mamm. 11:306-11.

1933　The insect food of the big brown bat. J. Mamm. 14: 155-56.

1941　Notes on some mammals of Lee County, Florida. Amer. Midl. Nat. 25:686-91.

1943　The mammals of eastern United States. Comstock Publ. Associates, Ithaca. 432 pp.

1949　The bacula of some North American vespertilionid bats. J. Mamm. 27:378-87.

Handley, C. O., Jr.

1955　New bats of the genus *Corynorhinus*. J. Washington Acad. Sci. 45:147-49.

1956　Bat versus ant. J. Mamm. 37:279.

1959　A revision of American bats of the genera *Euderma* and *Plecotus*. Proc. U. S. Natl. Mus. 110:95-246.

1960　Descriptions of new bats from Panama. Proc. U. S. Natl. Mus. 112:457-79.

Handley, C. O., Jr., and C. P. Patton
1947 Wild mammals of Virginia. Commission of Game and Inland Fisheries, Richmond. 220 pp.

Hardin, J. W.
1967 Waking periods and movement of *Myotis sodalis* during the hibernation season. M.S. Thesis, Univ. of Kentucky, Lexington.

Hardy, R.
1941 Some notes on Utah bats. J. Mamm. 22:289-95.
1949 Notes on mammals from Arizona, Nevada, and Utah. J. Mamm. 30:434-35.

Hargrave, L. L.
1944 Notes on three genera of bats from Arizona. J. Mamm. 25:312-13.

Harper, F.
1927 Mammals of Okefenokee swamp region of Georgia. Proc. Boston Soc. Nat. Hist. 38:191-396.
1929 Mammal notes from Randolph County, Georgia. J. Mamm. 10:84-85.
1961 Land and fresh-water mammals of the Ungava peninsula. Univ. Kansas Mus. Nat. Hist. Misc. Publ. No. 27. 178 pp.

Harris, A. H., and J. S. Findley
1962 Status of *Myotis lucifugus phasma* and comments on variation in *Myotis yumanensis*. J. Mamm. 43:192-99.

Hartman, C. G.
1933 On the survival of spermatozoa in the female genital tract of the bat. Quart. Rev. Biol. 8:185-93.

Harvey, M. J.
1965 Detecting animals tagged with Co^{60} through air, soil, water, wood, and stone. Trans. Kentucky Acad. Sci. 26:63-66.

Hassell, M. D.
1963 A study of homing in the Indiana bat, *Myotis sodalis*. Trans. Kentucky Acad. Sci. 24:1-4.

Hassell, M. D. (*continued*):
1967 Intra-cave activity of four species of bats hibernating in Kentucky. Ph.D. Thesis. Univ. Kentucky, Lexington.

Hassell, M. D., and M. J. Harvey
1965 Differential homing in *Myotis sodalis*. Amer. Midl. Nat. 74:501-503.

Hatfield, D. M.
1937 Notes on the behavior of the California leaf-nosed bat. J. Mamm. 18:96-97.

Hatt, R. T.
1923 Food habits of the Pacific pallid bat. J. Mamm. 4: 260-61.

Hays, H. A., and D. C. Bingman
1964 A colony of gray bats in southeastern Kansas. J. Mamm. 45:150.

Hays, H. A., and P. H. Ireland
1967 A big free-tailed bat (*Tadarida macrotis*) taken in southeastern Kansas. S. W. Nat. 12:196.

Hayward, B. J.
1961 Notes on *Plecotus phyllotis* from Arizona. J. Mamm. 42:402.
1963 A maternity colony of *Myotis occultus*. J. Mamm. 44:279.

Hayward, B. J., and R. Davis
1964 Flight speeds in western bats. J. Mamm. 45:236-42.

Hayward, J. S., and E. G. Ball
1966 Quantitative aspects of brown adipose tissue thermogenesis during arousal from hibernation. Biol. Bull. 131:94-103.

Henshaw, R. E.
1960 Responses of free-tailed bats to increases in cave temperature. J. Mamm. 41:396-98.

Henshaw, R. E., and G. E. Folk, Jr.
1966 Relation of thermoregulation to seasonally changing

Henshaw, R. E., and G. E. Folk, Jr. (continued):
microclimate in two species of bats (*Myotis lucifugus* and *M. sodalis*). Physiol. Zool. 39:223-36.

Heppenstall, C. A.
1960   A possible bat migration. J. Mamm. 41:509.

Herreid, C. F., Jr.
1959a   Sexual dimorphism in teeth of the free-tailed bat. J. Mamm. 40:538-41.
1959b   Notes on a baby free-tailed bat. J. Mamm. 40:609-10.
1960a   Comments on the odors of bats. J. Mamm. 41:396.
1960b   Roadrunner a predator of bats. Condor 62:67.
1961a   Temperature regulation and oxygen consumption of free-tailed bats in cave habitats. Diss. Abstr. 22:2520-21.
1961b   Snakes as predators of bats. Herpetologica 17:271-72.
1961c   Notes on the pallid bat in Texas. S. W. Nat. 6:13-20.
1963a   Survival of a migratory bat at different temperatures. J. Mamm. 44:431-33.
1963b   Temperature regulation and metabolism in Mexican freetail bats. Science 142:1573-74.
1963c   Temperature regulation of Mexican free-tailed bats in cave habitats. J. Mamm. 44:560-73.
1963d   Metabolism of the Mexican free-tailed bat. J. Cell. Comp. Physiol. 61:201-207.
1964   Bat longevity and metabolic rate. Exp. Geront. 1:1-9.
1967a   Temperature regulation, temperature preference and tolerance, and metabolism of young and adult free-tailed bats. Physiol. Zool. 40:1-22.
1967b   Mortality statistics of young bats. Ecology 48:310-12.

Herreid, C. F., Jr., and R. B. Davis
1966   Flight patterns of bats. J. Mamm. 47:78-86.

Herreid, C. F., Jr., R. B. Davis, and H. L. Short
1960   Injuries due to bat banding. J. Mamm. 41:398-400.

Herreid, C. F., Jr., and K. Schmidt-Nielsen
1966   Oxygen consumption, temperature, and water loss in bats from different environments. Am. J. Physiol. 211:1108-12.

Hibbard, C. W.
1936   Established colonies of the Mexican free-tailed bat in Kansas. J. Mamm. 17:167-68.

Hitchcock, H. B.
1943   Hoary bat, *Lasiurus cinereus*, at Southampton Island, N. W. T. Canadian Field-Nat. 57:86.
1949   Hibernation of bats in southeastern Ontario and adjacent Quebec. Canadian Field-Nat. 63:47-59.
1950   Sex ratios in hibernating bats. Bull. Natl. Speleolog. Soc. 12:26-28.
1955   A summer colony of the least bat, *Myotis subulatus leibii* (Audubon and Bachman). Canadian Field-Nat. 69:31.
1957   The use of bird bands on bats. J. Mamm. 38:402-405.
1963   An unintended bat trap. J. Mamm. 44:577-78.
1965   Twenty-three years of bat banding in Ontario and Quebec. Canadian Field-Nat. 79:4-14.

Hitchcock, H. B., and K. Reynolds
1942   Homing experiments with the little brown bat, *Myotis lucifugus lucifugus* (LeConte). J. Mamm. 23:258-67.

Hock, R. J.
1951   The metabolic rates and body temperatures of bats. Biol. Bull. 101:289-99.

Hoffmeister, D. F.
1954   Observations on mammals in southeastern Arizona. Nat. Hist. Misc. No. 129.
1955   Mammals new to Grand Canyon National Park, Arizona. Plateau 28:1-7.
1956   Mammals of the Graham (Pinaleno) Mountains, Arizona. Amer. Midl. Nat. 65:257-88.
1957   Review of the long-nosed bats of the genus *Leptonycteris*. J. Mamm. 38:454-61.
1959   Distributional records of certain mammals from southern Arizona. S. W. Nat. 4:14-19.

Hoffmeister, D. F., and W. L. Downes
1964   Blue jays as predators of red bats. S. W. Nat. 9:102-109.

269

Hoffmeister, D. F., and W. W. Goodpaster

1954   The mammals of the Huachuca Mountains, Southeastern Arizona. Univ. Illinois Press, Urbana. 152 pp.

1962   Observations on a colony of big-eared bats, *Plecotus rafinesquii*. Trans. Illinois Acad. Sci. 55:87-89.

Hoffmeister, D. F., and P. H. Krutzsch

1955   A new subspecies of *Myotis evotis* (H. Allen) from southeastern Arizona and Mexico. Nat. Hist. Misc. No. 151.

Hoffmeister, D. F., and C. O. Mohr

1957   Fieldbook of Illinois Mammals. Illinois Nat. Hist. Surv. Div., Urbana 233 pp.

Holsinger, J. R.

1963   *Plecotus* in Virginia. Bat Banding News 4:21.

Hooper, E. T.

1939   Notes on the sex ratio in *Nycticeius humeralis*. J. Mamm. 20:369-70.

Hough, F.

1957   Set hunting pattern of a little brown bat. J. Mamm. 38:121-22.

Howell, A. B.

1920a   Contribution to the life history of the California mastiff bat. J. Mamm. 1:111-17.

1920b   Some California experiences with bat roosts. J. Mamm. 1:169-77.

Howell, A. B., and L. Little

1924   Additional notes on California bats, with observations upon the young of *Eumops*. J. Mamm. 5:261-63.

Howell, A. H.

1921   A biological survey of Alabama. The mammals. N. Amer. Fauna No. 45. 88 pp.

Huey, L. M.

1925   Food of the California leaf-nosed bat. J. Mamm. 6:196-97.

1936   Desert pallid bats caught in mouse traps. J. Mamm. 17:285-86.

1954a   The mammals of Baja California, Mexico. Trans. San Diego Soc. Nat. Hist. 13:85-168.

1954b   *Choeronycteris mexicana* from southern California and Baja California, Mexico. J. Mamm. 35:436-37.

Humphrey, S. R.

1966   Flight behavior of *Myotis lucifugus* at nursery colonies. J. Mamm. 47:323.

Humphrey, S. R., and J. B. Cope

1964   Movements of *Myotis lucifugus lucifugus* from a colony in Boone County, Indiana. Proc. Indiana Acad. Sci. 72:268-71.

Hurst, R. N., and J. E. Wiebers

1967   Minimum body temperature extremes in the little brown bat *Myotis lucifugus*. J. Mamm. 48:465.

Husson, A. M.

1962   The bats of Suriname. Brill, Leiden. 282 pp.

Ingles, L. G.

1949   Hunting habits of the bat, *Myotis evotis*. J. Mamm. 30:197-98.

1965   Mammals of the Pacific states. Stanford Univ. Press, Stanford. 506 pp.

Irwin, D. W., and R. J. Baker

1967   Additional records of bats from Arizona and Sinaloa. S. W. Nat. 12:195.

Iwen, F. A.

1958   Hoary bat the victim of a barbed wire fence. J. Mamm. 39:438.

Jackson, H. H. T.

1922   The brown bat active in winter at Washington, D. C. J. Mamm. 3:52.

1926   Collecting bats with a net. J. Mamm. 7:230-31.

1961   The mammals of Wisconsin. Univ. Wisconsin Press, Madison. 504 pp.

Jameson, D. K.
1959 A survey of the parasites of five species of bats. S. W. Nat. 4:61-65.

Jegla, T. C., and J. S. Hall
1962 A pleistocene deposit of the free-tailed bat in Mammoth Cave, Kentucky. J. Mamm. 43:477-81.

Jennings, W. L.
1958 The ecological distribution of bats in Florida. Ph.D. Thesis. Univ. Florida, Gainesville. 126 pp.

Jepsen, G. L.
1966 Early Eocene bat from Wyoming. Science 154:1333-39.

Jewett, S. G.
1955 Free-tailed bats, and melanistic mice in Oregon. J. Mamm. 36:458-59.

Jobling, B.
1949 Host-parasite relationship between the American Streblidae and the bats, with a new key to the American genera and a record of the Streblidae from Trinidad, British West Indies (Diptera). Parasitology 39:315-29.

Johnson, C. E.
1932 Notes on a family of red bats in captivity. J. Mamm. 13:132-35.

Johnson, P. B.
1933 Accidents to bats. J. Mamm. 14:156-57.

Jones, C.
1961 Additional records of bats in New Mexico. J. Mamm. 42:538-39.
1965 Ecological distribution and activity periods of bats of the Mogollon Mountains area of New Mexico and adjacent Arizona. Tulane Stud. in Zool. 12:93-100.
1966 Changes in populations of some western bats. Amer. Midl. Nat. 76:522-28.
1967 Growth, development, and wing loading in the evening bat, *Nycticeius humeralis* (Rafinesque). J. Mamm. 48:1-19.

Jones, C., and J. S. Findley
1963 The long-nosed bat in New Mexico. S. W. Nat. 8:174-75.

Jones, G. F.
1948 A summer aggregation of lump-nosed bats at Lake Pend Oreille, Idaho. J. Mamm. 29:416.

Jones, J. K., Jr.
1963 Additional records of mammals from Durango, Mexico. Trans. Kansas Acad. Sci. 66:750-53.
1964 Distribution and taxonomy of mammals of Nebraska. Univ. Kansas Publ., Mus. Nat. Hist. 16:1-356.
1966 Records of bats from western North Dakota. Trans. Kansas Acad. Sci. 69:88-90.

Jones, J. K., Jr., and J. F. Downhower
1963 Second record of *Myotis grisescens* in Kansas. S. W. Nat. 8:174.

Jones, J. K., Jr., E. D. Fleharty, and P. B. Dunnigan
1967 The distributional status of bats in Kansas. Univ. Kansas Mus. Nat. Hist. Misc. Publ. No. 46. 33 pp.

Jones, J. K., Jr., and H. H. Genoways
1966 Records of bats from western North Dakota. Trans. Kansas Acad. Sci. 69:88-90.
1967a A new subspecies of the fringed-tailed bat, *Myotis thysanodes,* from the Black Hills of South Dakota and Wyoming. J. Mamm. 48:231-35.
1967b Annotated checklist of bats from South Dakota. Trans. Kansas Acad. Sci. 70:194-96.

Jones, J. K., Jr., J. D. Smith, and T. Alvarez
1965 Notes on bats from the cape region of Baja California. Trans. San Diego Soc. Nat. Hist. 14:53-56.

Jones, J. K., Jr., and W. C. Stanley
1962 *Myotis subulatus* in North Dakota. J. Mamm. 43:263.

Judd, F. W.
1967 Notes on some mammals from Big Bend National Park. S. W. Nat. 12:192-94.

Kallen, F. C.
1960   Vascular changes related to hibernation in the vesper-
        tilionid bat *Myotis lucifugus*. Bull. Mus. Comp. Zool.
        124:373-86.
1964   Some aspects of water balance in the hibernating bat.
        Ann. Acad. Sci. Fennicae Ser. A.IV Biologica 71:259-
        67.

Kayser, C.
1961   The physiology of natural hibernation. Pergamon Press,
        New York. 325 pp.

Killpack, M. L., and M. A. Goates
1963   Bat captured in snap trap. J. Mamm. 44:125-26.

Kinsey, C.
1961   Leopard frog attacks bat. J. Mamm. 42:408.

Klite, P. D., and M. Kourany
1965   Isolation of salmonellae from a neotropical bat. J.
        Bacteriol. 90:831.

Klite, P. D., and R. V. Young
1965   Bats and histoplasmosis. Ann. Int. Med. 62:1263-71.

Klugh, A. B.
1924   Notes on *Eptesicus fuscus*. J. Mamm. 5:42-43.

Koestner, E. J.
1941   An annotated list of mammals collected in Nuevo Leon,
        Mexico, in 1938. Great Basin Nat. 2:9-15.
1942   A method of collecting bats. J. Tennessee Acad. Sci.
        17:301.

Koford, C. B., and M. R. Koford
1948   Breeding colonies of bats, *Pipistrellus hesperus* and
        Myotis subulatus melanorhinus. J. Mamm. 29:417-
        18.

Koopman, K. F.
1963   The identity of bats (genus *Myotis*) collected in
        Arizona by Miller, Price, and Condit in 1894. Amer.
        Mus. Novitates No. 2140.
1965   A northern record of the yellow bat. J. Mamm. 46:695.

Koopman, K. F., and F. Gudmundsson
1966   Bats in Iceland. Amer. Mus. Novitates No. 2262.

Koopman, K. F., M. K. Hecht, and E. Ledecky-Janecek
1957   Notes on the mammals of the Bahamas with special
        reference to the bats. J. Mamm. 38:164-74.

Krutzsch, P. H.
1944a   California lyre snake feeding on the pocketed bat.
        J. Mamm. 25:410.
1944b   Notes on the little known pocketed bat. J. Mamm.
        25:201.
1944c   Fourth record of the pocketed bat in California. J.
        Mamm. 25:413-14.
1945   Observations on a colony of molossids. J. Mamm. 26:
        196.
1946   Some observations on the big brown bat in San Diego
        County, California. J. Mamm. 27:240-42.
1954   Notes on the habits of the bat, *Myotis californicus*.
        J. Mamm. 35:539-45.
1955a   Observations on the Mexican free-tailed bat, *Tadarida
        mexicana*. J. Mamm. 36:236-42.
1955b   Ectoparasites from some species of bats from western
        North America. J. Mamm. 36:457-58.
1955c   Observations on the California mastiff bat. J. Mamm.
        36:407-14.
1961   A summer colony of male little brown bats. J. Mamm.
        42:529-30.
1966   Remarks on silver-haired and Leib's bats in eastern
        United States. J. Mamm. 47:121.

Krutzsch, P. H., and C. A. Heppenstall
1955   Additional distributional records of bats in Utah. J.
        Mamm. 36:126-27.

Krutzsch, P. H., and A. H. Hughes
1959   Hematological changes with torpor in the bat. J.
        Mamm. 40:547-54.

Krutzsch, P. H., and S. E. Sulkin
1958   The laboratory care of the Mexican free-tailed bat. J.
        Mamm. 39:262-65.

Krutzsch, P. H., and T. A. Vaughan

1955   Additional data on the bacula of North American bats. J. Mamm. 36:96-100.

Krutzsch, P. H., and W. W. Wells

1960   Androgenic activity in the interscapular brown adipose tissue of the male hibernating bat (Myotis lucifugus). Proc. Soc. Exp. Biol. Med. 105:578-81.

Krzanowski, A.

1958.   Bat attacking an owl. Przeglad Zoologiczny 2:44-45.

Kunz, T. H.

1965   Notes on some Nebraskan bats. Trans. Kansas Acad. Sci. 68:201-203.

1966   Evening bat in Iowa. J. Mamm. 47:341.

Lane, H. K.

1946   Notes on Pipistrellus subflavus subflavus (F. Cuvier) during the season of parturition. Proc. Pennsylvania Acad. Sci. 20:57-61.

Lange, K. I.

1960   Mammals of the Santa Catalina Mountains, Arizona. Amer. Midl. Nat. 64:436-58.

LaVal, R. K.

1967   Records of bats from the southeastern United States. J. Mamm. 48:645-48.

Layne, J. N.

1955   Seminole bat, Lasiurus seminolus, in central New York. J. Mamm. 36:453.

1958   Notes on mammals of southern Illinois. Amer. Midl. Nat. 60:219-54.

Leitner, P.

1966   Body temperature, oxygen consumption, heart rate and shivering in the California mastiff bat, Eumops perotis. Comp. Biochem. Physiol. 19:431-43.

Lewis, J. B.

1940   Mammals of Amelia County, Virginia. J. Mamm. 21:422-28.

Licht, P., and P. Leitner

1967a   Behavioral responses to high temperatures in three species of California bats. J. Mamm. 48:52-61.

1967b   Physiological responses to high environmental temperatures in three species of microchiropteran bats. Comp. Biochem. Physiol. 22:371-87.

Lidicker, W. Z., Jr., and W. H. Davis

1955   Changes in splenic weight associated with hibernation in bats. Proc. Soc. Exp. Biol. Med. 89:640-42.

Lindsay, D. M.

1956a   Additional records of Nycticeius in Indiana. J. Mamm. 37:282.

1956b   Some bat records from southeastern Indiana. J. Mamm. 37:543-45.

Little, L.

1920   Some notes concerning the mastiff bat. J. Mamm. 1:182.

Long, C. A.

1964   Red bat impaled on barbed wire. Trans. Kansas Acad. Sci. 67:201.

1965   The mammals of Wyoming. Univ. Kansas Publ., Mus. Nat. Hist. 14:493-758.

Long, C. A., and C. J. Jones

1966   Variation and frequency of occurrence of the baculum in a population of Mexican free-tailed bats. S. W. Nat. 11:290-95.

Long, C. A., and P. Kamensky

1967   Osteometric variation and function of the high-speed wing of the free-tailed bat. Amer. Midl. Nat. 77:452-61.

Long, W. S.

1940   Notes on the life histories of some Utah mammals. J. Mamm. 21:170-80.

Longhurst, W. M.

1940   The mammals of Napa County, California. California Fish and Game 26:240-70.

Loomis, R. B., and J. K. Jones, Jr.
1964   The northern yellow bat in Sinaloa, Mexico. Bull. So. California Acad. Sci. 63:32.

Luckens, M. M., and W. H. Davis
1964   Bats: Sensitivity to DDT. Science 146:948.
1965   Toxicity of dieldrin and endrin in bats. Nature 207: 879-80.

Lukens, P. W., Jr., and W. B. Davis
1957   Bats of Mexican state of Guerrero. J. Mamm. 38:1-14.

Lyon, M. W.
1925   Bats caught by burdocks. J. Mamm. 6:280.
1936   Mammals of Indiana. Amer. Midl. Nat. 17:1-384.

Mackiewicz, J.
1956   Oceanic records of *Lasionycteris noctivagans* and *Lasiurus borealis*. J. Mamm. 37:442-43.

Macy, R. M., and R. W. Macy
1939   Hawks as enemies of bats. J. Mamm. 20:252.

Maly, R. G.
1962   Second record of eastern big-eared bat in Ohio. J. Mamm. 43:108.

Manville, R. H., and S. P. Young
1965   Distribution of Alaskan mammals. Circular 211, U. S. Dept. Interior, Fish & Wildl. Serv. Bur. Sport Fisheries and Wildl. 74 pp.

Martin, R. L.
1961a   Vole predation on bats in an Indiana cave. J. Mamm. 42:540-41.
1961b   Bat transmitted rabies. Iowa State Univ. Vet. 24:79-82.

Martin, R. L., J. T. Pawluk, and T. B. Clancy
1966   Observations on hibernation of *Myotis subulatus*. J. Mamm. 47:348-49.

Maslin, T. P., Jr.
1938   Fringed-tailed bat in British Columbia. J. Mamm. 19:373.

McClure, H. E.
1939   Red bats at Lewis, Iowa. J. Mamm. 20:501-502.
1942   Summer activities of bats (genus *Lasiurus*) in Iowa. J. Mamm. 23:430-34.

McCue, J. J. G.
1961   How bats hunt with sound. Natl. Geographic Mag. 119:547-88.

McKeever, S.
1951   A survey of the mammals of West Virginia. Cons. Comm. of West Virginia. 126 pp.

Menaker, M.
1959   Endogenous rhythms of body temperature in hibernating bats. Nature 184:1251.
1961   The free running period of the bat clock; seasonal variations at low body temperature. J. Cell. Comp. Physiol. 57:81-86.
1962   Hibernation-hypothermia: an annual cycle of response to low temperature in the bat *Myotis lucifugus*. J. Cell. Comp. Physiol. 59:163-73.
1964   Frequency of spontaneous arousal from hibernation in bats. Nature 203:540-41.

Merriam, C. H.
1884   The mammals of the Adirondack region, northeastern New York. Privately published, New York. 316 pp.
1888   Do any Canadian bats migrate? Evidence in the affirmative. Trans. Royal Soc. Canada 1887 Sec. 4:85-87.

Michael, E. D., and J. B. Birch
1967   First Texas record of *Plecotus rafinesquii*. J. Mamm. 48:672.

Miller, G. S., Jr.
1897a   Migration of bats on Cape Cod, Massachusetts. Science. n.s. 5:541-43.
1897b   North American bats of the family Vespertilionidae. N. Amer. Fauna, No. 13. 136 pp.
1939   Note on the lectotype of *Lasiurus semotus* (H. Allen). J. Mamm. 20:369.

Miller, G. S., Jr., and G. M. Allen
  1928   The American bats of the genera *Myotis* and *Pizonyx*. Bull. U. S. Natl. Mus. No. 144. 207 pp.

Miller, R. E.
  1939   The reproductive cycle in male bats of the species *Myotis lucifugus lucifugus* and *Myotis grisescens*. J. Morph. 64:267-95.

Milstead, W. W., and D. W. Tinkle
  1959   Seasonal occurrence and abundance of bats (Chiroptera) in northwestern Texas. S. W. Nat. 4:134-42.

Mitchell, H. A.
  1963   Ammonia tolerance of the California leaf-nosed bat. J. Mamm. 44:543-51.
  1965   Investigations of the cave atmosphere of a Mexican bat colony. J. Mamm. 45:568-77.

Mitchell, O. G.
  1956   *Trypanosoma vespertilionis* from some southern California bats. J. Mamm. 37:443-44.

Mohos, S. C.
  1961   Bats as laboratory animals. Anat. Rec. 139:369-78.

Mohr, C. E.
  1932   *Myotis grisescens* and *Myotis sodalis* in Tennessee and Alabama. J. Mamm. 13:272-73.
  1933   Observations on the young of cave-dwelling bats. J. Mamm. 14:49-53.
  1936   Notes on the least bat *Myotis subulatus leibii*. Proc. Pennsylvania Acad. Sci. 10:62-65.
  1952   A survey of bat banding in North America, 1932-1951. Amer. Caver 14:3-13.

Moor, K., F. Stay, and W. G. Bradley
  1965   Mexican free-tailed bat and western pipistrelle found roosting in sedges. J. Mamm. 46:507.

Moore, J. C.
  1949   Putnam County and other Florida mammal notes. J. Mamm. 30:57-66.

Morse, R. C., and B. P. Glass
  1960   The taxonomic status of *Antrozous bunkeri*. J. Mamm. 41:10-15.

Mossman, A. S., and W. K. Clark
  1958   Winter records of bats in Alaska. J. Mamm. 39:585.

Mueller, H. C.
  1965   Homing and distance-orientation in bats. Z. Tierpsychol. 23:403-21.

Mueller, H. C., and J. T. Emlen, Jr.
  1957   Homing in bats. Science 126:307-308.

Muir, T. J., and E. Polder
  1960   Notes on hibernating bats in Dubuque County caves. Iowa Acad. Sci. 67:602-606.

Mulaik, S.
  1943   Notes on bats of the Southwest. J. Mamm. 24:269.

Mumford, R. E.
  1957   *Myotis occultus* and *Myotis yumanensis* breeding in New Mexico. J. Mamm. 38:260.
  1958   Population turnover in wintering bats in Indiana. J. Mamm. 39:253-61.
  1963a   A concentration of hoary bats in Arizona. J. Mamm. 44:272.
  1963b   Unusual dentition in *Myotis occultus*. J. Mamm. 44:275.

Mumford, R. E., and L. L. Calvert
  1960   *Myotis sodalis* evidently breeding in Indiana. J. Mamm. 41:512.

Mumford, R. E., and J. B. Cope
  1958   Summer records of *Myotis sodalis* in Indiana. J. Mamm. 39:586-87.
  1964   Distribution and status of the Chiroptera of Indiana. Amer. Midl. Nat. 72:473-89.

Mumford, R. E., L. L. Oakley, and D. A. Zimmerman
  1964   June bat records from Guadalupe Canyon, New Mexico. S. W. Nat. 9:43-45.

Mumford, R. E., and D. A. Zimmerman
1962   Notes on *Choeronycteris mexicana.* J. Mamm. 43: 101-102.
1963   The southern yellow bat in New Mexico. J. Mamm. 44:417-18.

Munyer, E. A.
1967   A parturition date for the hoary bat, *Lasiurus c. cinereus,* in Illinois and notes on the newborn young. Trans. Illinois Acad. Sci. 60:95-97.

Murphy, R. C., and J. T. Nichols
1913   Long Island fauna and flora. I. The bats. Mus. Brooklyn Inst. Arts and Sciences. Science Bull. No. 2. 15 pp.

Musser, G. G., and S. D. Durrant
1960   Notes on *Myotis thysanodes* in Utah. J. Mamm. 41:393-94.

Myers, R. F.
1960   *Lasiurus* from Missouri caves. J. Mamm. 41:114-17.

Nason, E. S.
1948   Morphology of hair of eastern North American bats. Amer. Midl. Nat. 39:345-61.

Neil, R. W.
1940   The pocketed bat in California. J. Mamm. 21:356.

Neill, W. T.
1952   Hoary bat in a squirrel's nest. J. Mamm. 33:113.

Nelson, C. E.
1966   The deciduous dentition of the central American phyllostomid bats *Macrotus waterhousii* and *Pteronotus suapurensis.* S. W. Nat. 11:142-43.

Nelson, E. W.
1918   Smaller mammals of North America. Natl. Geographic Mag. 33:371-493.

Nelson, E. W., and E. A. Goldman
1909   Eleven new mammals from Lower California. Proc. Biol. Soc. Washington 22:23-28.

Nero, R. W.
1957a   Saskatchewan silver-haired bat records. Blue Jay 15: 38-46.
1957b   New silver-haired bat records. Blue Jay 15:121.
1958   Hoary bat parturition date. Blue Jay 16:130-31.
1959   Winter records of bats in Saskatchewan. Blue Jay 17:78.
1960   Long-eared myotis found in Saskatchewan. Blue Jay 18:181.

Novakowski, N. S.
1956   Additional records of bats in Saskatchewan. Canadian Field-Nat. 70:142.

Novick, A.
1965   Echolocation of flying insects by the bat, *Chilonycteris psilotis.* Biol. Bull. 128:297-314.

Nyholm, E. S.
1965   Zur Okologie von *Myotis mystacinus* und *M. daubentoni.* Ann. Zool. Fennici. 2:77-123.

O'Farrell, M. J., W. G. Bradley, and G. W. Jones
1967   Fall and winter bat activity at a desert spring in southern Nevada. S. W. Nat. 12:163-74.

Olson, A. C., Jr.
1947   First record of *Choeronycteris mexicana* in California. J. Mamm. 28:183-84.

Orr, R. T.
1950a   Unusual behavior and occurrence of a hoary bat. J. Mamm. 31:456-57.
1950b   Notes on the seasonal occurrence of red bats in San Francisco. J. Mamm. 31:457-58.
1954   Natural history of the pallid bat, *Antrozous pallidus* (LeConte). Proc. California Acad. Sci. 28:165-246.
1958   Keeping bats in captivity. J. Mamm. 39:339-44.

Packard, R. L.
1966   *Myotis austroriparius* in Texas. J. Mamm. 47:128.

Packard, R. L., and F. W. Judd
1967   Two noteworthy records of bats from Chihuahua. S. W. Nat. 12:330.

Paradiso, J. L., and A. M. Greenhall
  1967 Longevity records for American bats. Amer. Midl. Nat. 78:251-52.

Parker, H. C.
  1932 Notes on mammals of the Carlsbad Cavern region. J. Mamm. 13:70.

Pearson, E. W.
  1962 Bats hibernating in silica mines in southern Illinois. J. Mamm. 43:27-33.

Pearson, O. P., M. R. Koford, and A. K. Pearson
  1952 Reproduction of the lump-nosed bat (*Corynorhinus rafinesquii*) in California. J. Mamm. 33:273-320.

Perry, A. E.
  1965 Population analysis of the guano bat *Tadarida brasiliensis mexicana* (Saussure) using the lens-weight method of age determination. Ph.D. Thesis. Oklahoma State Univ., Stillwater. 60 pp.

Perry, A. E., and G. Rogers
  1964 Predation by great horned owl (*Bubo virginianus*) on young Mexican free-tailed bats (*Tadarida brasiliensis mexicana*) in Major County, Oklahoma. S. W. Nat. 9:205.

Peterson, R. L.
  1966 The mammals of eastern Canada. Oxford, New York. 465 pp.

Phillips, G. L.
  1966 Ecology of the big brown bat (Chiroptera: Vespertilionidae) in northeastern Kansas. Amer. Midl. Nat. 75:168-98.

Pirlot, P.
  1967 Nouvelle recolte de chiropteres dans l'ouest du Venezuela. Mammalia 31:260-74.

Pittman, H. H.
  1924 Notes on the feeding habits of the little brown bat (*Myotis lucifugus*). J. Mamm. 5:231-32.

Poole, E. L.
  1932 A survey of the mammals of Berks County, Pennsylvania. Reading Public Mus. & Art Gallery Bull. No. 13. 74 pp.
  1938 Notes on the breeding of *Lasiurus* and *Pipistrellus* in Pennsylvania. J. Mamm. 19:249.

Provost, E. E., and C. M. Kirkpatrick
  1952 Observations on the hoary bat in Indiana and Illinois. J. Mamm. 33:110-13.

Punt, A., and P. J. van Nieuwenhoven
  1957 The uses of radioactive bands in tracing hibernating bats. Experientia 13:51-54.

Quay, W. B.
  1948 Notes on some bats from Nebraska and Wyoming. J. Mamm. 29:181-82.

Quay, W. B., and J. S. Miller
  1955 Occurrence of the red bat, *Lasiurus borealis*, in caves. J. Mamm. 36:454-55.

Radovsky, F. J.
  1967 The Macronyssidae and Laelapidae (Acarina:Mesostigmata) parasitic on bats. Univ. California Publ. Entomol. 46:1-288.

Rageot, R. H.
  1955 A new northernmost record of the yellow bat, *Dasypterus floridanus*. J. Mamm. 36:456.

Ramage, M. C.
  1947 Notes on keeping bats in captivity. J. Mamm. 28:60-62.

Raun, G. G.
  1960 A mass die-off of the Mexican brown bat, *Myotis velifer*, in Texas. S. W. Nat. 5:104.
  1961 The big free-tailed bat in southern Texas. J. Mamm. 42:253.

Raun, G. G., and J. K. Baker
  1958 Some observations of Texas cave bats. S. W. Nat. 3:102-106.

Rausch, R.
1946   Collecting bats in Ohio. J. Mamm. 27:275-76.

Reeder, W. G.
1949   Hibernating temperature of the bat, *Myotis californicus pallidus*. J. Mamm. 30:51-53.
1965   Occurrence of the big brown bat in southwestern Alaska. J. Mamm. 46:332-33.

Reeder, W. G., and R. B. Cowles
1951   Aspects of thermoregulation in bats. J. Mamm. 32:389-403.

Reite, O. B., and W. H. Davis
1966   Thermoregulation in bats exposed to low ambient temperatures. Proc. Soc. Exp. Biol. Med. 121:1212-15.

Rice, D. W.
1955   A new race of *Myotis austroriparius* from the upper Mississippi Valley. J. Florida Acad. Sci. 18:67-68.
1957   Life history and ecology of *Myotis austroriparius* in Florida. J. Mamm. 38:15-32.

Richardson, J. H., R. L. Ramsey, and L. E. Starr
1966   Bat rabies in Georgia, 1956-65. Pub. Health Repts. 81:1031-36.

Rippy, C. L.
1965   The baculum in *Myotis sodalis* and *Myotis austroriparius austroriparius*. Trans. Kentucky Acad. Sci. 26:19-21.

Rippy, C. L., and M. J. Harvey
1965   Notes on *Plecotus townsendii virginianus* in Kentucky. J. Mamm. 46:499.

Roeder, K. D., and A. E. Treat
1961   The detection and evasion of bats by moths. Smithsonian Rept. for 1961. 455-64.

Ross, A. J.
1961a   Biological studies on bat ectoparasites of the genus *Trichobius* (Diptera: Streblidae) in North America, north of Mexico. Wasman J. Biol. 19:229-46.
1961b   Notes on the food habits of bats. J. Mamm. 42:66-71.

Ryberg, O.
1947   Studies on bats and bat parasites. Svensk Natur, Stockholm. 330 pp.

Rysgaard, G. N.
1941   Bats killed by severe storm. J. Mamm. 22:452-53.
1942   A study of the cave bats of Minnesota with especial reference to the large brown bat, *Eptesicus fuscus fuscus* (Beauvois) Amer. Midl. Nat. 28:245-67.

Sanborn, C. C.
1932   The bats of the genus *Eumops*. J. Mamm. 13:347-57.
1943   External characters of the bats of the subfamily Glossophaginae. Field Mus. Nat. Hist., Zool. Ser. 24:271-77.
1951   Colonies of Illinois bats invaded by business. Bull. Chicago Nat. Hist. Mus. 22:4-5.
1954   Bats of the United States. Publ. Health Repts. 69:17-28.

Sanborn, C. C., and J. A. Crespo
1957   El murcielago blanquizco (*Lasiurus cinereus*) y sus subespecies. Bol. Mus. Cien. Nat. No. 4. 13 pp.

Saunders, W. E.
1930   Bats in migration. J. Mamm. 11:225.

Schramm, P.
1957   A new homing record for the little brown bat. J. Mamm. 38:514-15.

Schwartz, A.
1955   The status of the species of the *brasiliensis* group of the genus *Tadarida*. J. Mamm. 36:106-109.

Schwartz, C. W., and E. R. Schwartz
1959   The wild mammals of Missouri. Univ. Missouri Press, Columbia. 341 pp.

Sealander, J. A., Jr.
1951   Lump-nosed bat in Arkansas. J. Mamm. 32:465.
1956   A provisional check-list and key to the mammals of Arkansas (annotated). Amer. Midl. Nat. 56:257-96.

Sealander, J. A., Jr. (*continued*):

1960   Some noteworthy records of Arkansas mammals. J. Mamm. 41:525-26.

1967   First record of small-footed myotis in Arkansas. J. Mamm. 48:666.

Sealander, J. A., Jr., and A. J. Hoiberg

1954   Occurrence of the seminole bat in Arkansas. J. Mamm. 35:584.

Sealander, J. A., Jr., and J. F. Price

1964   Free-tailed bat in Arkansas. J. Mamm. 45:152.

Sealander, J. A., Jr., and H. Young

1955   Preliminary observations on the cave bats of Arkansas. Arkansas Acad. Sci. 7:21-31.

Seton, E. T.

1922   A roving band of Say's bats. J. Mamm. 3:52.

Sherman, A. R.

1929   Summer outings of bats during fourteen seasons. J. Mamm. 10:319-26.

Sherman, H. B.

1930   Birth of the young of *Myotis austroriparius*. J. Mamm. 11:495-503.

1935   Food habits of the seminole bat. J. Mamm. 16:223-24.

1937   Breeding habits of the free-tailed bat. J. Mamm. 18:176-87.

1939   Notes on the food of some Florida bats. J. Mamm. 20:103-104.

Short, H. L.

1961   Growth and development of Mexican free-tailed bats. S. W. Nat. 6:156-63.

Short, H. L., R. B. Davis, and C. F. Herreid, Jr.

1960   Movements of Mexican free-tailed bats in Texas. S. W. Nat. 5:208-16.

Silver, J.

1928   Pilot black-snake feeding on the big brown bat. J. Mamm. 9:149.

Simmons, N. M.

1966   Observations of mammals in the Cabeza Prieta Game Range area, Arizona. J. Mamm. 47:122.

Sims, R. A., R. Allen, and S. E. Sulkin

1963   Studies on the pathogenesis of rabies in insectivorous bats. III. Influence of the gravid state. J. Infectious Dis. 112:17-27.

Smead, J. L.

1938   Second Colorado record of *Tadarida macrotis*. J. Mamm. 19:104.

Smith, E.

1954   Studies on the life history of non-cave-dwelling bats in northeastern Ohio. Ohio J. Sci. 54:1-12.

1957   Experimental study of factors affecting sex ratios in the little brown bat. J. Mamm. 38:32-39.

Smith, E., and W. Goodpaster

1958   Homing in nonmigratory bats. Science 127:644.

1960   A free-tailed bat found in Ohio. J. Mamm. 41:117.

Smith, P. W., and P. W. Parmallee

1954   Notes on distribution and habits of some bats from Illinois. Trans. Kansas Acad. Sci. 57:200-205.

Snyder, W. E.

1902   A list with brief notes of the mammals of Dodge Co., Wisconsin. Bull. Wisconsin Nat. Hist. Soc. 2:113-26.

Sperry, C. C.

1933   Opossum and skunk eat bats. J. Mamm. 14:152-53.

Sprunt, A., Jr.

1950   Hawk predation at the bat caves of Texas. Texas J. Sci. 2:462-70.

Stager, K. E.

1939   Status of *Myotis velifer* in California, with notes on its life history. J. Mamm. 20:225-28.

1942   The cave bat as the food of the California lyre snake. J. Mamm. 23:92.

Stager, K. E. (*continued*):

1943a Remarks on *Myotis occultus* in California. J. Mamm. 24:197-99.

1943b Notes on the roosting place of *Pipistrellus hesperus*. J. Mamm. 24:266-67.

1943c California leaf-nosed bat trapped by desert shrub. J. Mamm. 24:396.

1945 *Tadarida mexicana* in Oregon. J. Mamm. 26:196.

1948 Falcons prey on Nye Cave bats. Bull. Natl. Speleolog. Soc. 10:97-99.

1957 Records of the spotted bat from California and Arizona. J. Mamm. 38:260.

Stains, H. J.

1965 Female red bat carrying four young. J. Mamm. 46:333.

Stains, H. J., and R. H. Baker

1954 Deciduous teeth in the hognose bat, *Choeronycteris mexicana*. J. Mamm. 35:437-38.

Stiles, C. W., and M. O. Nolan

1931 Key catalogue of parasites reported for Chiroptera (bats) with their possible public health importance. Natl. Inst. Health Bull. 155:603-742.

Stones, R. C.

1965 Laboratory care of little brown bats at thermal neutrality. J. Mamm. 46:681-83.

Stones, R. C., and J. E. Wiebers

1965a Body temperature cycling of winter little brown bats in cold following heat exposure. Experientia 21:1-6.

1965b Seasonal changes in food consumption of little brown bats held in captivity at a "neutral" temperature of 92° F. J. Mamm. 46:18-22.

1965c Activity and body weight of *Myotis lucifugus* at a low temperature. J. Mamm. 46:94-95.

1965d A review of temperature regulation in bats (Chiroptera). Amer. Midl. Nat. 74:155-67.

1966 Body weight and temperature regulation of *Myotis lucifugus* at a low temperature of 10° C. J. Mamm. 47:520-21.

Storer, T. I.

1926a Bats, bat towers, and mosquitoes. J. Mamm. 7:85-90.

1926b What is the northward limit of range for the mastiff bat? J. Mamm. 7:131.

1931 A colony of Pacific pallid bats. J. Mamm. 12:244-47.

Strandtmann, R. W.

1962 *Nycteriglyphus bifolium* n. sp., a new cavernicolous mite associated with bats (Chiroptera) (Acarina: Glycyphagidae). Acarologia 4:623-31.

Studier, E. H.

1966 Studies on the mechanisms of ammonia tolerance of the guano bat. J. Exp. Zool. 163:79-86.

Studier, E. H., L. R. Beck, and R. C. Lindeborg

1967 Tolerance and initial metabolic response to ammonia intoxication in selected bats and rodents. J. Mamm. 48:564-72.

Stuewer, F. W.

1948 A record of red bats mating. J. Mamm. 29:180-81.

Sulkin, S. E., R. Allen, R. Sims, P. H. Krutzsch, and C. Kim

1959 Studies on the pathogenesis of rabies in insectivorous bats. I. Role of brown adipose tissue. J. Exp. Med. 110:369-88.

1960 Studies on the pathogenesis of rabies in insectivorous bats. II. Influence of environmental temperature. J. Exp. Med. 112:595-617.

Sulkin, S. E., P. Krutzsch, C. Wallis, and R. Allen

1957 Role of brown fat in pathogenesis of rabies in insectivorous bats (*Tadarida b. mexicana*). Proc. Soc. Exp. Biol. Med. 96:461-64.

Suthers, R. A.

1965 Acoustic orientation by fish-catching bats. J. Exp. Zool. 158:319-48.

1966 Optomotor responses by echolocating bats. Science 152:1102-1104.

1967 Comparative echolocation by fishing bats. J. Mamm. 48:79-87.

Suthers, R. A., and J. Chase
1966   Visual pattern discrimination by an echolocating bat. Amer. Zool. 6:309.

Swanson, G., and C. Evans
1936   The hibernation of certain bats in southern Minnesota. J. Mamm. 17:39-43.

Taylor, J.
1964   Noteworthy predation on the guano bat. J. Mamm. 45:300-301.

Tenaza, R. R.
1966   Migration of hoary bats on South Farallon Island, California. J. Mamm. 47:533-35.

Terres, J. K.
1956   Migration record of the red bat *Lasiurus borealis*. J. Mamm. 37:442.

Tesh, R. B., and A. A. Arata
1967   Bats as laboratory animals. Health Lab. Sci. 4:106-12.

Tesh, R. B., and J. D. Schneidau, Jr.
1966   Experimental infection of North American insectivorous bats (*Tadarida brasiliensis*) with *Histoplasma capsulatum*. Amer. J. Trop. Med. Hygiene 15:544-50.

Thomas, O.
1921   Bats on migration. J. Mamm. 2:167.

Tibbetts, T.
1956   Homing instincts of two bats, *Eptesicus fuscus* and *Tadarida mexicana* (Mammalia: Chiroptera). S. W. Nat. 1:194.

Tinkle, D. W., and W. W. Milstead
1960   Sex ratios and population density in hibernating *Myotis*. Amer. Midl. Nat. 63:327-34.

Tinkle, D. W., and I. G. Patterson
1965   A study of hibernating populations of *Myotis velifer* in northwestern Texas. J. Mamm. 46:612-33.

Toner, G. C.
1935   A note on *Eptesicus fuscus*. J. Mamm. 16:147.

de la Torre, L.
1955   Bats from Guerrero, Jalisco and Oaxaca, Mexico. Fieldiana: Zool. 37:695-701.

de la Torre, L., and M. P. Dysart
1966   A method for photographing teeth of small mammals. J. Mamm. 47:515-18.

Trapido, H., and J. Kezer
1941   The acadian bat in New Jersey. J. Mamm. 22:449-50.

Tuttle, M. D.
1961   Notes on the bats of eastern Tennessee. Bat Banding News 2:13-14.
1964   *Myotis subulatus* in Tennessee. J. Mamm. 45:148-49.

Twente, J. W.
1954   Predation on bats by hawks and owls. Wilson Bull. 66:135-36.
1955a   Some aspects of habitat selection and other behavior of cavern-dwelling bats. Ecology 36:706-32.
1955b   Aspects of a population study of cavern-dwelling bats. J. Mamm. 36:379-90.
1956   Ecological observations on a colony of *Tadarida mexicana*. J. Mamm. 37:42-47.
1959   Swimming behavior of bats. J. Mamm. 40:440-41.
1960   Environmental problems involving the hibernation of bats in Utah. Proc. Utah Acad. Sci. 37:67-71.

Twente, J. W., and J. A. Twente
1964   An hypothesis concerning the evolution of heterothermy in bats. Ann. Acad. Sci. Fennicae 71:435-42.

Tyson, E. L.
1964   Two new records of bats (Molossidae) from Panama. J. Mamm. 45:495-96.

Ubelaker, J. E.
1966   Parasites of the gray bat, *Myotis grisescens*, in Kansas. Amer. Midl. Nat. 75:199-204.

Van Deusen, H. M.
1961   Yellow bat collected over south Atlantic. J. Mamm. 42:530-31.

Van Gelder, R. G.
1956   Echolocation failure in migratory bats. Trans. Kansas Acad. Sci. 59:220-22.

Van Gelder, R. G., and W. W. Goodpaster
1952   Bats and birds competing for food. J. Mamm. 33:491.

Van Gelder, R. G., and D. B. Wingate
1961   The taxonomy and status of bats in Bermuda. Amer. Mus. Novitates No. 2021.

Vaughan, T. A.
1954   Mammals of the San Gabriel Mountains of California. Univ. Kansas Publ., Mus. Nat. Hist. 7:513-82.

1959   Functional morphology of three bats: *Eumops*, *Myotis*, *Macrotus*. Univ. Kansas Publ., Mus. Nat. Hist. 12:1-153.

1966   Morphology and flight characteristics of molossid bats. J. Mamm. 47:249-60.

Vaughan, T. A., and P. H. Krutzsch
1954   Seasonal distribution of the hoary bat in southern California. J. Mamm. 35:431-32.

Vercammen-Grandjean, P. H., and S. G. Watkins
1966   A new genus and species (*Albeckia albecki*) of North American bat (*Antrozous pallidus*, Vesperlilionidae) chiggers. Acarologia 8:74-77.

Villa, B.
1956a   *Tadarida brasiliensis mexicana* (Saussure), el murcielago guanero, es una subespecie migratoria. Acta Zool. Mex. 1:1-11.

1956b   Una extrana mortandad de murcielagos *Mormoops megalophylla* en el norte de Mexico. An. Inst. Biol. Mex. 26:547-52.

1967   Los murcielagos de Mexico. Univ. Nac. Aut. Mexico, Mexico, D.F.   491 pp.

Villa, B., and E. L. Cockrum
1962   Migration in the guano bat *Tadarida brasiliensis mexicana* (Saussure). J. Mamm. 43:43-64.

Villa B., and A. Jiminez
1961   Acerca de la position taxonomic de *Mormoops megalophylla senicula* Rehn, y la presencia de virus rabico en estos murcielagos insectivoros. An. Inst. Biol. Mex. 31:501-509.

Von Bloeker, J. C., Jr.
1932   The roosting-place of *Pipistrellus hesperus*. J. Mamm. 13:273.

Walton, D. W., and N. J. Siegel
1966   The histology of the pararhinal glands of the pallid bat, *Antrozous pallidus*. J. Mamm. 47:357-60.

Ward, H. L.
1891   Descriptions of three new species of Mexican bats. Amer. Nat. 25:743-53.

Warner, D. W., and J. R. Beer
1957   Birds and mammals of the mesa de San Diego, Puebla, Mexico. Acta Zool. Mex. 2:1-21.

Webb, O. L., and J. K. Jones, Jr.
1952   An annotated checklist of Nebraskan bats. Univ. Kansas Publ., Mus. Nat. Hist. 5:269-79.

Webster, F. A.
1963   Active energy radiating systems: The bat and ultrasonic principles. II; Acoustical control of airborne interceptions by bats. Proc. Int. Cong. Technol. Blindness 1:49-135.

Webster, F. A., and O. G. Brazier
1965   Experimental studies on target detection, evaluation and interception by echolocating bats. Aerospace Med. Res. Lab. Publ., Wright-Patterson AFB, Ohio.   135 pp.

Webster, F. A., and D. R. Griffin
1962   The role of the flight membranes in insect capture by bats. Anim. Beh. 10:332-40.

Werner, H. J.

1966   Observations on the facial glands of the guano bat *Tadarida brasiliensis mexicana* (Saussure). Proc. Louisiana Acad. Sci. 29:156-60.

Wetmore, A.

1933   The red bat in the Washington region in winter. J. Mamm. 14:157-58.

1936   Hibernation of the brown bat. J. Mamm. 17:130-31.

Whelden, R. M.

1941   Hibernation of *Eptesicus fuscus* in a New Hampshire building. J. Mamm. 22:203.

Whitaker, J. O.

1967   Hoary bat apparently hibernating in Indiana. J. Mamm. 48:663.

Whitlow, W. B., and E. R. Hall

1933   Mammals of the Pocatello region of southeastern Idaho. Univ. California Publ. Zool. 40:235-76.

Williams, T. C., and J. M. Williams

1967   Radio tracking of homing bats. Science 155:1435-36.

Williams, T. C., J. M. Williams, and D. R. Griffin

1966a   Visual orientation in homing bats. Science 152:677.

1966b   The homing ability of the neotropical bat *Phyllostomus hastatus* with evidence for visual orientation. Anim. Beh. 14:468-73.

Wilson, N.

1958   Another instance of bat versus ant. J. Mamm. 39:438.

1960   A northernmost record of *Plecotus rafinesquii* Lesson (Mammalia; Chiroptera). Amer. Midl. Nat. 64:500.

1965   Red bats attracted to insect light traps. J. Mamm. 46:704-705.

Wimsatt, W. A.

1944a   Further studies on the survival of spermatozoa in the female reproductive tract of the bat. Anat. Rec. 88:193-204.

1944b   Growth of the ovarian follicle and ovulation in *Myotis lucifugus lucifugus*. Amer. J. Anat. 74:129-73.

1944c   An analysis of implantation in the bat *Myotis lucifugus lucifugus*. Amer. J. Anat. 74:355-411.

1945   Notes on breeding behavior, pregnancy, and parturition in some vespertilionid bats of the eastern United States. J. Mamm. 26:23-33.

1960a   An analysis of parturition in Chiroptera, including new observations on *Myotis l. lucifugus*. J. Mamm. 41:183-200.

1960b   Some problems of reproduction in relation to hibernation in bats. Bull. Mus. Comp. Zool. 124:249-67.

Wimsatt, W. A., and F. C. Kallen

1957   The unique maturation response of the graafian follicles of hibernating vespertilionid bats and the question of its significance. Anat. Rec. 129:115-32.

Wimsatt, W. A., P. H. Krutzsch, and L. Napotitano

1966   Studies on sperm survival mechanisms in the female reproductive tract of hibernating bats. Amer. J. Anat. 119:25-59.

Zimmerman, F. R.

1937   Migration of little brown bats. J. Mamm. 18:363.

Index